I0709635

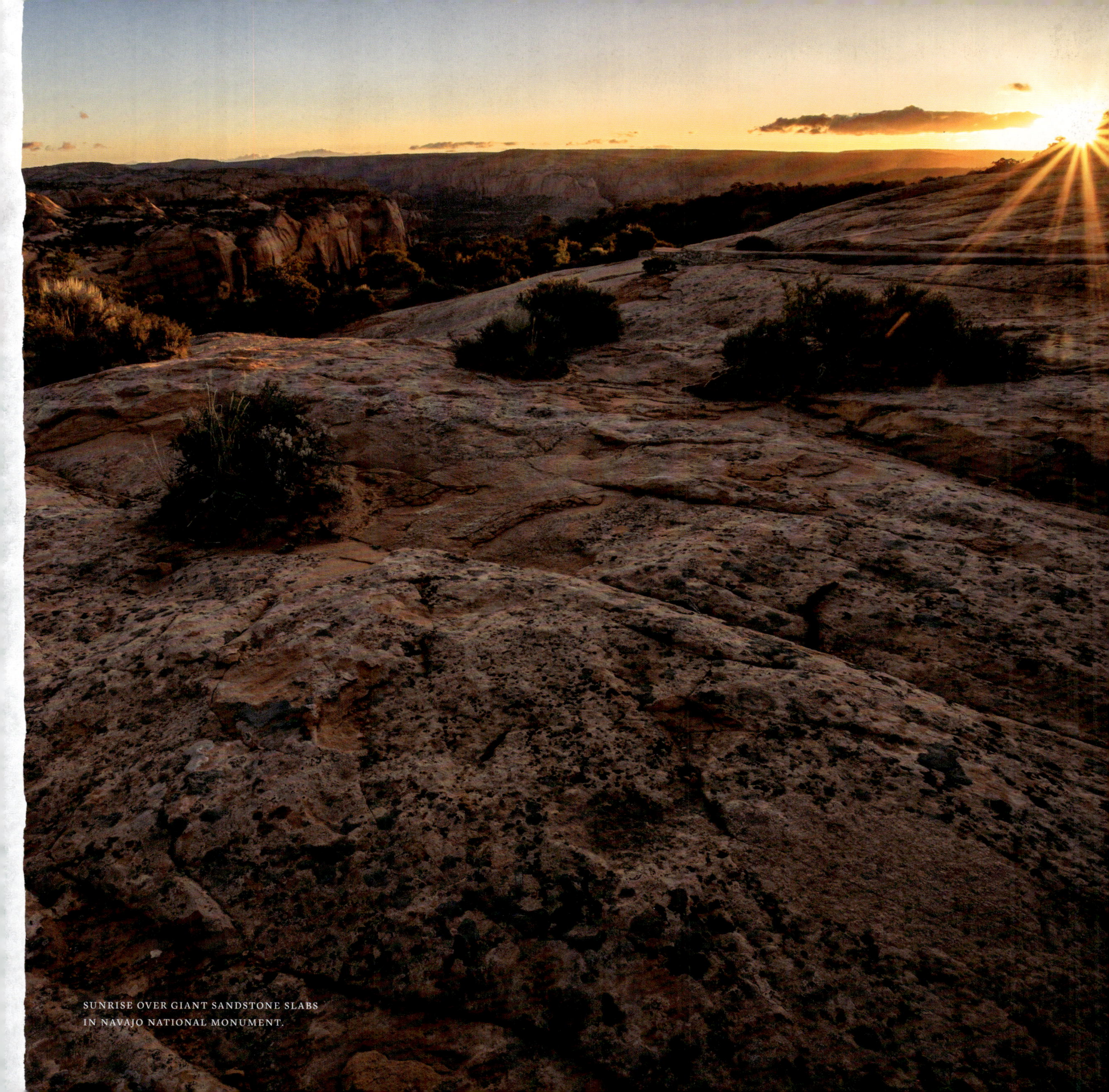

SUNRISE OVER GIANT SANDSTONE SLABS
IN NAVAJO NATIONAL MONUMENT.

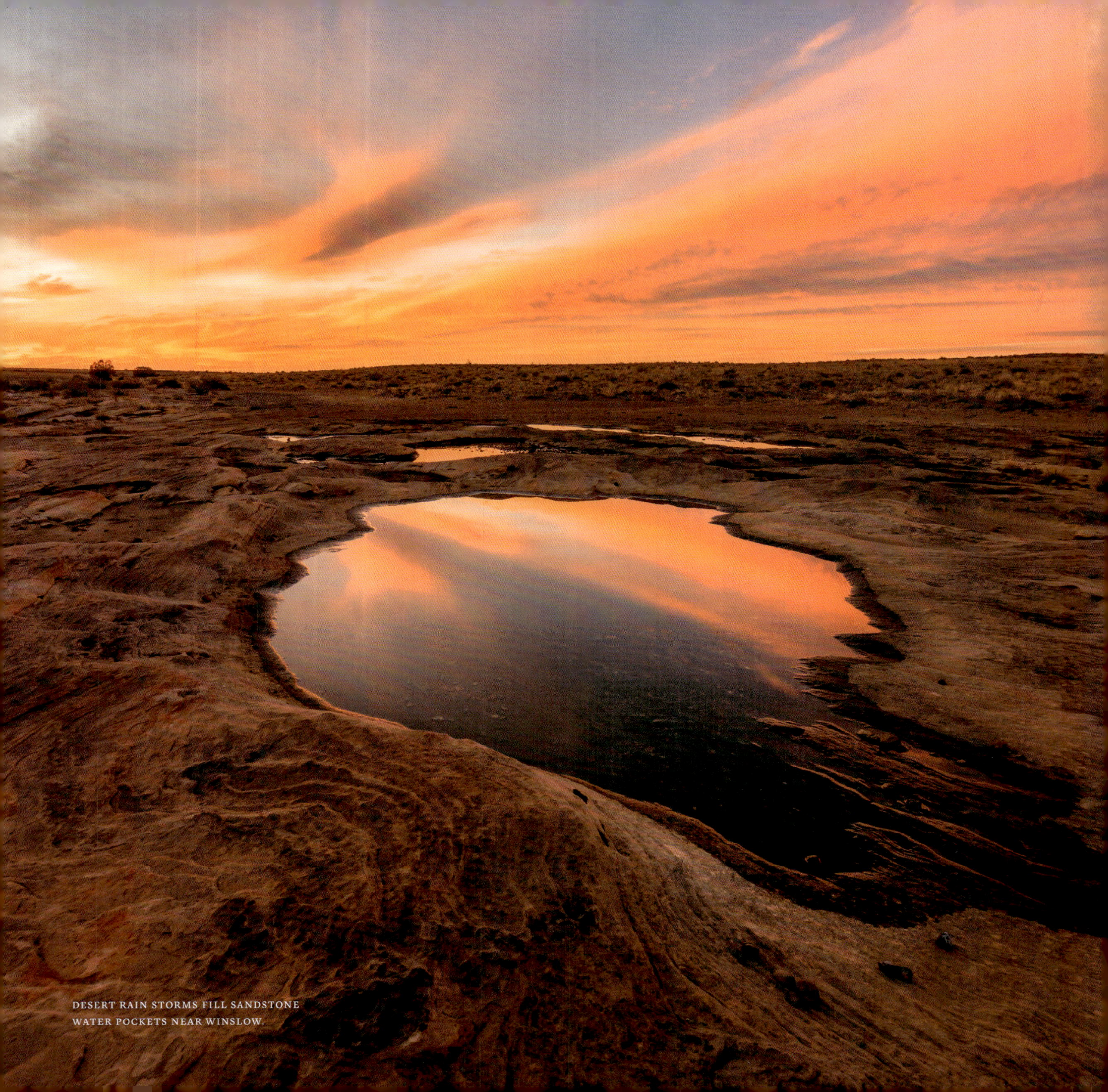


DESERT RAIN STORMS FILL SANDSTONE
WATER POCKETS NEAR WINSLOW.

# ARIZONA

THE GRAND CANYON STATE

PHOTOGRAPHS BY MARK LISK

Copyright © 2025 by Mark Lisk
All rights reserved.

Published by Familius LLC, www.familius.com

Familius books are available at special discounts for bulk purchases,
whether for sales promotions or for family or corporate use. For more information,
contact Familius Sales at orders@familius.com.

Reproduction of this book in any manner, in whole or in part,
without written permission of the publisher is prohibited.

Library of Congress Control Number: 2025939255

Print ISBN 9798893960631
Ebook ISBN 9798893960709

Printed in China

Edited by Peg Sandkam and Leah Welker
Cover and book design by Derek George, Carlos Mireles-Guerrero, and Brooke Jorden

10 9 8 7 6 5 4 3 2 1

First Edition

MIX
Paper
FSC   FSC® C188448

# CONTENTS


WELCOME TO ARIZONA . . . . . . . . 7

GRAND CANYON—COLORADO PLATEAU . . . . 9

MOGOLLON RIM—TRANSITION . . . . . 97

MOJAVE DESERT . . . . . . . . . 127

SONORAN DESERT . . . . . . . . . 145

CHIHUAHUAN DESERT . . . . . . . . 203

ABOUT THE AUTHOR . . . . . . . . 239

ABOUT FAMILIUS . . . . . . . . . 240

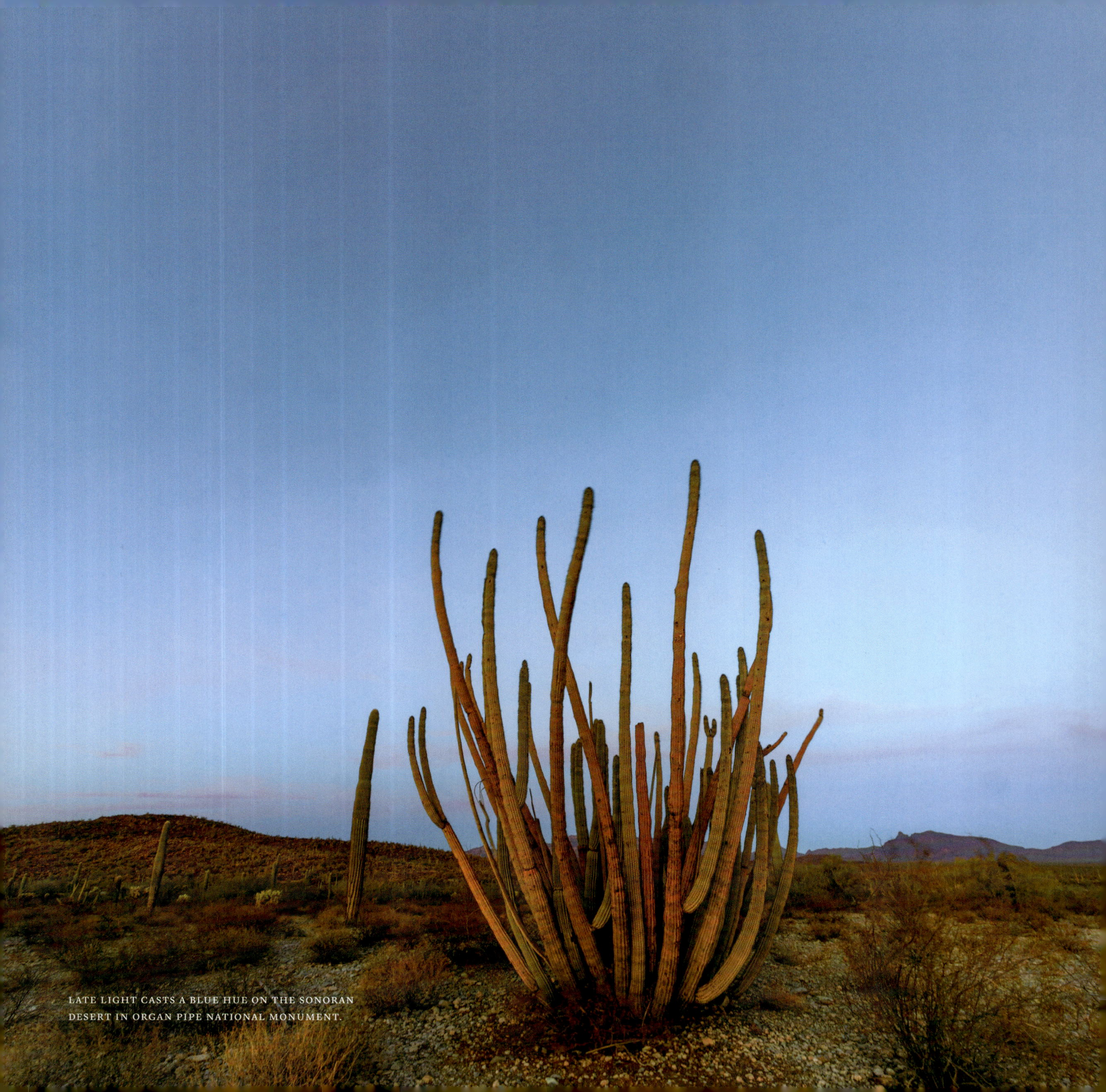

LATE LIGHT CASTS A BLUE HUE ON THE SONORAN
DESERT IN ORGAN PIPE NATIONAL MONUMENT.

THE RAVEN SPEAKS, CALLING FROM THE walls of the vertical sedimentary cliffs that drop away then down to the river. Slashing upward, the sinister ebony silhouette enters the deep blue sky above the rim, soaring above the cliff edge into an area known as Marble Canyon. The raven's echo welcomes me back to this place.

From the Rainbow Bridge Overlook, the mighty Colorado River passes below, cutting deep into the earth, crossing through one of the greatest of America's national parks, Grand Canyon National Park. It was here that my photographic journey took a turn from the mountains of the northwest to the vibrant, arid deserts of the Southwest. Exploring fantastic shapes and colors in a magnificent country full of forested ridges, river gorges and slot canyons.

Arizona has 4 of the 5 North American deserts: the Colorado Plateau, Sonoran, Mojave, and Chihuahuan touch various regions of the sixth largest state in the US. Virtually all of Arizona lies within the Colorado River drainage system. The Gila River, with its major feeder streams—the Salt and the Verde—is by far the Colorado River's main Arizona tributary, with the little Colorado draining the high transition zone of the Mogollon Rim. Water is the force that shapes these deserts. The slow and constant rhythm continues to change and evolve the landscape of these amazing and unique places.

From my camp across the river from Deer Creek, I have an amazing view of Deer Creek Falls that spills 180 feet from an incision in the red wall to the Colorado River. I follow a raven, circling above the mist and smooth sandstone then disappearing into the mysterious opening to the slot above, revealing the entrance into the cliff face. The small water-filled slot along the sheer walled opening takes me to a hidden alcove, a place of power—a place I can peer into the past, through the eye of my camera, into the deep blue sky where the ravens speak.

—**MARK LISK**

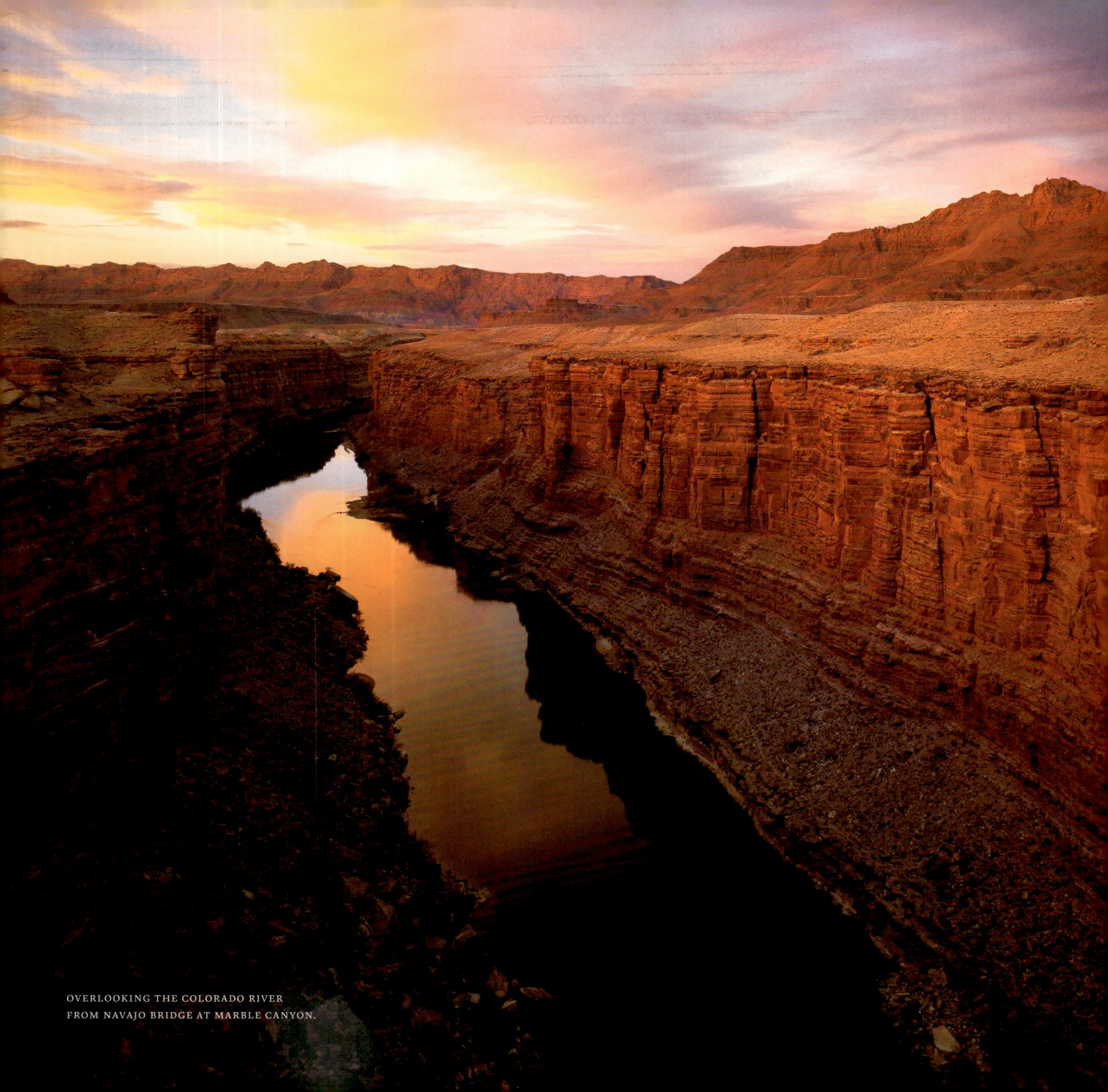
OVERLOOKING THE COLORADO RIVER
FROM NAVAJO BRIDGE AT MARBLE CANYON.

# GRAND CANYON—
# COLORADO PLATEAU

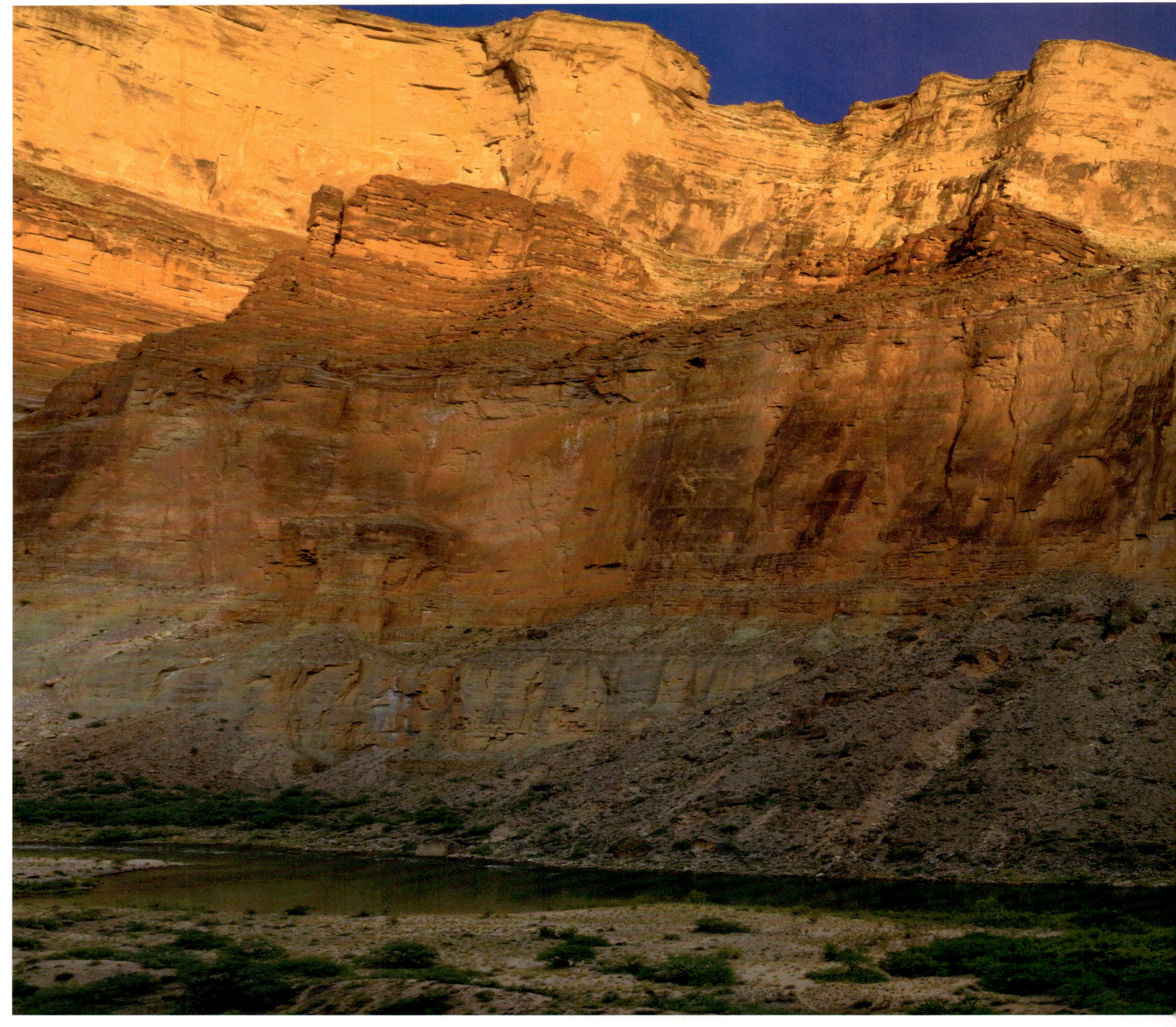

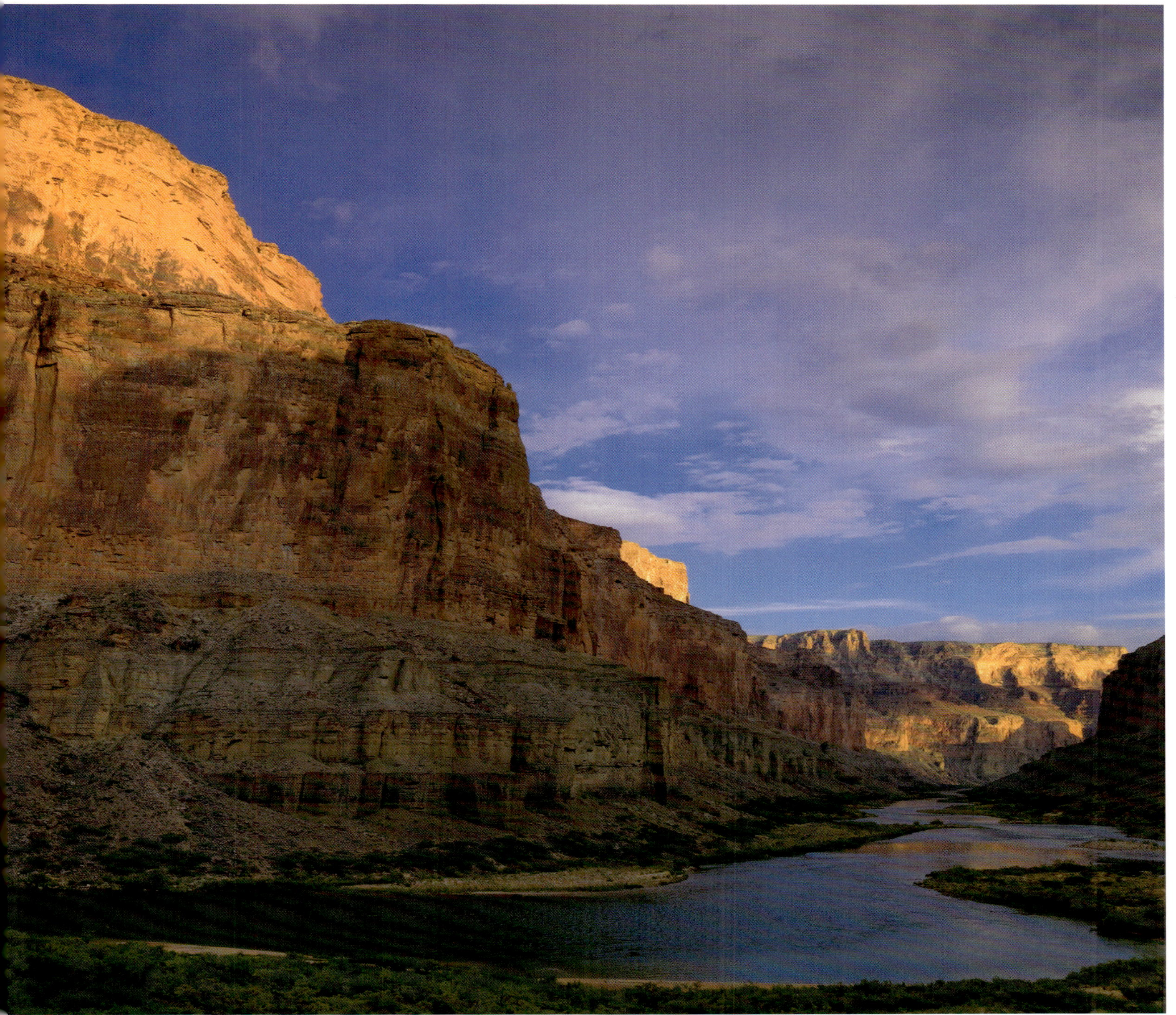

THE CLASSIC VIEW OF THE CANYON DOWNSTREAM OF NANKOWEAP MESA.

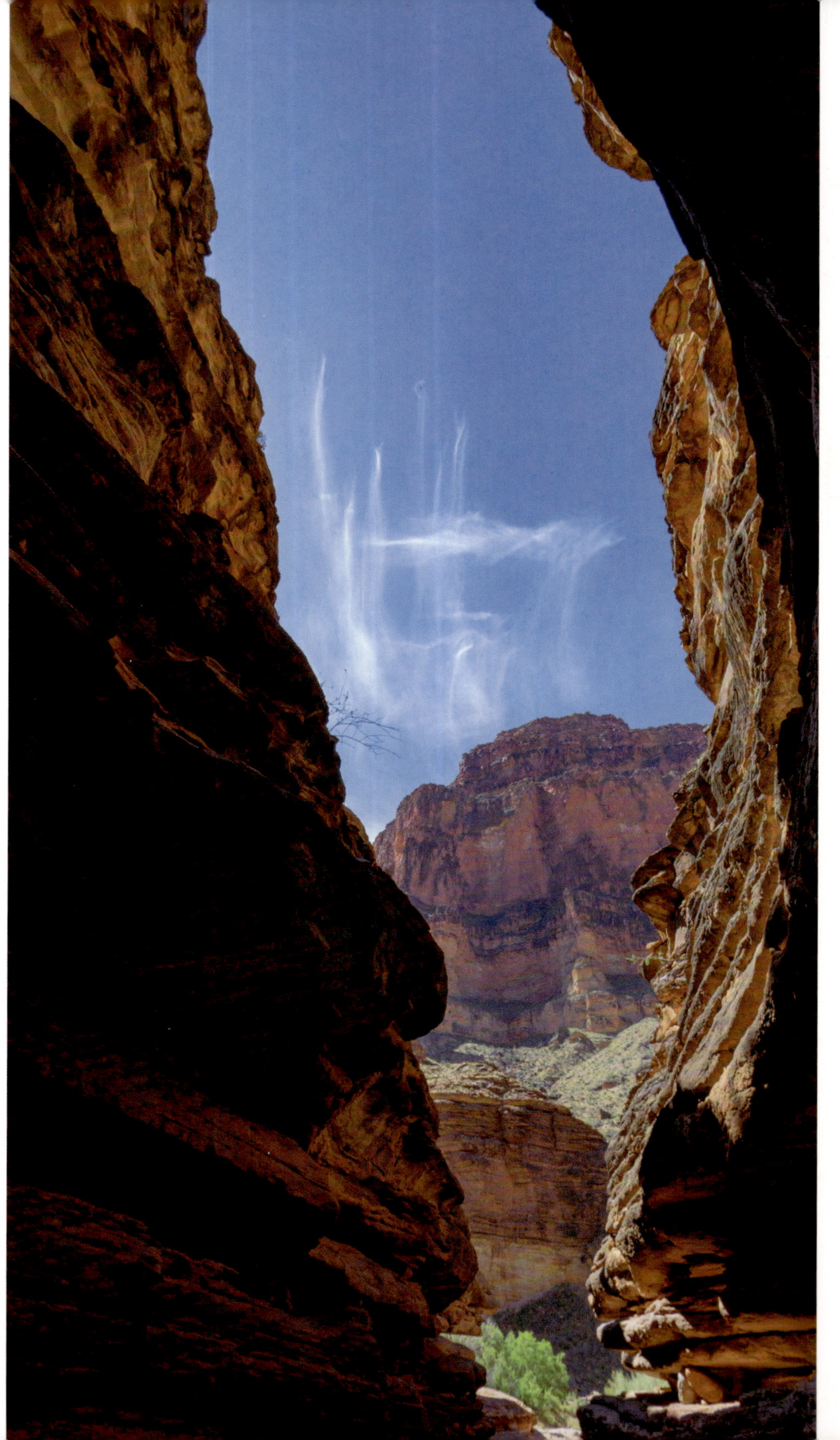

BLACKTAIL CANYON, A POPULAR HIKE
AND CAMP ON THE COLORADO RIVER.

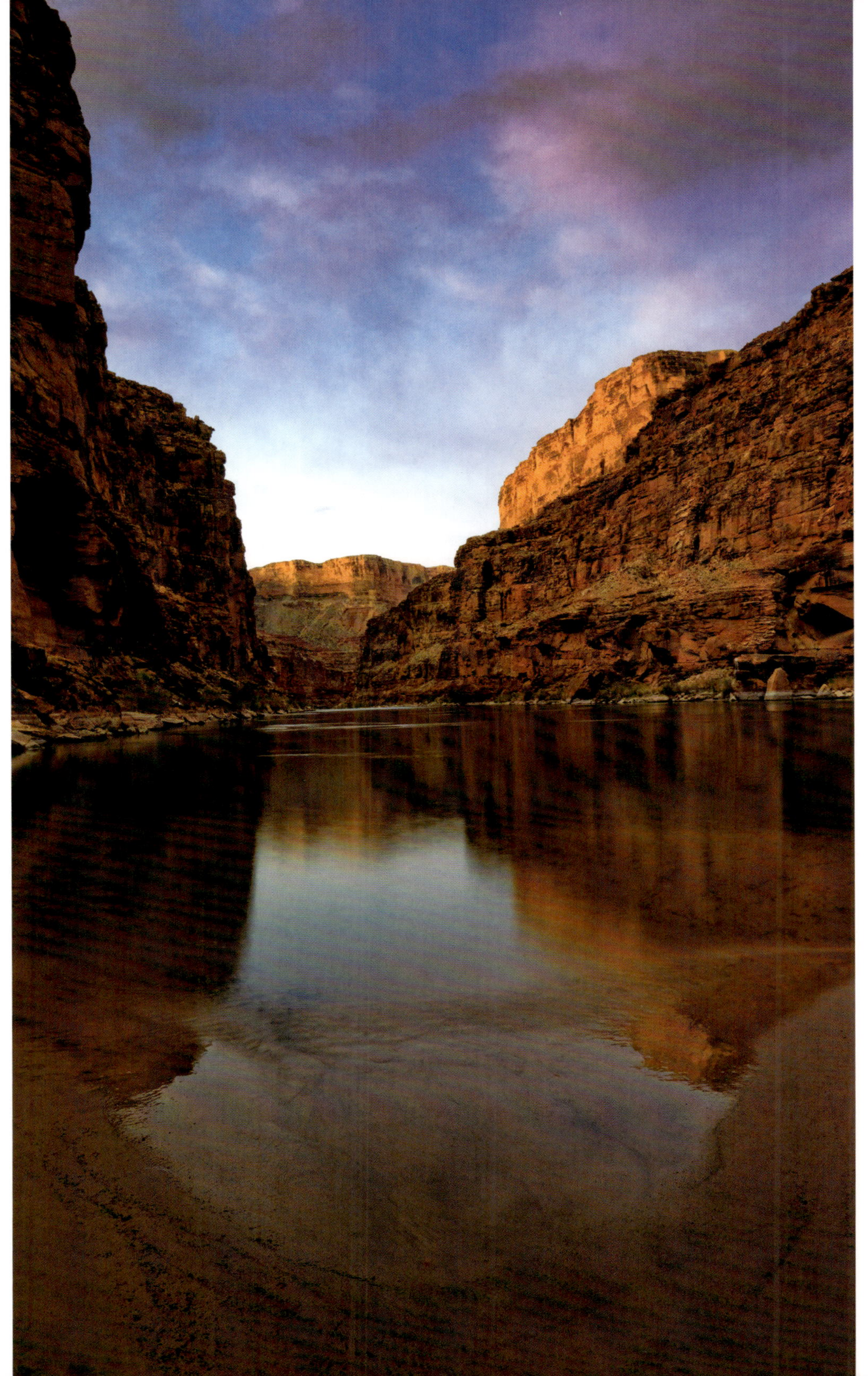

LOOKING DOWNSTREAM FROM HOT NA NA
CAMP, GRAND CANYON NATIONAL PARK.

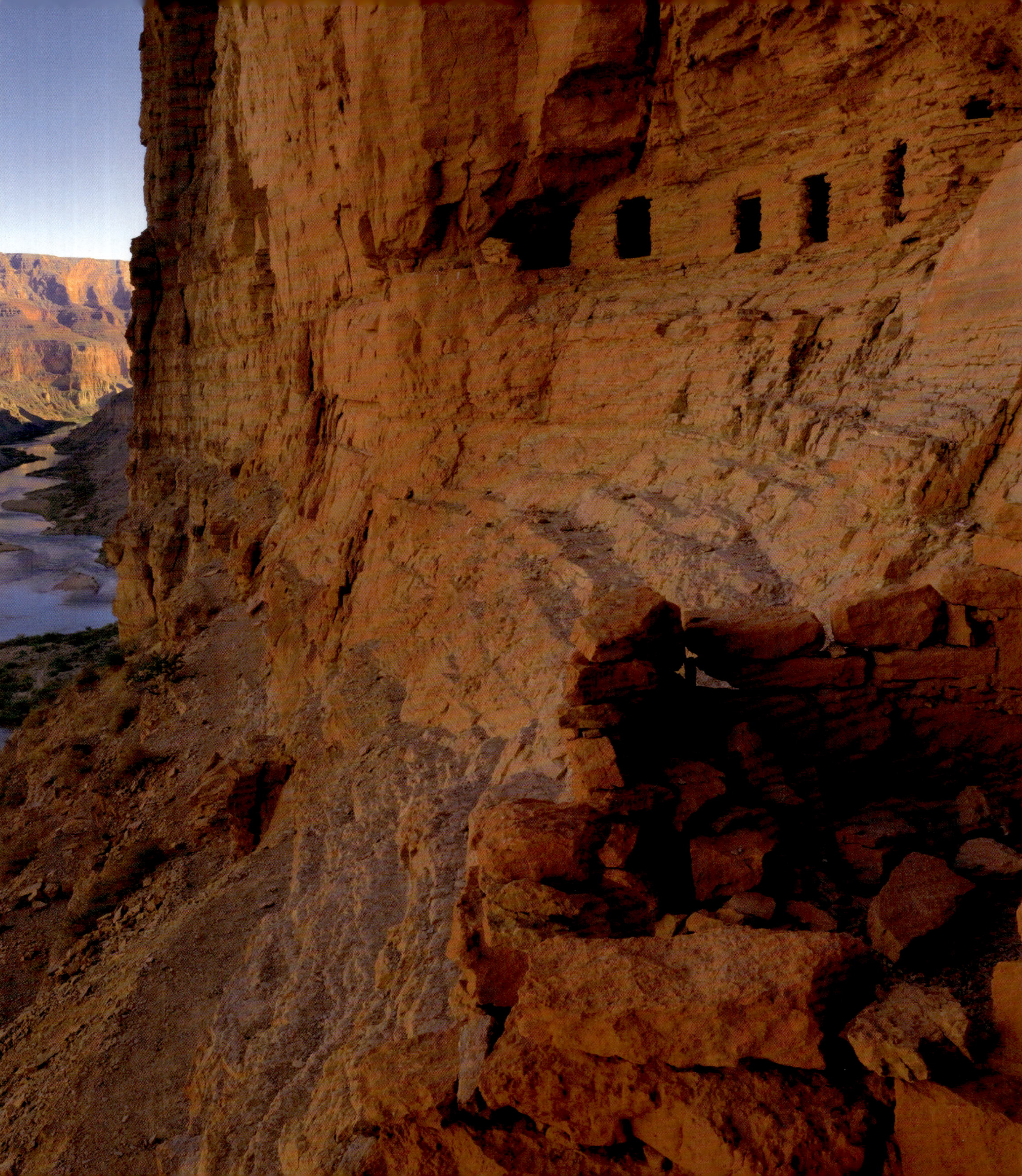

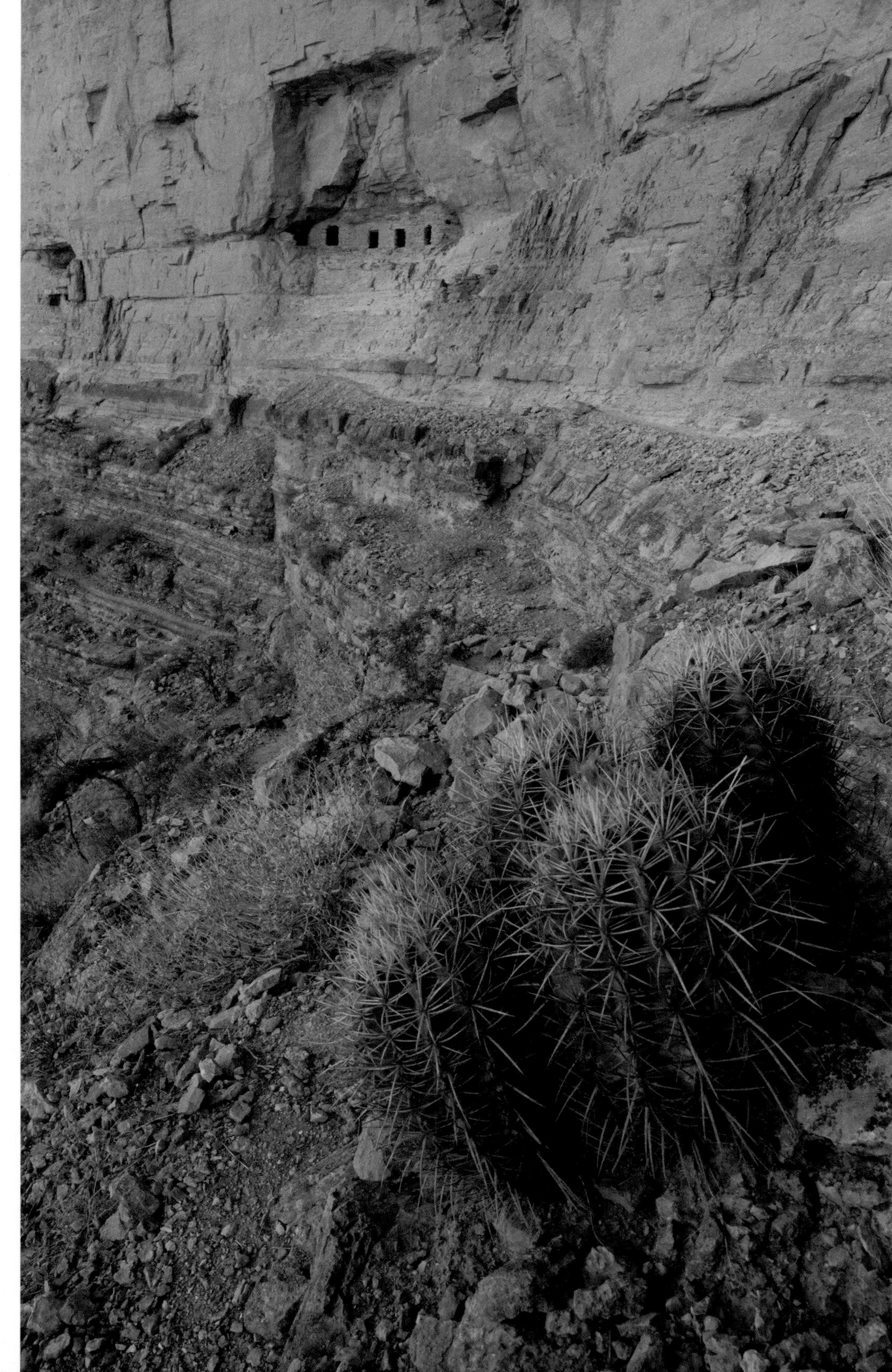


CLIFF DWELLINGS SIT BELOW
NANKOWEAP MESA, A CLASSIC
VIEW OF THE COLORADO RIVER.

CLIFF DWELLINGS HIGH IN THE
WALL ABOVE NANKOWEAP CREEK.

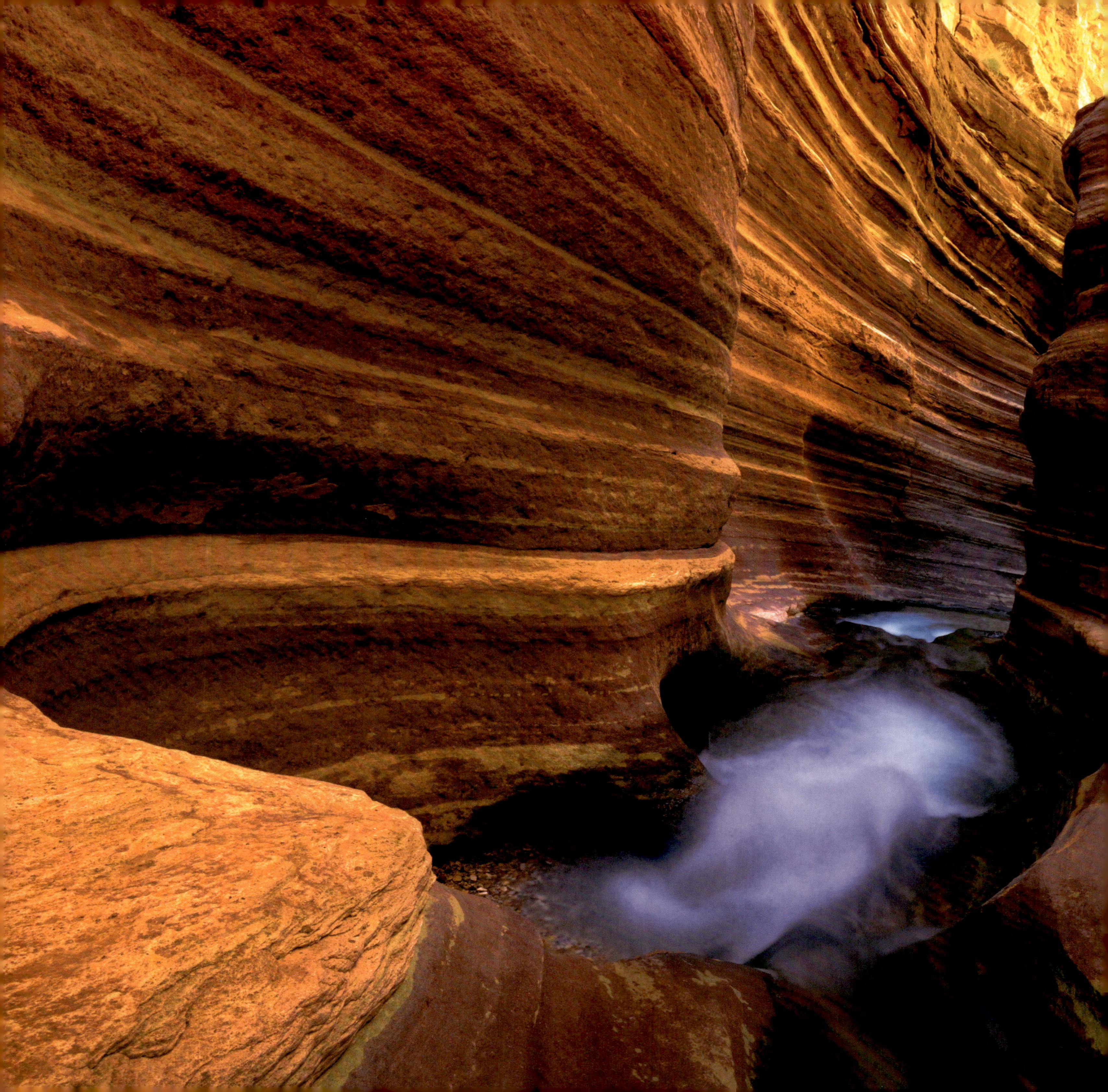

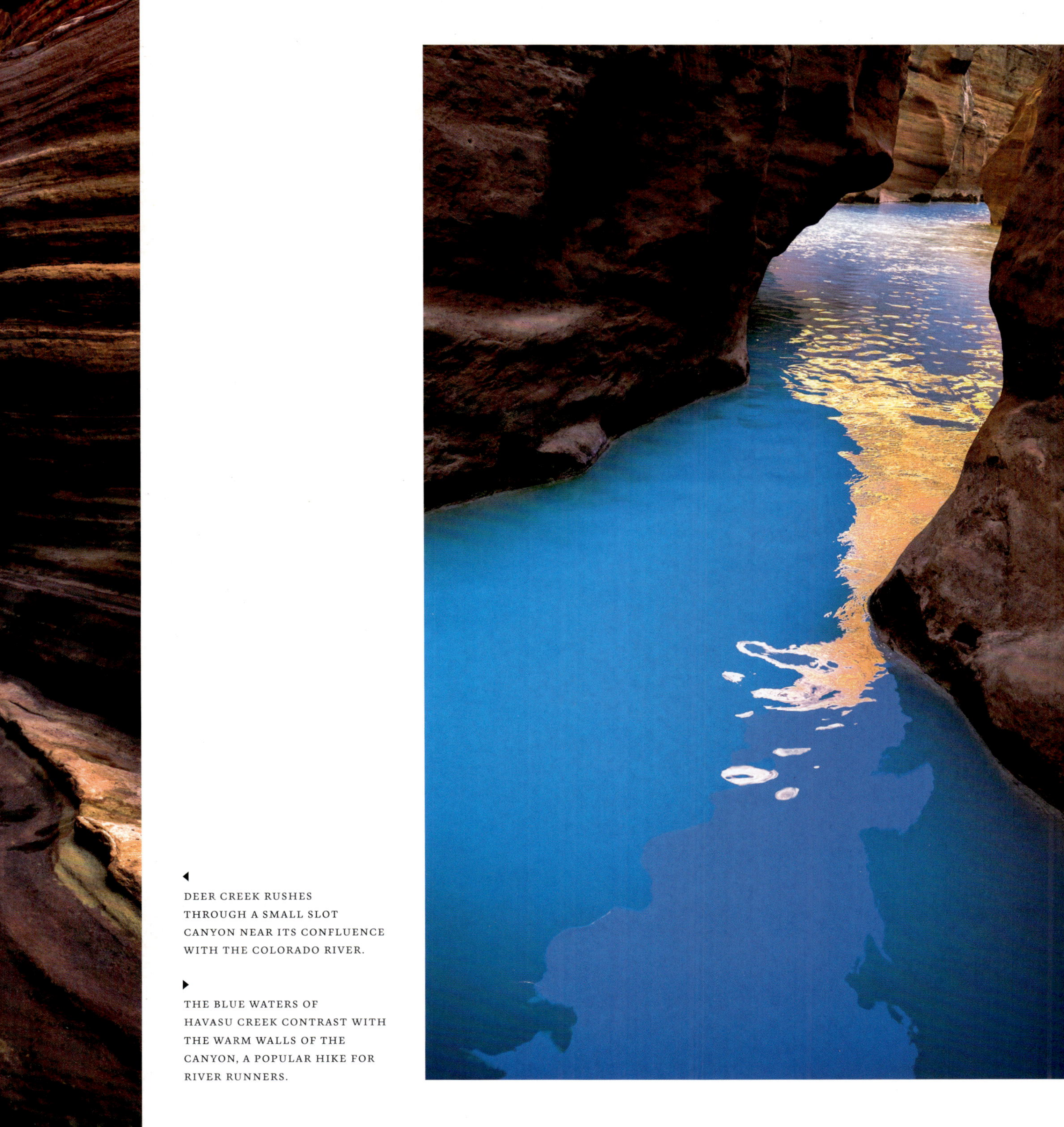

DEER CREEK RUSHES
THROUGH A SMALL SLOT
CANYON NEAR ITS CONFLUENCE
WITH THE COLORADO RIVER.

THE BLUE WATERS OF
HAVASU CREEK CONTRAST WITH
THE WARM WALLS OF THE
CANYON, A POPULAR HIKE FOR
RIVER RUNNERS.

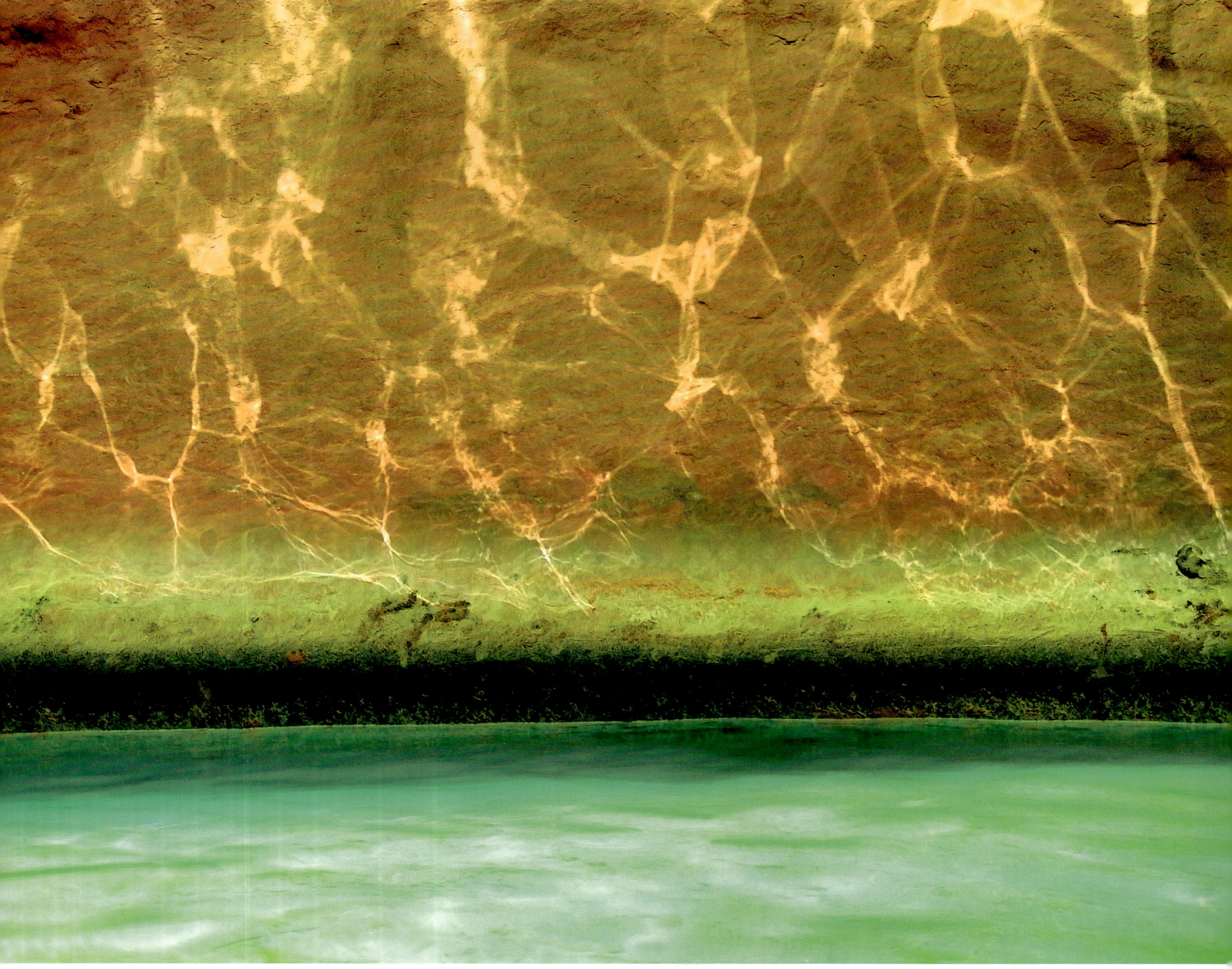



GRAPHIC PATTERNS FROM THE AZURE WATER OF HAVASU CREEK REFLECT ON THE WALLS OF THE GRAND CANYON.

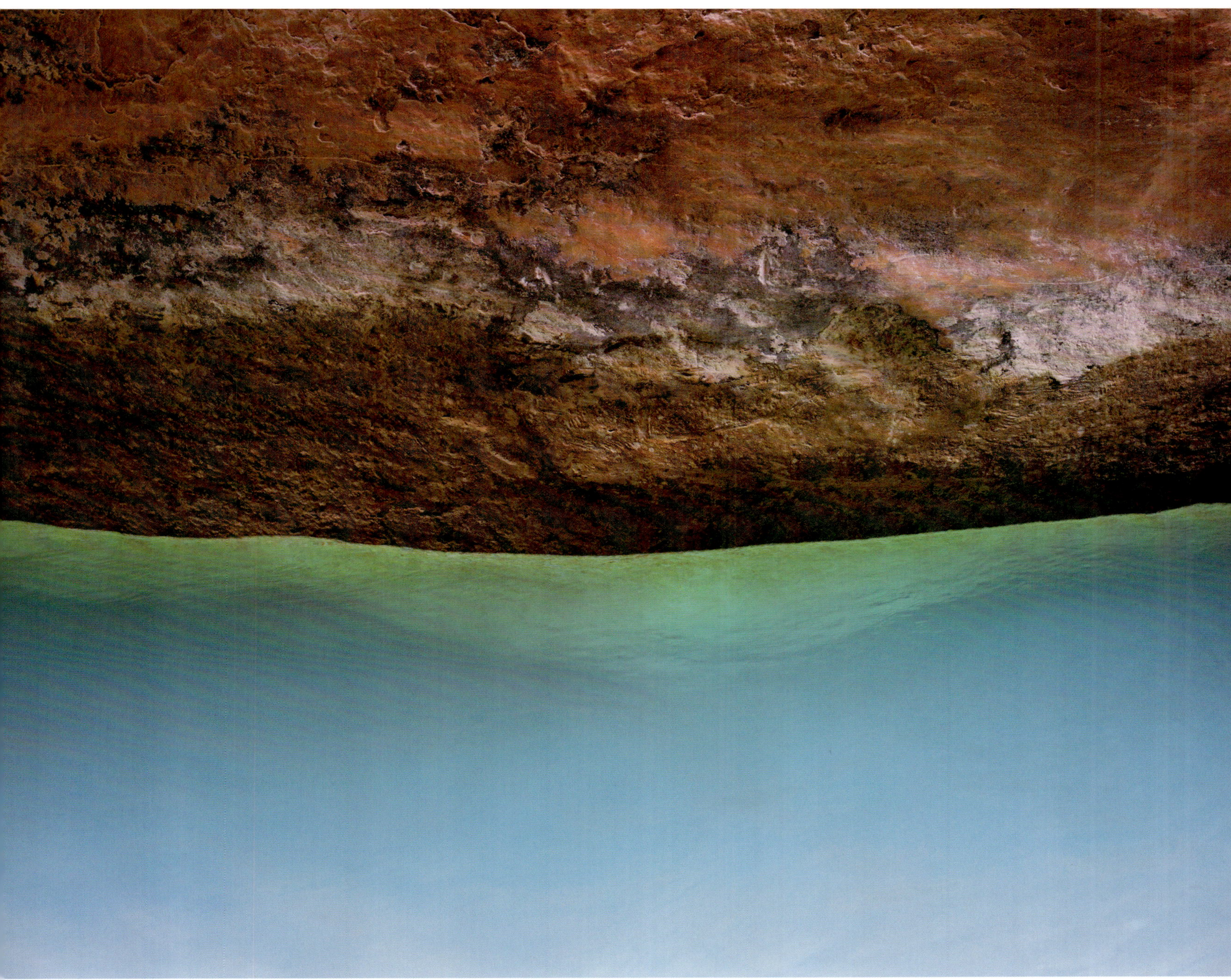

TURQUOISE WATER CARESSES THE WARM SANDSTONE WALLS AT THE CONFLUENCE OF HAVASU CREEK IN GRAND CANYON NATIONAL PARK.

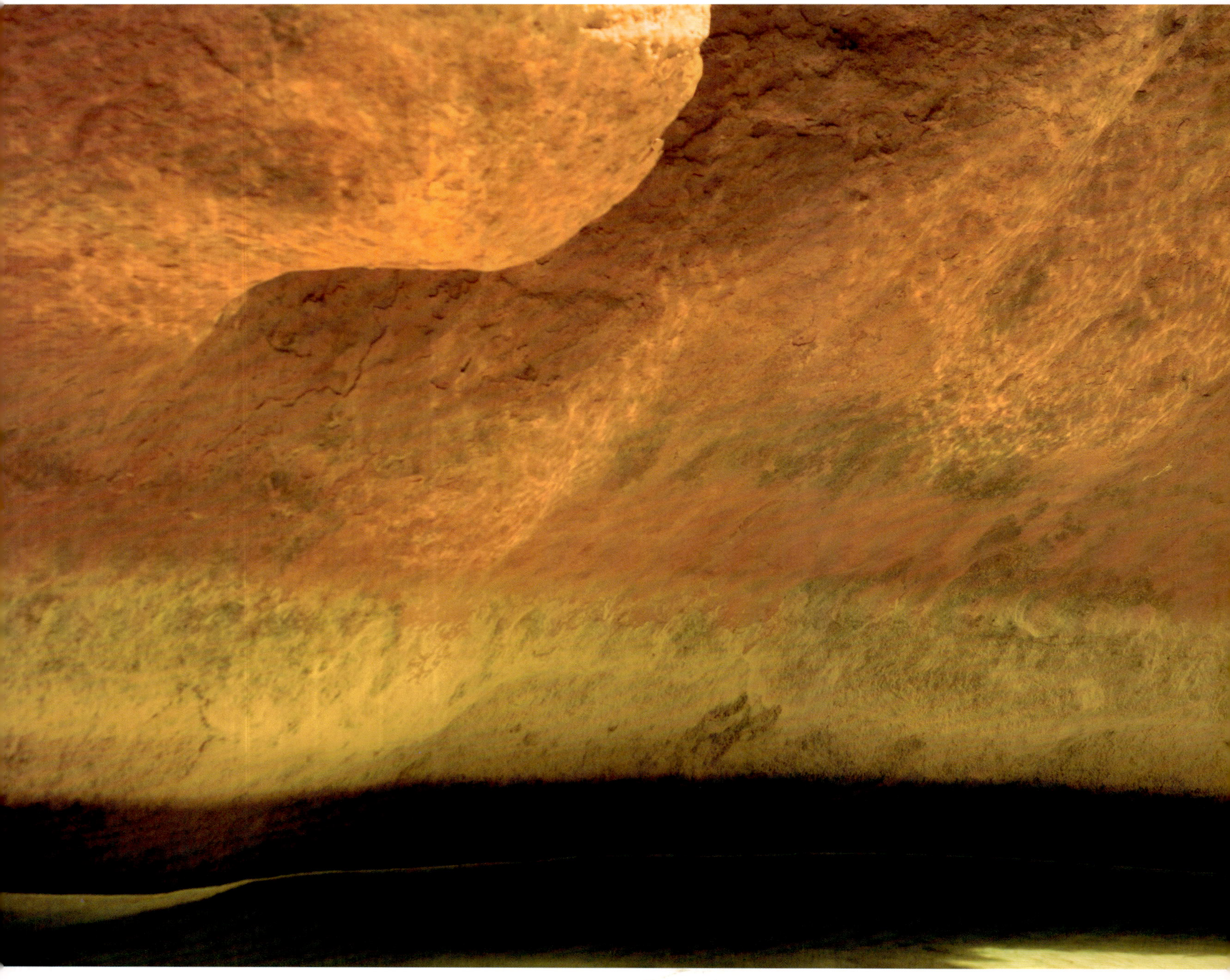



GOLDEN WATER TOUCHES THE WARM SANDSTONE WALLS AT THE CONFLUENCE OF HAVASU CREEK IN GRAND CANYON NATIONAL PARK.

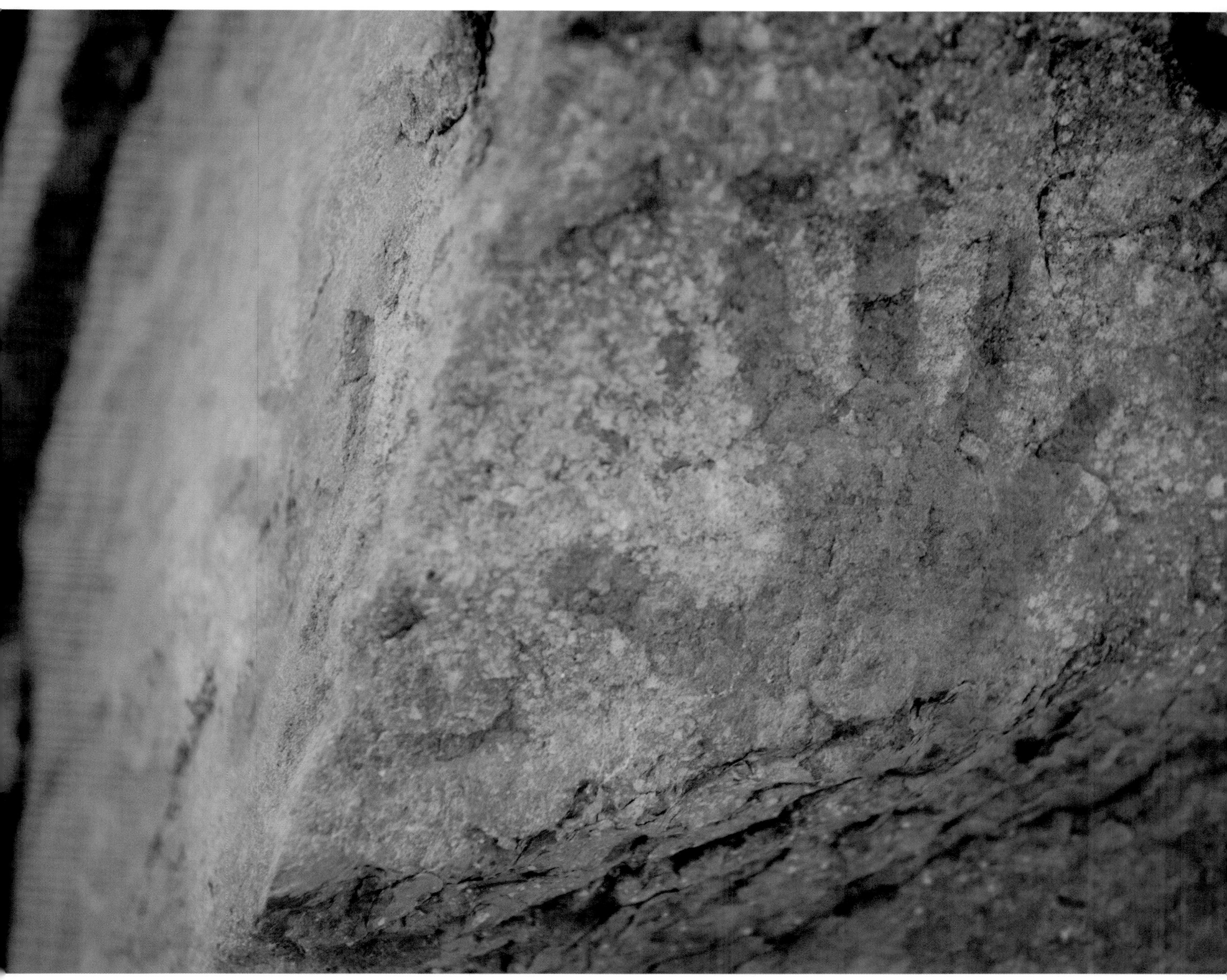

HANDPRINTS FROM ANCIENT PUEBLOAN PEOPLE LINE THE STEEP WALLS OF DEER CREEK CANYON.

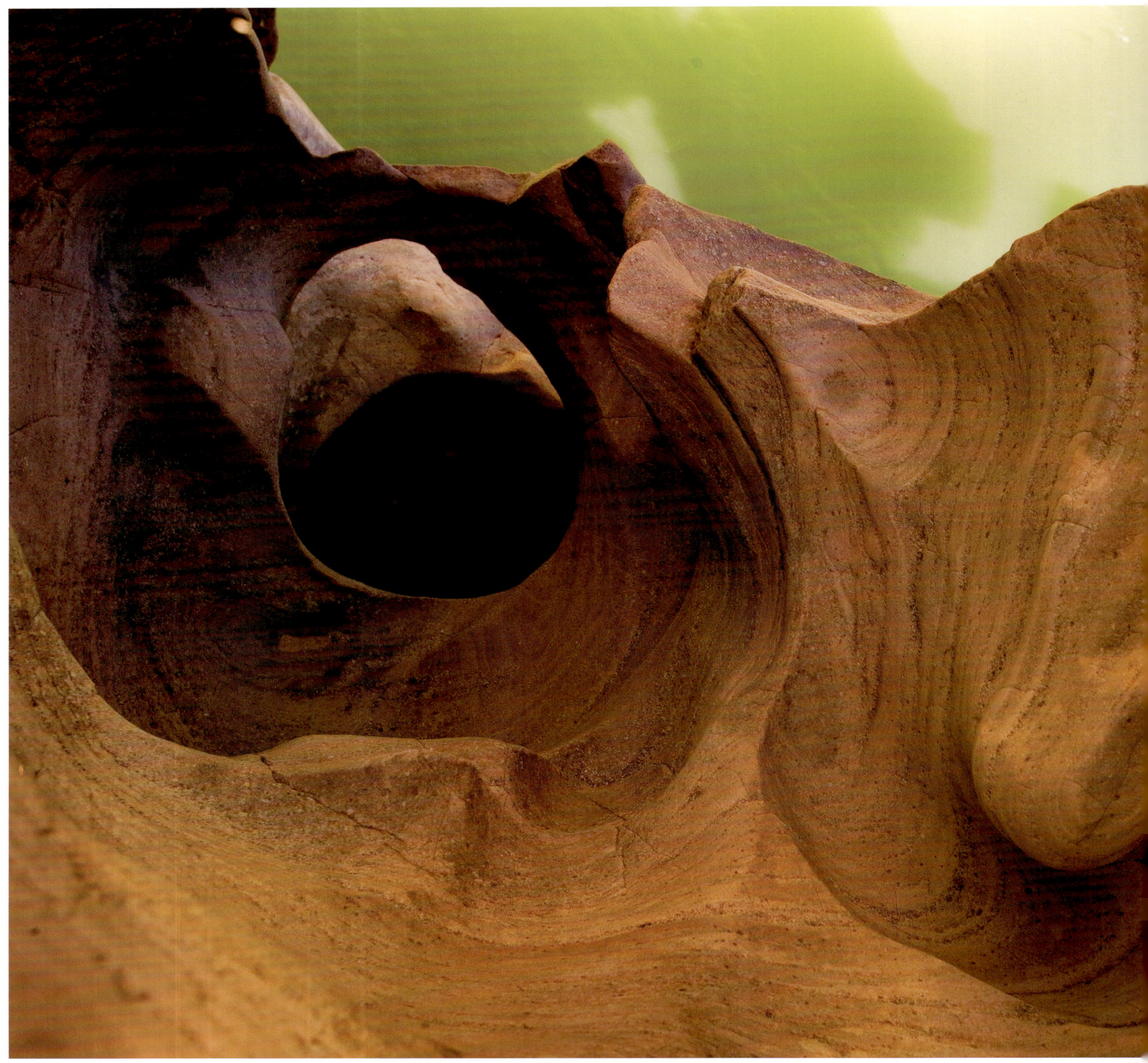

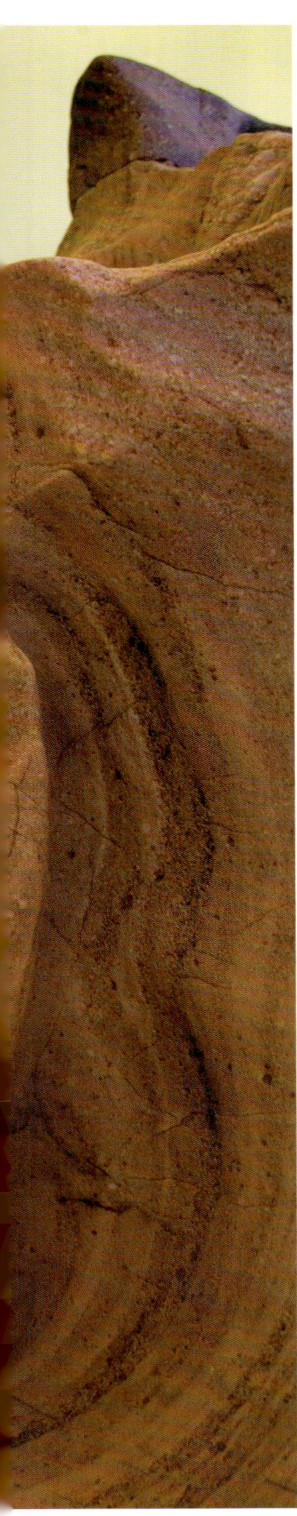

◀

GRAPHIC PATTERNS AND
SHAPES CARVED BY THE MIGHTY
COLORADO RIVER EMERGE NEAR
PUMPKIN SPRING IN GRAND
CANYON NATIONAL PARK.

▶

TURQUOISE WATER AND
GOLDEN CANYON WALLS AT THE
CONFLUENCE OF HAVASU CREEK
AND THE COLORADO RIVER.

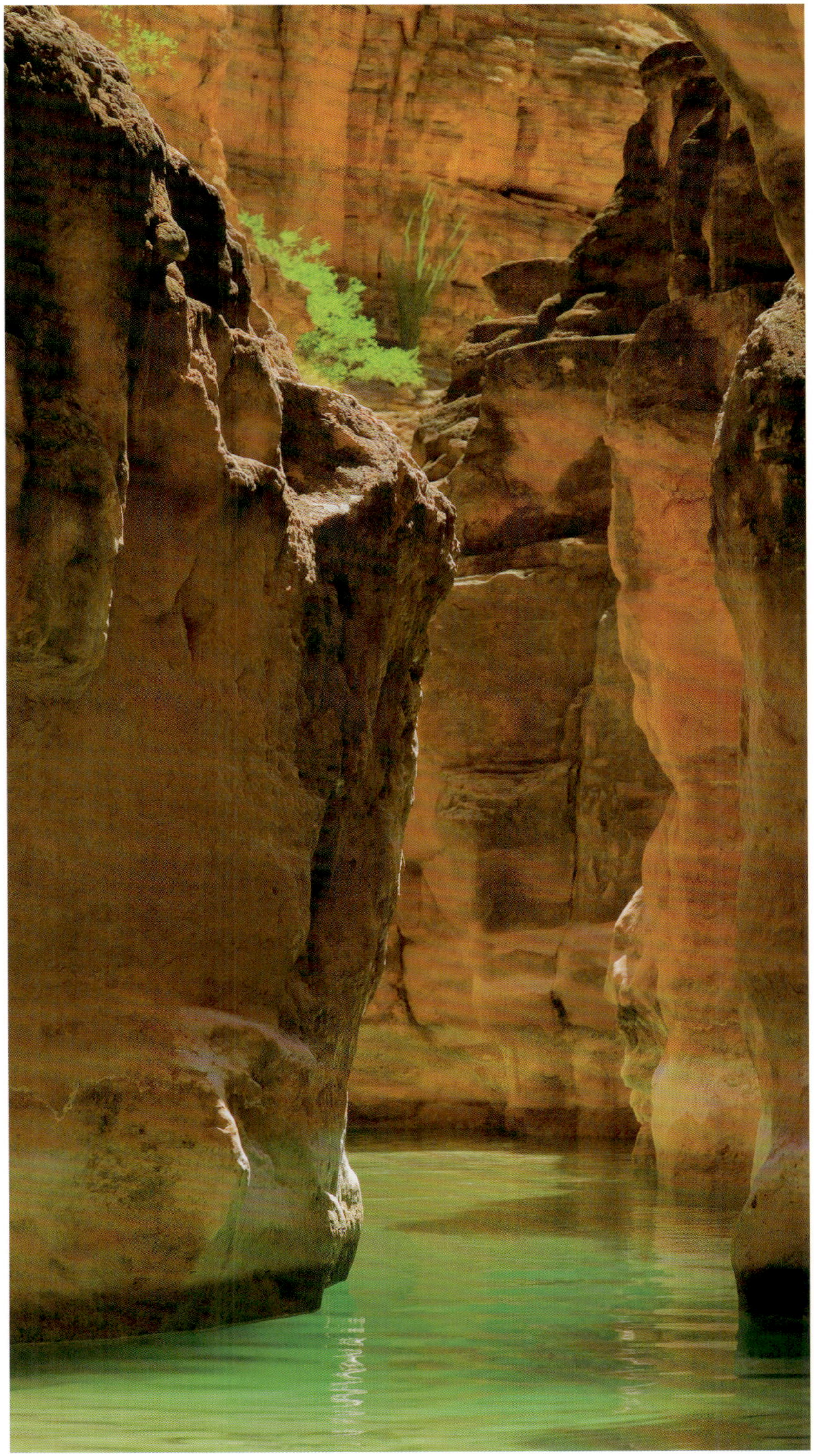

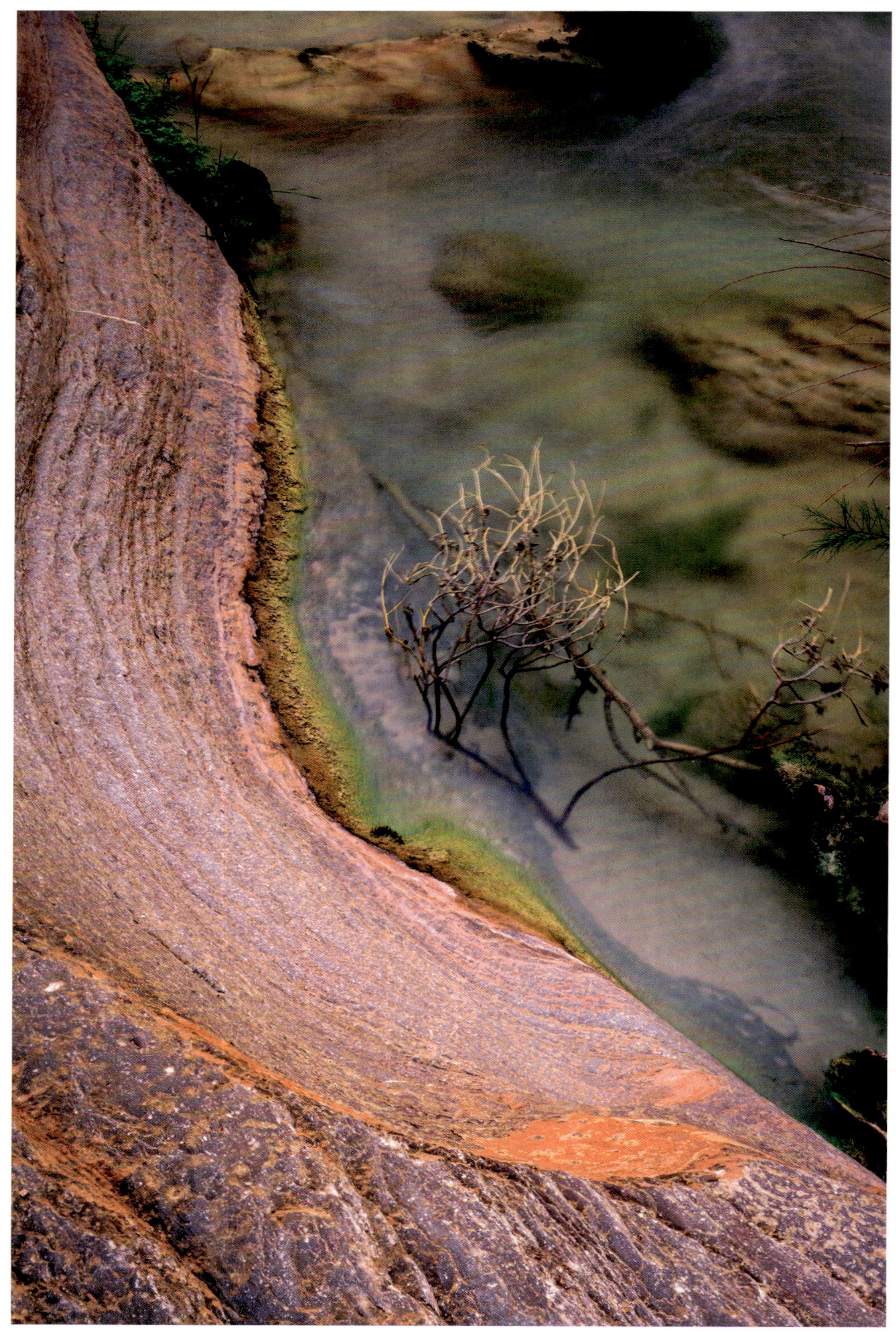

◀

HAVASU CREEK FLOWS CLEAR
ON ITS WAY TO THE CONFLUENCE
WITH THE COLORADO RIVER.

▶

SUSPENDED MINERALS AND SILT
GIVE HAVASU CREEK A GHOSTLY
APPEARANCE.

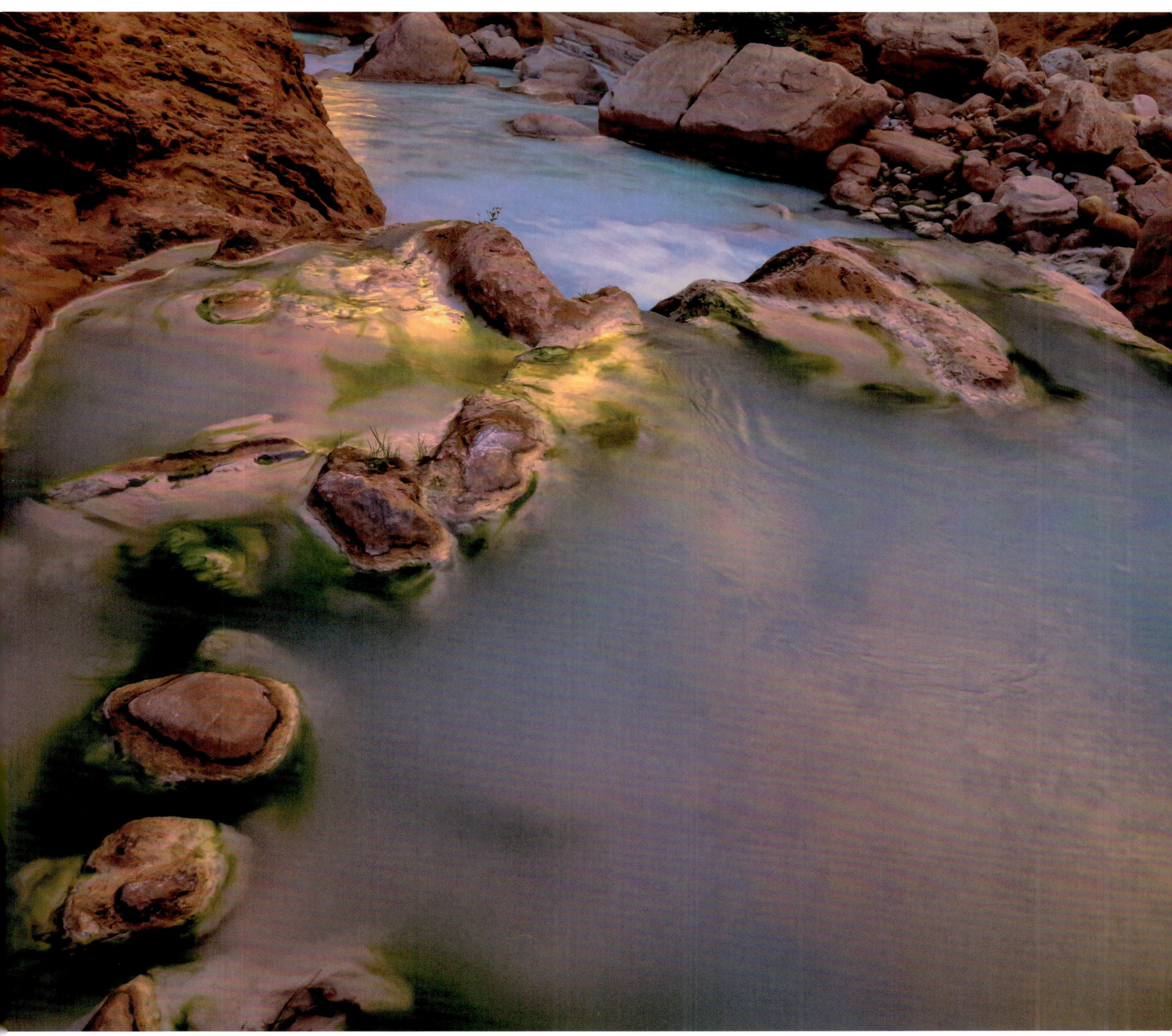

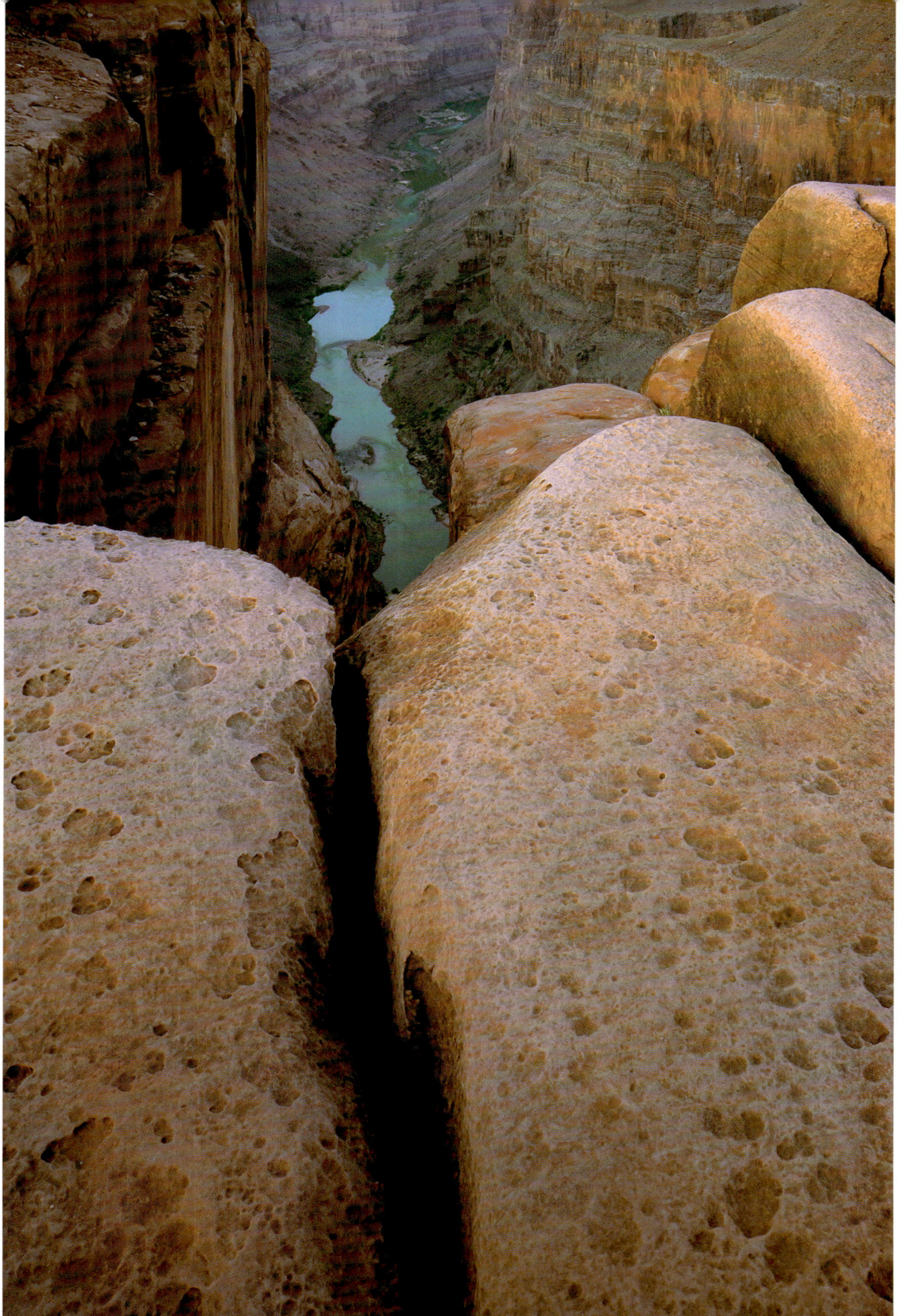

BREAD LOAF-SHAPED
ROCKS HIGH ABOVE THE
COLORADO RIVER AT THE
TOROWEAP OVERLOOK.

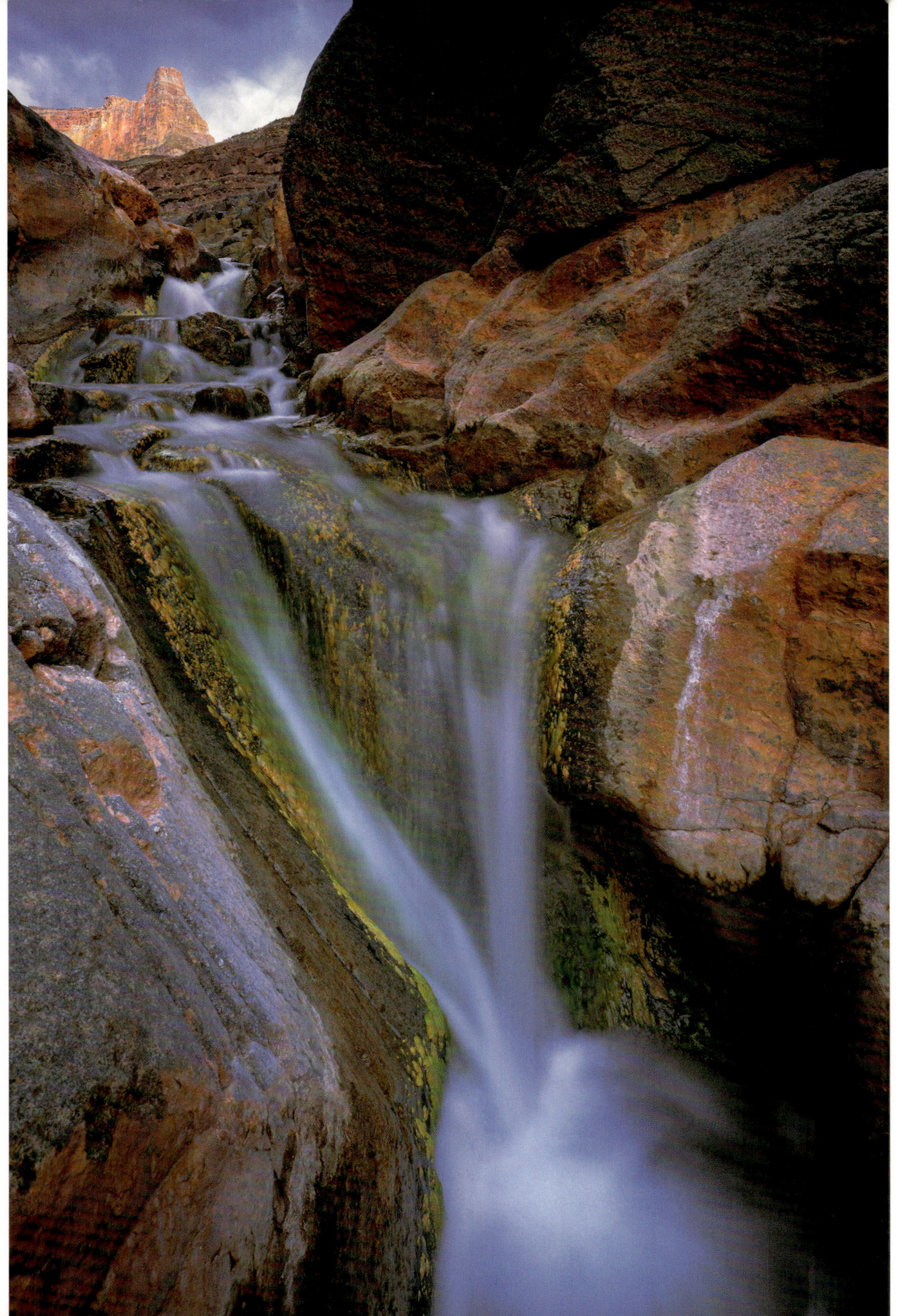

RED SANDSTONE FORMATIONS SPIRE UPWARDS ABOVE A WATERFALL ON STONE CREEK.

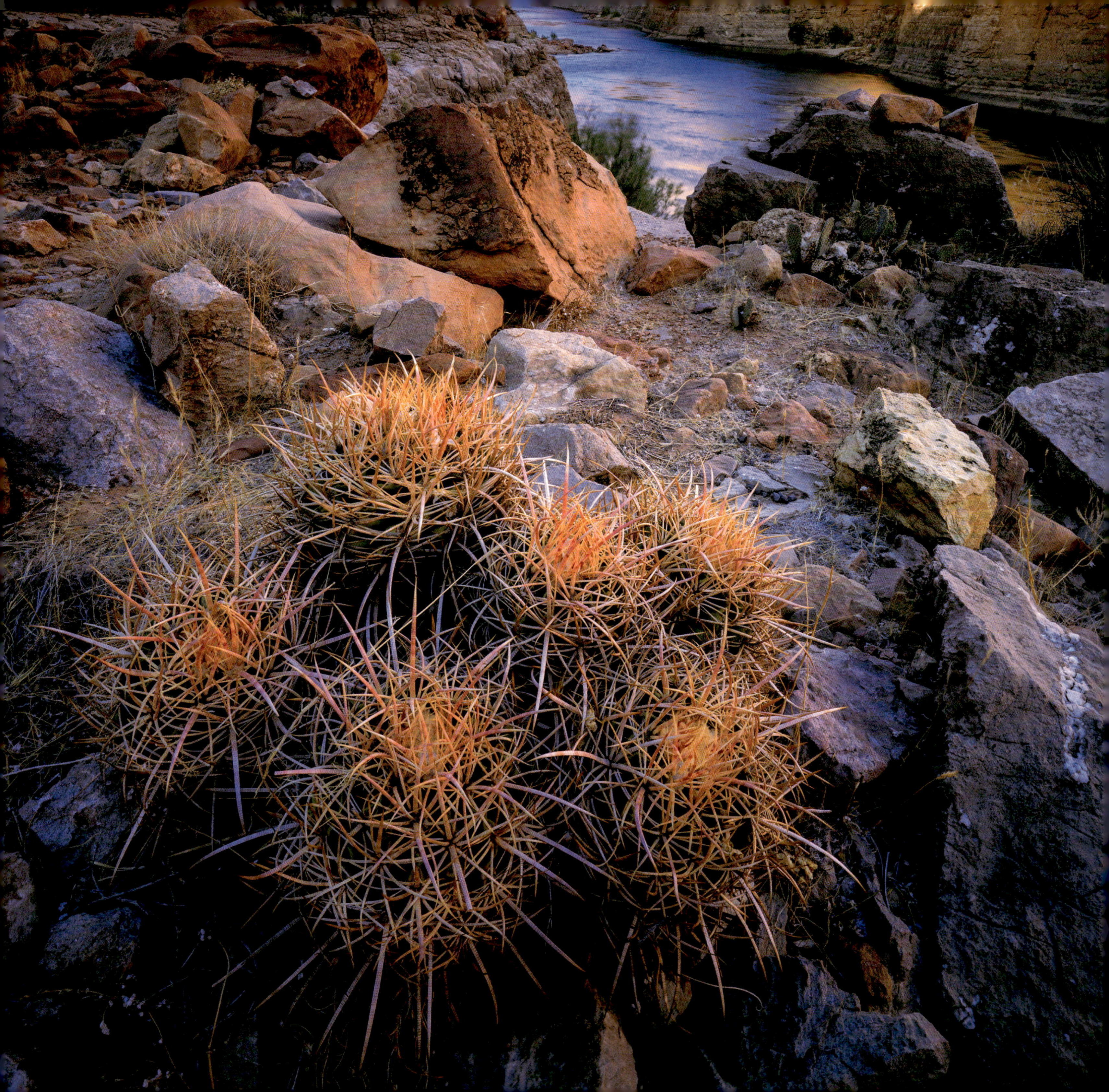

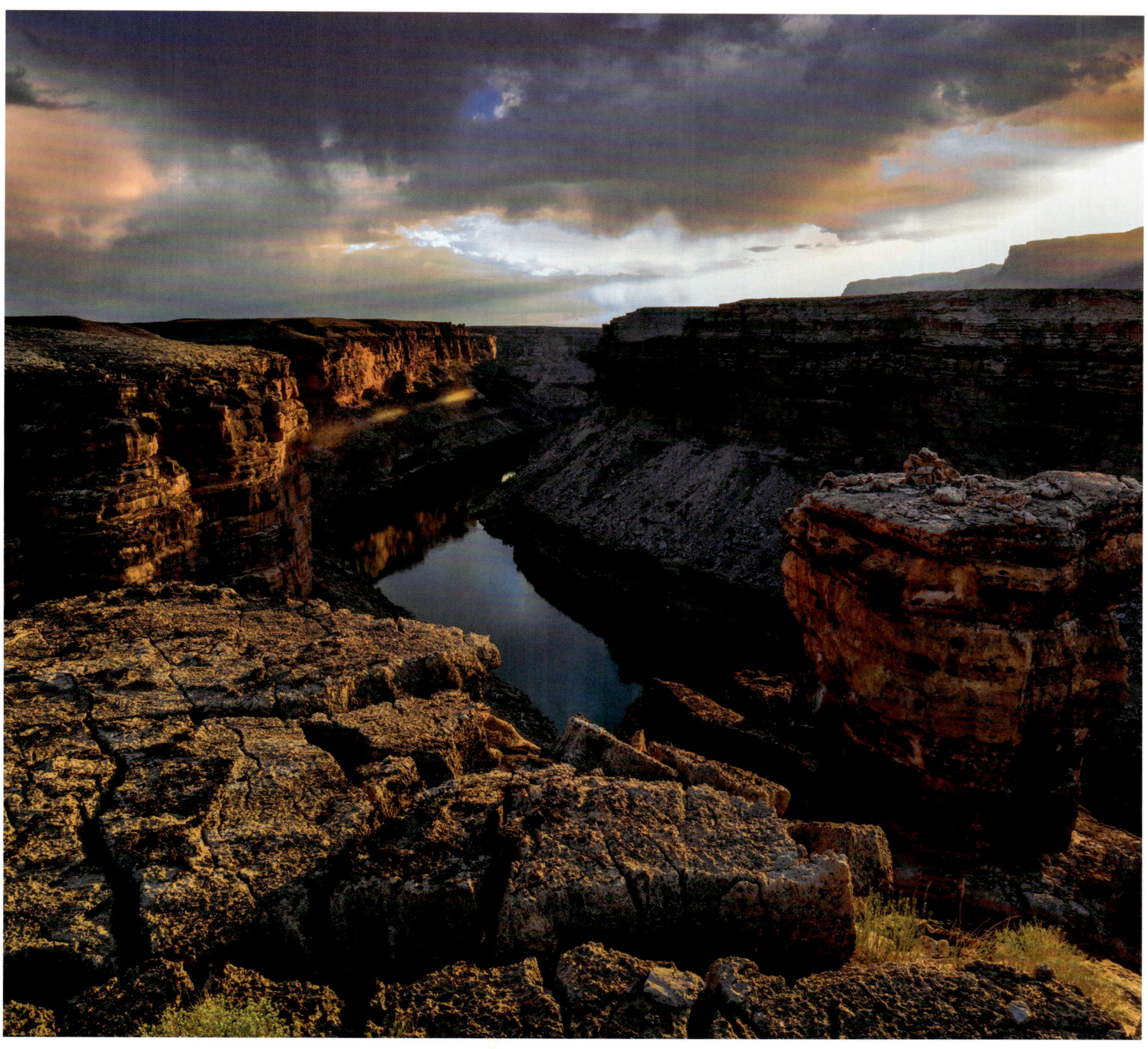

BARREL CACTI BLOOM ON THE LEDGES
ABOVE SOUTH CANYON CAMP.

WARM LIGHT SPILLS ACROSS A LIMESTONE LEDGE
IN THE UPPER REACHES OF MARBLE CANYON.

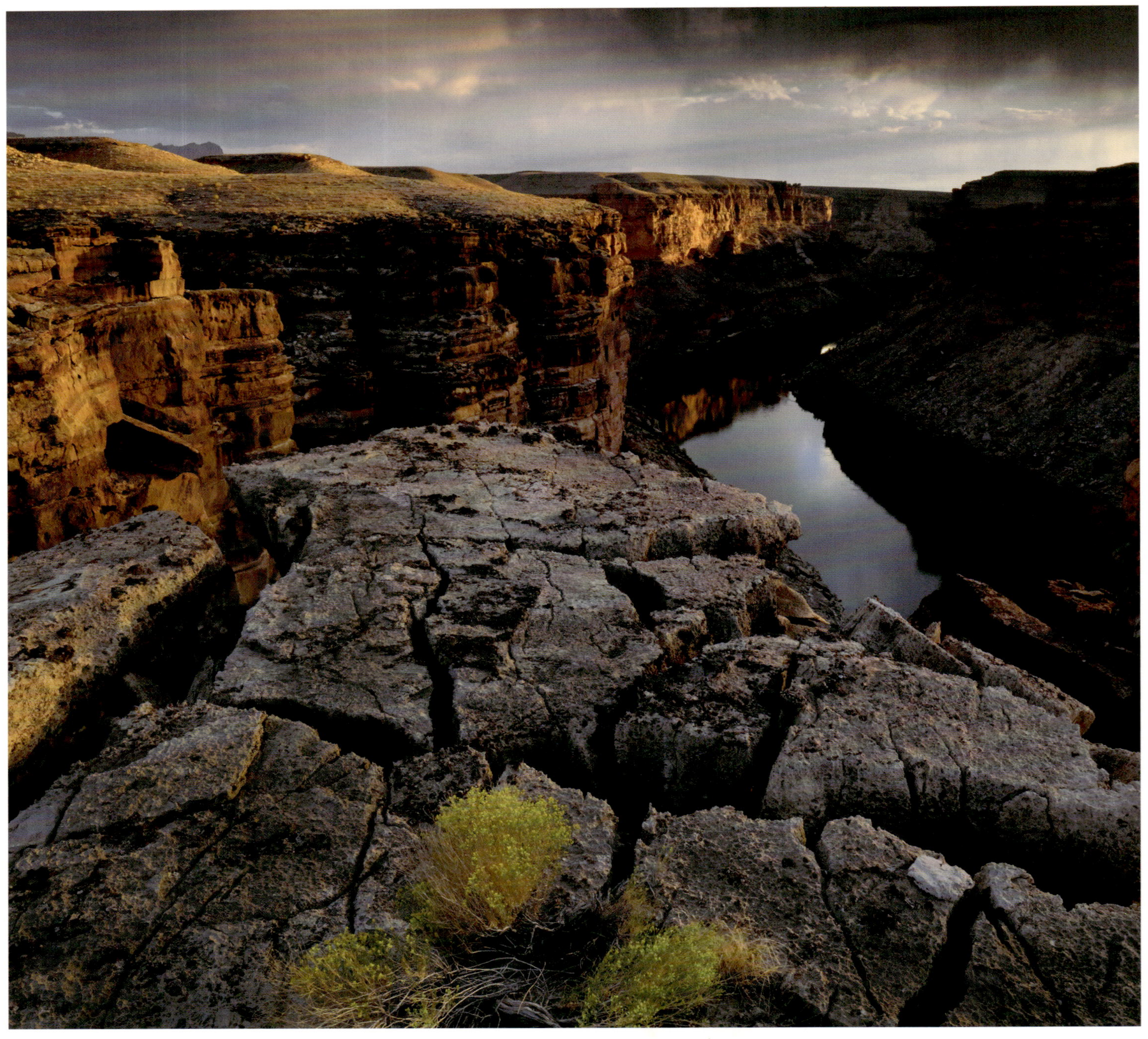

STORM CLOUDS RACE OVER MARBLE CANYON NEAR THE NAVAJO BRIDGE.

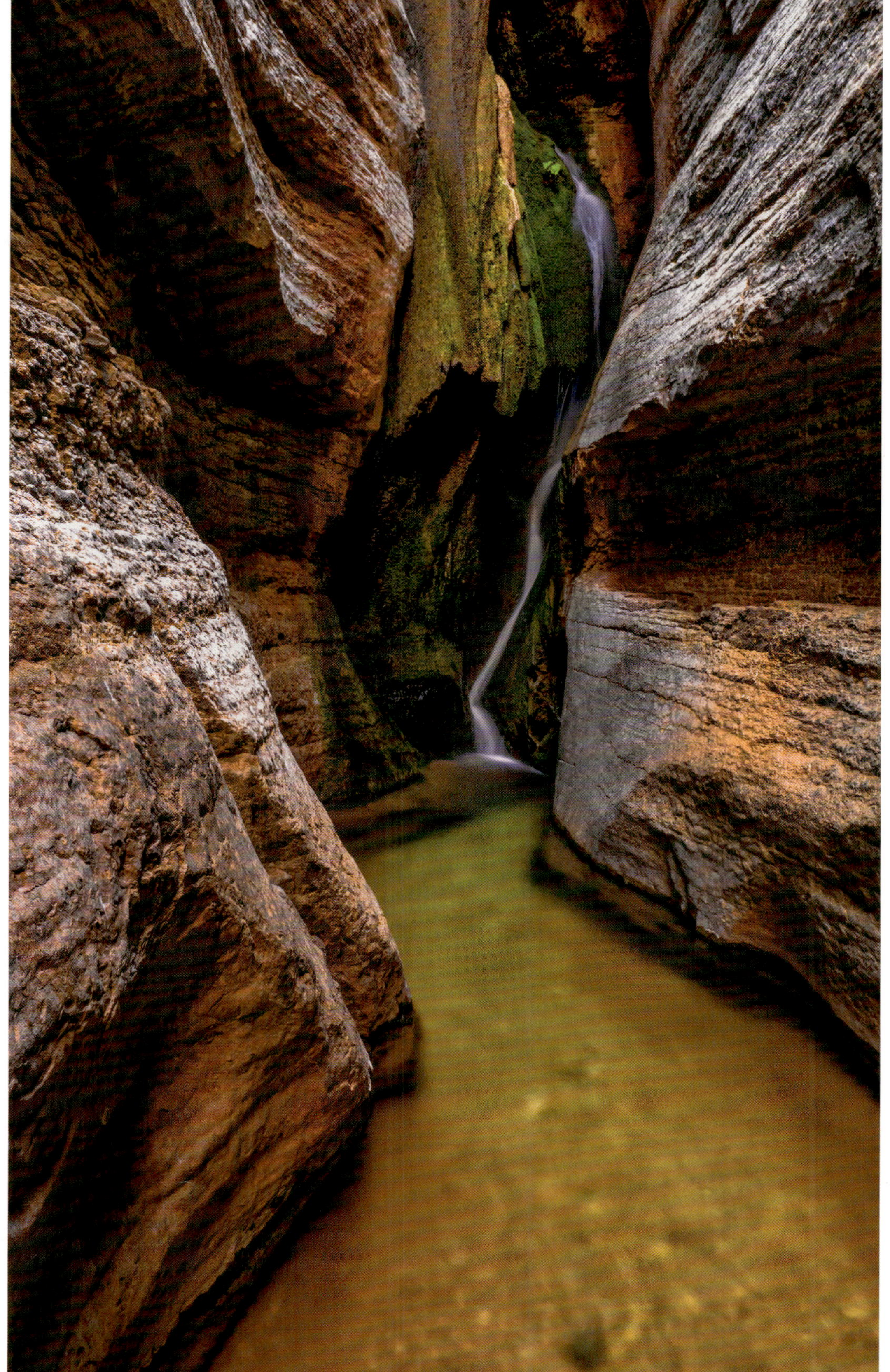

NATURAL SPRINGS PROVIDE ENOUGH
WATER IN SADDLE CANYON TO
PRODUCE A BEAUTIFUL WATERFALL
NEAR ITS CONFLUENCE WITH THE
COLORADO RIVER.

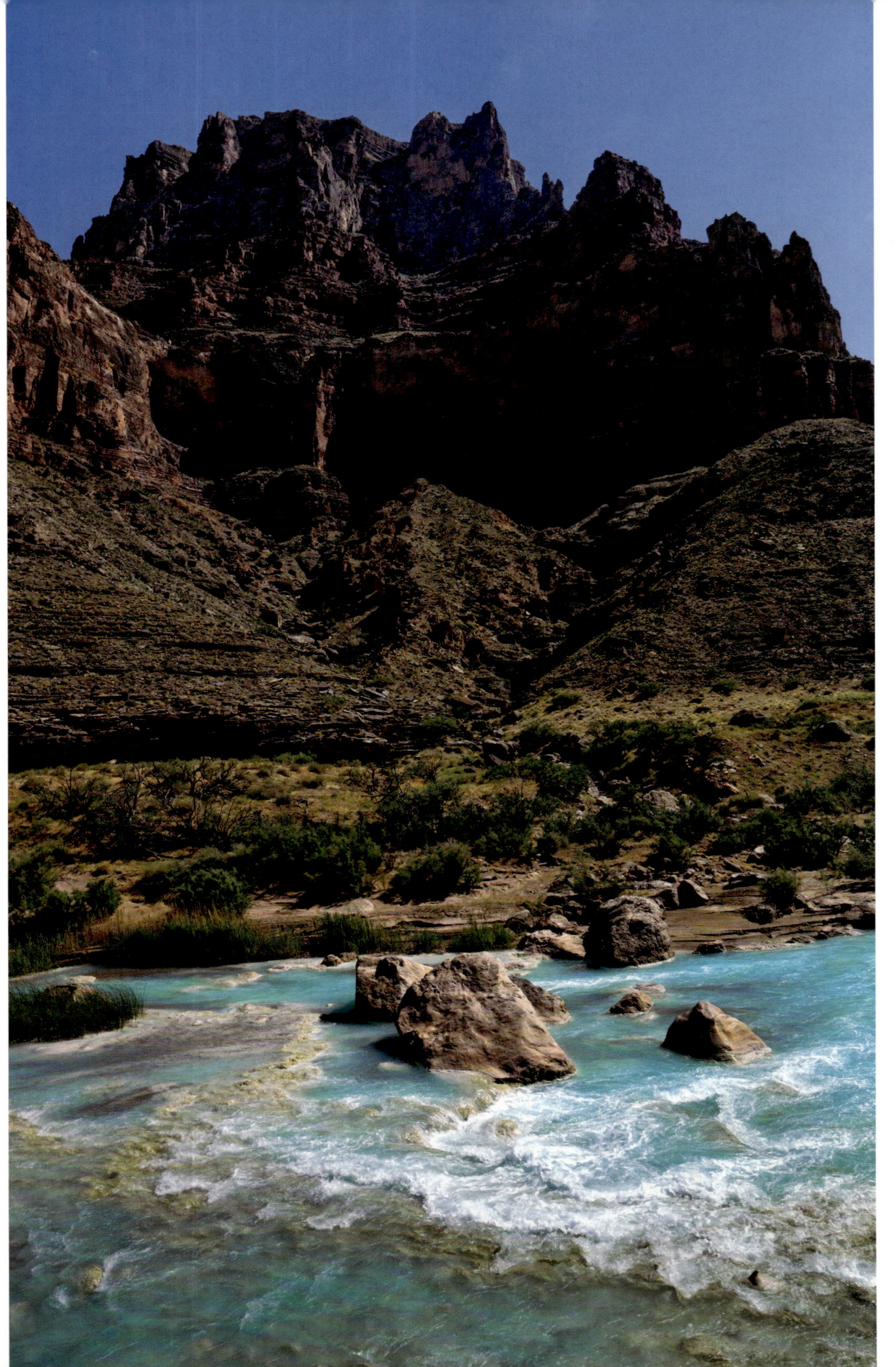

AZURE WATERS OF THE
LITTLE COLORADO RIVER NEAR
ITS CONFLUENCE WITH THE
COLORADO RIVER.

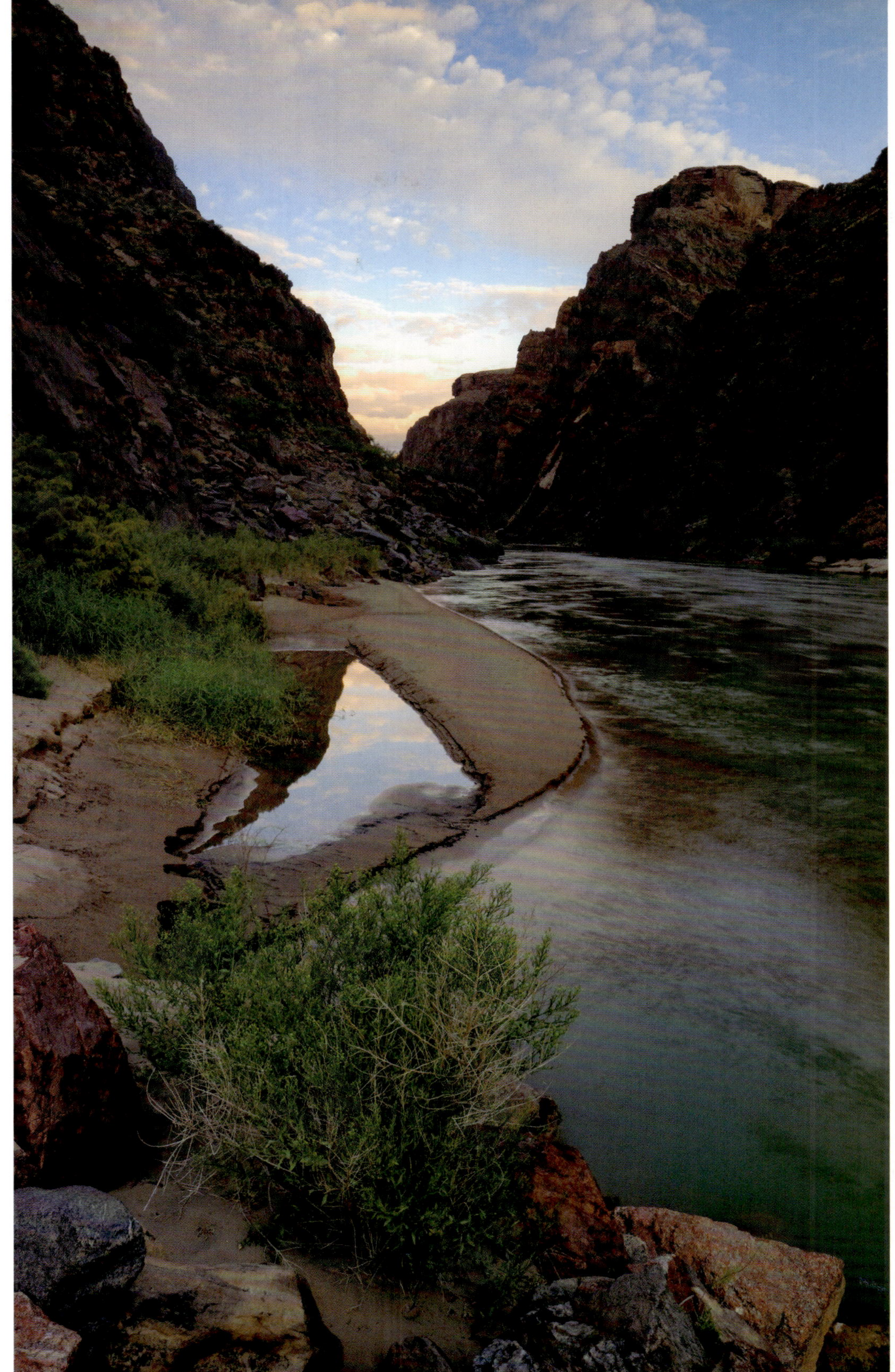

LARGE SANDBARS LIKE THIS ONE
ABOVE GRAPEVINE RAPID ARE
POPULAR CAMPS FOR RIVER RUNNERS
IN THE GRAND CANYON.

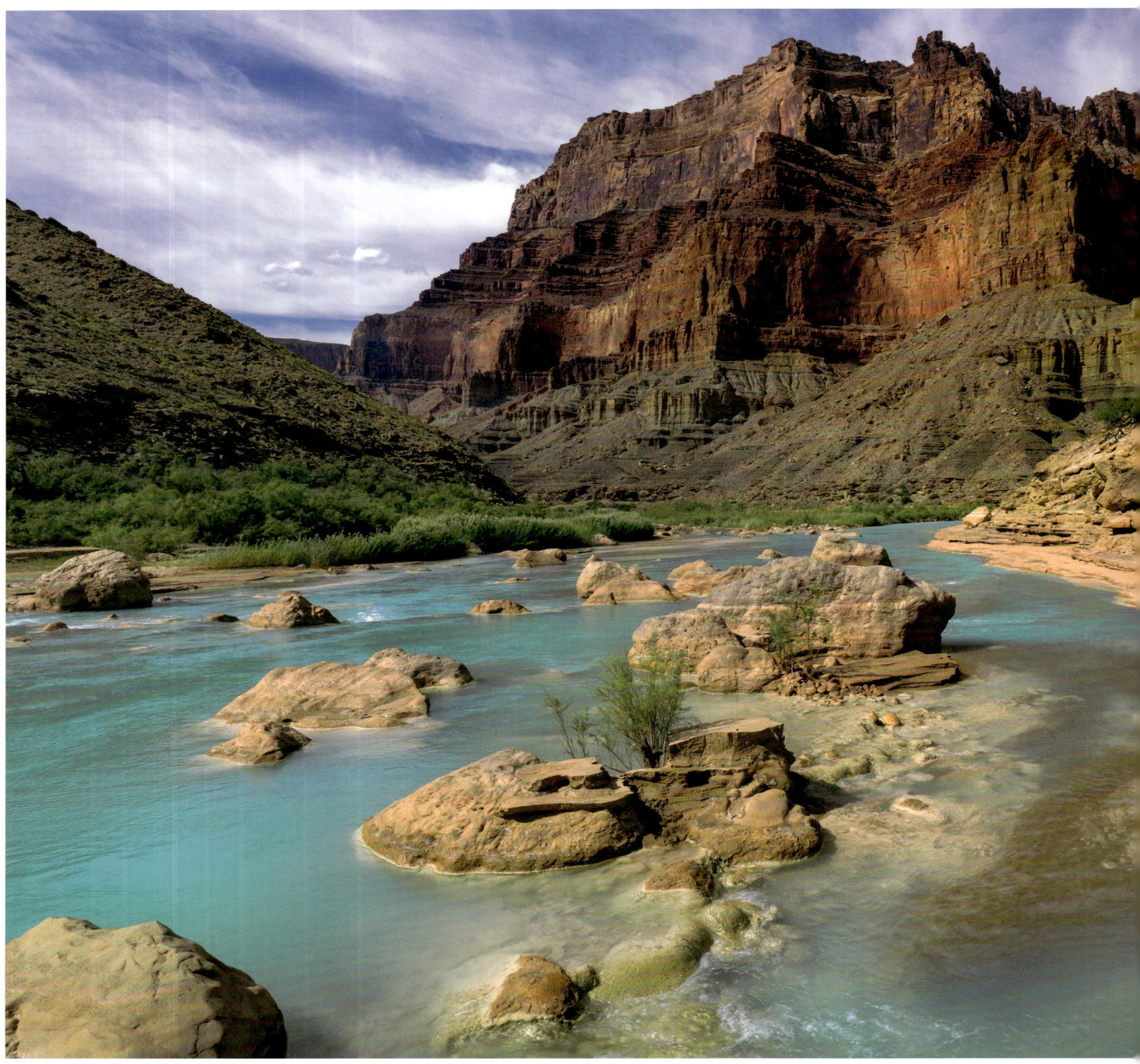

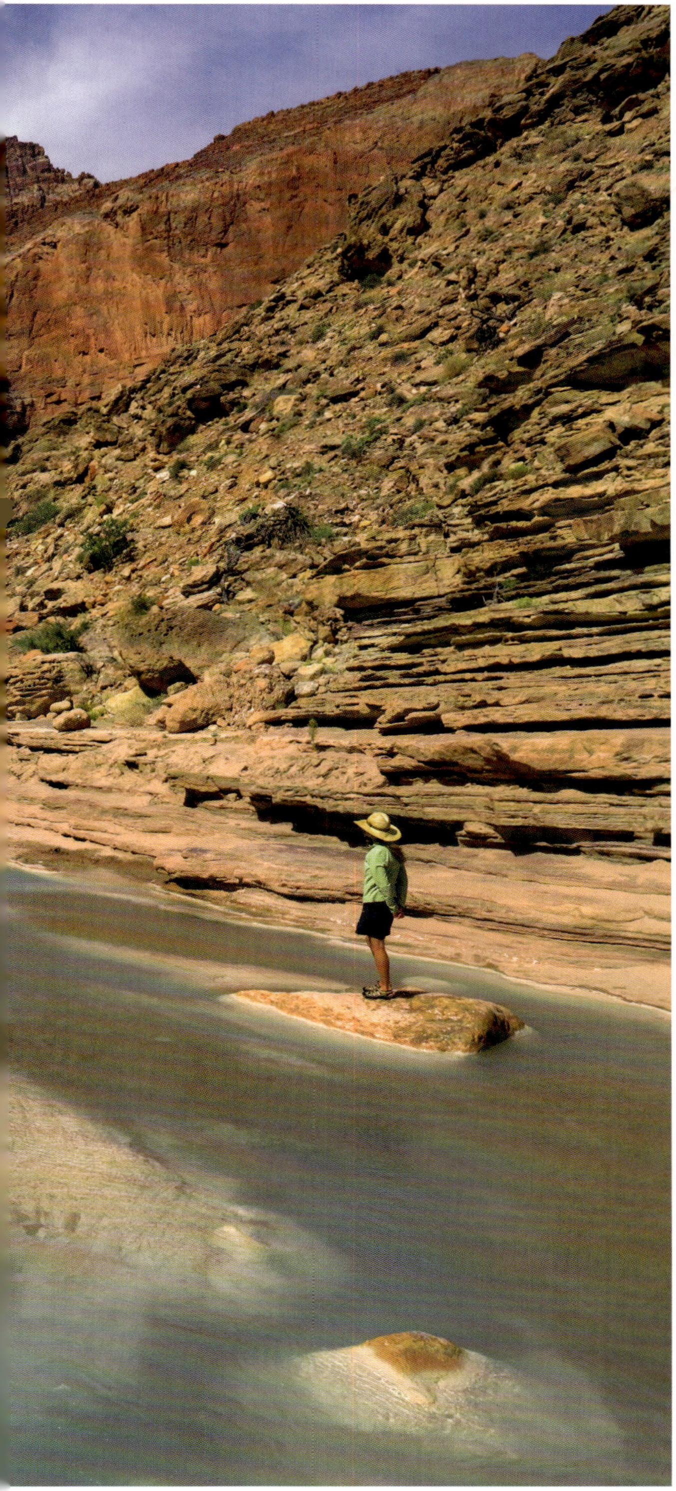

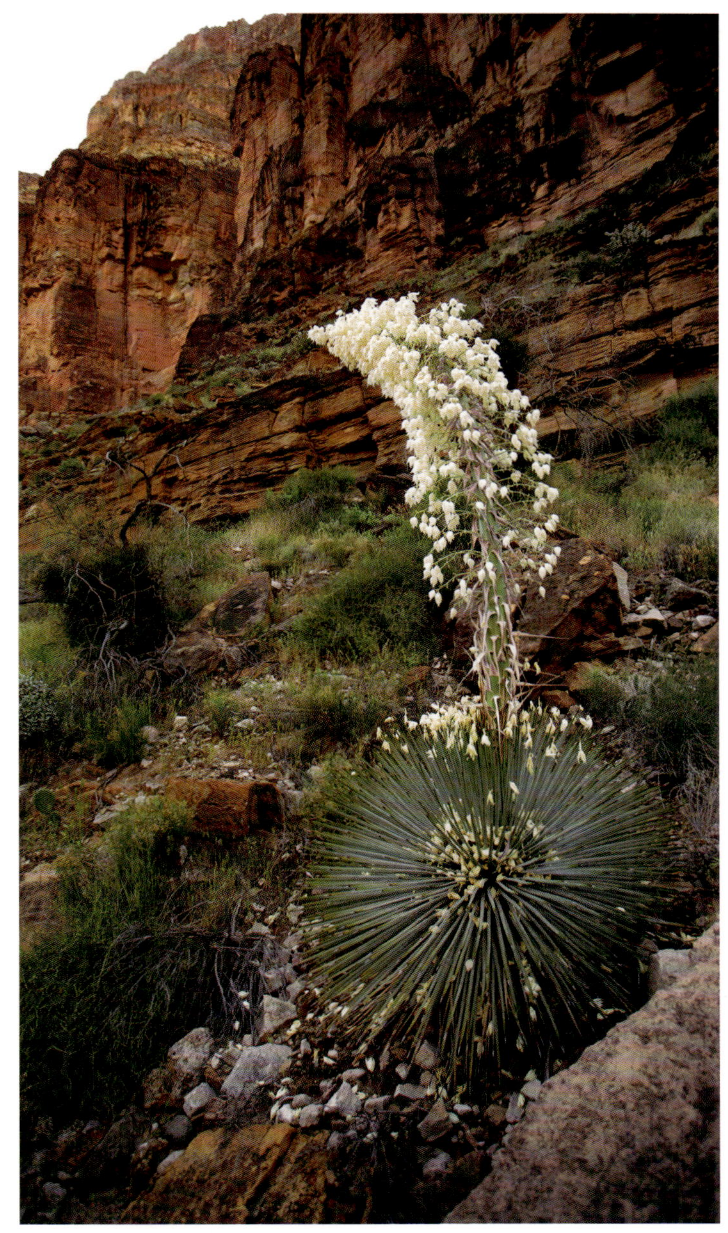



▲

THE WALLS OF THE CANYON HOLD HEAT, ALLOWING CENTURY PLANTS TO BLOOM IN THE SPRING-LIKE CONDITIONS.

◄

HIKERS ENJOY THE AZURE COLOR OF THE LITTLE COLORADO RIVER NEAR ITS CONFLUENCE WITH THE COLORADO RIVER IN GRAND CANYON NATIONAL PARK.

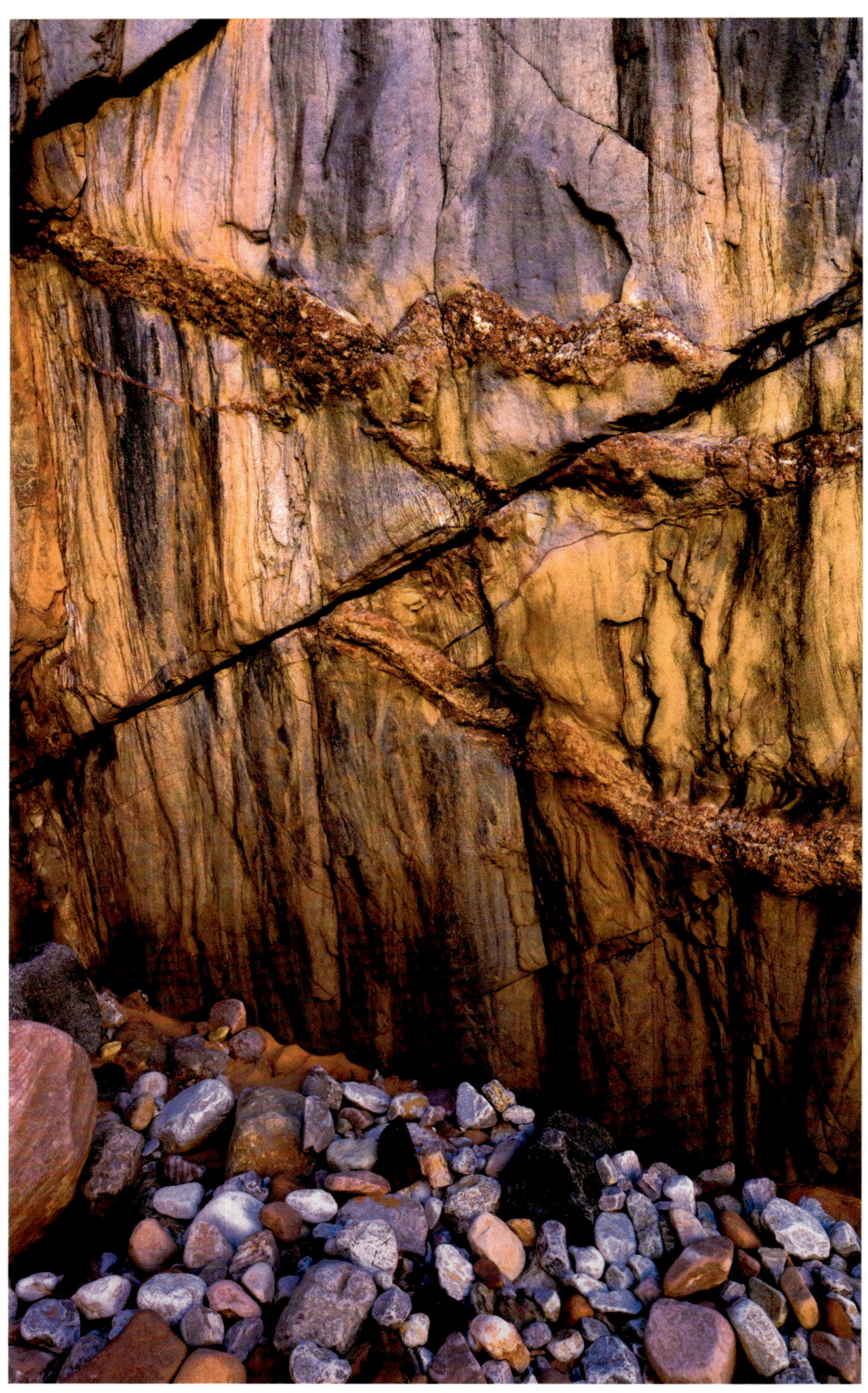

THE POLISHED GRANITE WALLS OF HAKATAI
CANYON LOOK ALMOST METALLIC IN MANY OF THE
SIDE CREEKS OF THE GRAND CANYON.

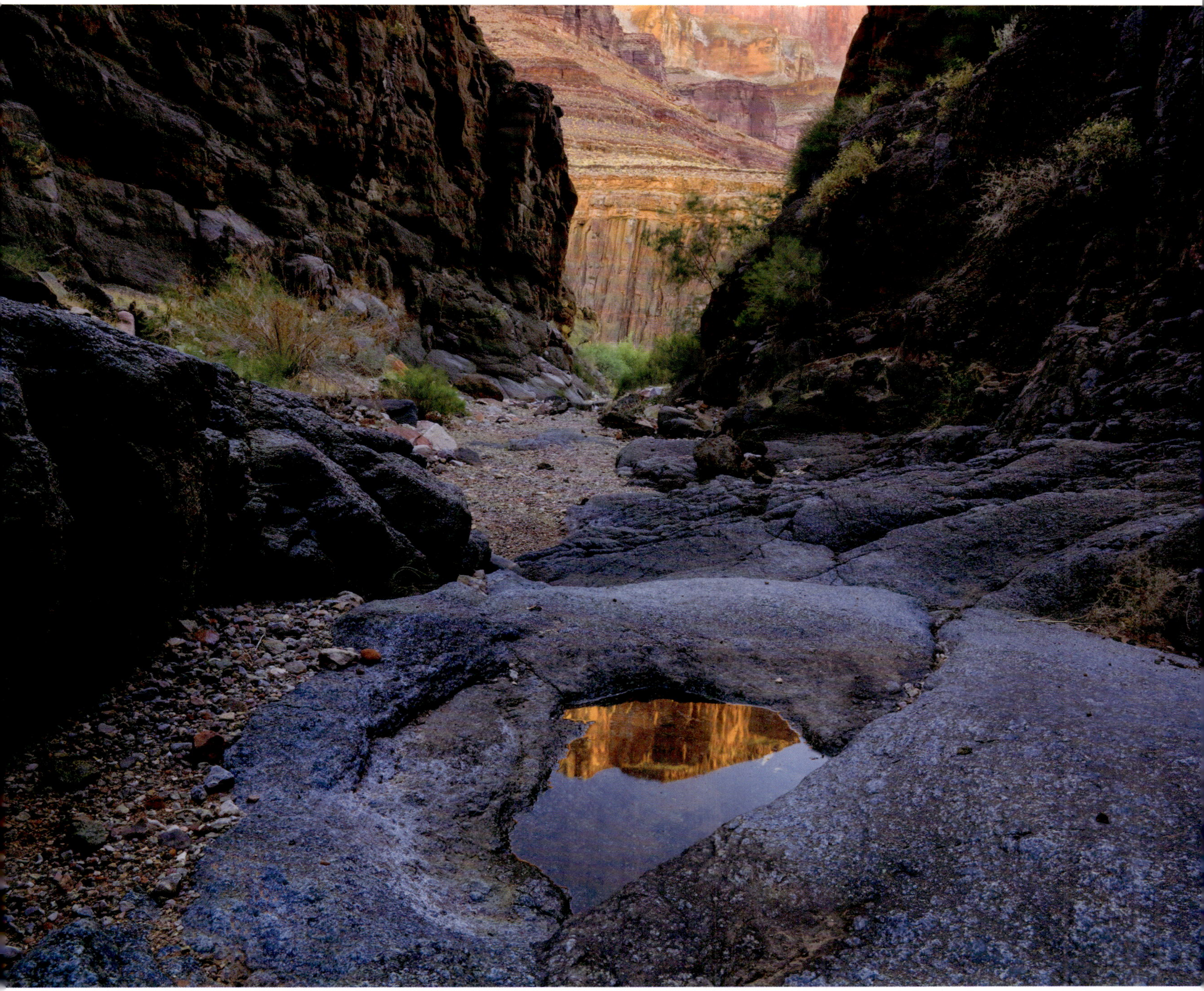

A SMALL WATER POCKET REFLECTS THE CANYON WALLS OF THE GRAND CANYON NEAR TALKING HEADS CAMP.

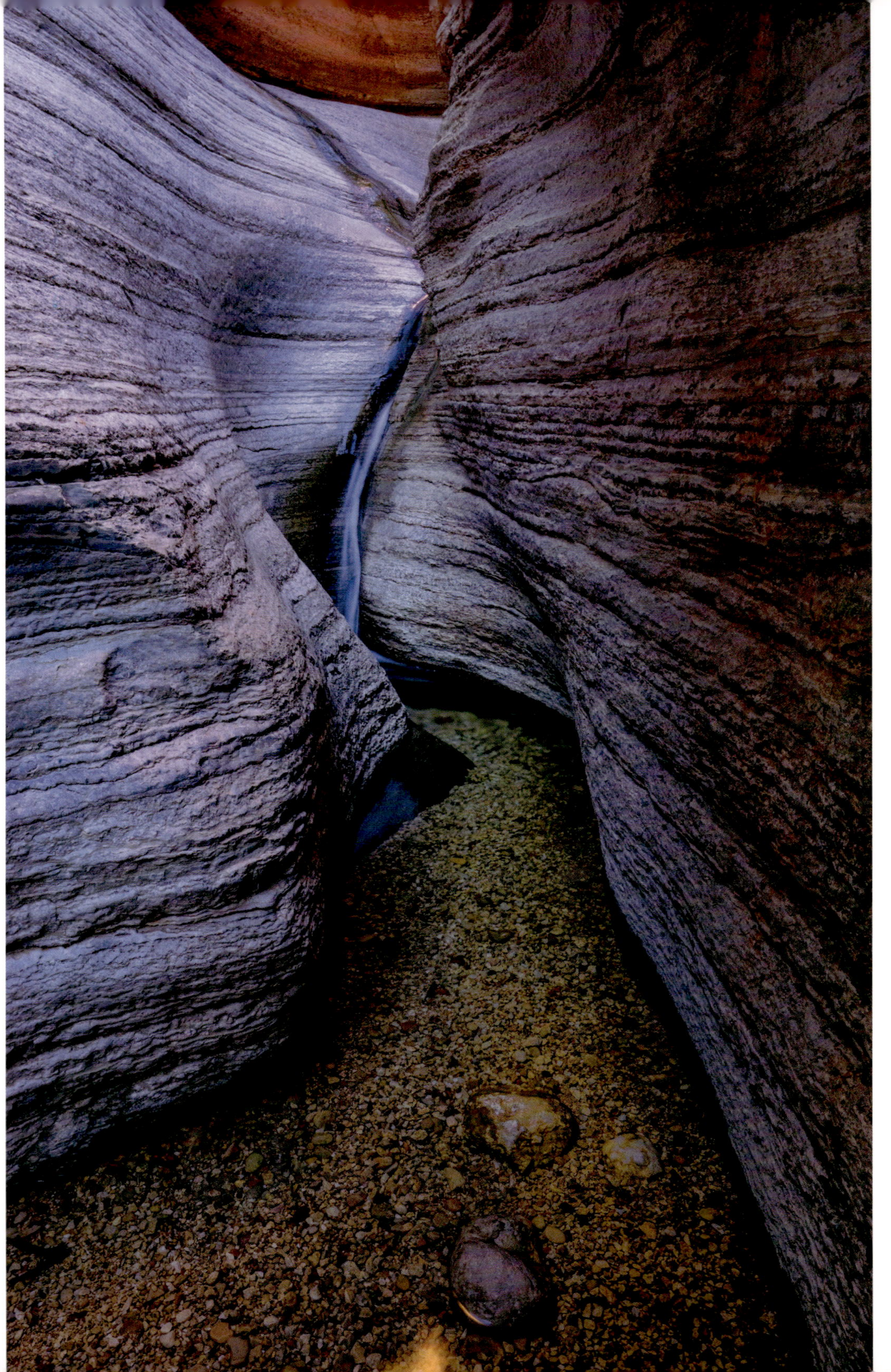

WATER CUTS THROUGH A
MUAV LIMESTONE SHELF,
FORMING A BEAUTIFUL
WATERFALL IN NATIONAL CANYON.

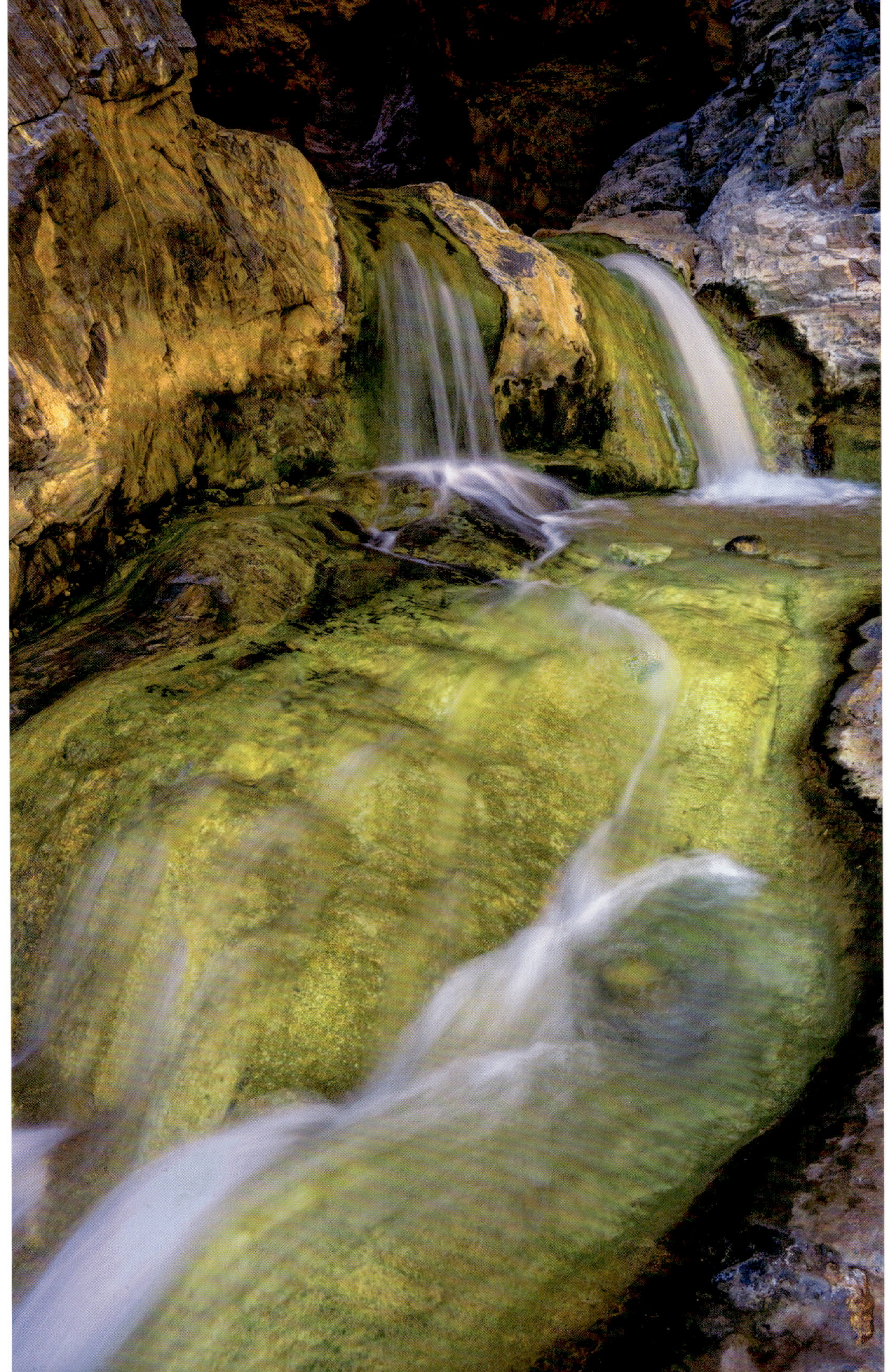

WATER SPILLS OVER THE TRAVERTINE
SHELVES OF TRAVERTINE CANYON IN
LOWER GRANITE GORGE.

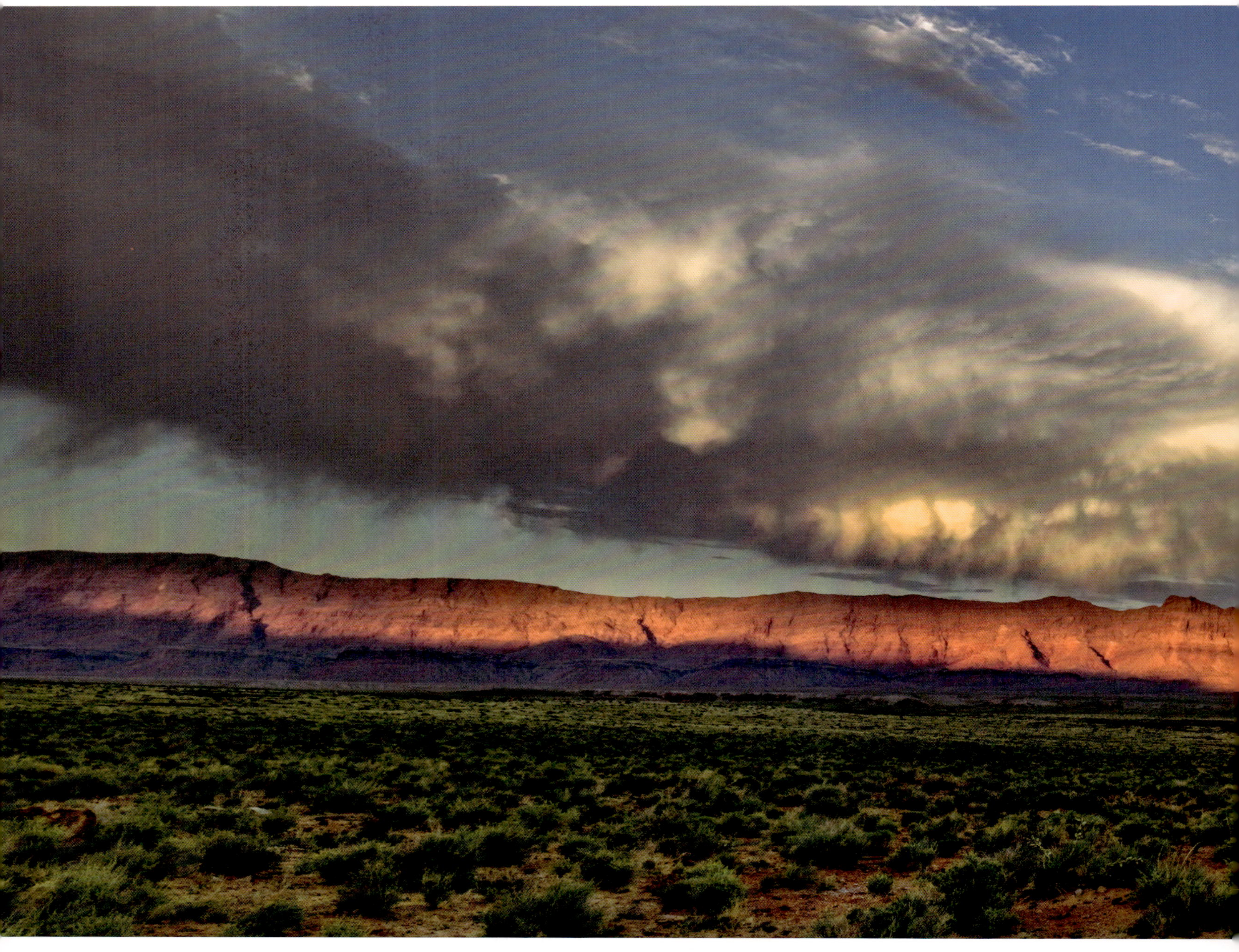

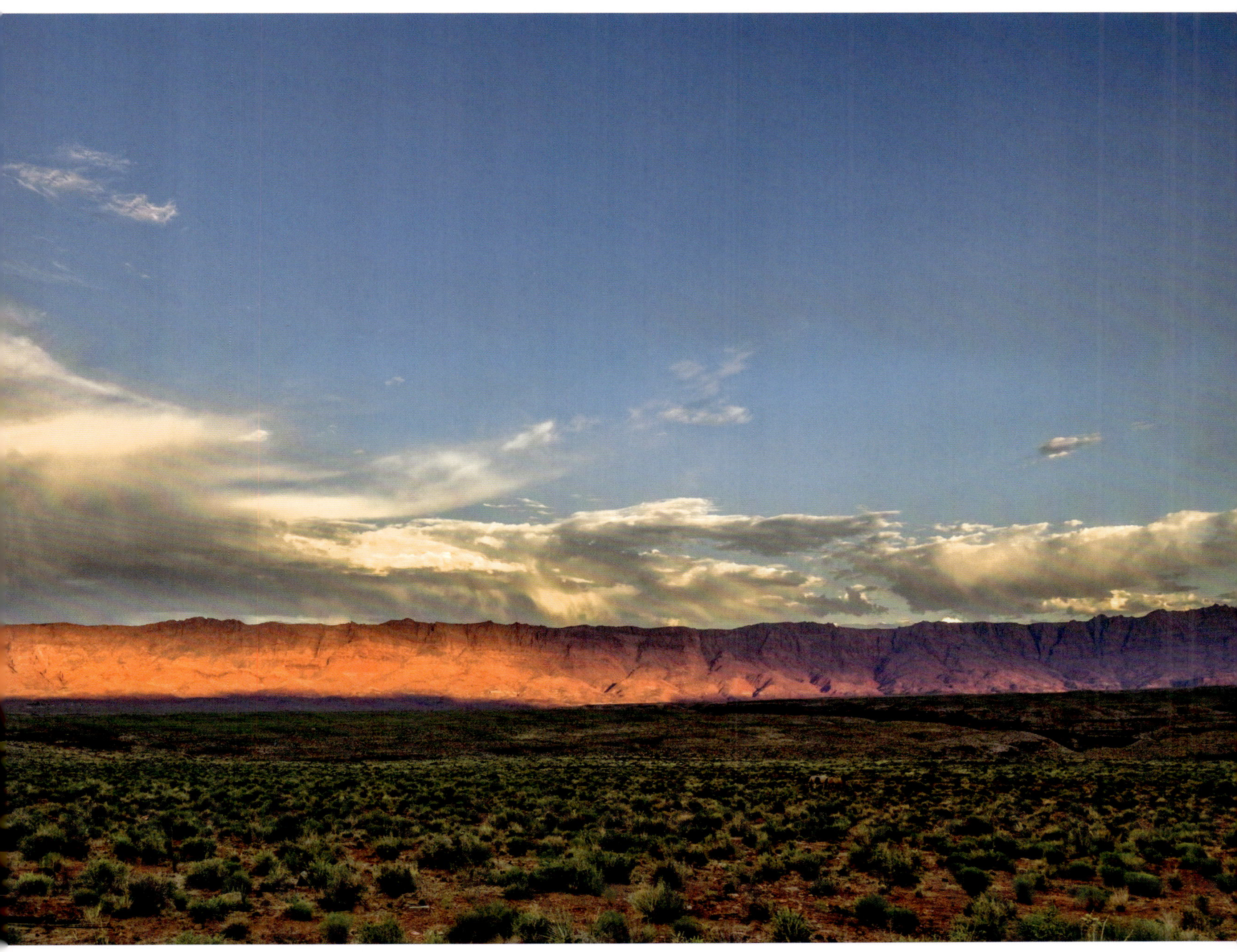

STORM CLOUDS FILTER THE LIGHT FALLING ON THE CLIFF LINE ABOVE THE COLORADO RIVER AT VERMILLION CLIFFS.

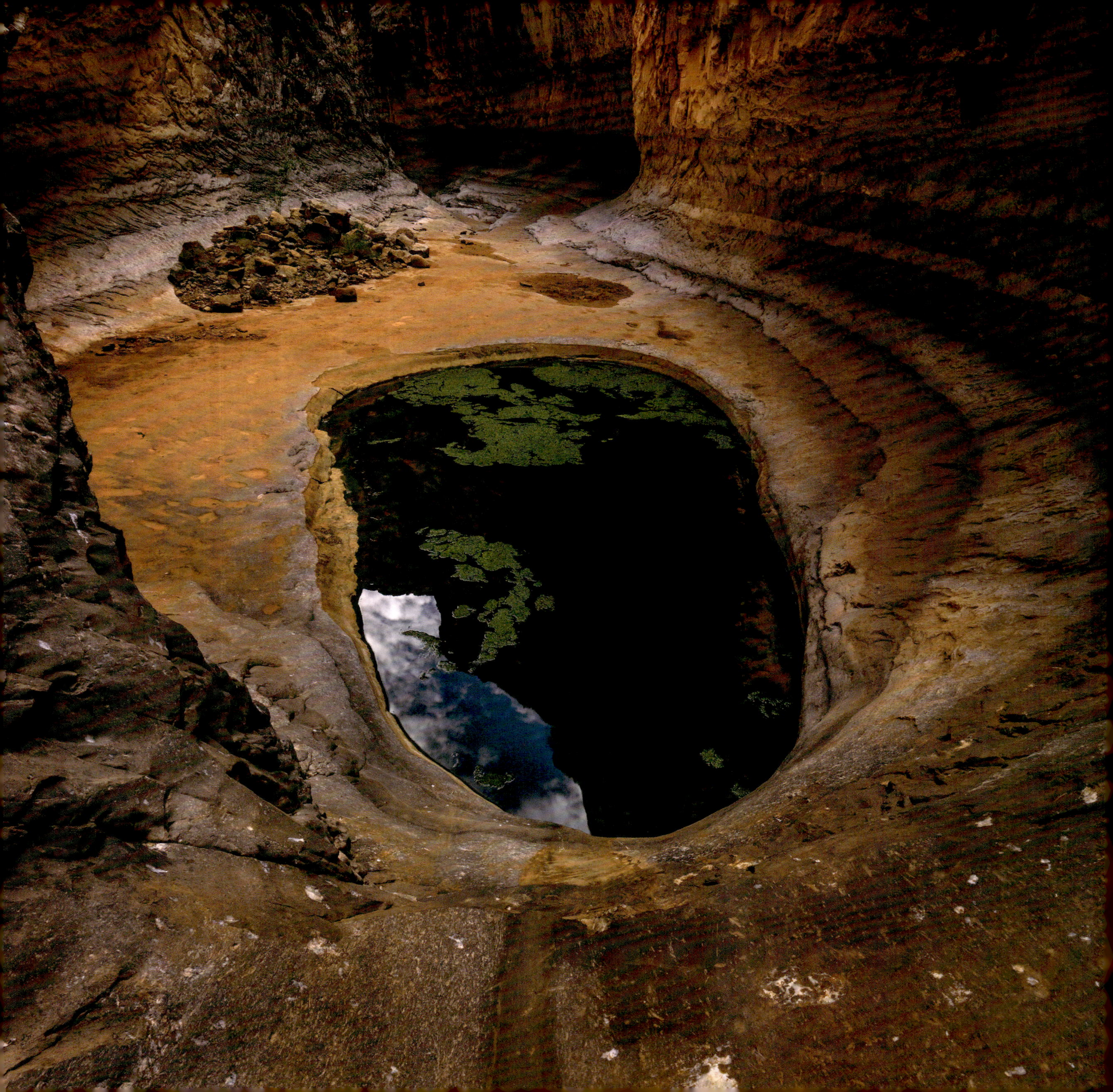

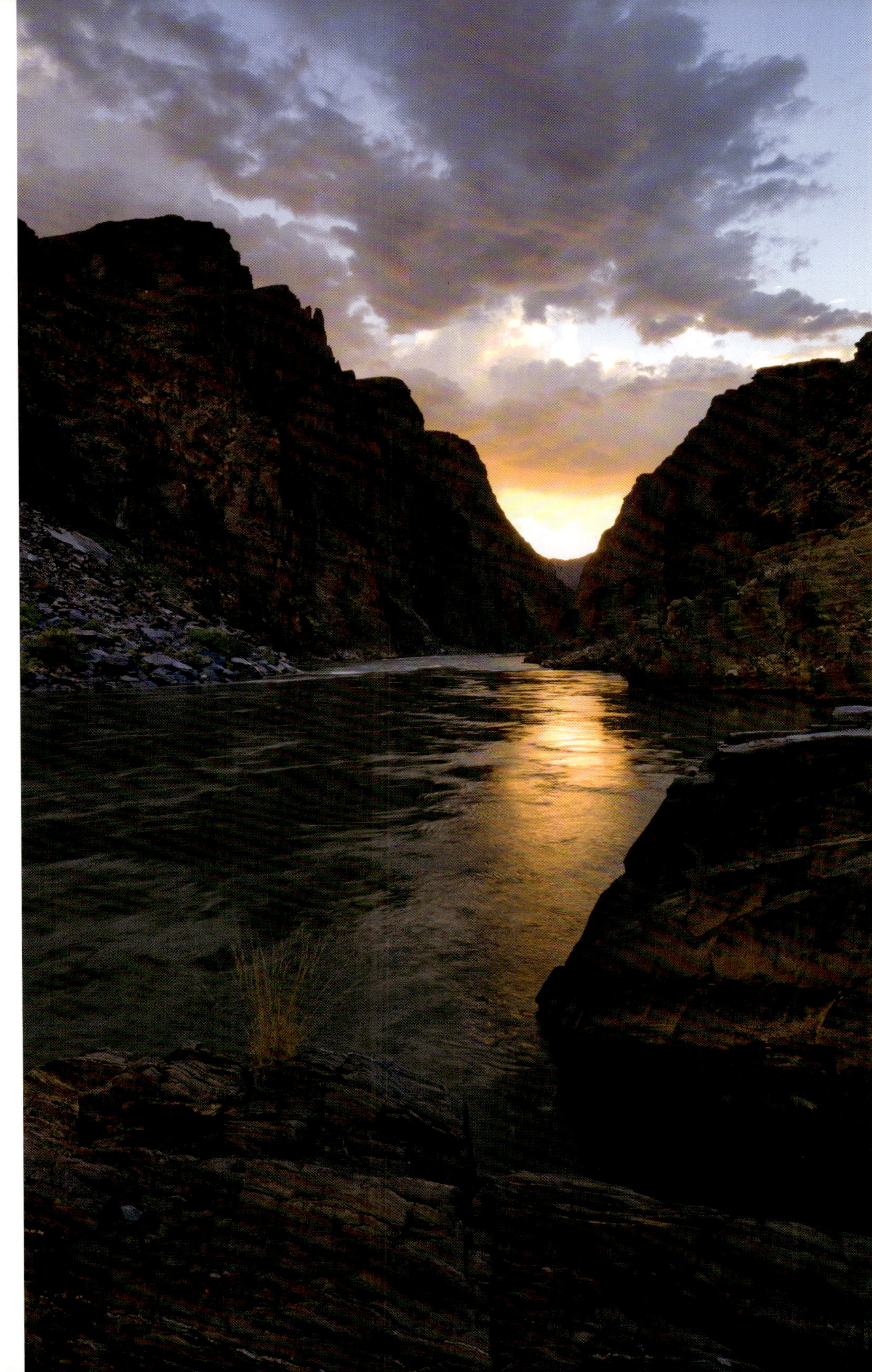

DEEP, COLD POOLS FILL THE
LIMESTONE BASINS IN SILVER GROTTO.

THUNDERHEADS BUILD IN THE
SUMMER SKY NEAR CLEAR CREEK CAMP
ON THE COLORADO RIVER.

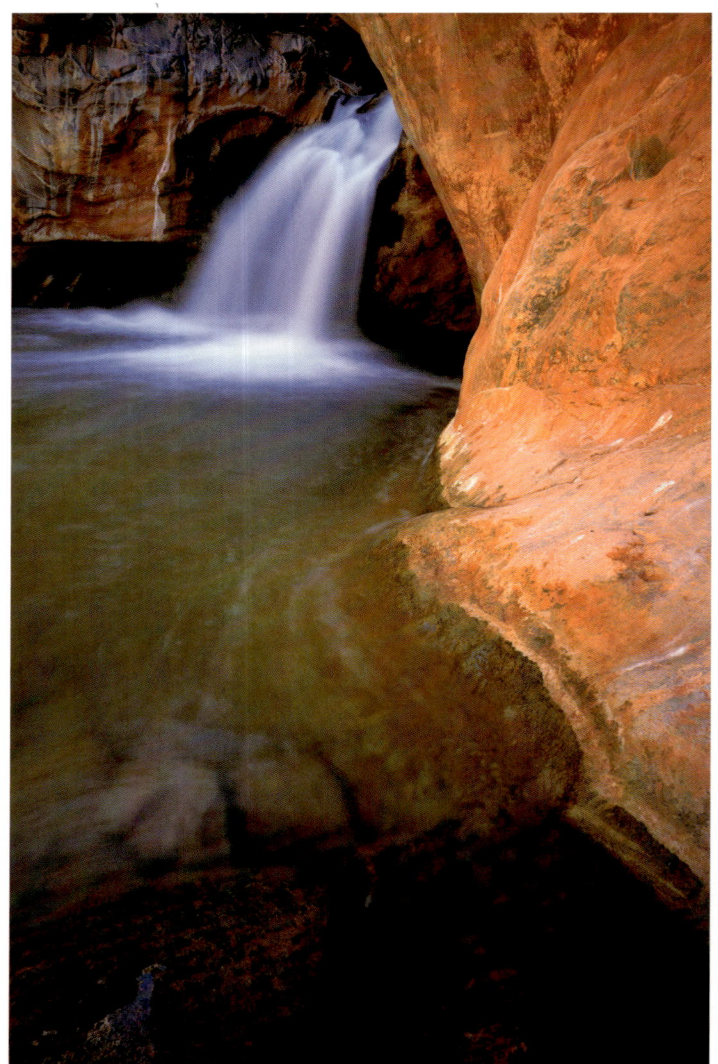



SHINUMO CREEK POURS FROM A SLOT IN THE RED
SANDSTONE WALLS ALONG THE LOWER NORTH BASS TRAIL.

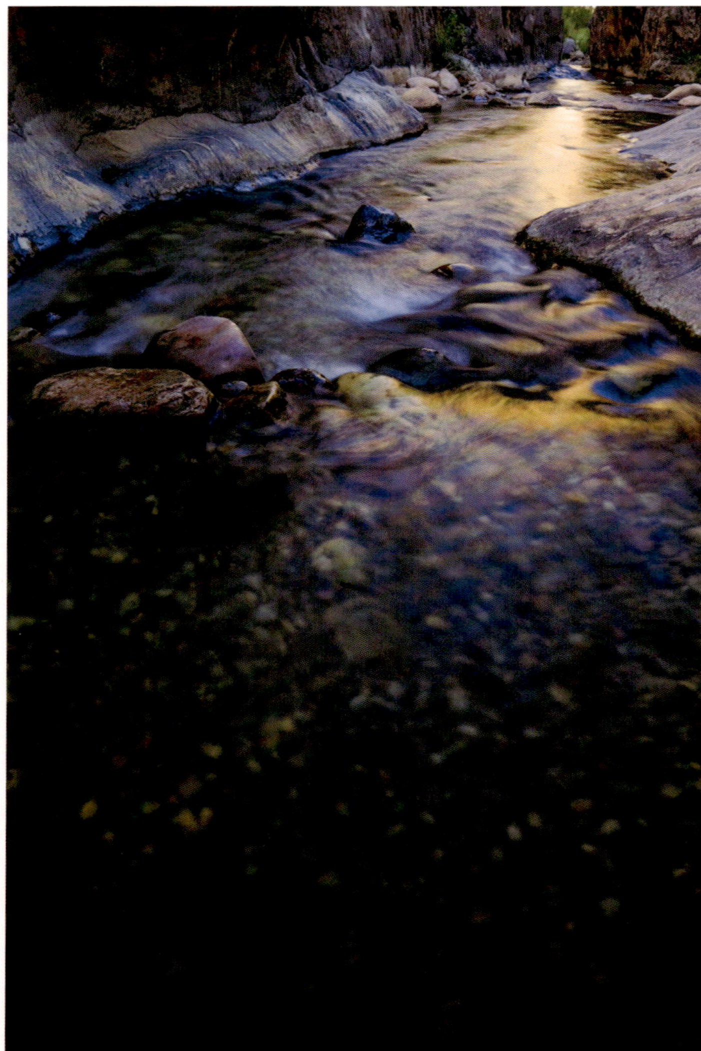

SHINUMO CREEK POURS OVER A COBBLE FLOOR NEAR
ITS CONFLUENCE WITH THE COLORADO RIVER.

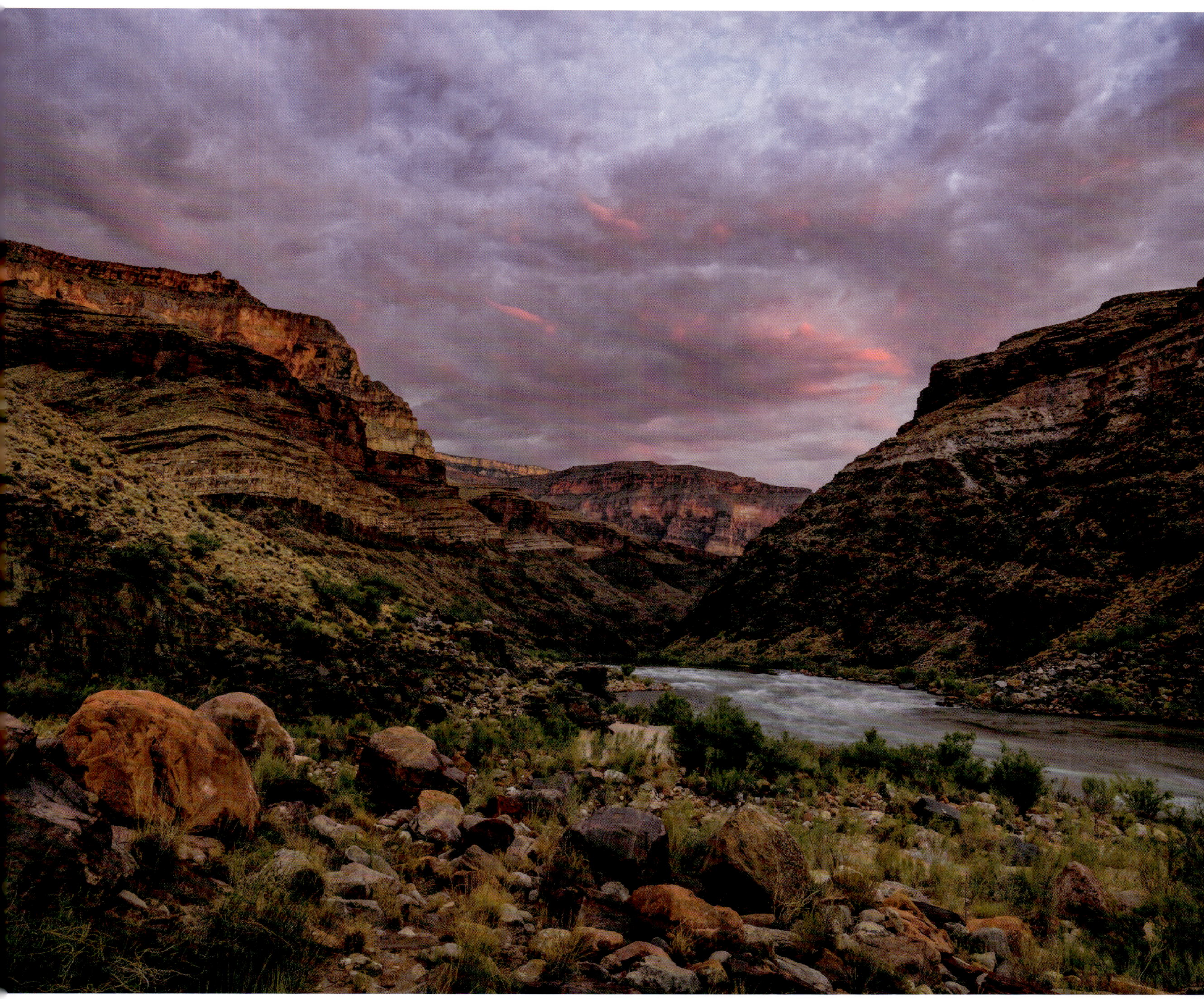

MAGENTA CLOUDS FILL THE SKY UPSTREAM OF STONE CREEK, IN THE GRAND CANYON.

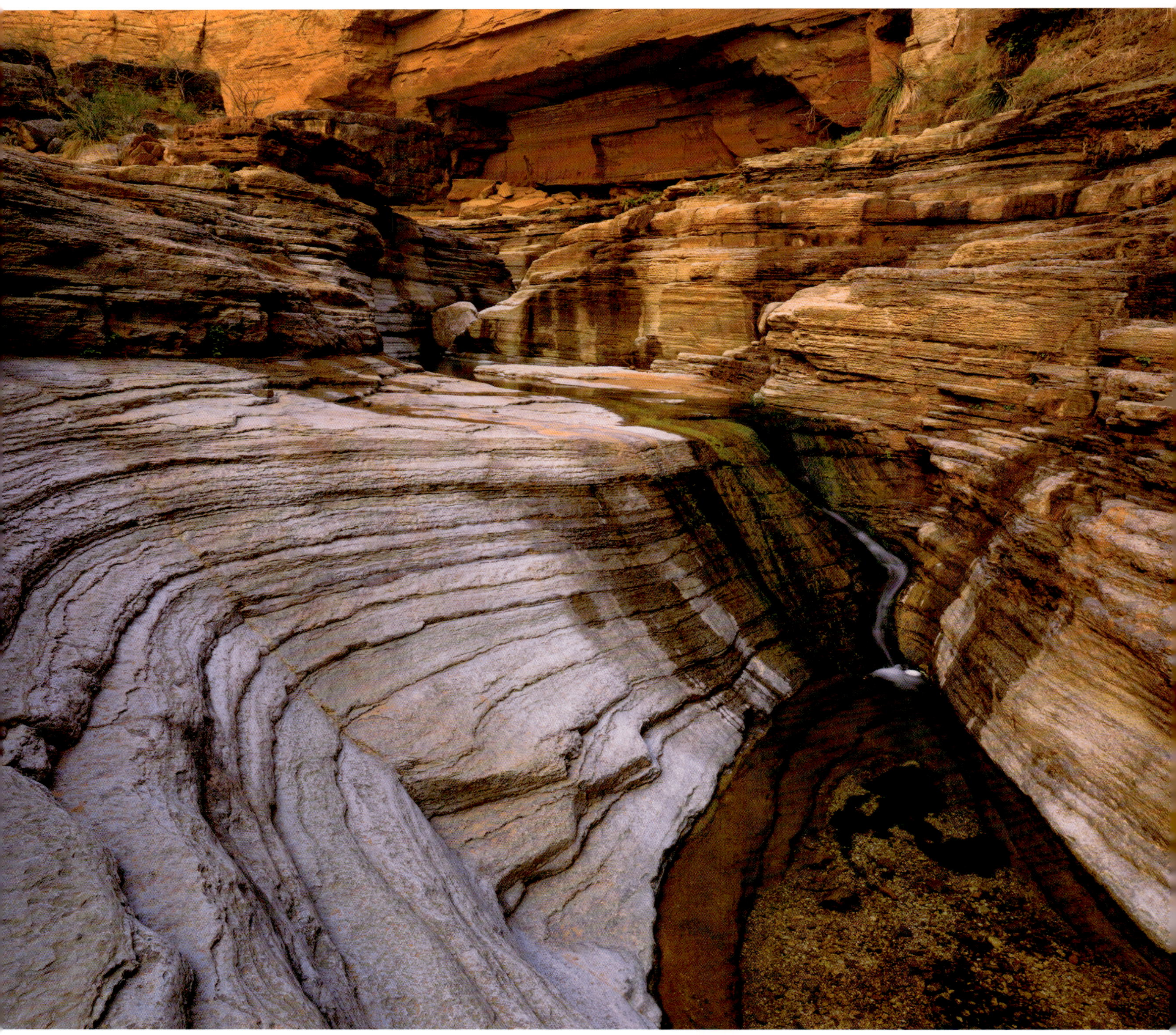

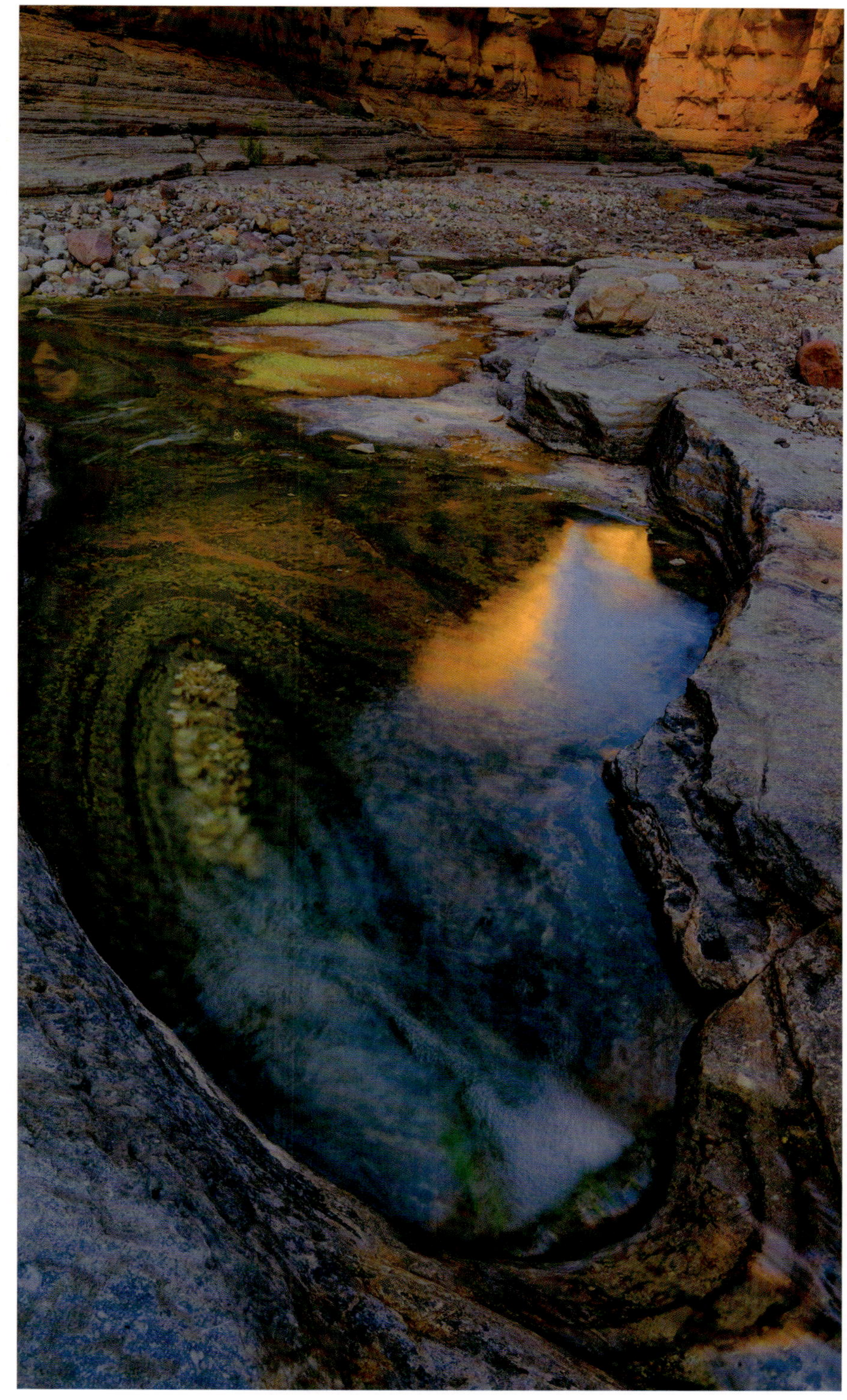

◄
WATER FALLS OVER LIMESTONE
SHELVES IN MATKATAMIBA CANYON.

►
WATER CARVES OUT RHYTHMIC
PATTERNS IN THE LIMESTONE FLOOR
OF NATIONAL CANYON.

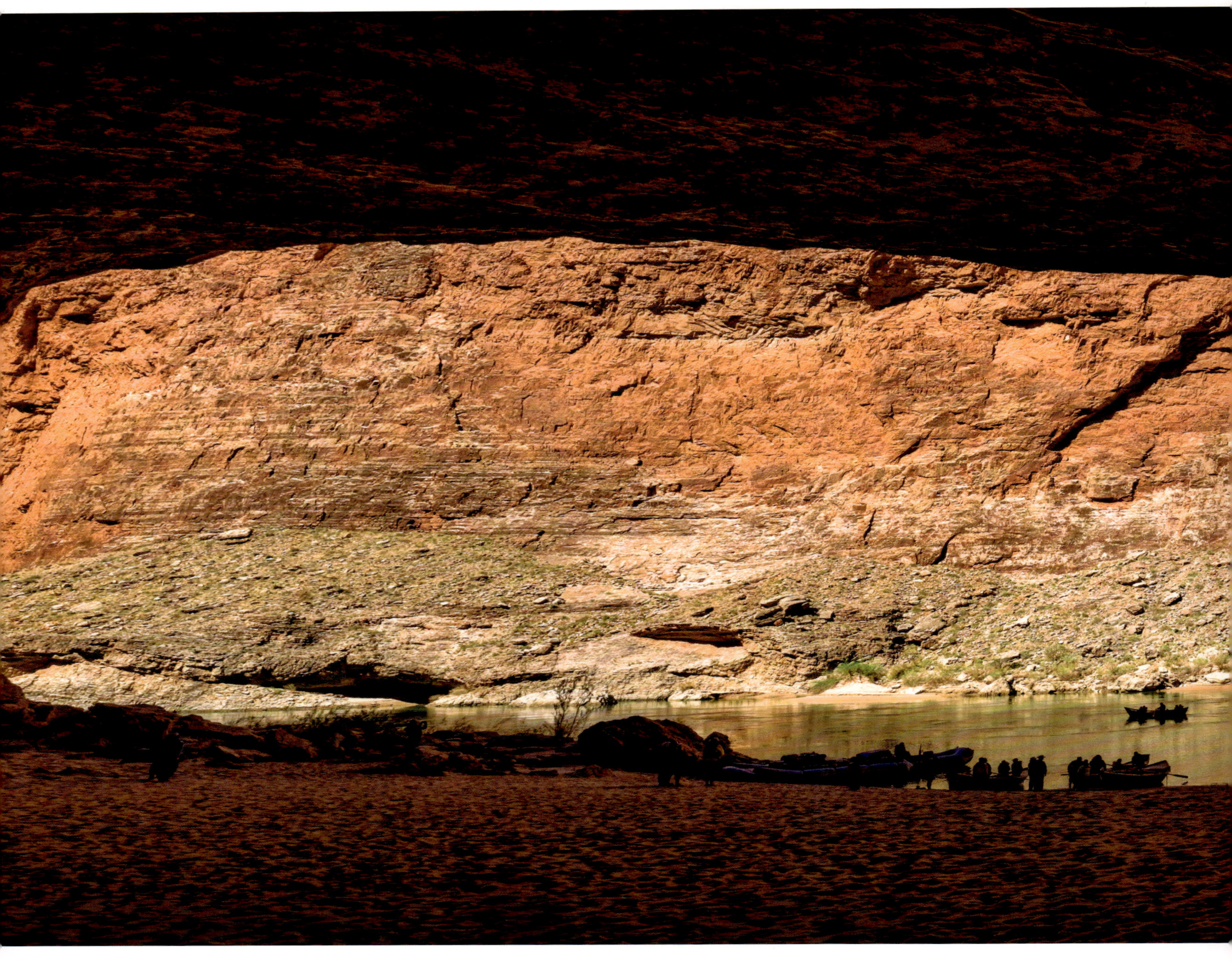

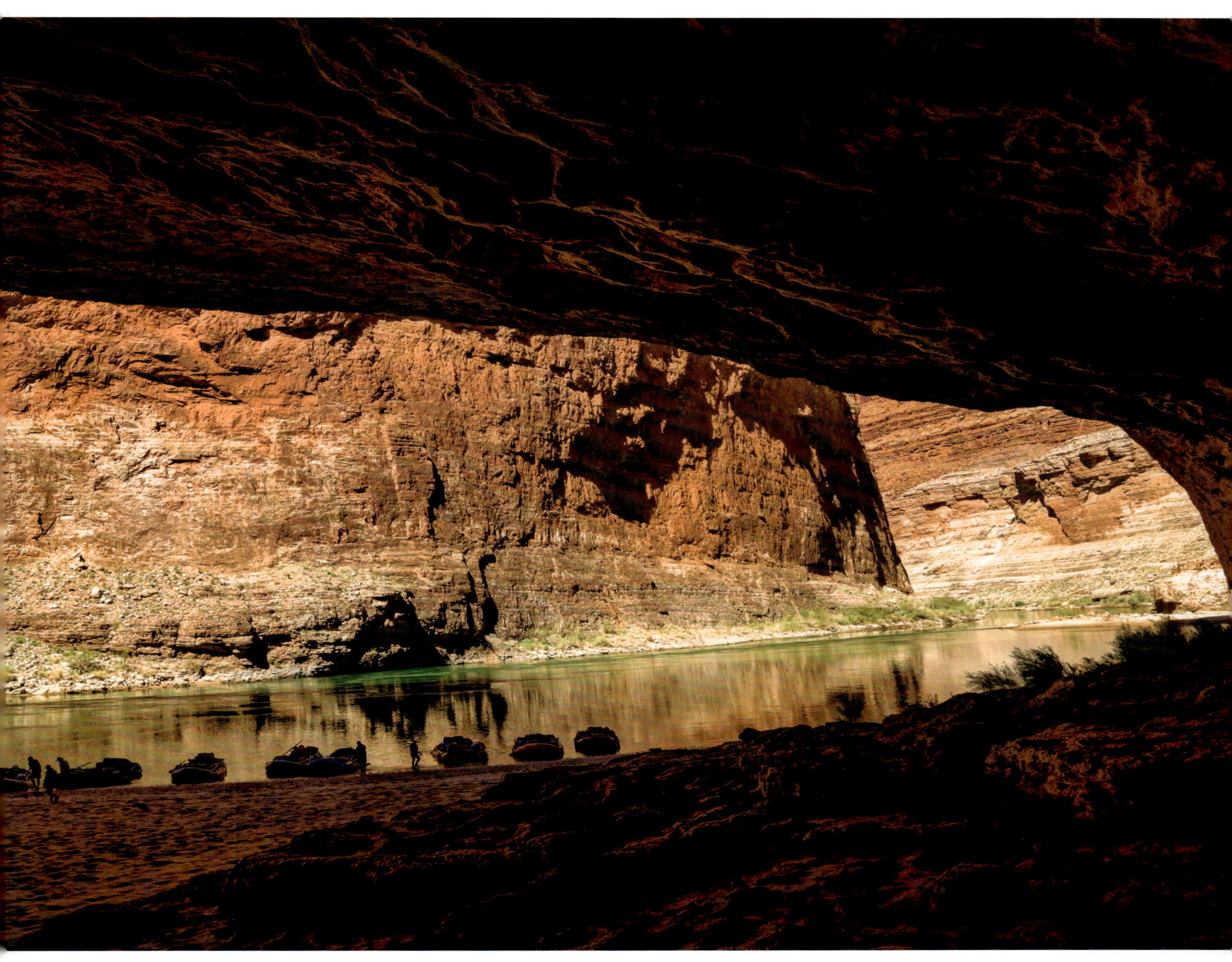

RIVER RUNNERS VISIT RED WALL CAVERN.

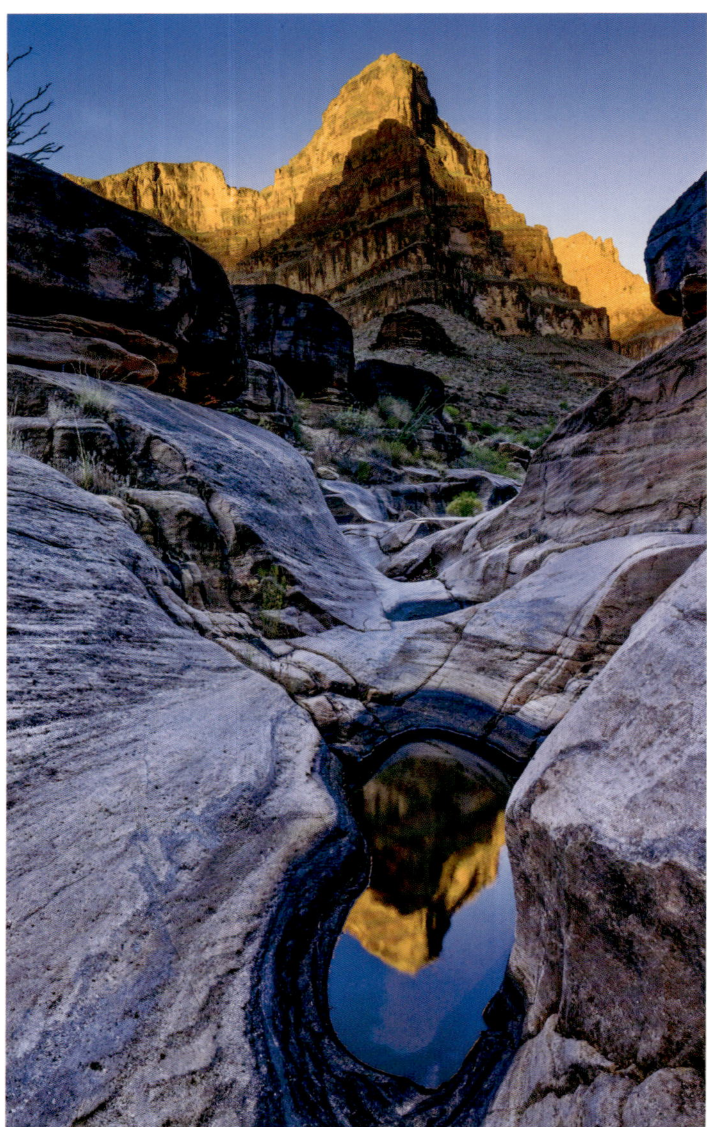



214 MILE CREEK, A SMALL CAMP AT LOW
WATER NEAR PUMPKIN SPRING.

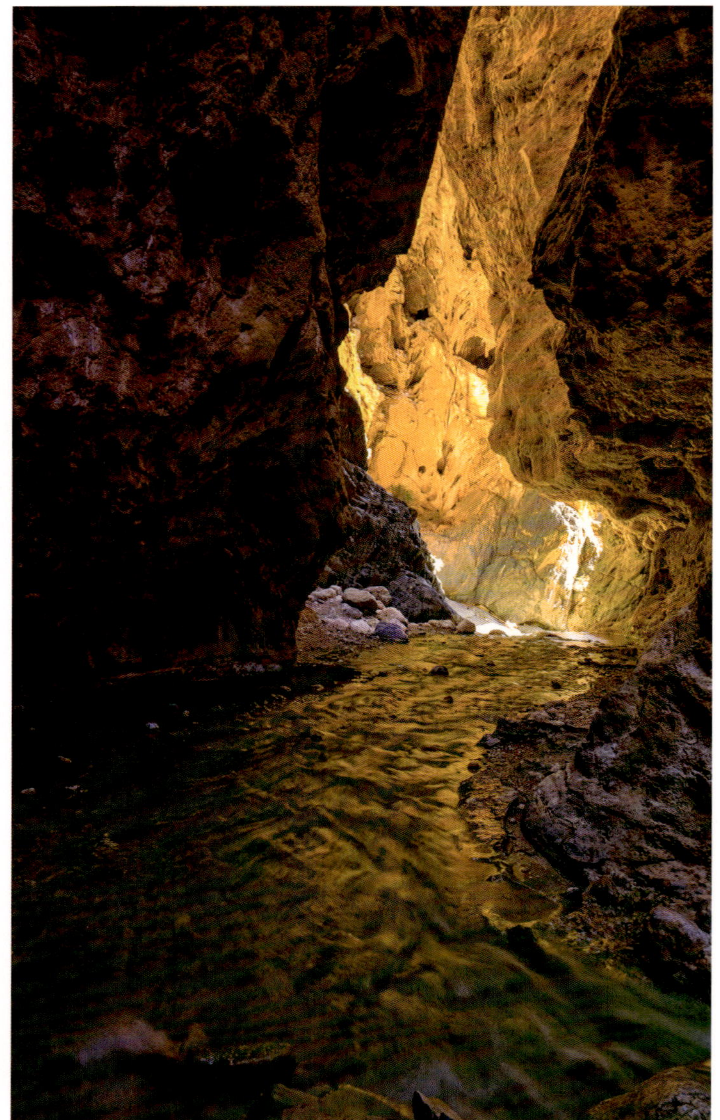

TRAVERTINE FALLS ON THE HUALAPAI
NATION IN LOWER GRANITE GORGE.

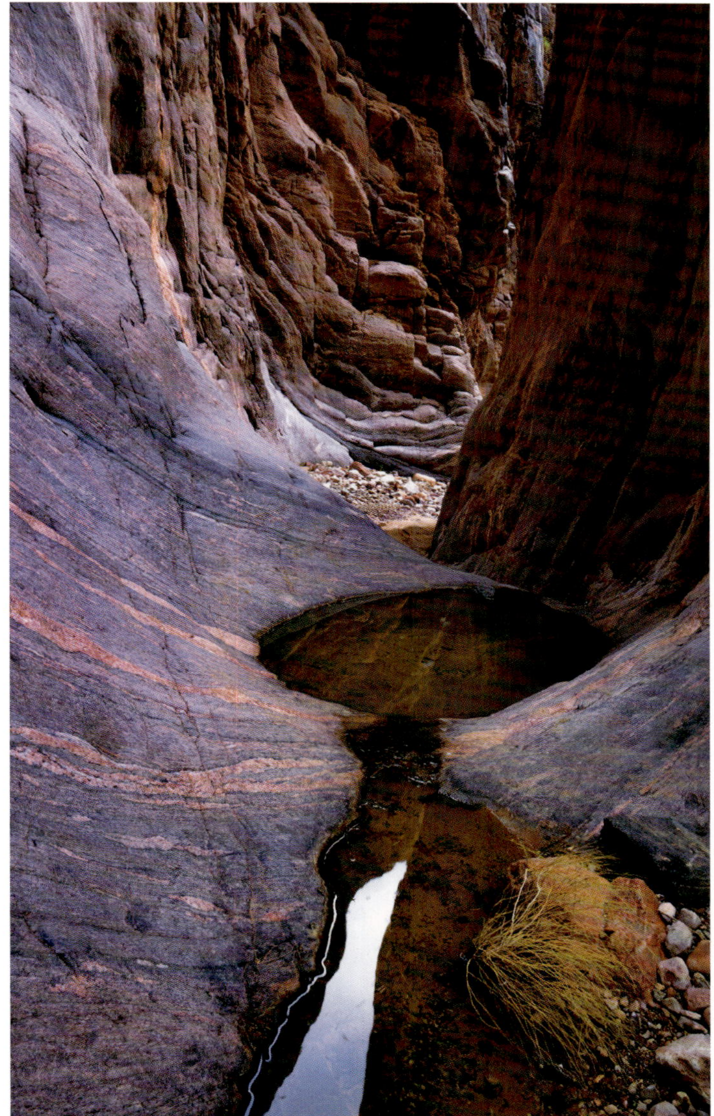

GRAPHIC PATTERNS DECORATE THE
GRANITE WALLS OF TRINITY CREEK WASH.

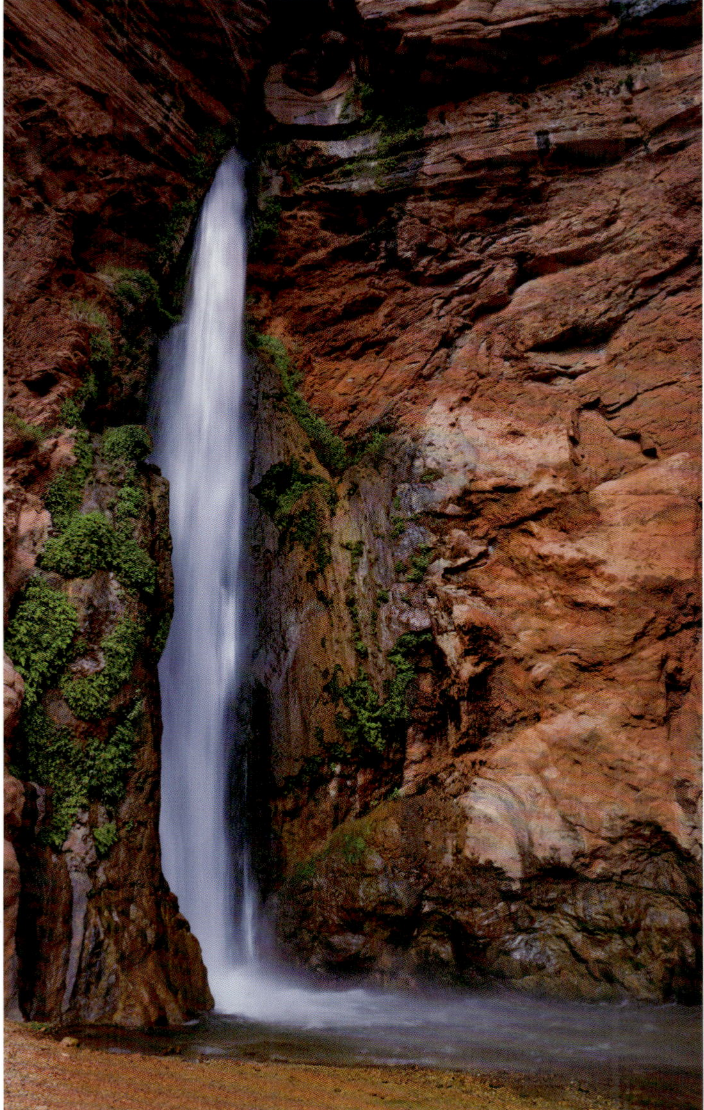

DEER CREEK FALLS POURS FROM A SLOT HIGH IN
THE CANYON WALL TO THE COLORADO RIVER BELOW.

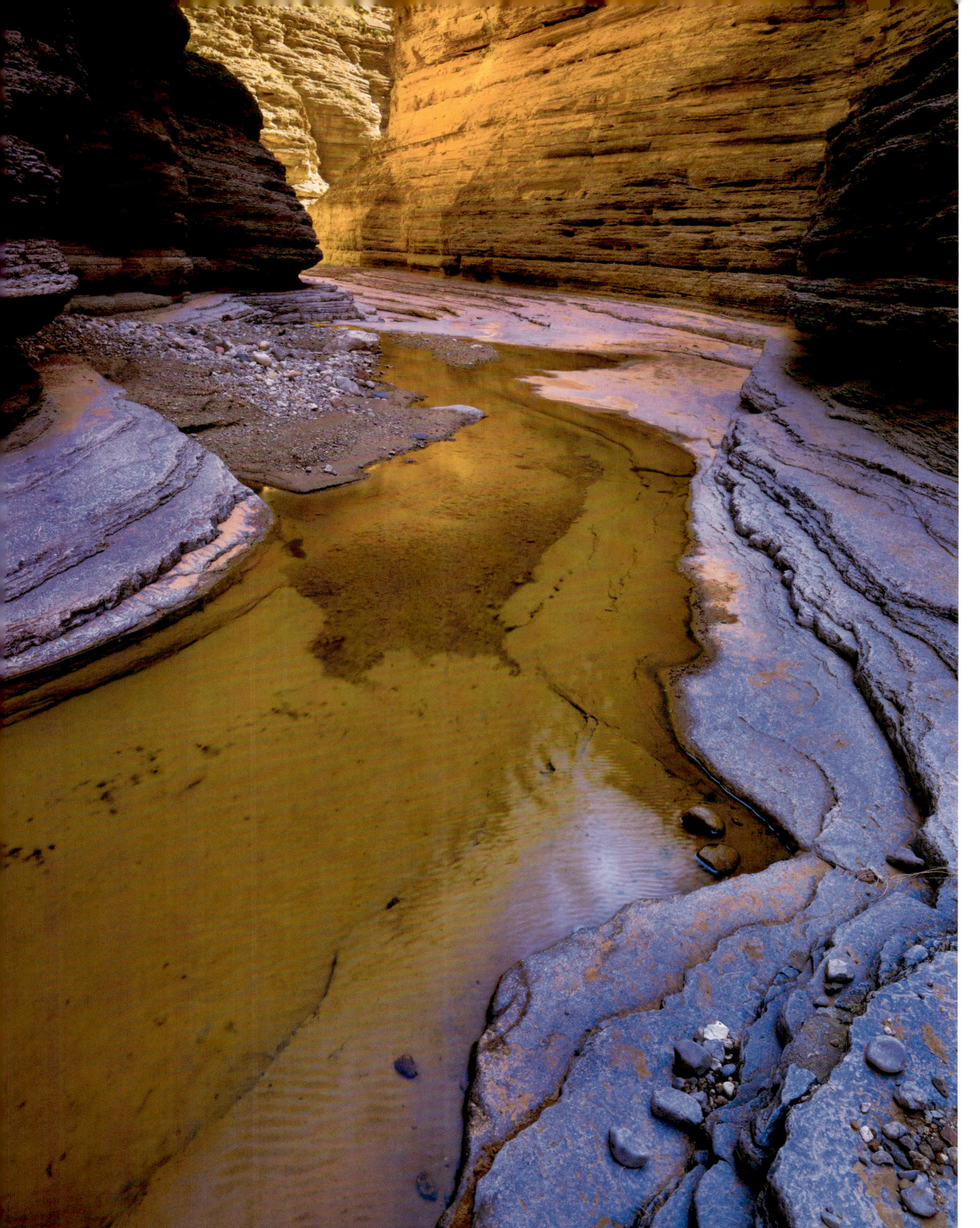

TUCKUP CANYON
AT RIVER MILE 165
OFFERS GOOD HIKING
FOR RIVER RUNNERS.

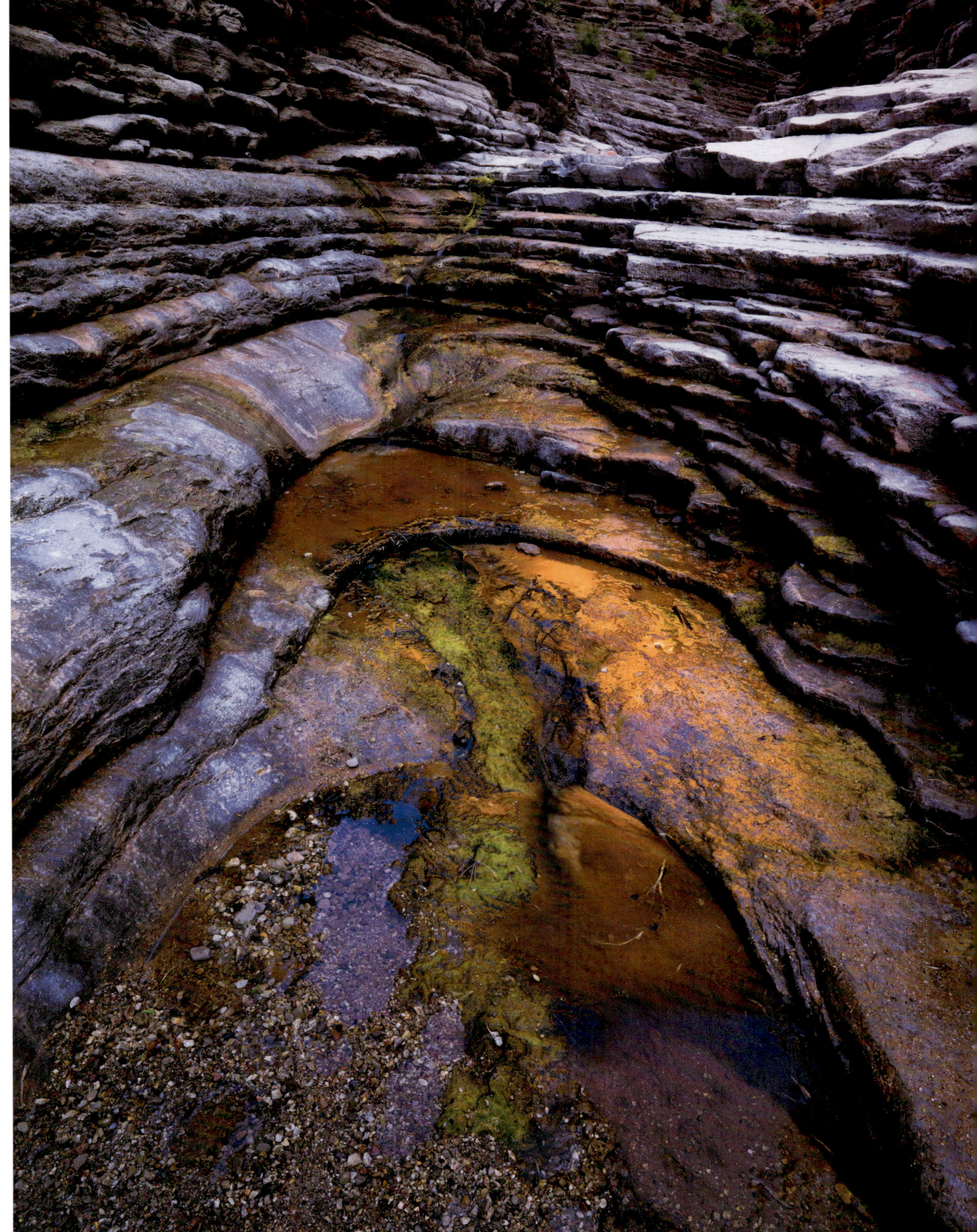

LIMESTONE STEPS IN
TUCKUP CANYON.

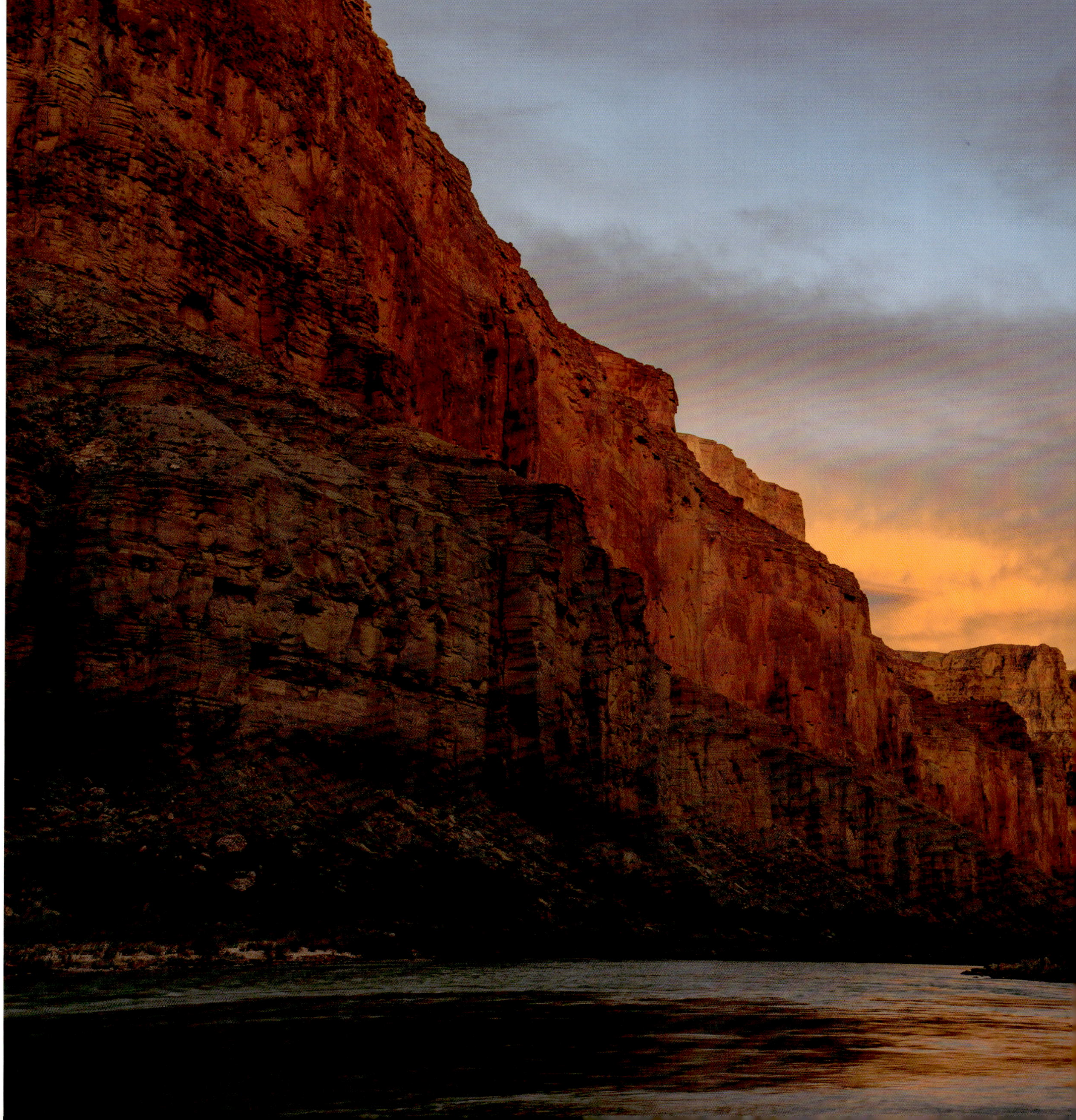

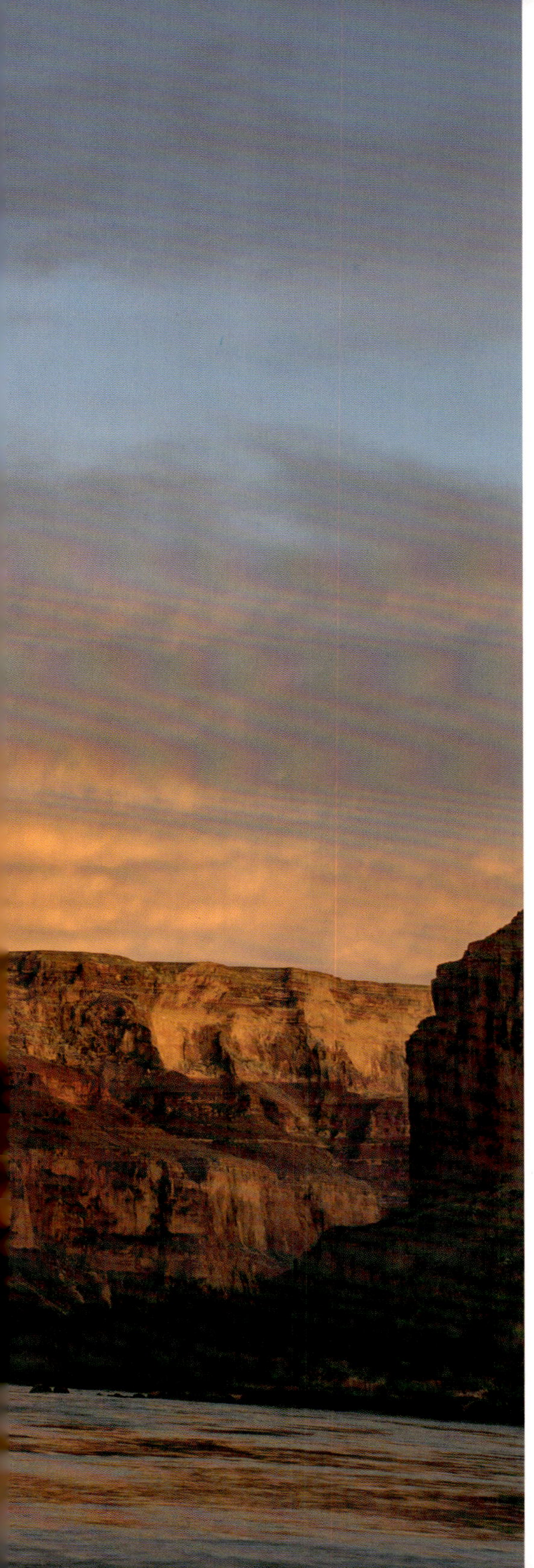

◀

THE CLIFFS OF THE SOUTH RIM GLOW
IN THE SUNSET ABOVE CARBON CAMP.

▶

A THIN LINE IN THE STEEP RED WALLS
OF BLACKTAIL CANYON.

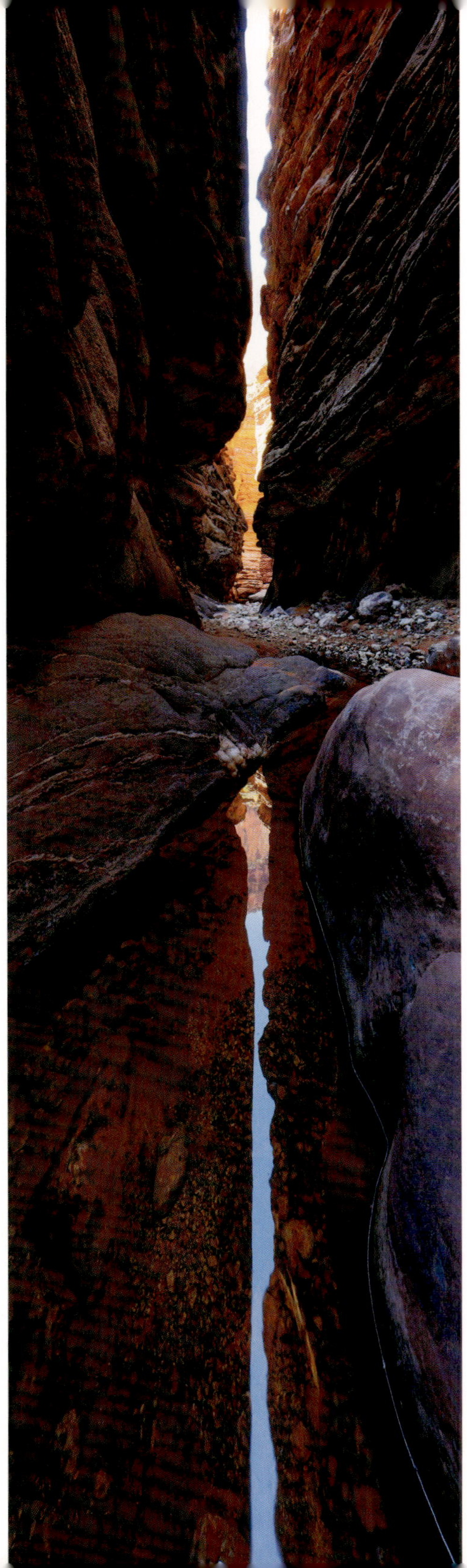

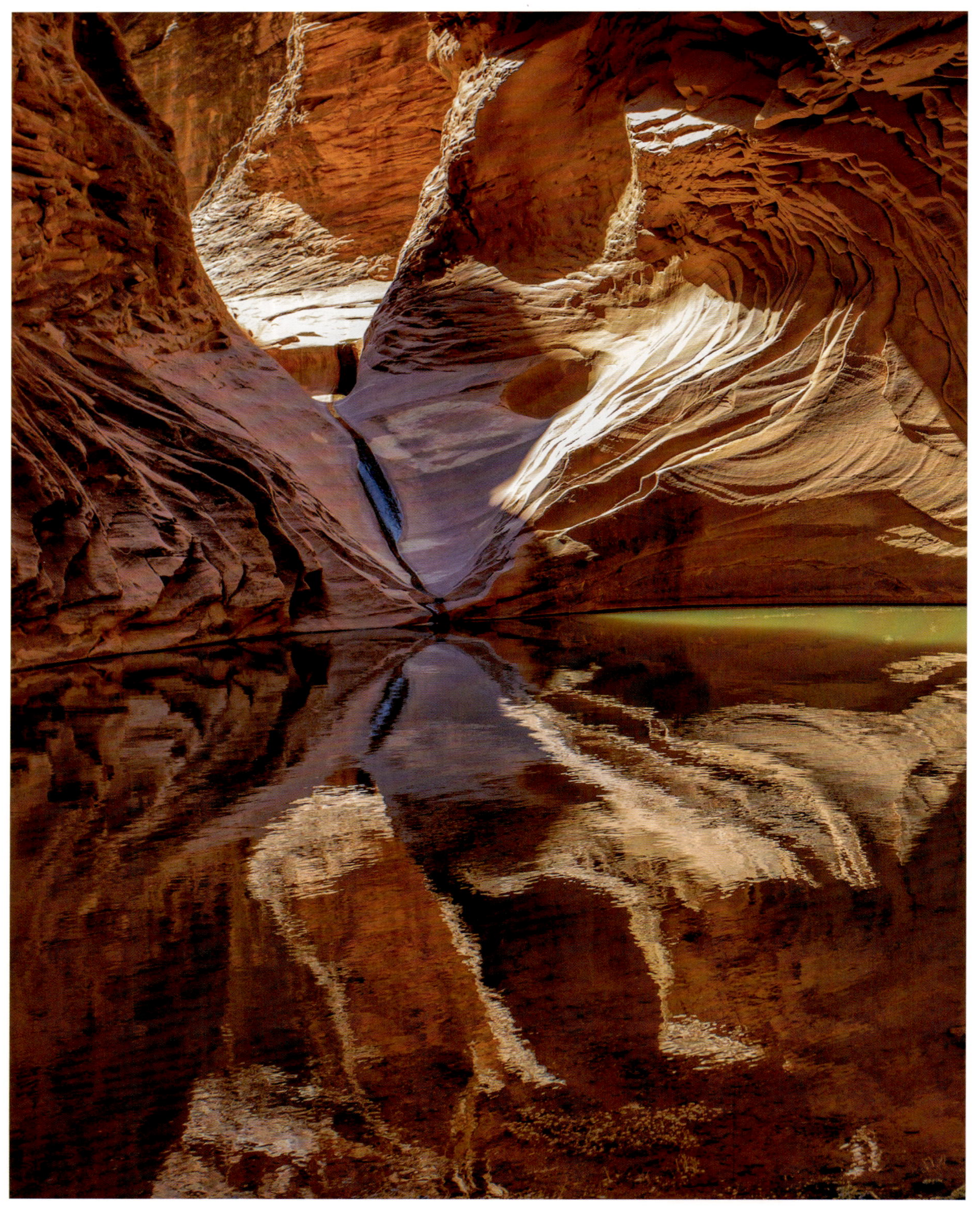

◄

WOMB OF WOMAN,
A TRANQUIL FEATURE
IN NORTH CANYON.

►

ELECTRIC GREEN
ALGAE EMPHASIZES
THE BEAUTY OF
THIS WATERFALL IN
BRIDGE CANYON.

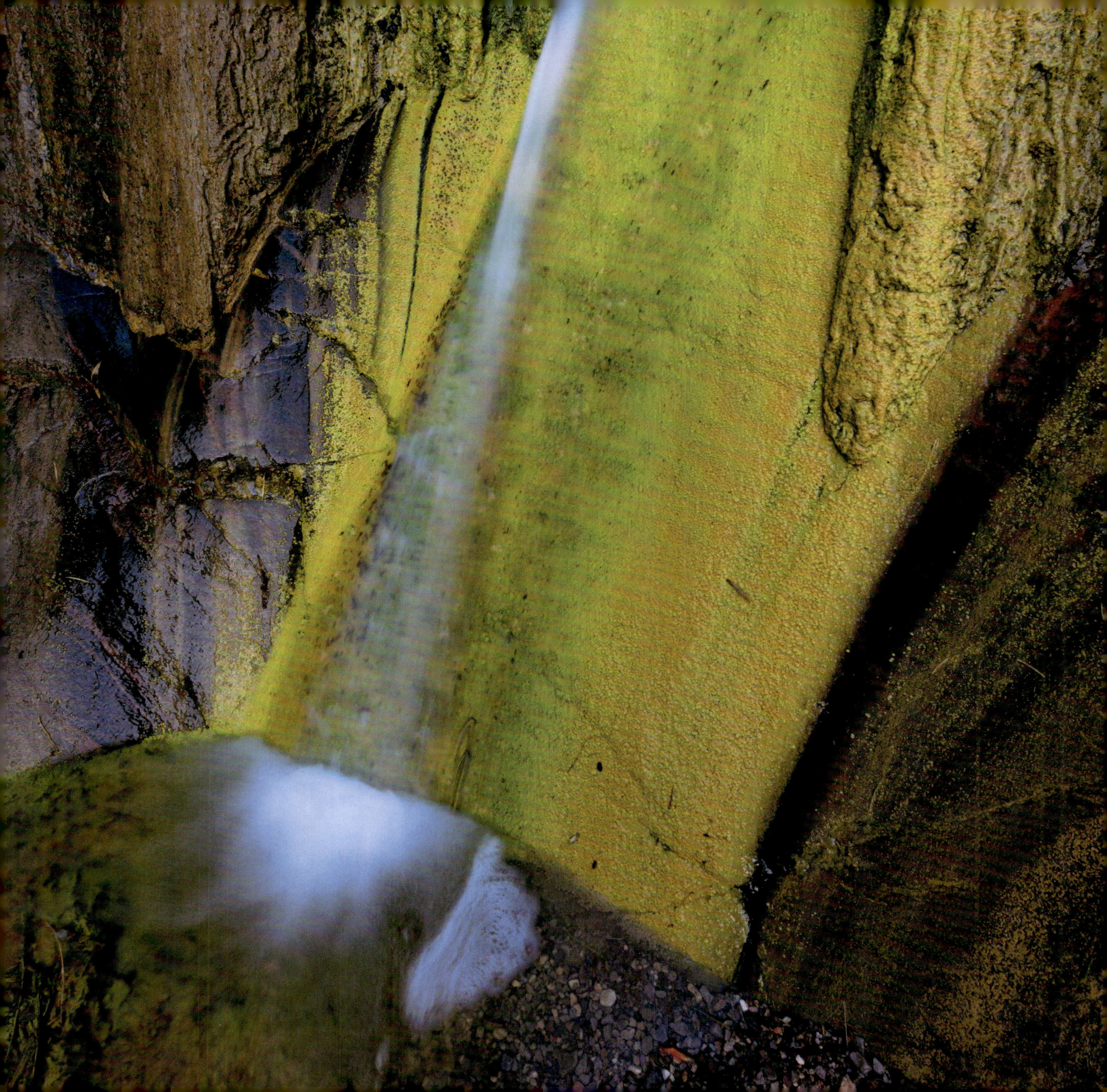

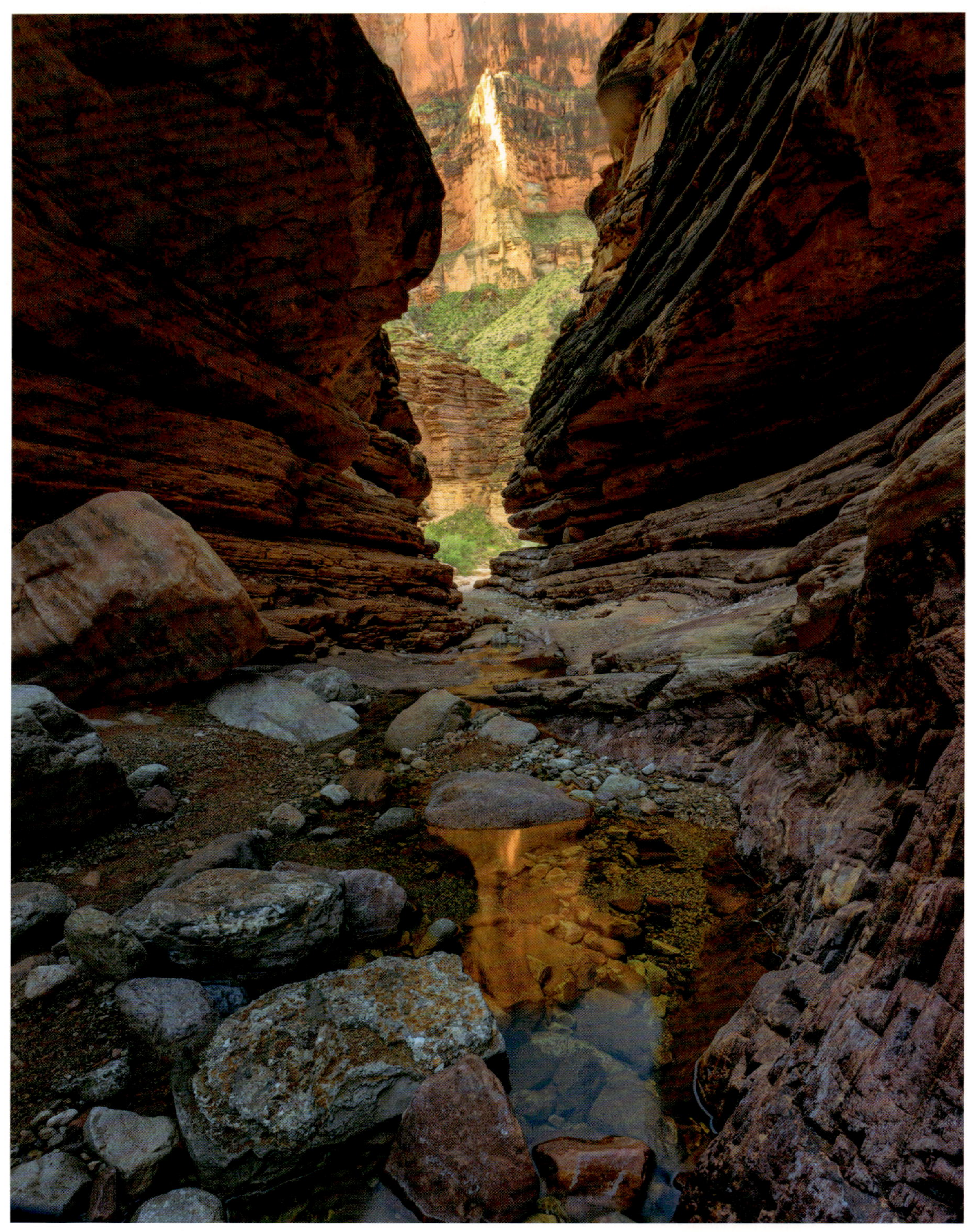

REFLECTIONS AT
THE ENTRANCE OF
BLACKTAIL CANYON.

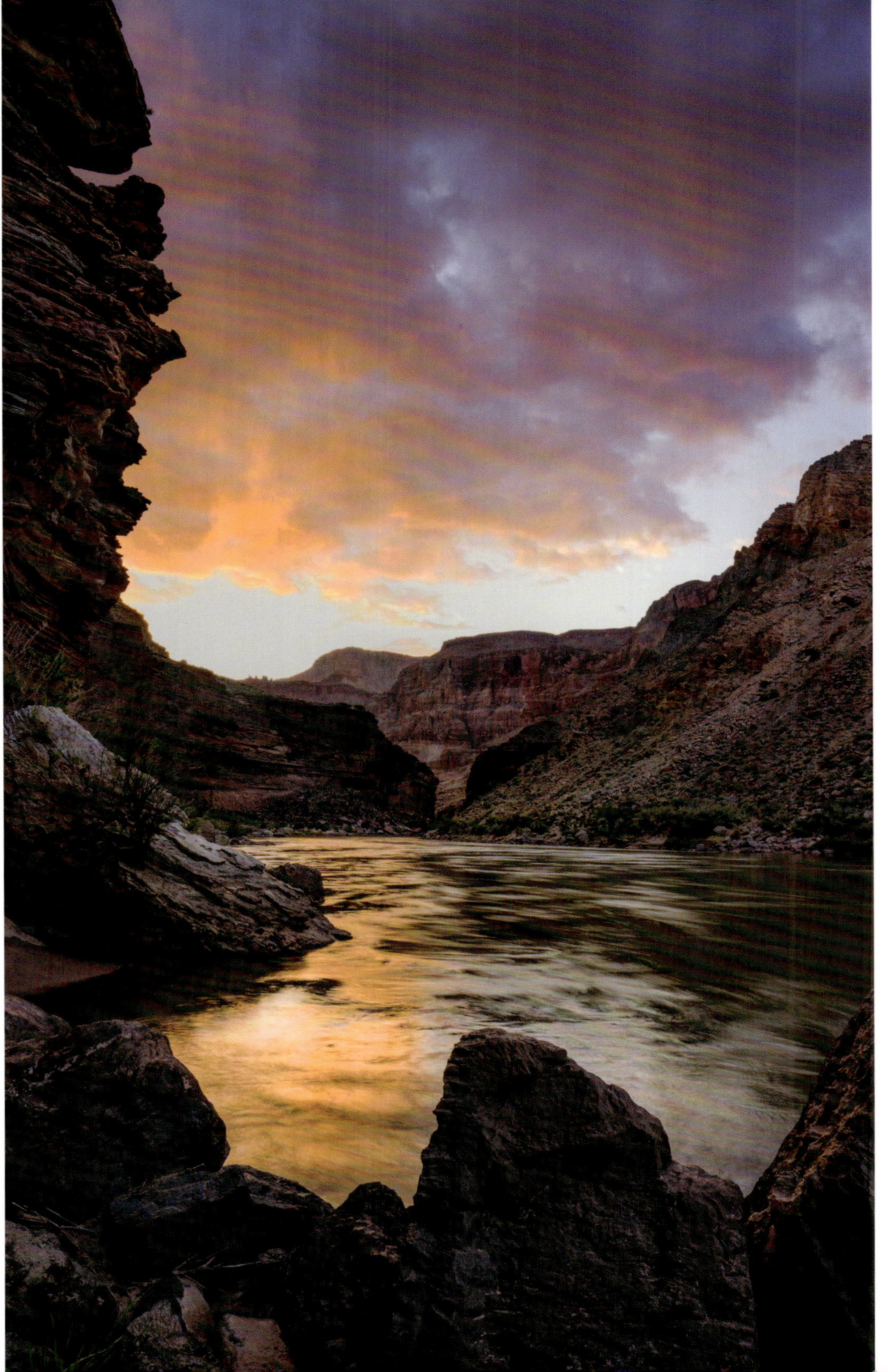

SUNSET AT PANCHO'S KITCHEN,
A POPULAR CAMP BELOW DEER CREEK.

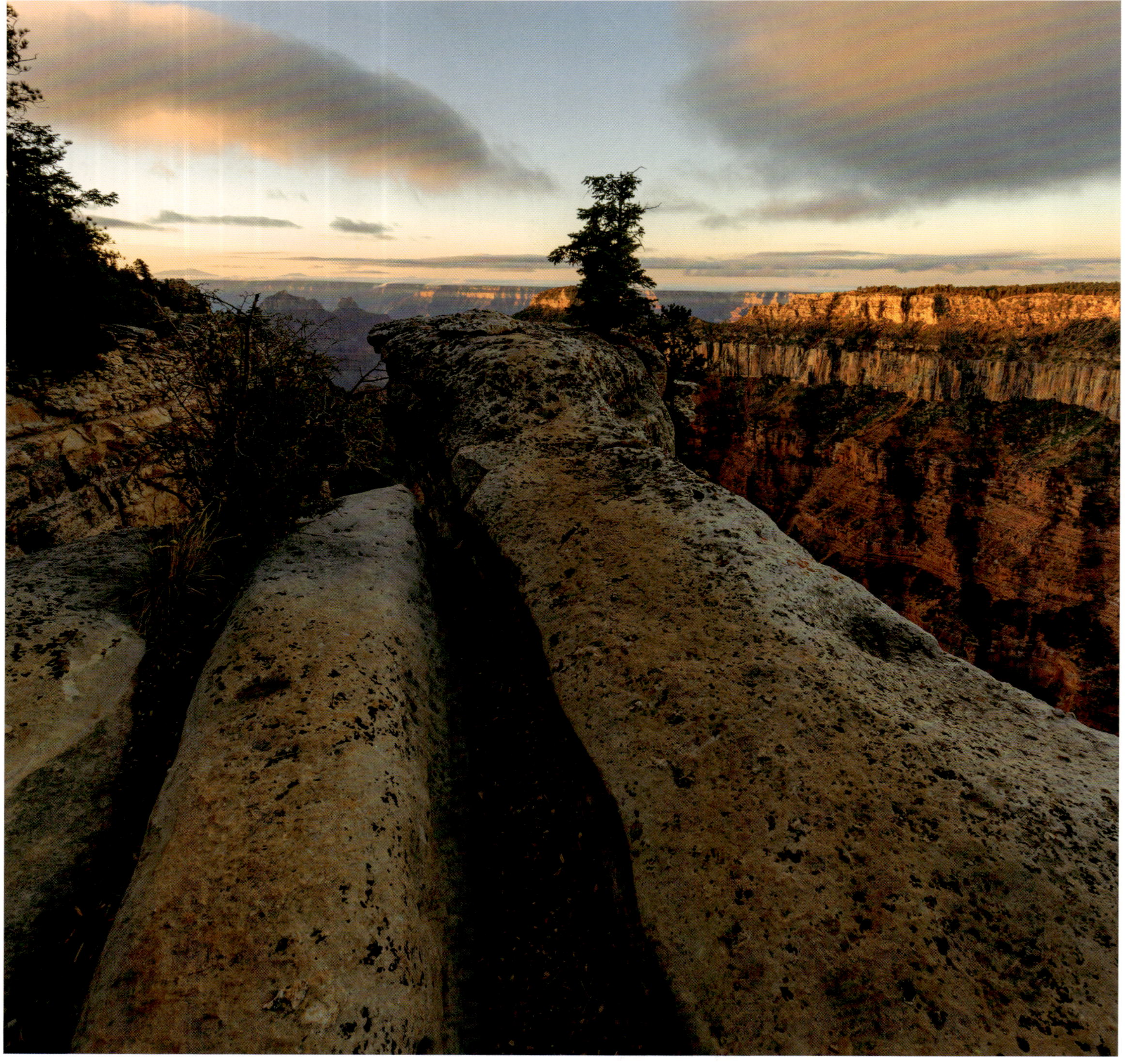



PINE TREES REST ON THE ROCKY EDGE OF THE NORTH RIM NEAR BRIGHT ANGEL POINT.

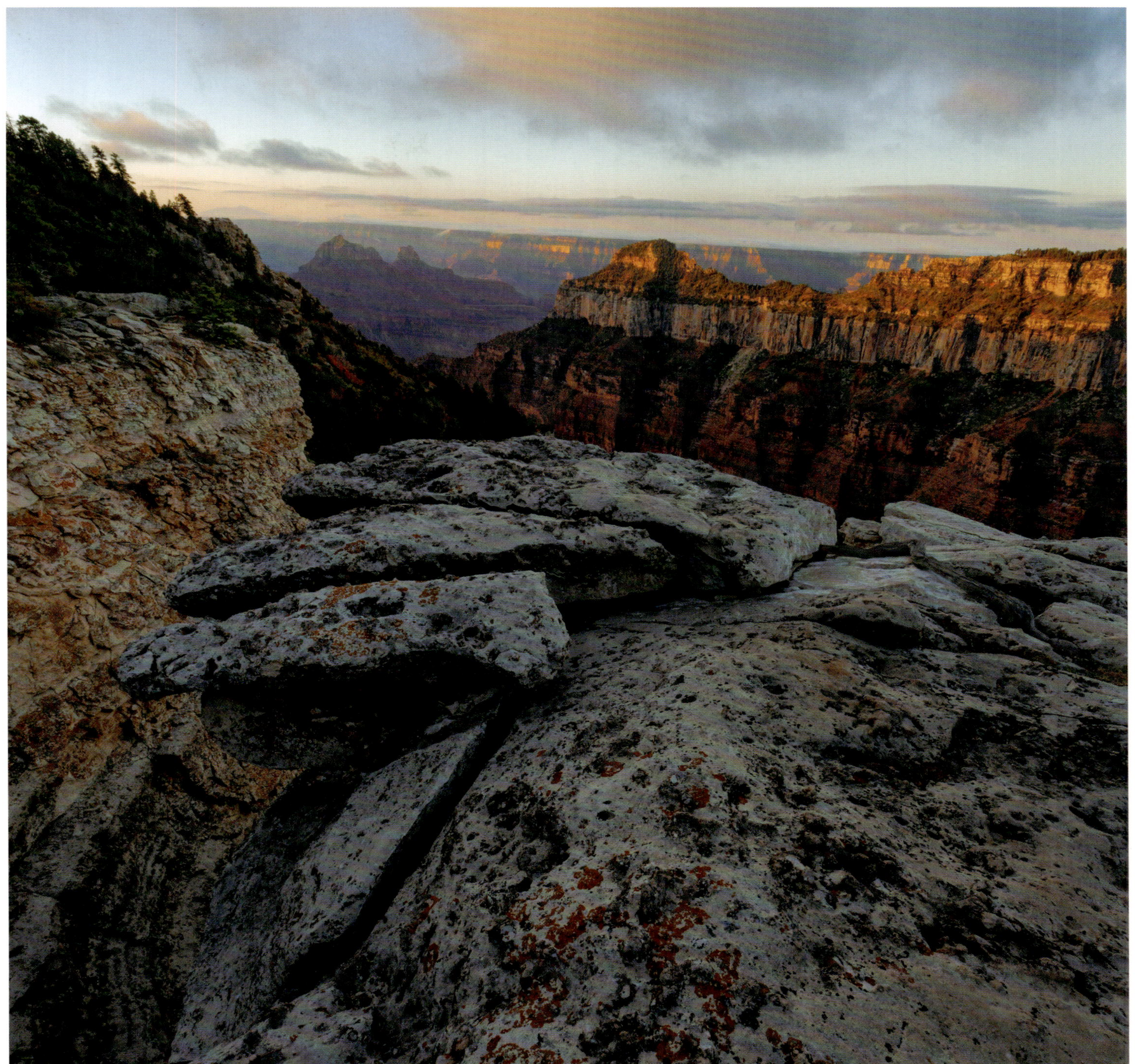

OZA BUTTE SITS AT 8065 FEET ON THE NORTH RIM.

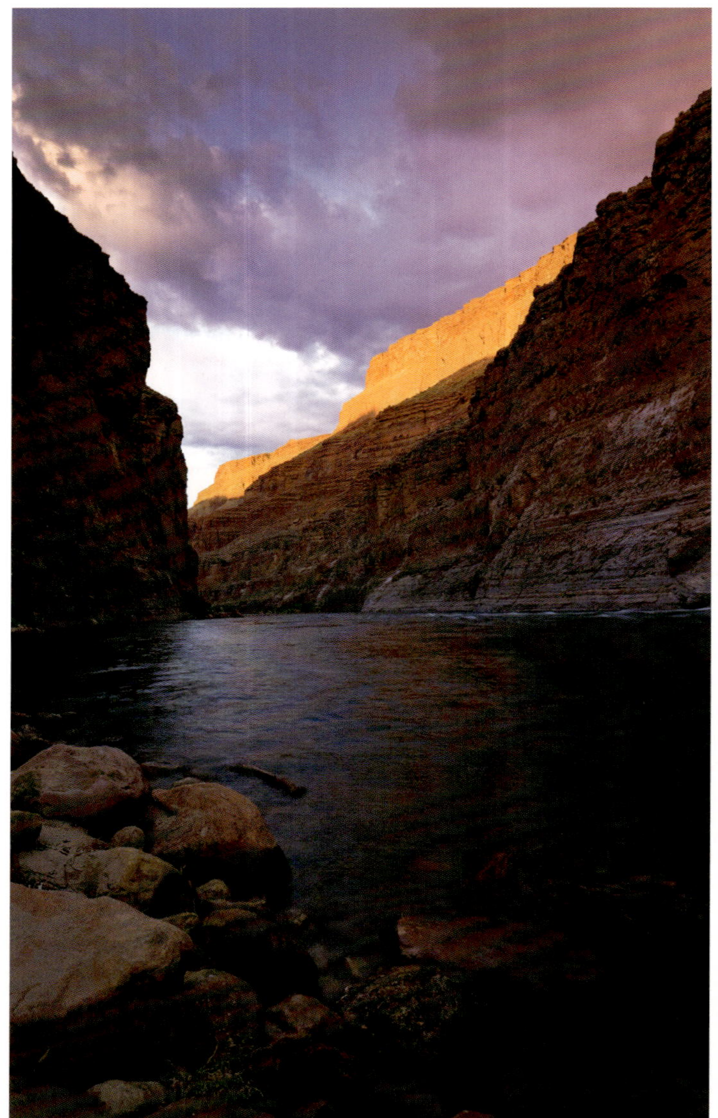



SUNRISE ILLUMINATES THE CLIFFS
ABOVE SHINUMO WASH CAMP.

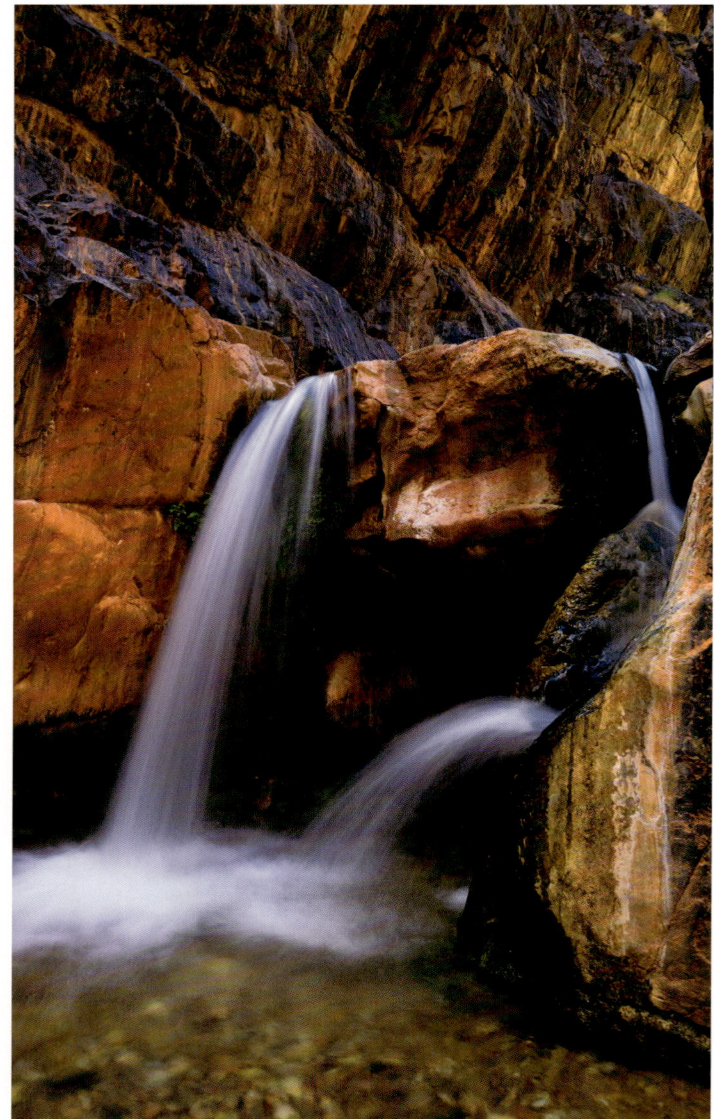

CLEAR CREEK WATERFALL POURS OVER BOULDERS
NEAR THE CONFLUENCE OF THE COLORADO RIVER.

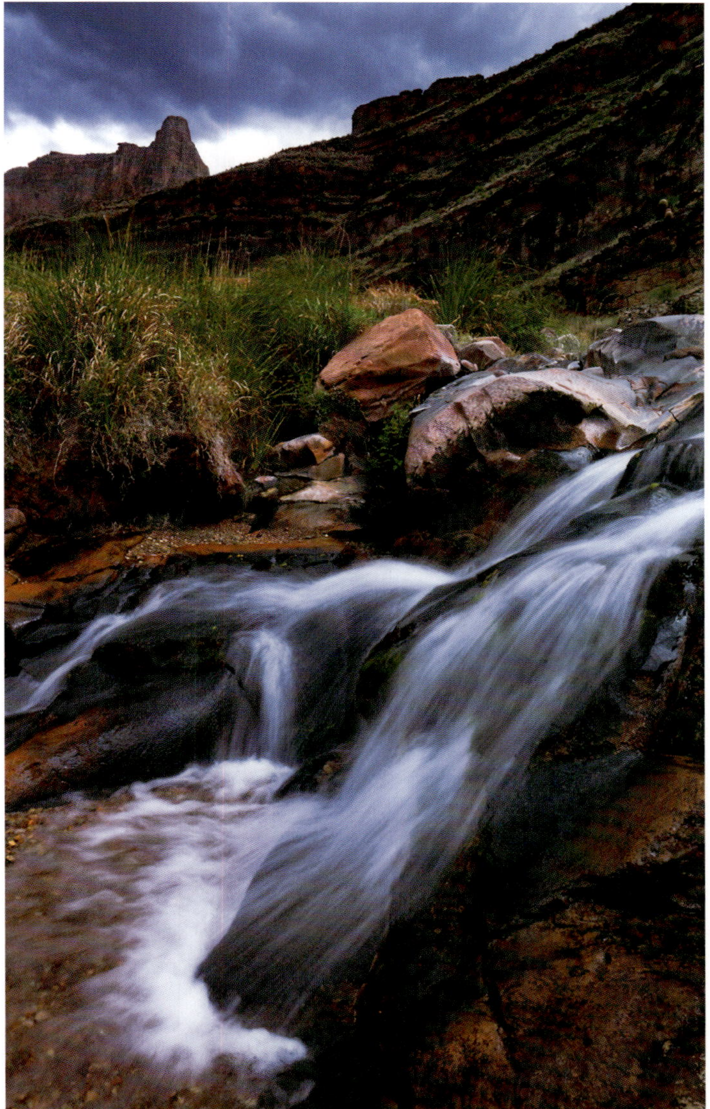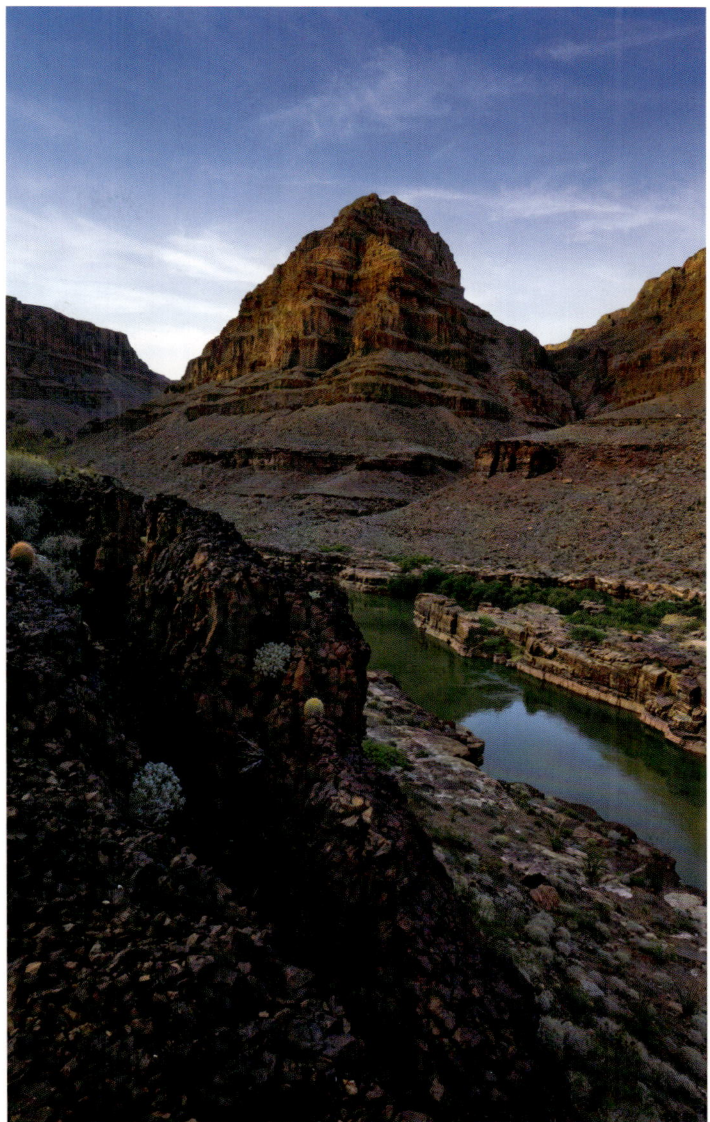



LAVA INTRUSIONS ALONG THE
COLORADO RIVER AT 214 MILE CAMP.

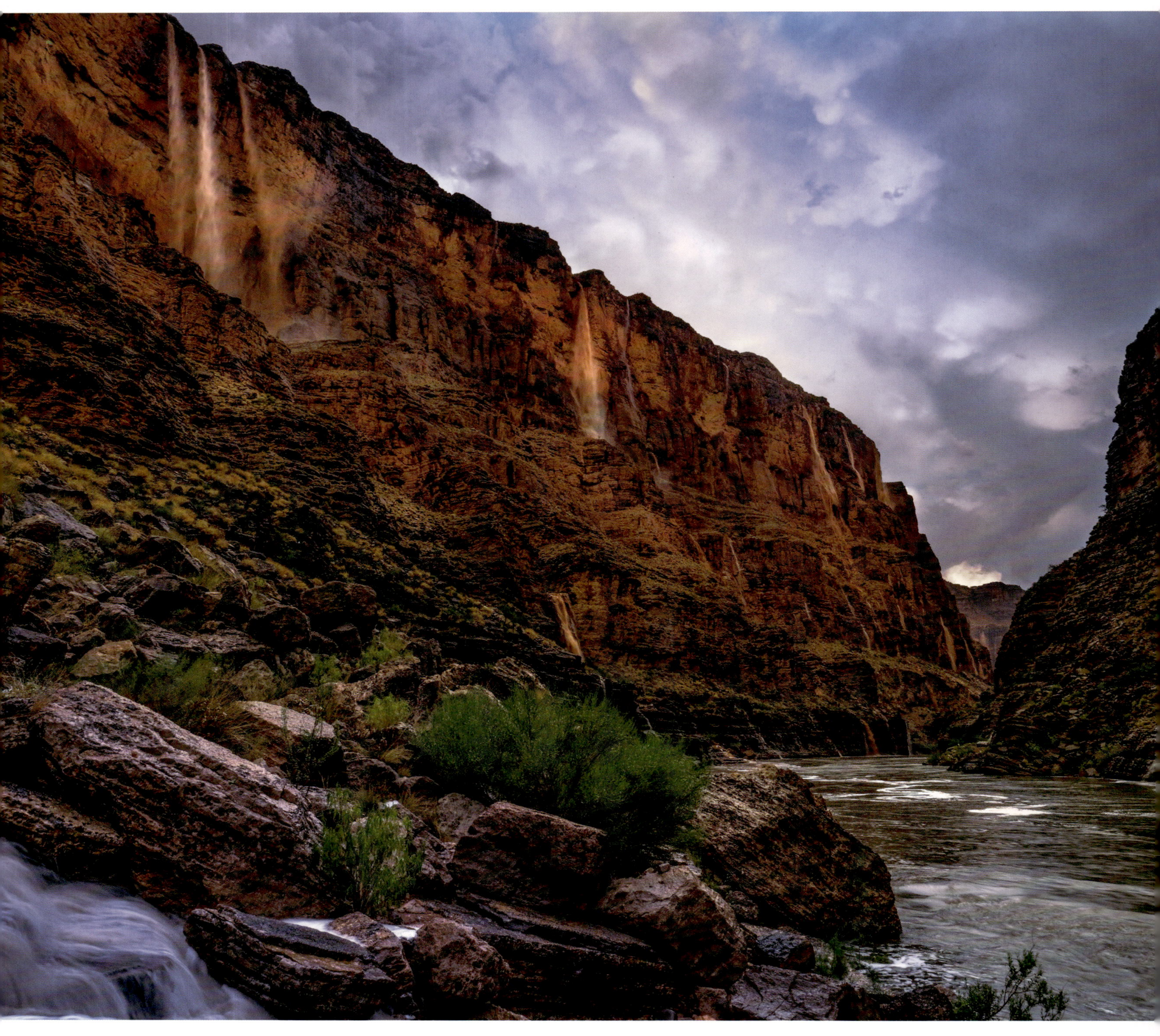

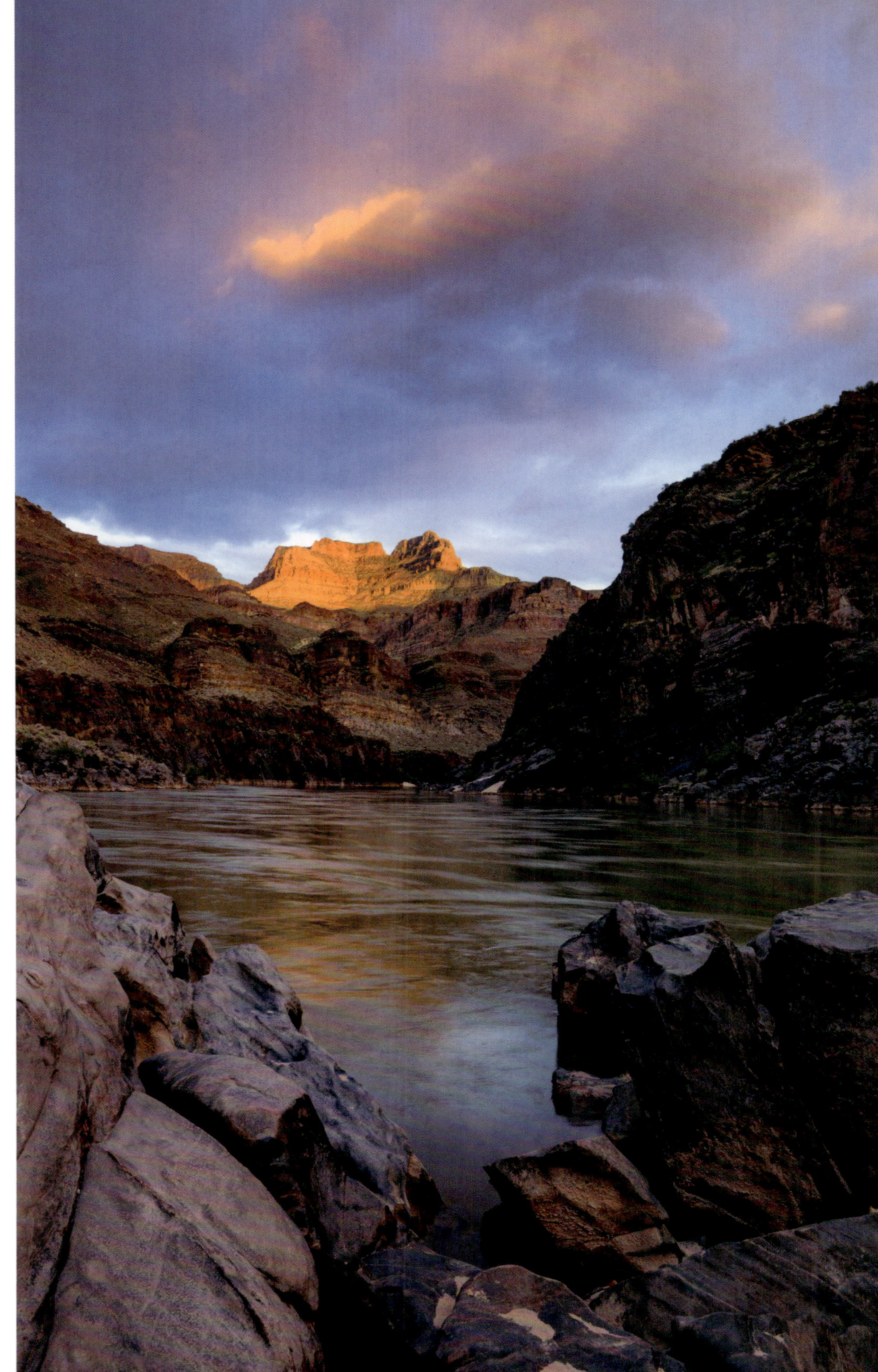

MONSOON RAINS CREATE
WATERFALLS THAT POUR OVER
THE RIMROCK OF THE GRAND
CANYON AT LEDGES CAMP.

FLUTED ROCKS AT THE RIVER'S
EDGE NEAR BASS CAMP.

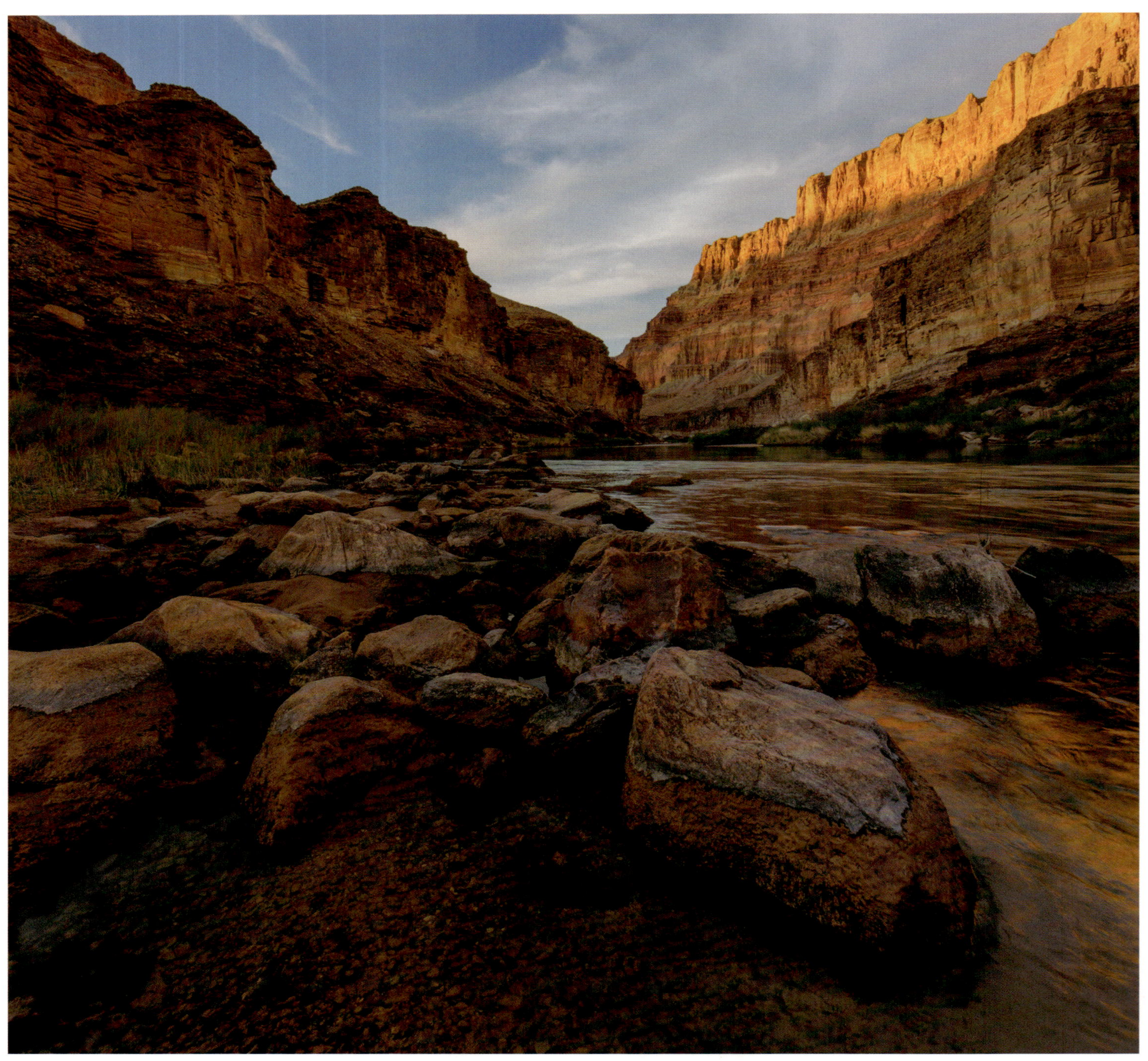



GOLDEN LIGHT REFLECTS FROM THE CLIFFS ONTO
THE BOULDERS AT RIVER LEVEL NEAR CARBON CANYON.



BACKWATER IS TRAPPED BETWEEN A SANDBAR AND
TAPEATS SANDSTONE AT MILE 120.9 CAMP.

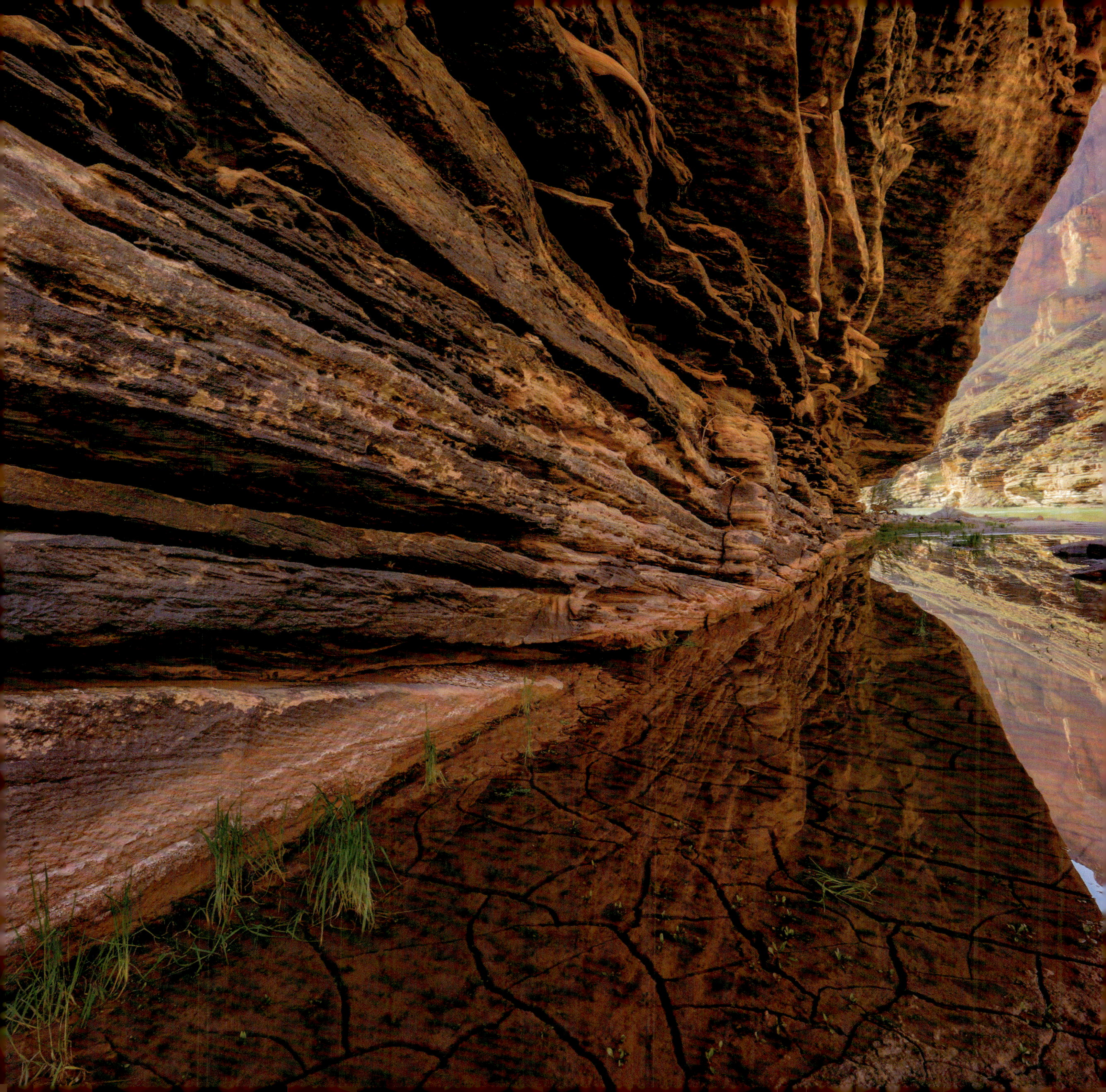

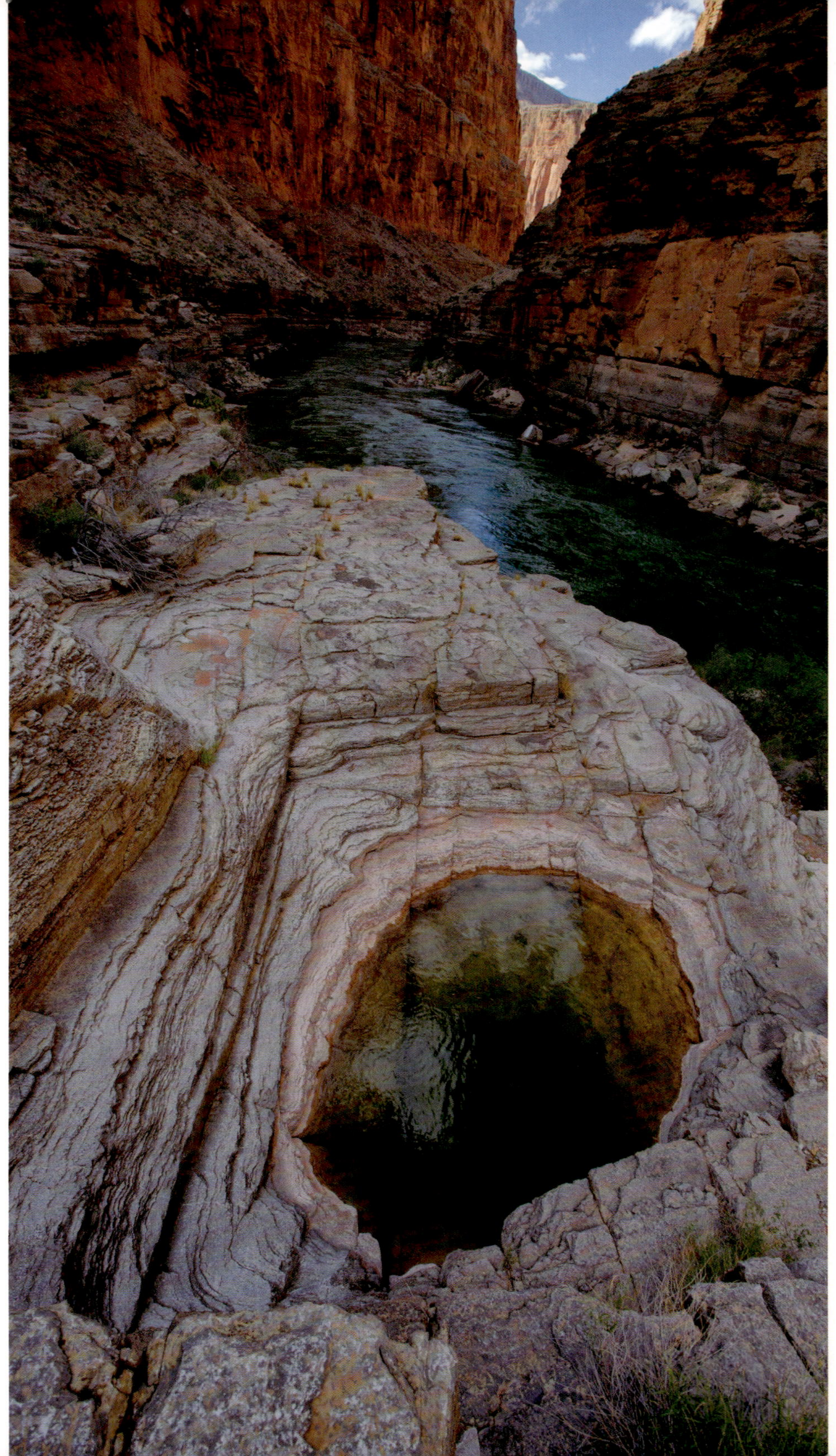

◄

A STILL POOL SITS ON A LIMESTONE
LEDGE JUST ABOVE THE COLORADO
RIVER BELOW MATCAT HOTEL.

▶

A SHORT BUT SWEET SUNRISE ACROSS
FROM DEER CREEK CAMP, AT MILE 136.8.

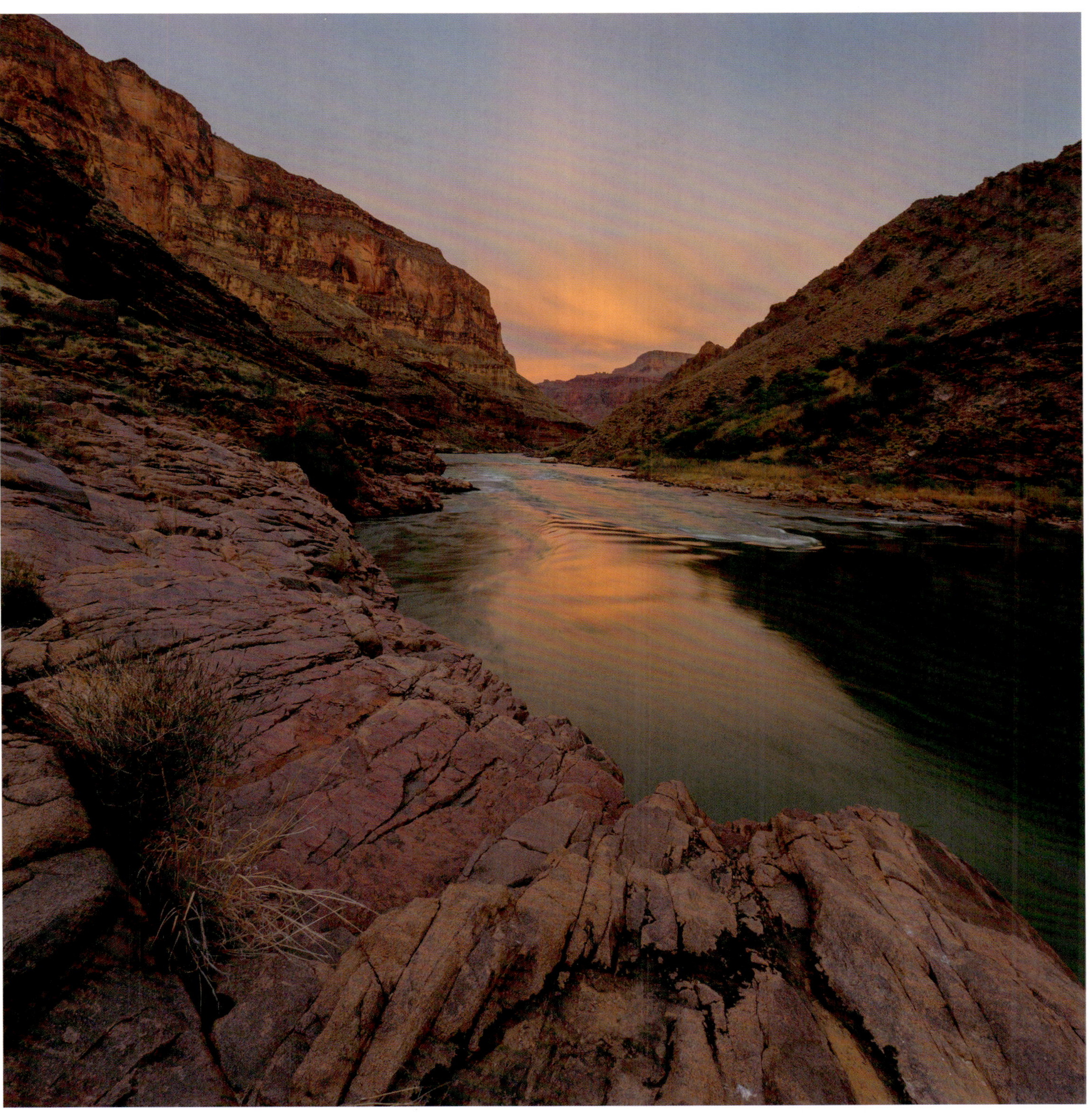

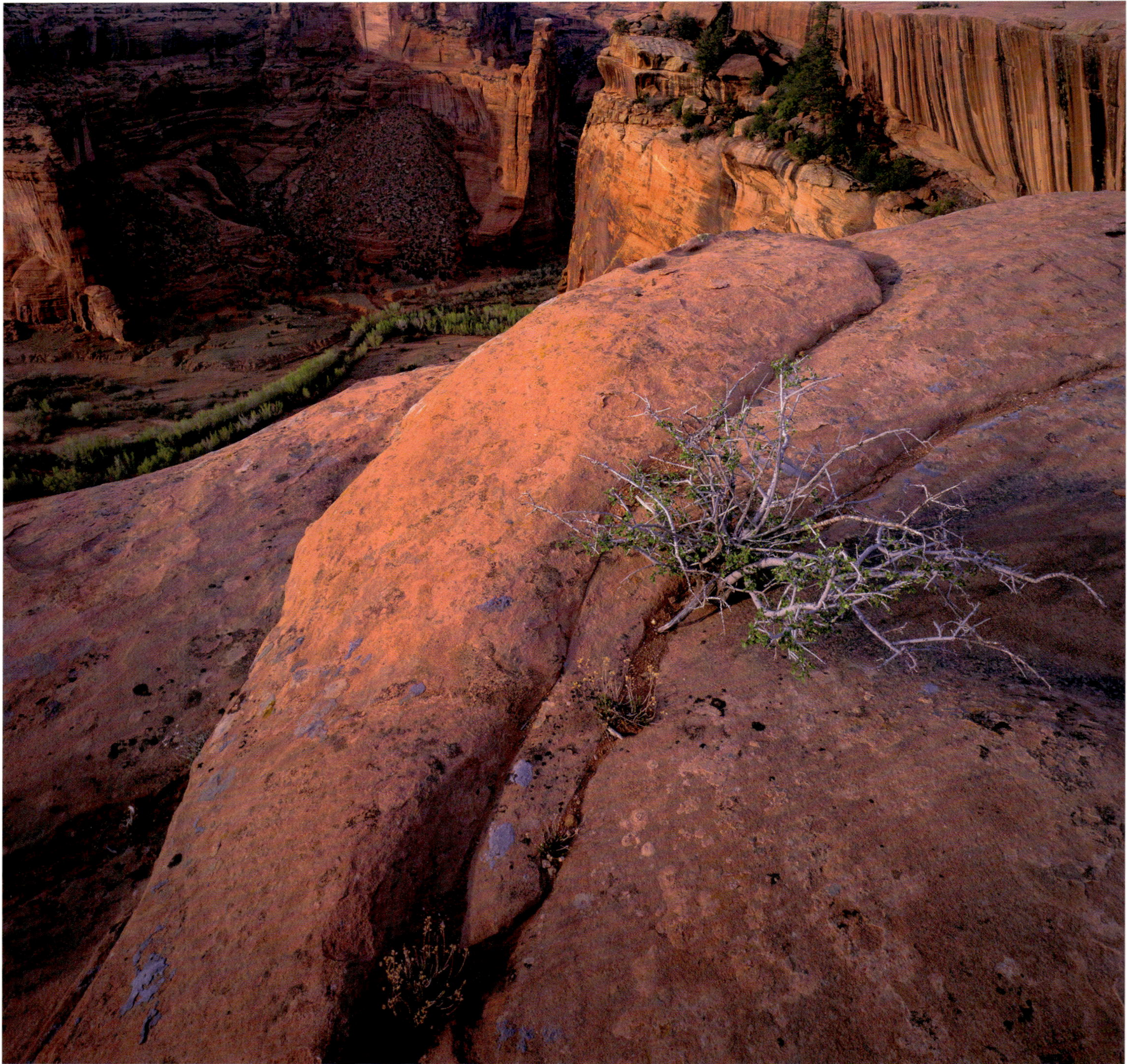


GRAPHIC PATTERNS IN SANDSTONE AT SPIDER ROCK OVERLOOK IN CANYON DE CHELLY NATIONAL MONUMENT.

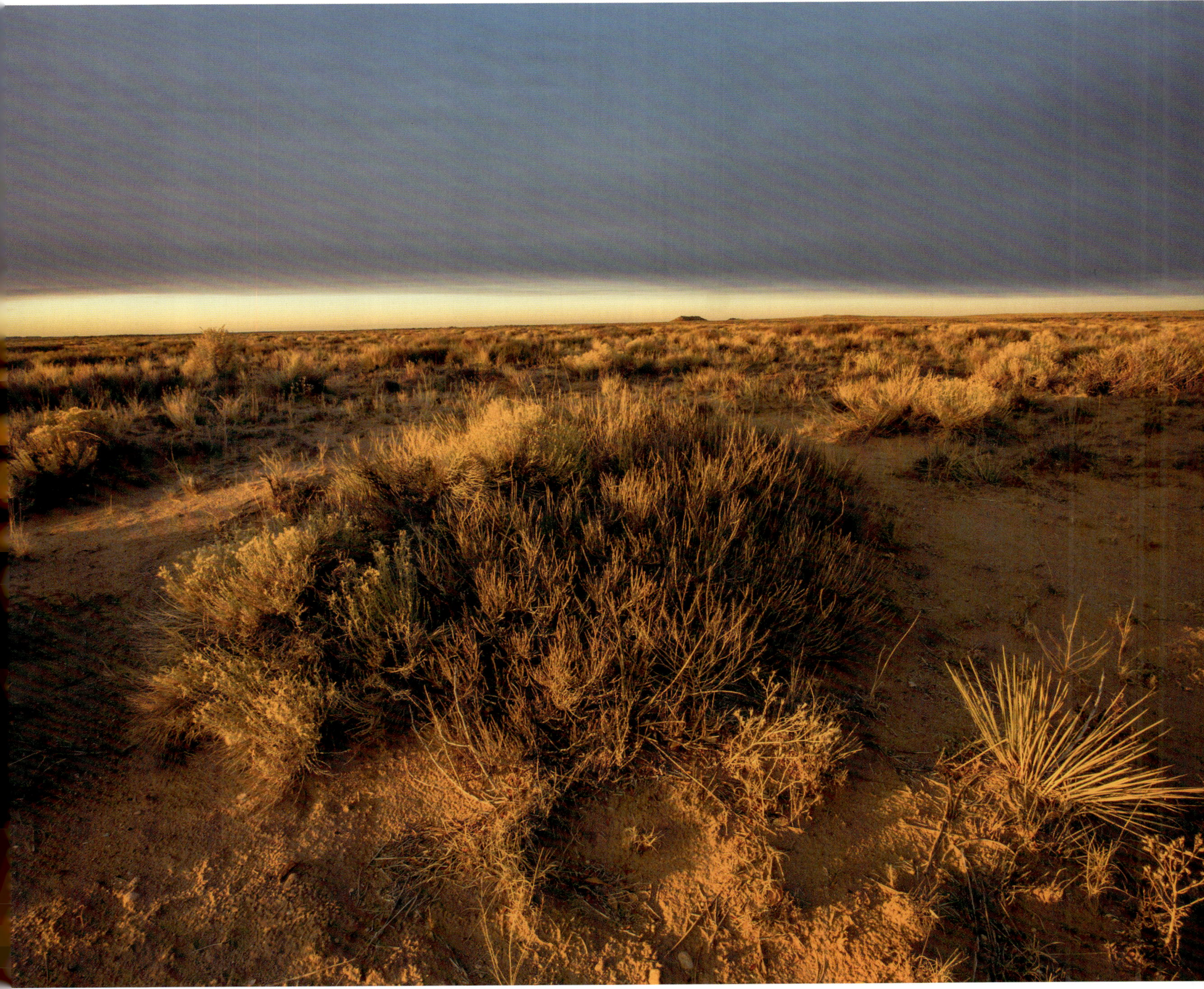

A LATE FALL STORM STRETCHES ACROSS THE HORIZON AT HOMOLOVI STATE PARK.

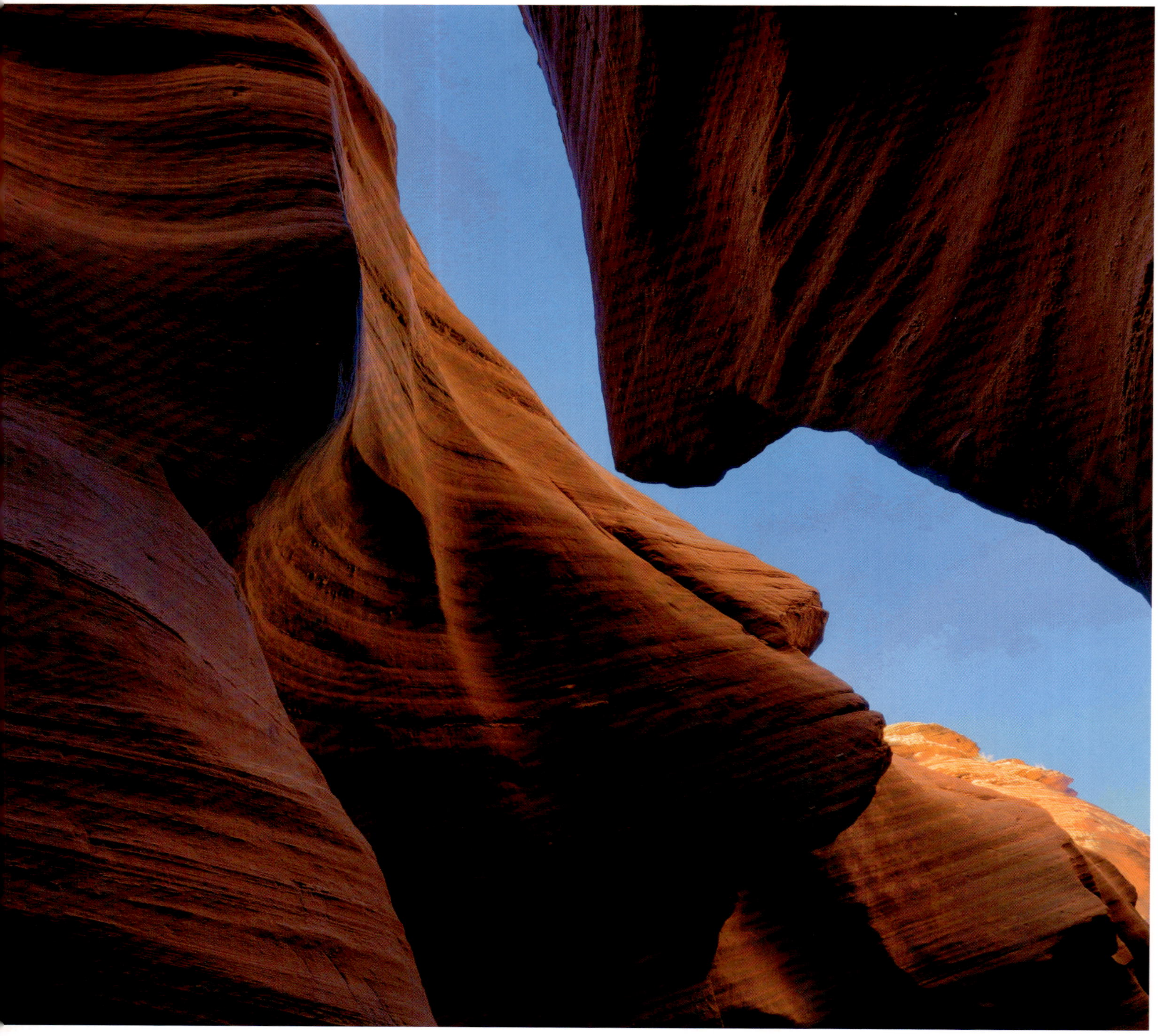



SMOOTH SANDSTONE WALLS IN THE SLOTS OF WATERHOLE CANYON NEAR PAGE, ARIZONA.

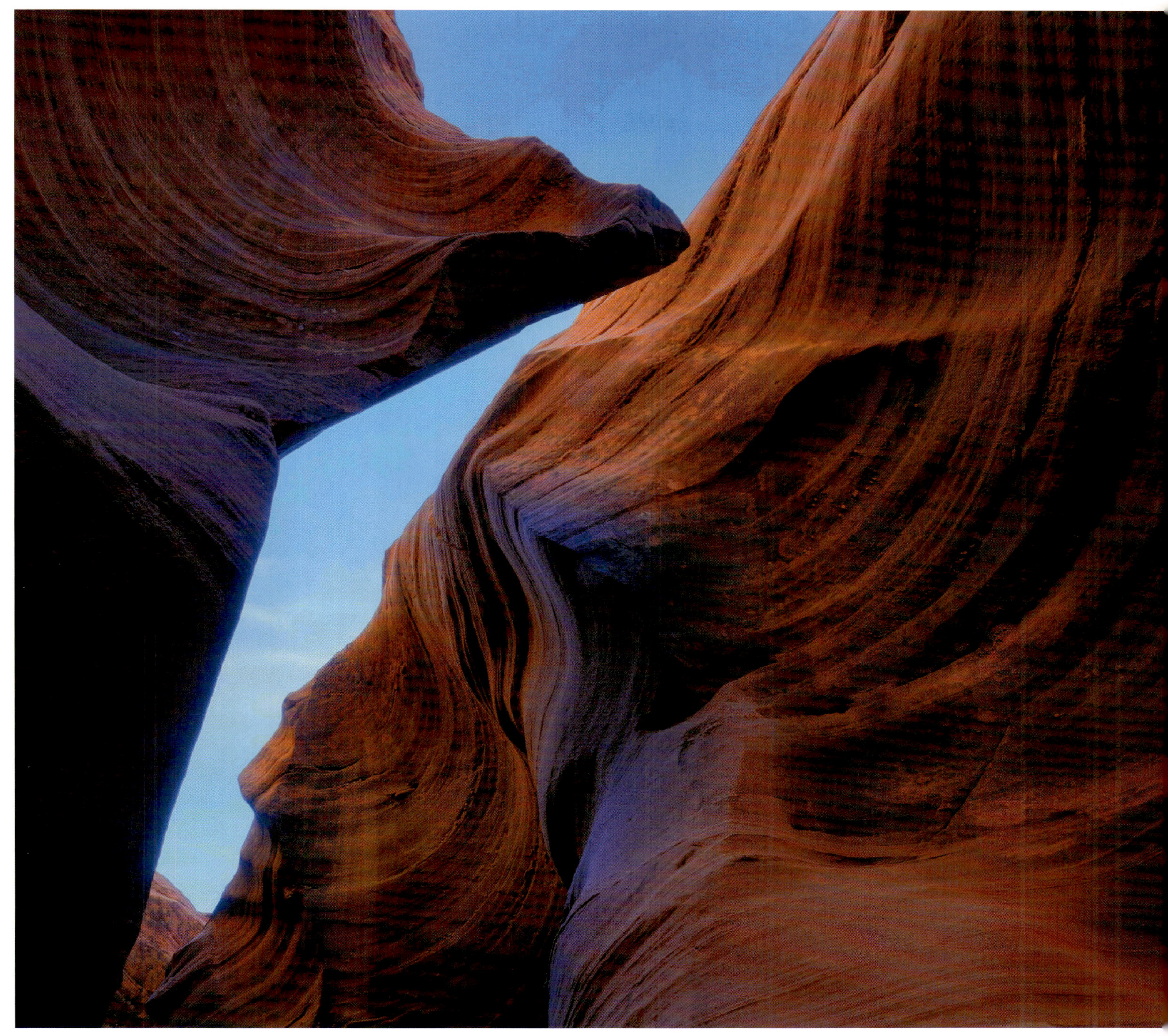

AMAZINGLY GRAPHIC PATTERN ON THE SMOOTH WALLS OF WATERHOLE SLOT CANYON.

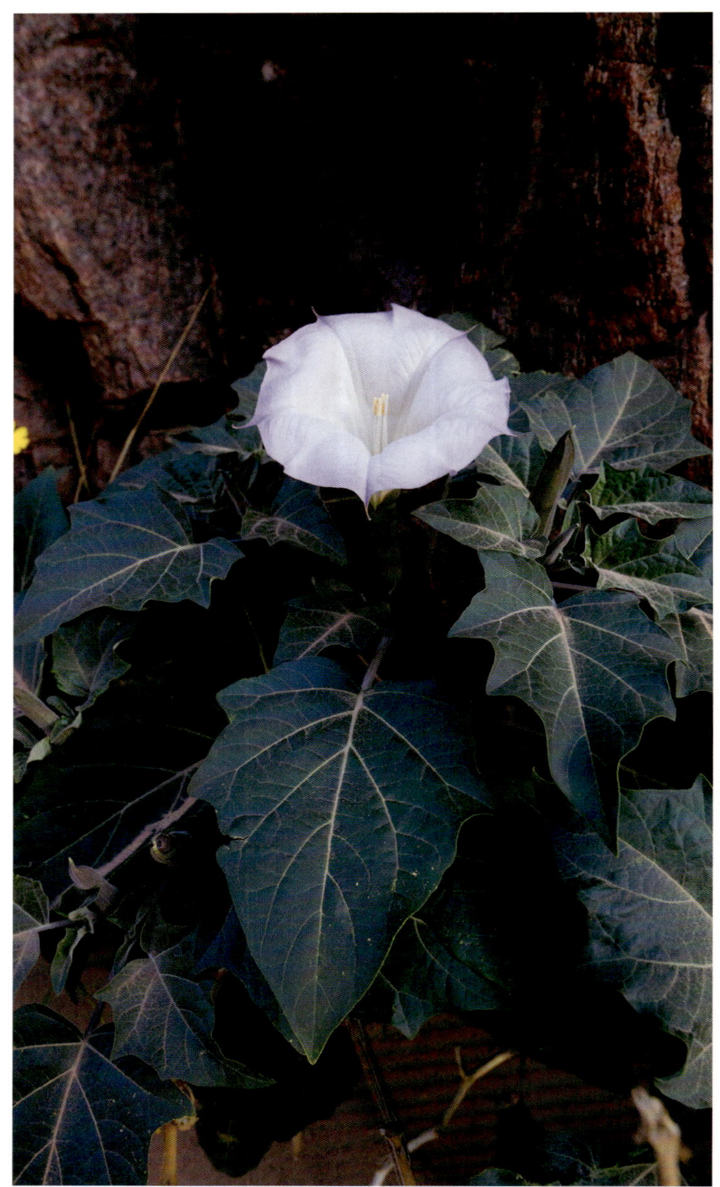



DATURA BLOOMS NEAR A GRANITE
WALL AT TRINITY CREEK.

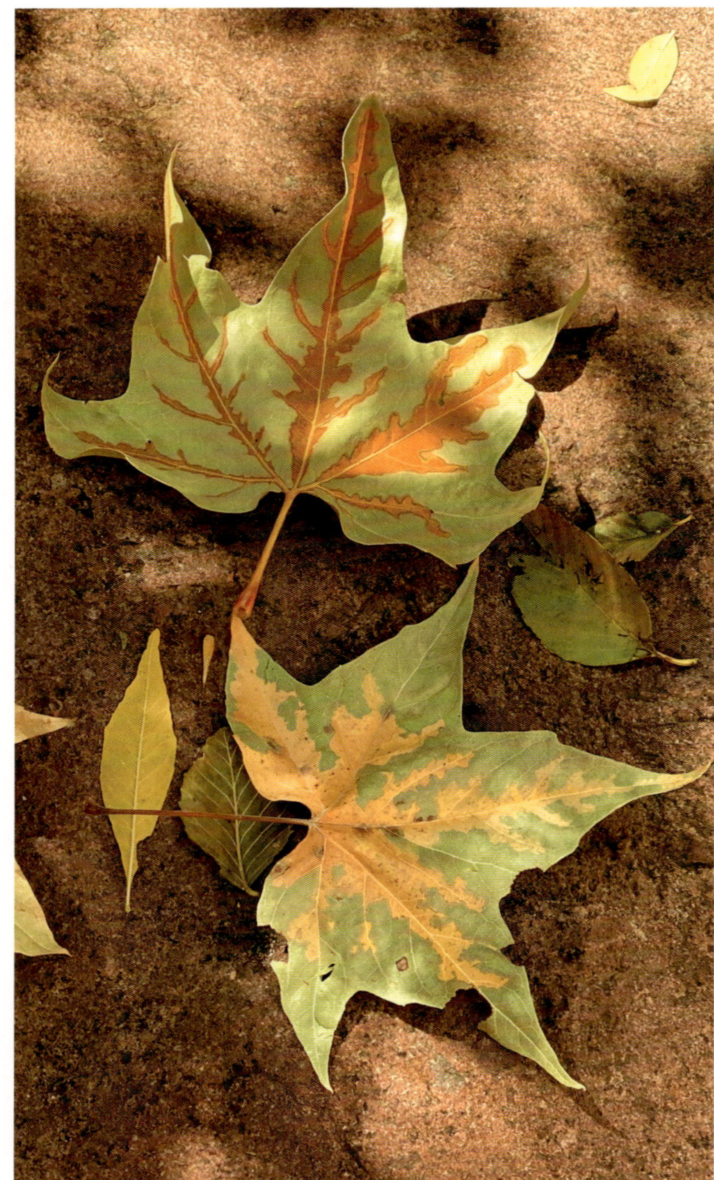

DETAIL OF WHITE SYCAMORE LEAVES IN
THE RED ROCK CANYONS NEAR SEDONA.

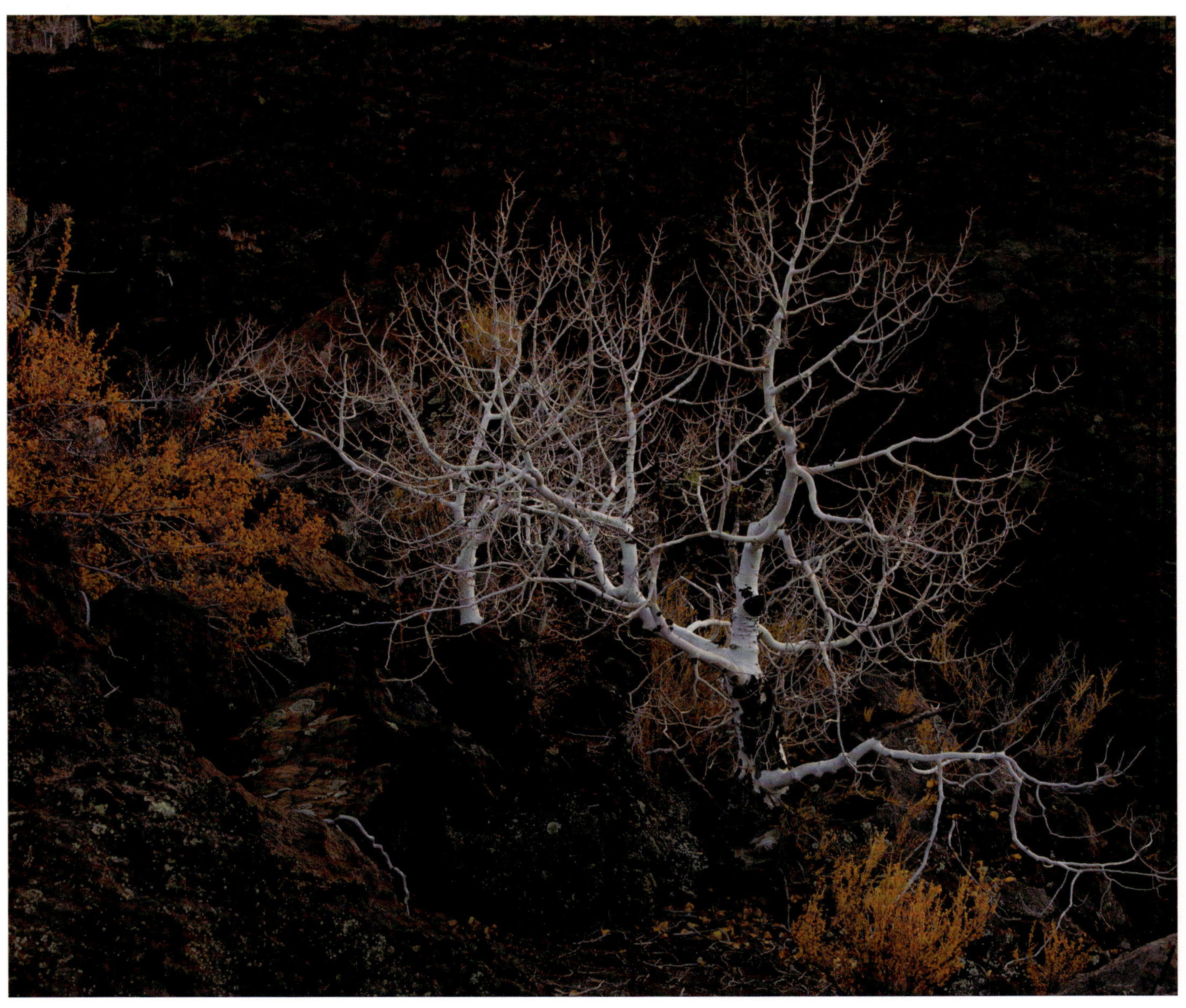

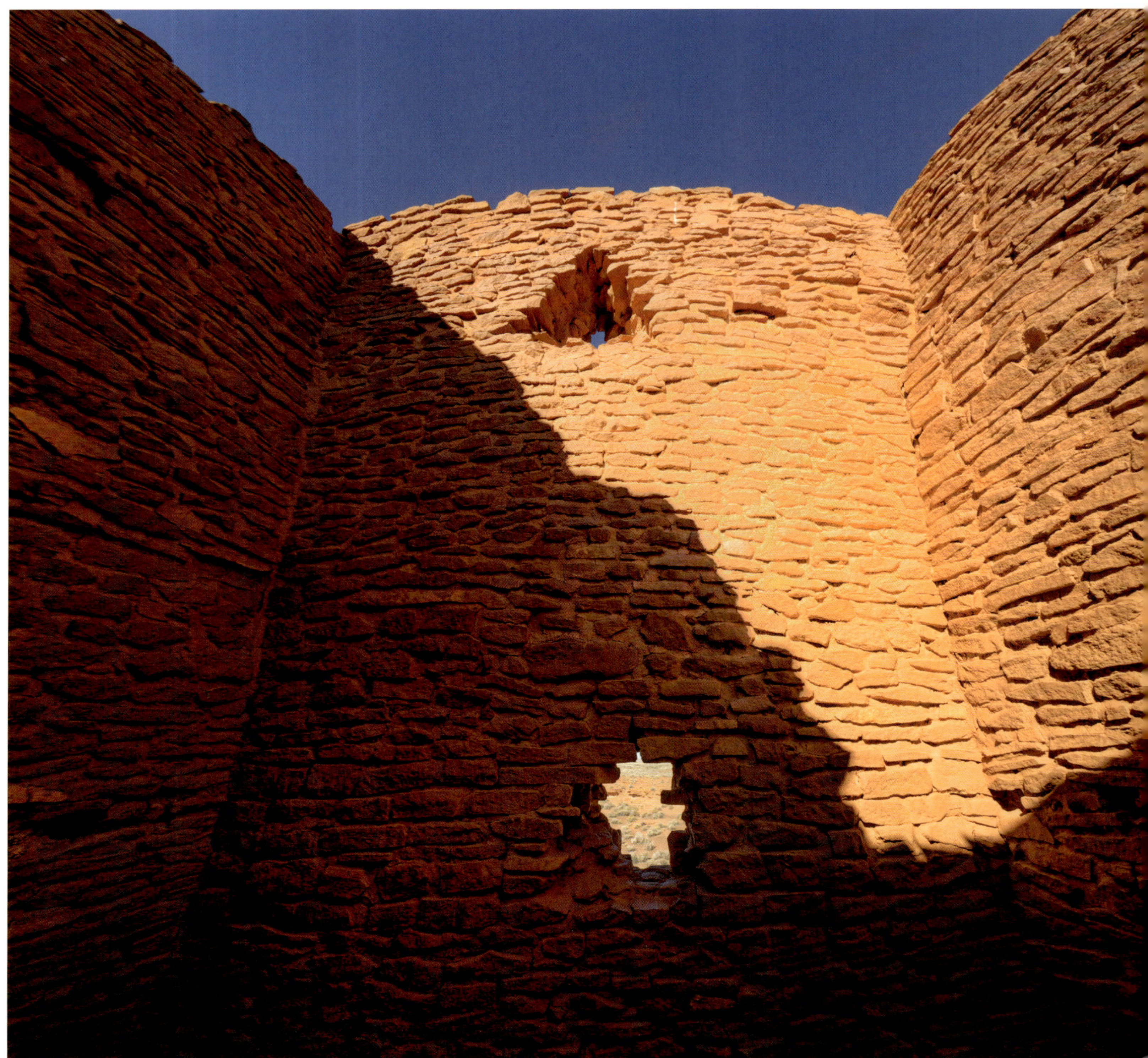

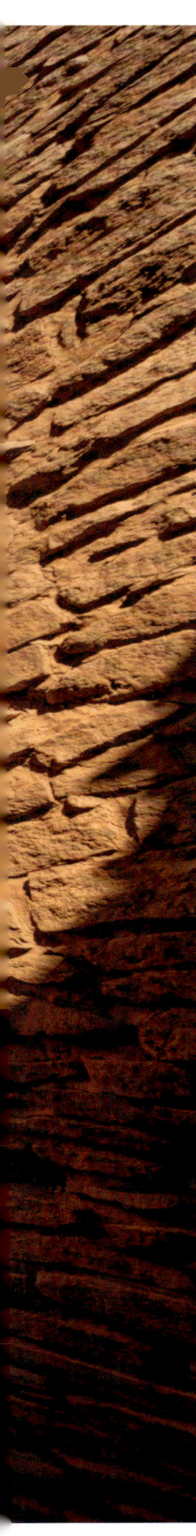

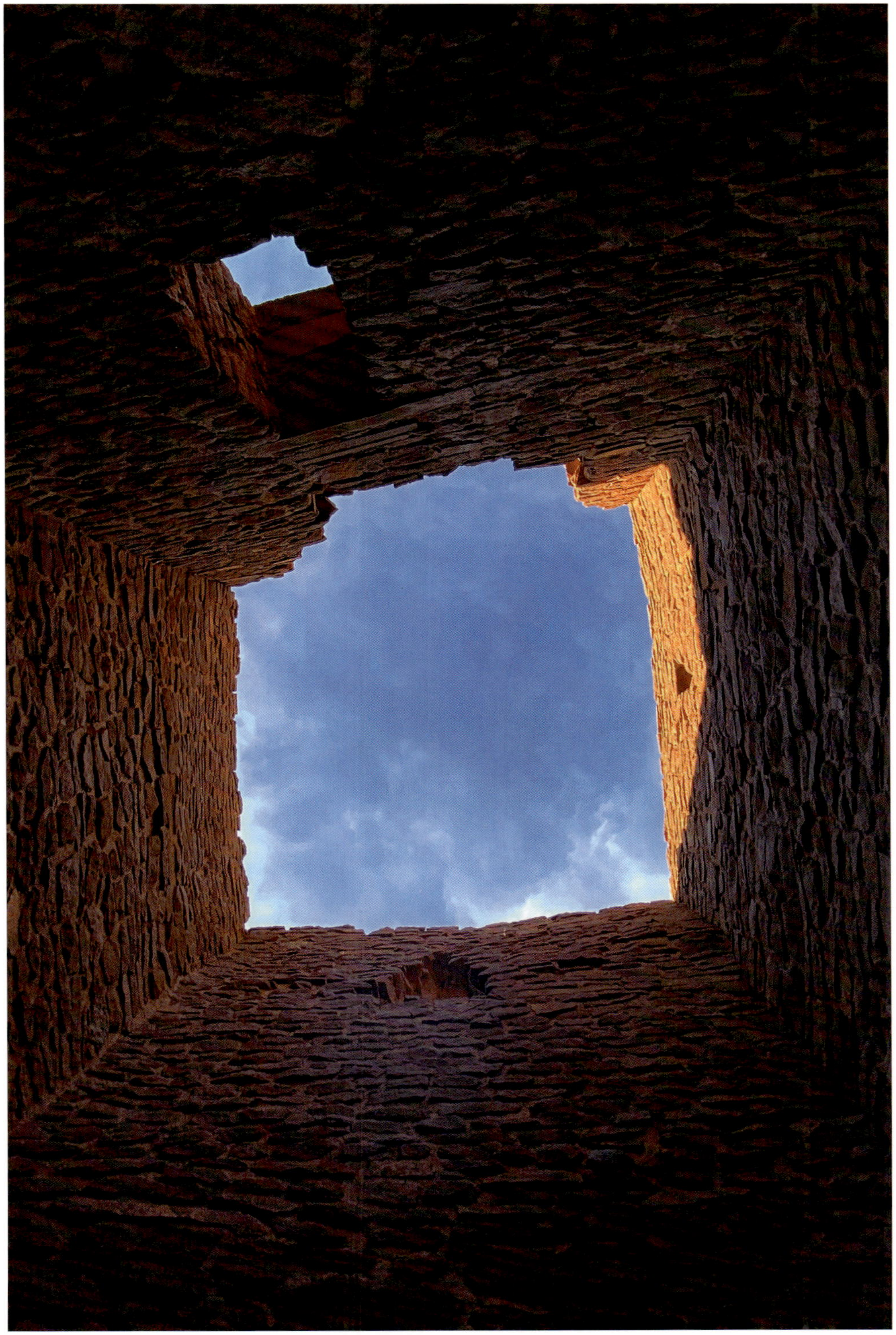

◀

DETAILS AT THE LOMAKI
RUINS IN WUPATKI NATIONAL
MONUMENT.

▶

DETAIL OF THE TOWER AT
THE LOMAKI RUINS IN WUPATKI
NATIONAL MONUMENT.

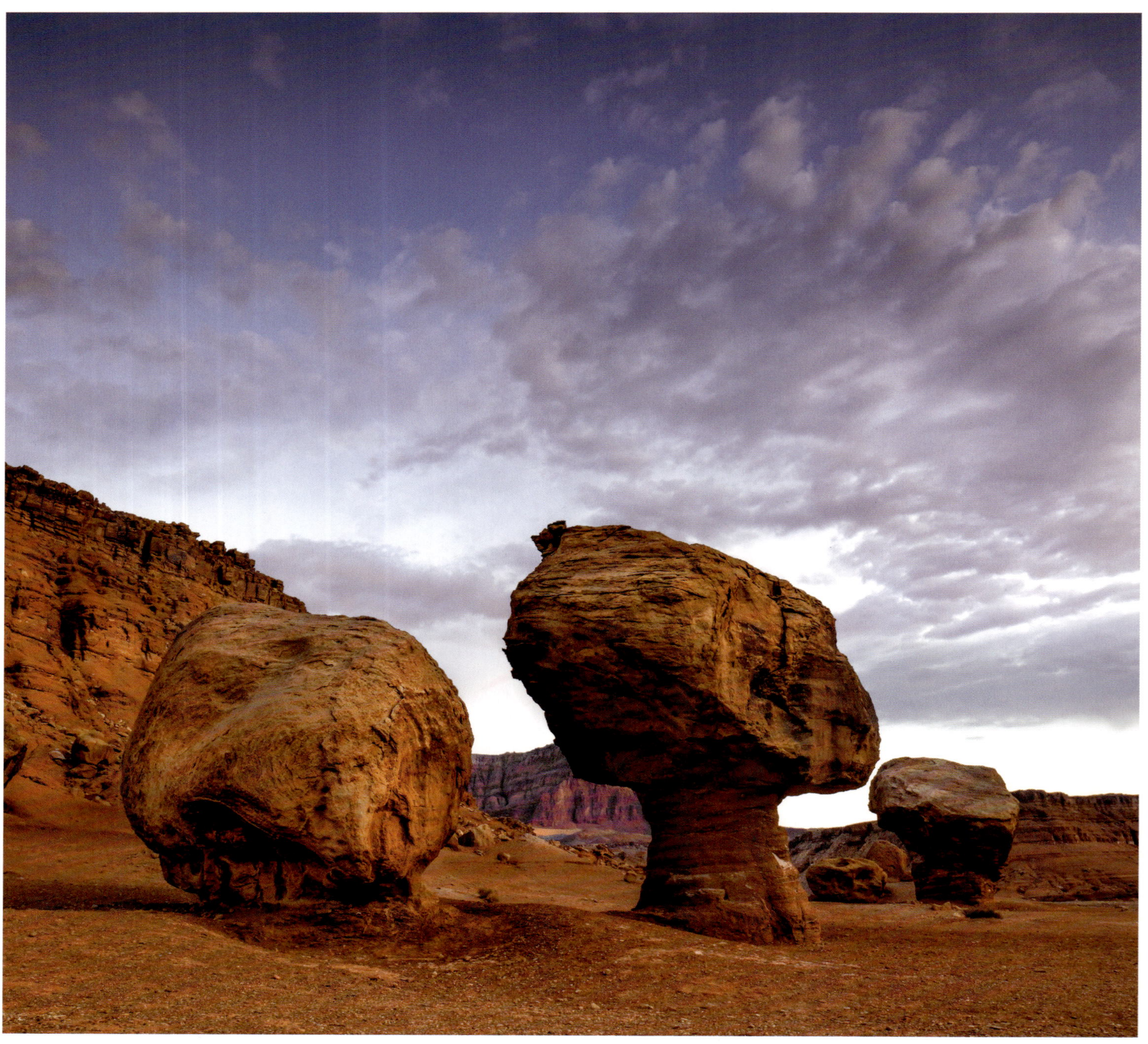

SANDSTONE HOODOOS REST BELOW VERMILLION CLIFFS.

LONELY LOMAKI RUIN AT THE WUPATKI NATIONAL MONUMENT.

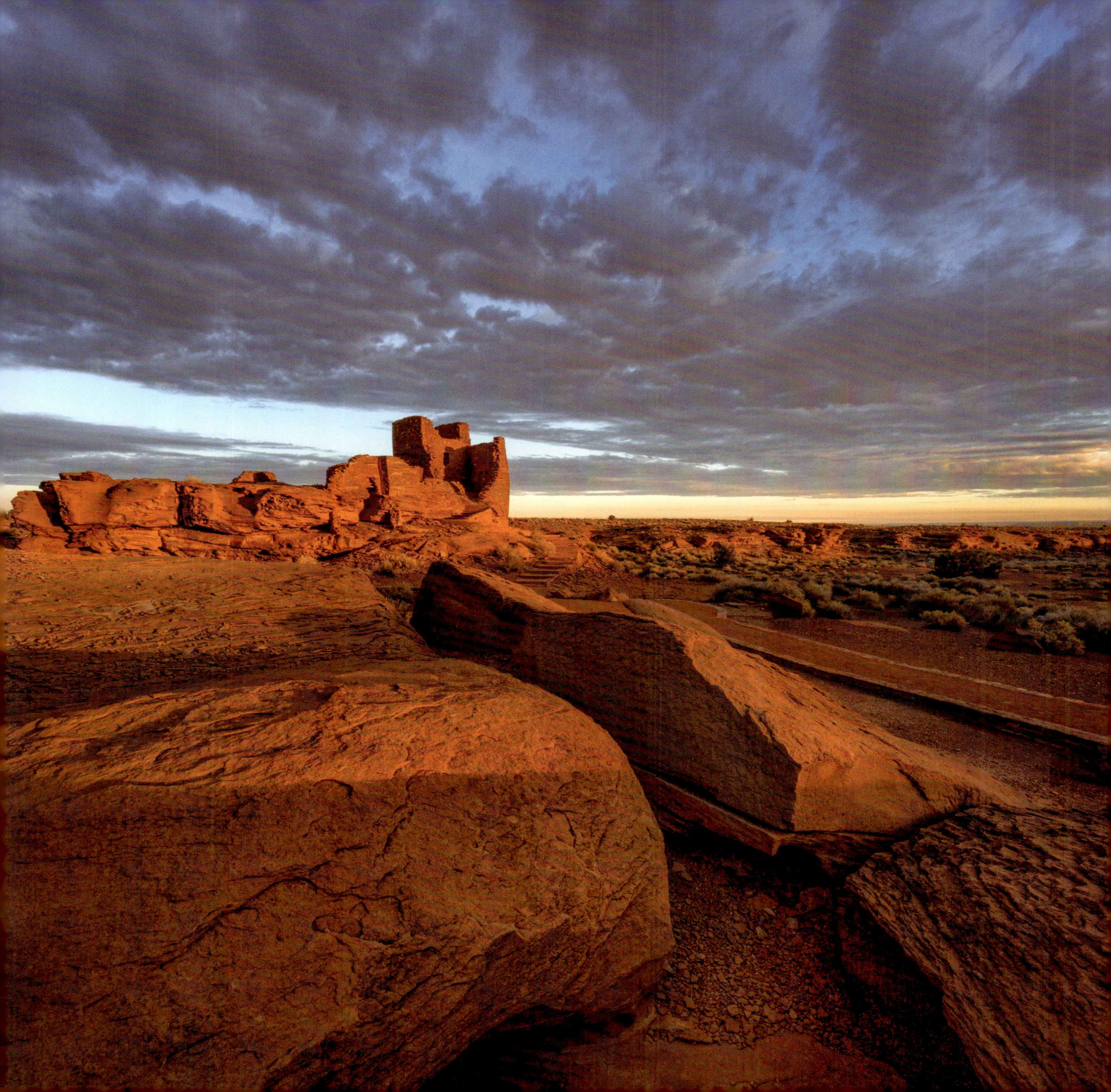

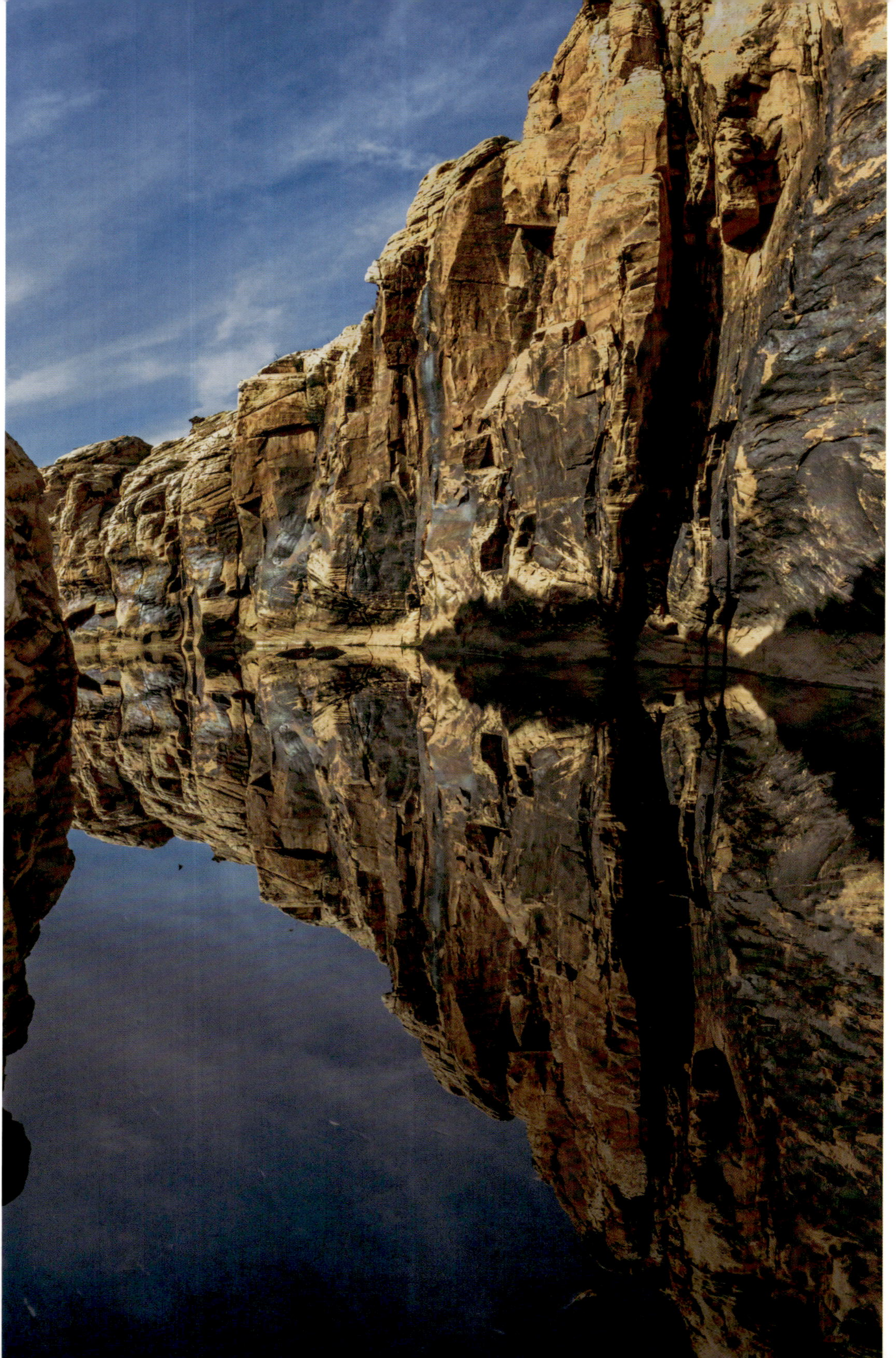

DEEP BLUE POOLS ALONG THE
SANDSTONE WALLS OF CHEVELON
CREEK NEAR WINSLOW.

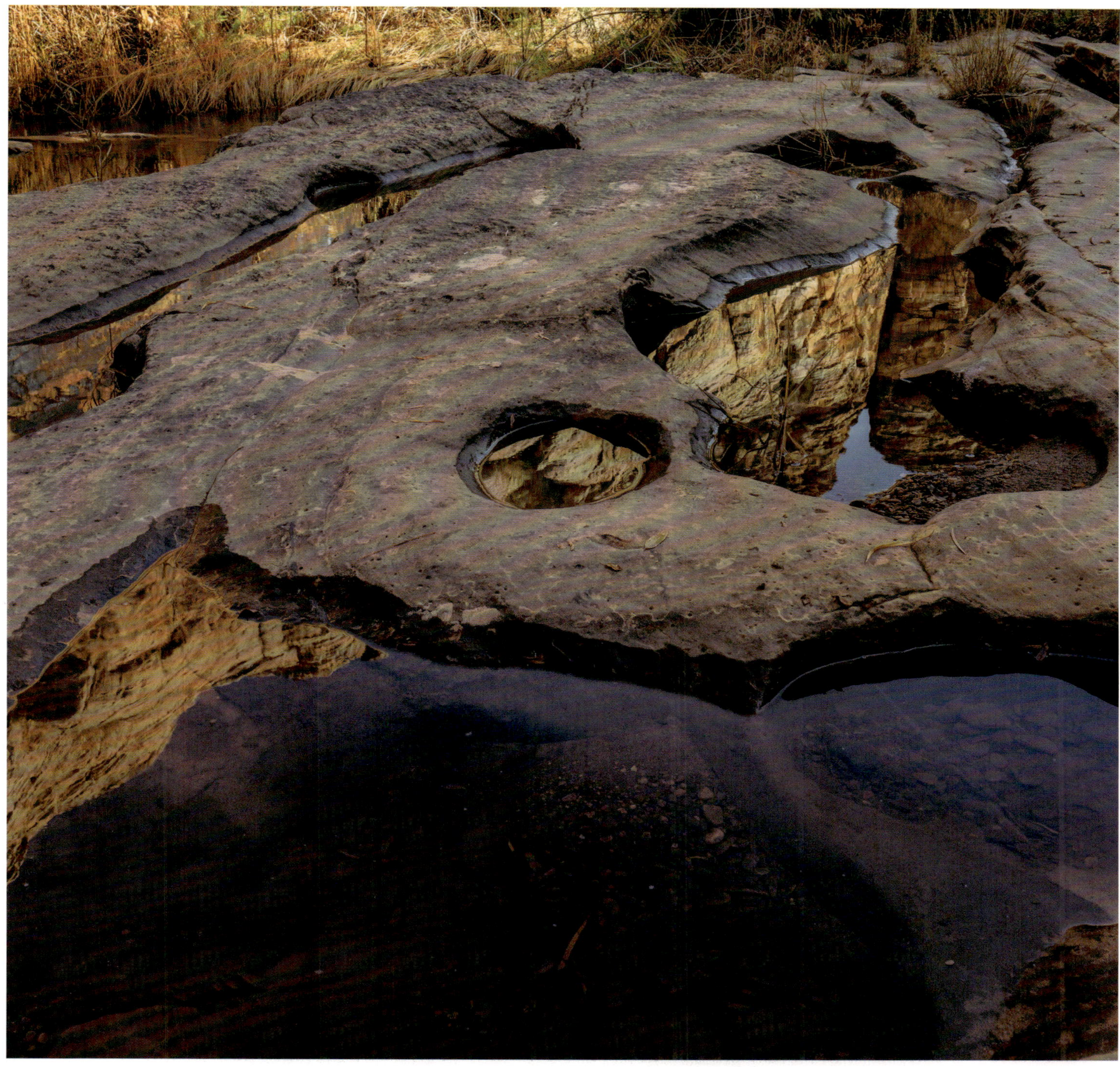

THE YEAR-ROUND FLOW OF CHEVELON CREEK CUTS DEEP PATTERNS IN THE SANDSTONE BEDROCK.

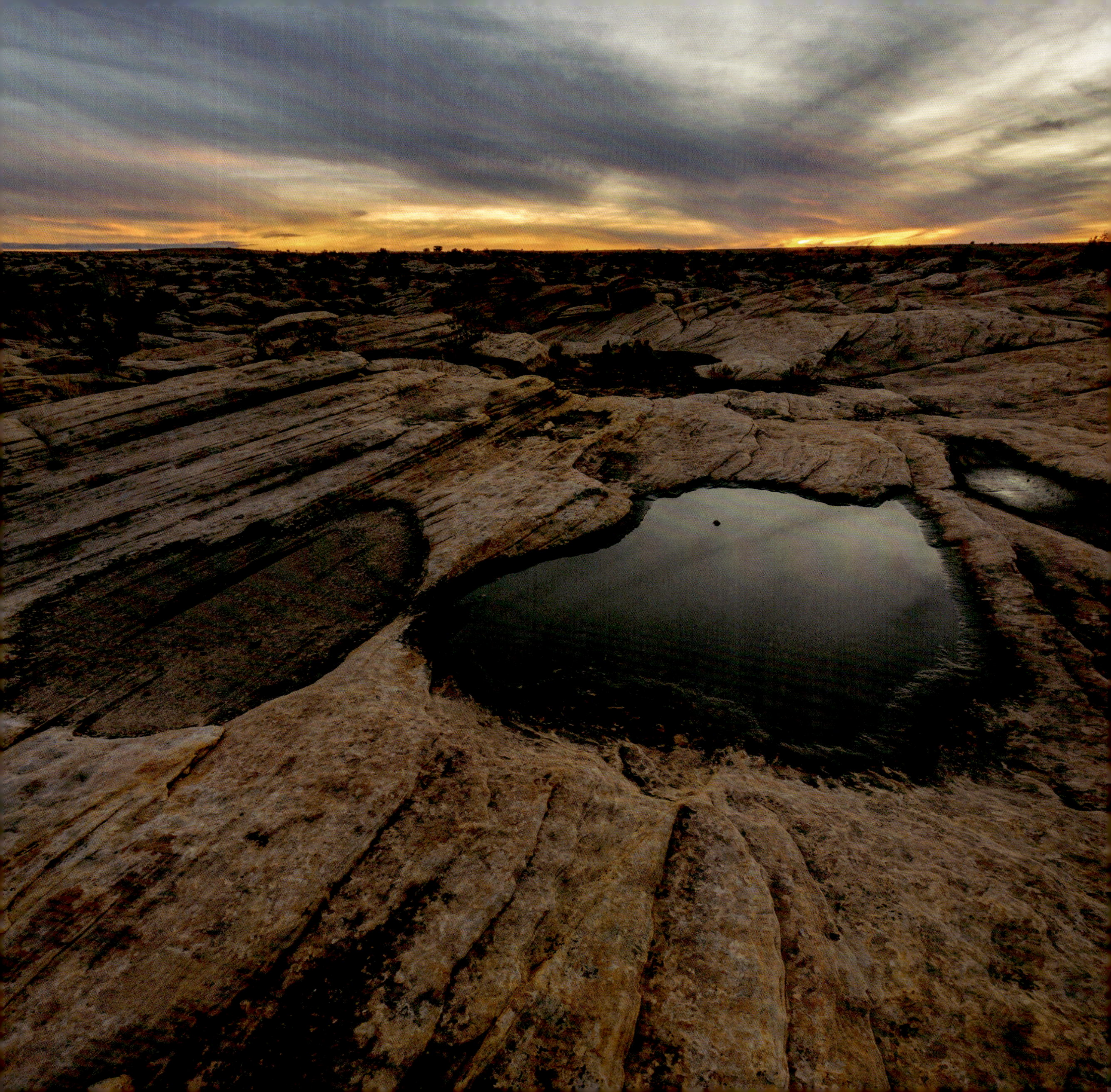

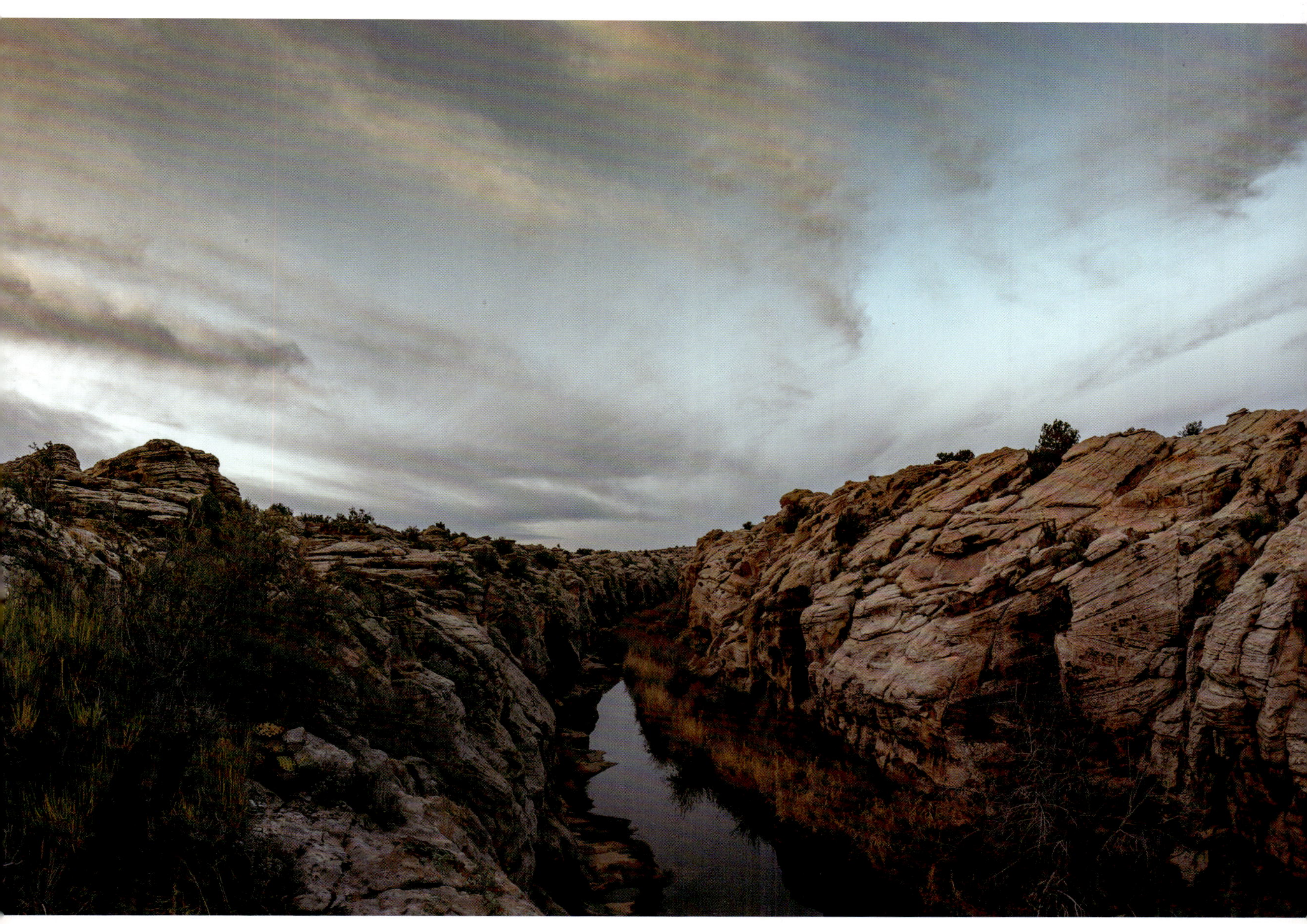



CHEVELON CREEK CUTS INTO THE DESERT FLOOR
AS IT FLOWS FROM THE MOGOLLON RIM TO ITS
CONFLUENCE WITH THE LITTLE COLORADO RIVER.

◀

SANDSTONE COLLECTS WINTER RAINS IN THE
CHEVELON CANYON WILDLIFE AREA.

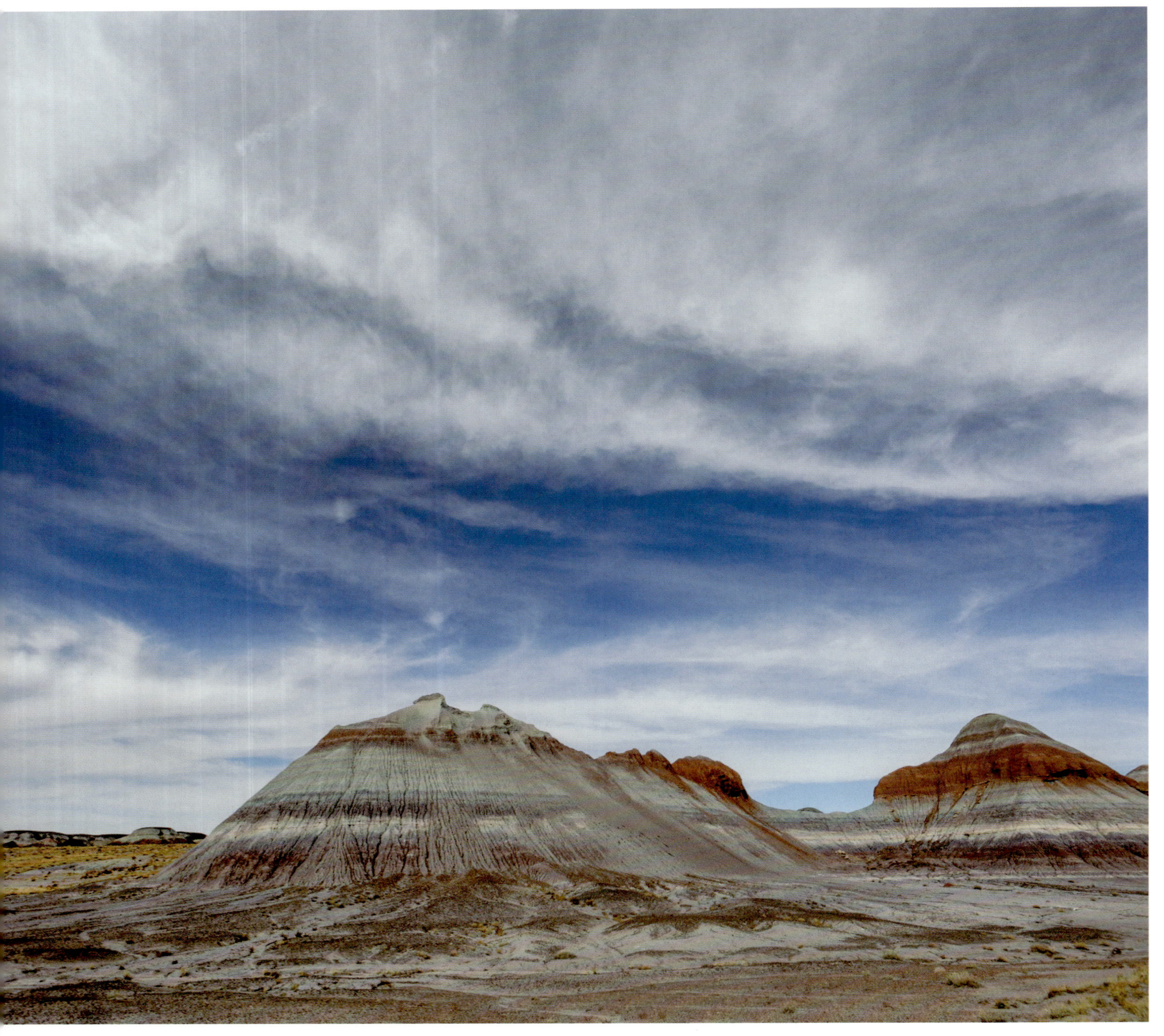



MULTICOLORED EARTHEN BUTTES OF THE CHINLE FORMATION IN PETRIFIED FOREST NATIONAL PARK.

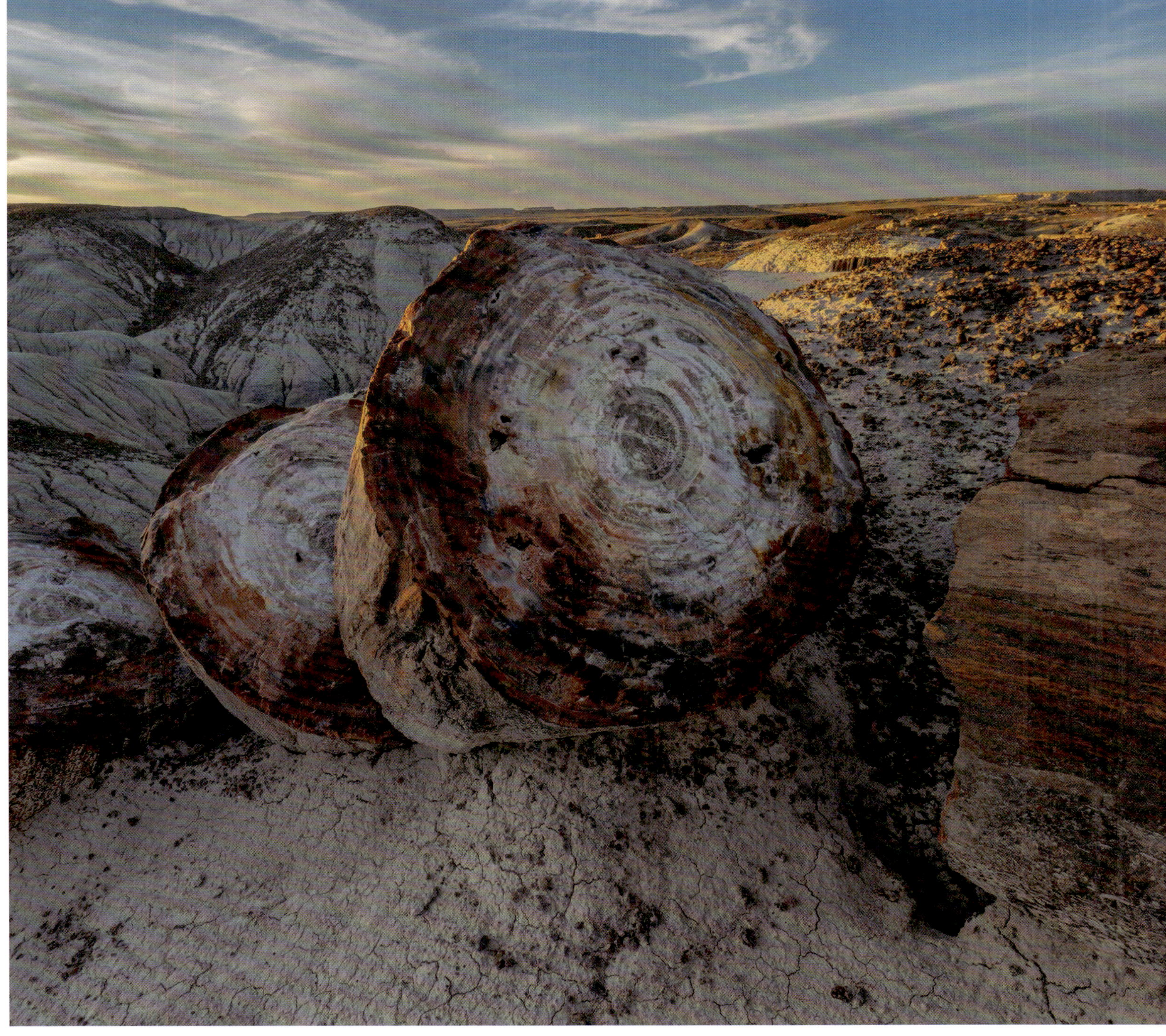

HUGE PETRIFIED LOGS COVER THE PARCHED DESERT EARTH IN PETRIFIED FOREST NATIONAL PARK.

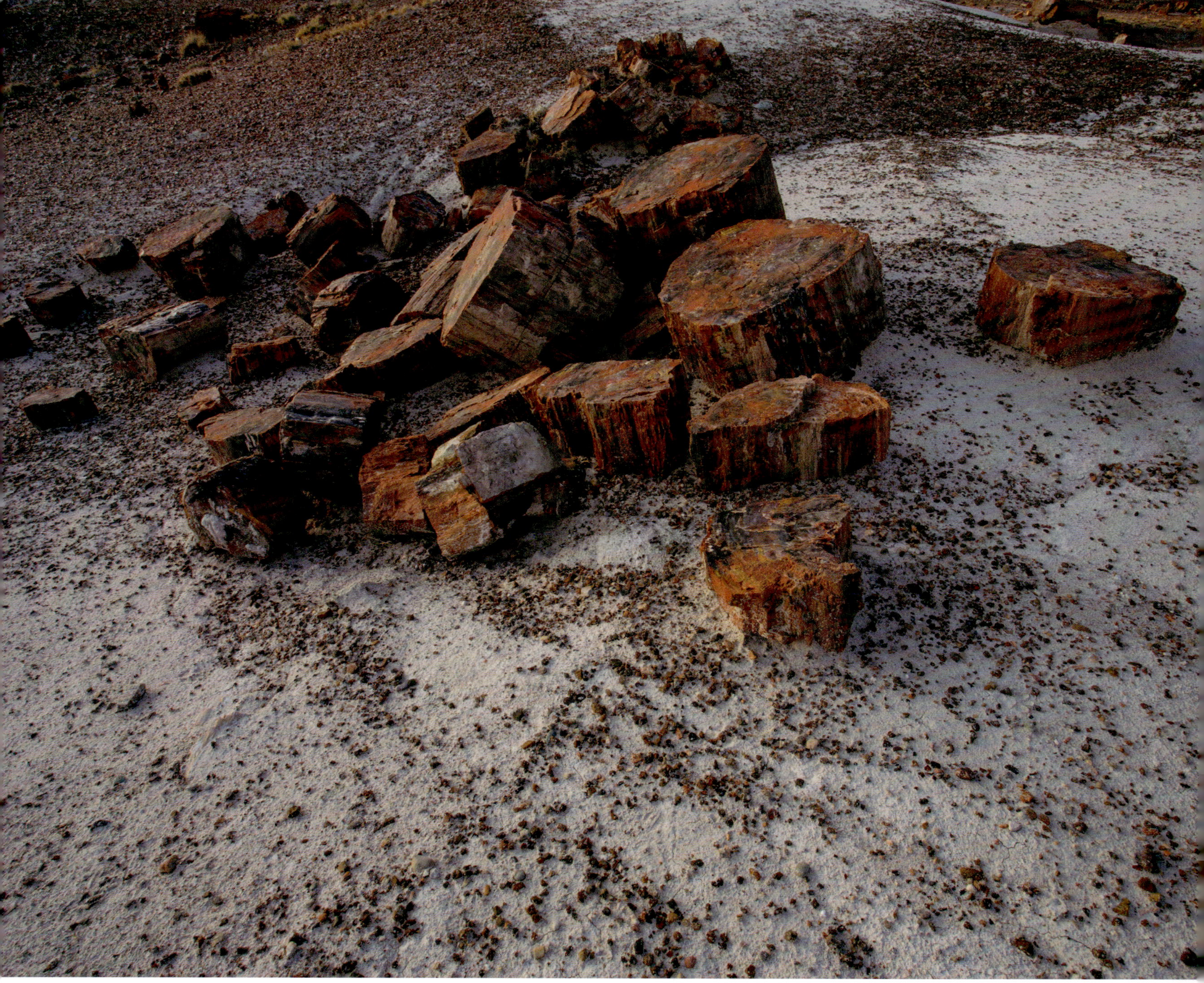



PETRIFIED WOOD STACKED NEATLY BY NATURE IN THE CRYSTAL FOREST OF PETRIFIED FOREST NATIONAL PARK.

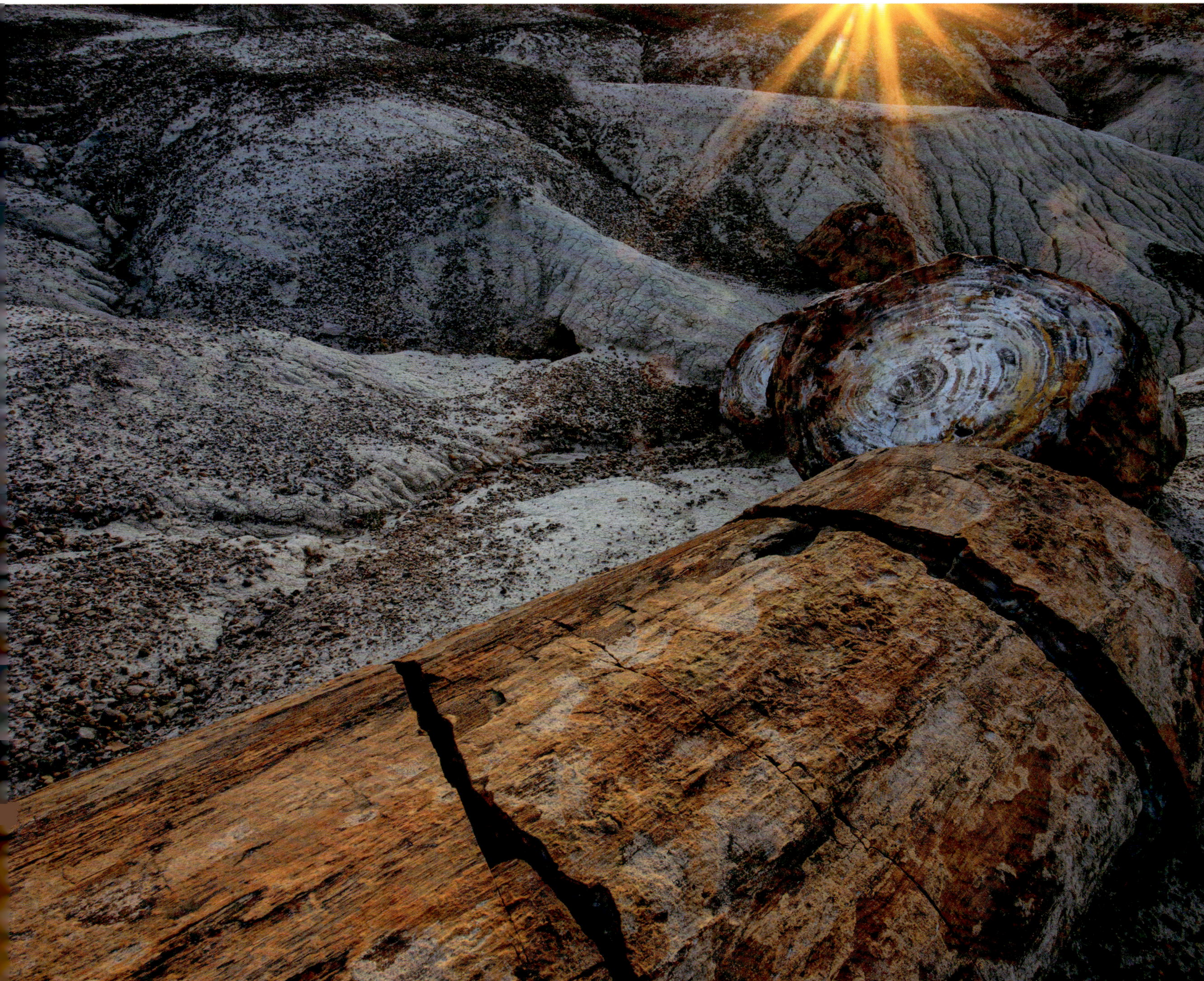

GIANT LOGS LAY AS THEY FELL IN PETRIFIED FOREST NATIONAL PARK.

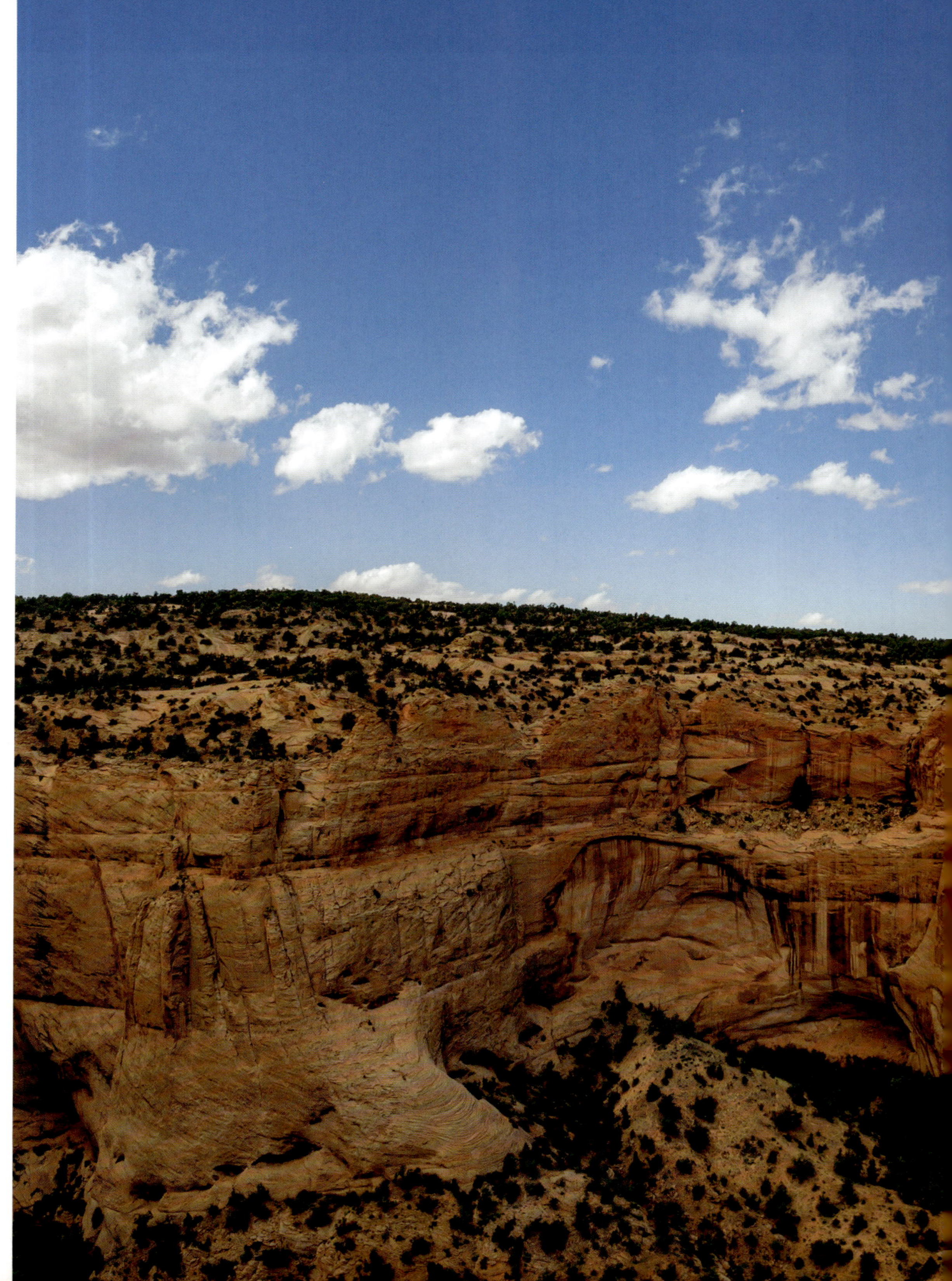

ANCIENT PUEBLOS NESTLE
UNDER WARM SANDSTONE
LEDGES IN NAVAJO
NATIONAL MONUMENT.

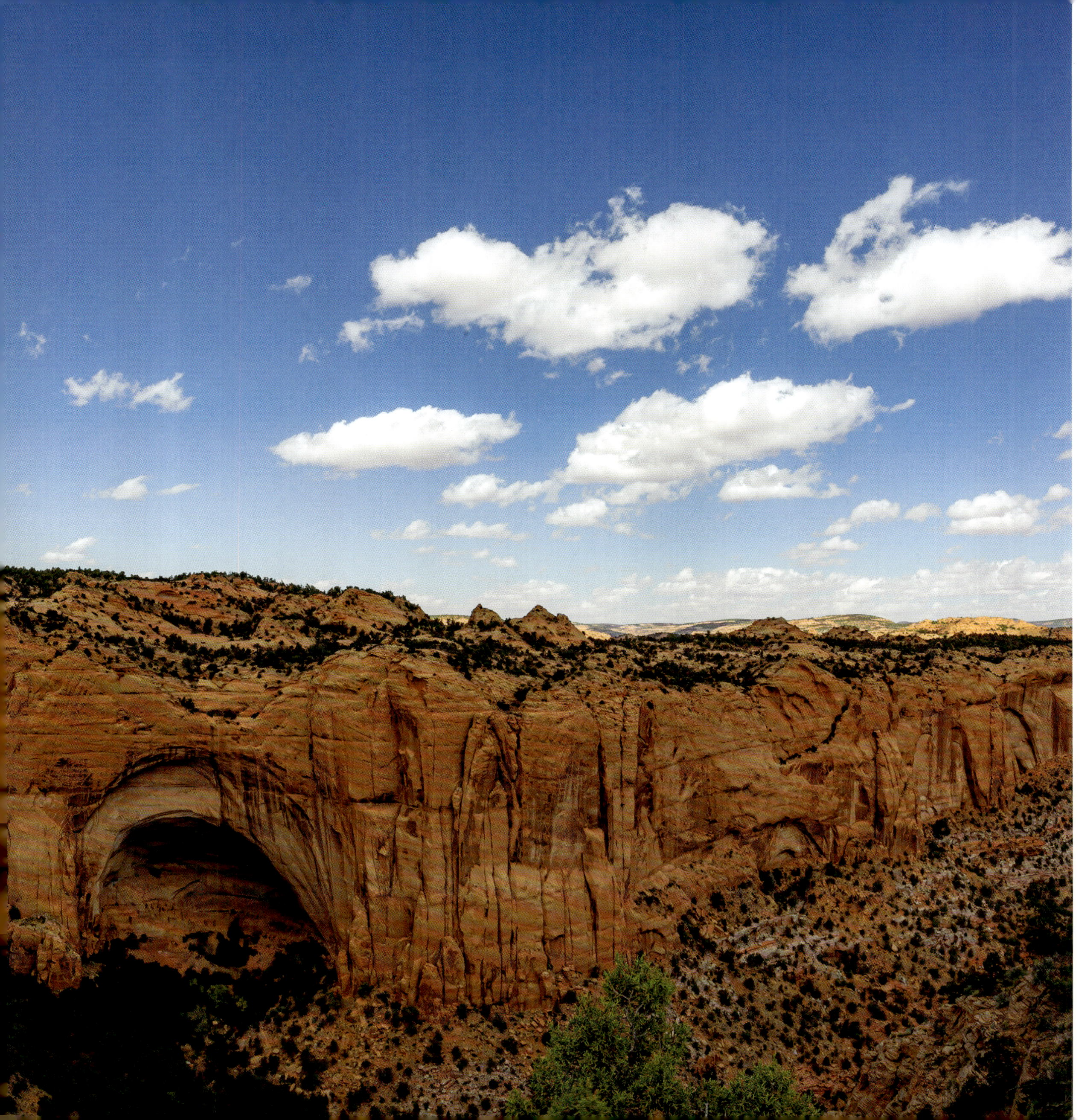

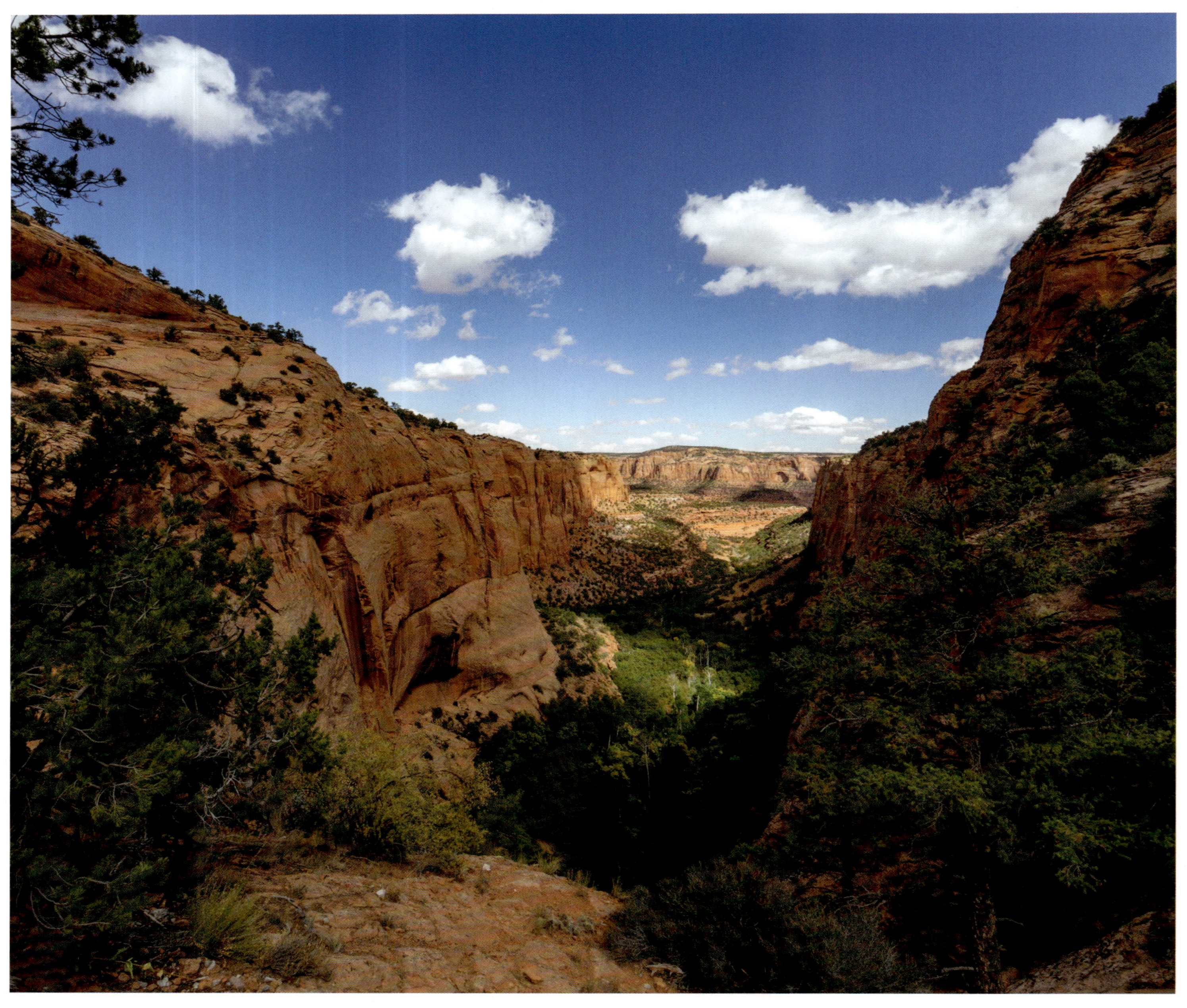

GIANT SANDSTONE FORMATIONS CREATE WONDERFUL
CANYONS IN NAVAJO NATIONAL MONUMENT.

CLOUDS ROLL ACROSS THE DESERT SKY IN NAVAJO NATIONAL MONUMENT.

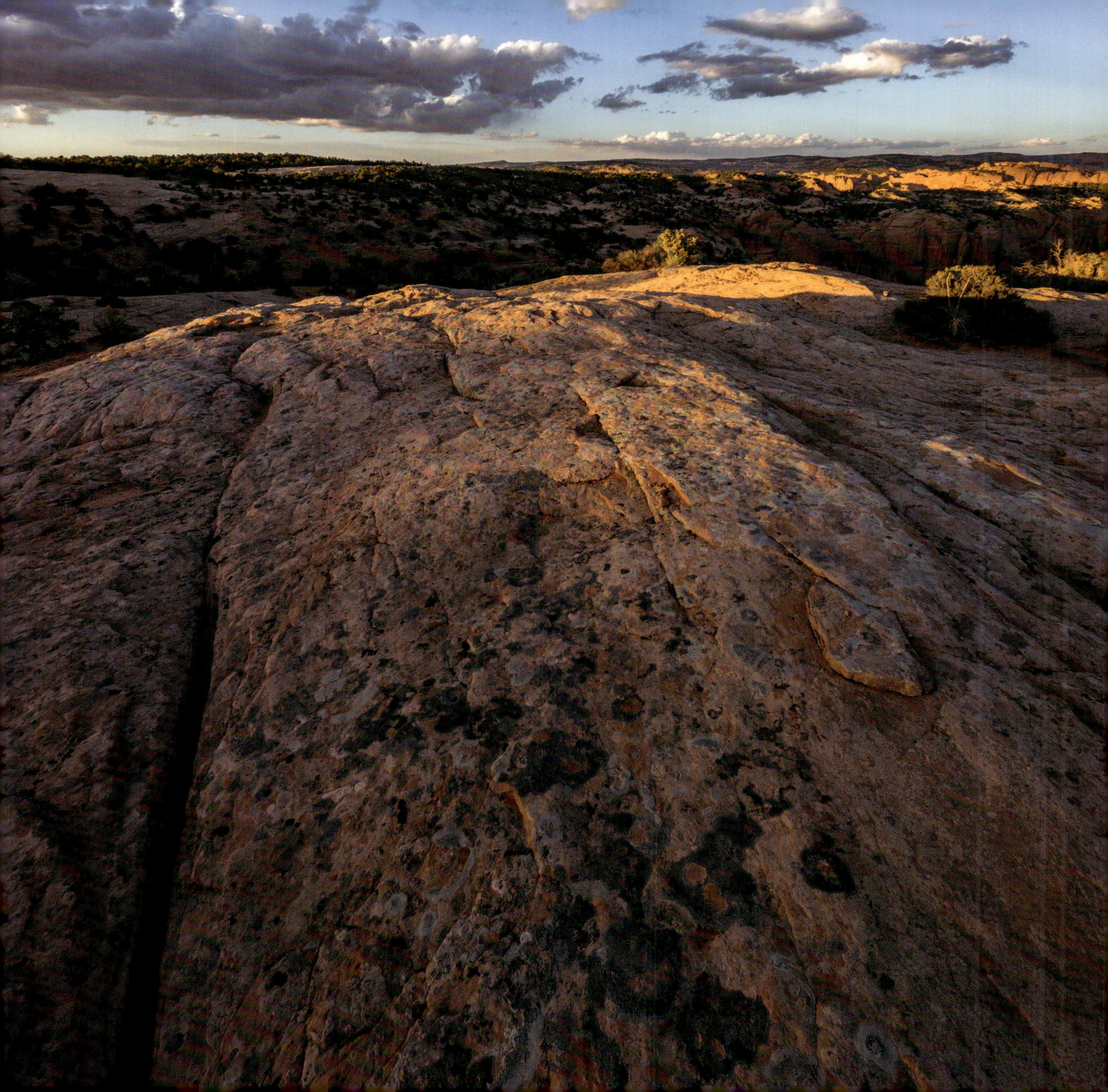

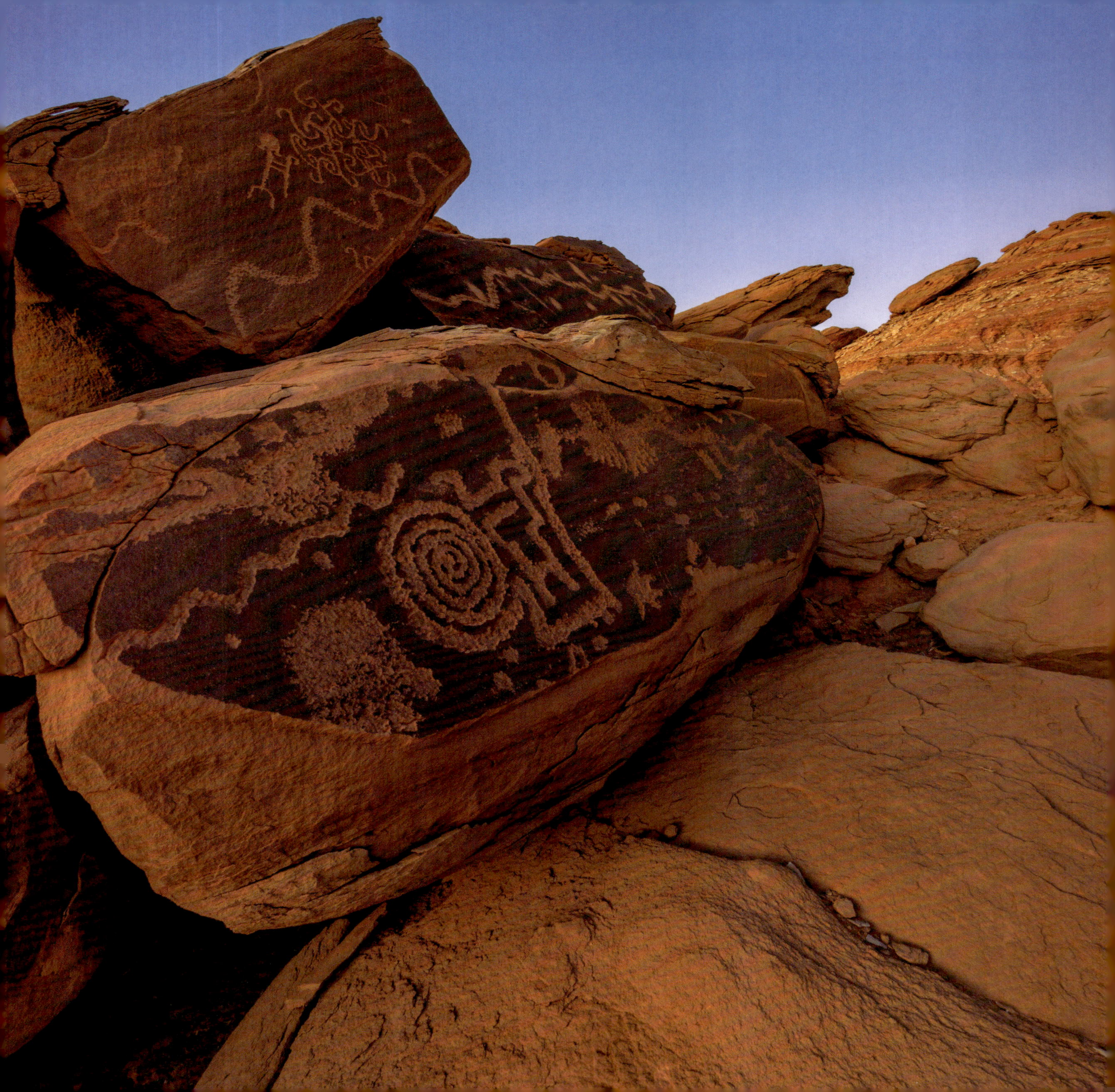

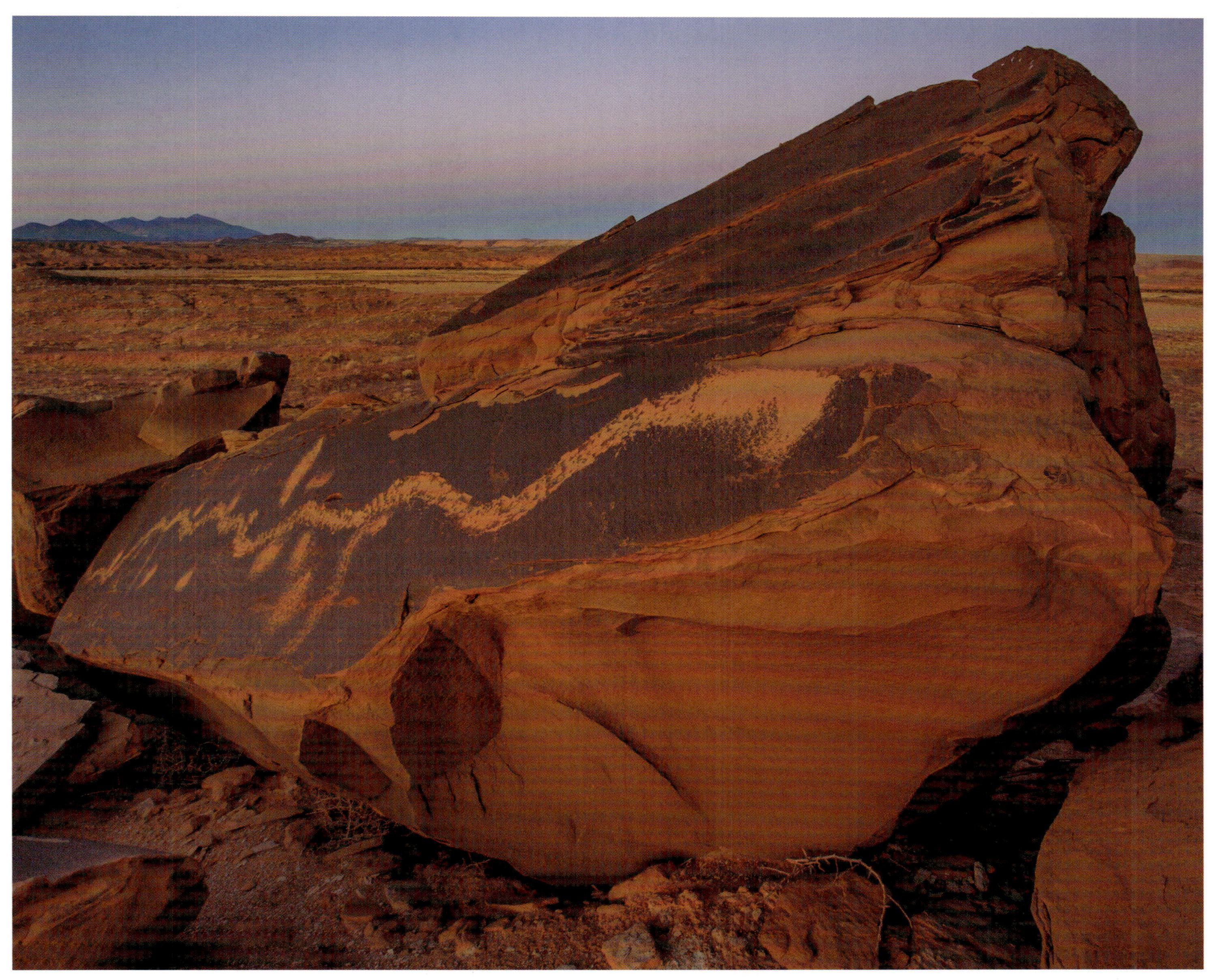

THIS ROCK INSCRIPTION MAY SERVE AS A MAP TO
THE LITTLE COLORADO RIVER VALLEY BELOW.

INDIAN ROCK ART AT INSCRIPTION POINT ALONG
THE LITTLE COLORADO RIVER.

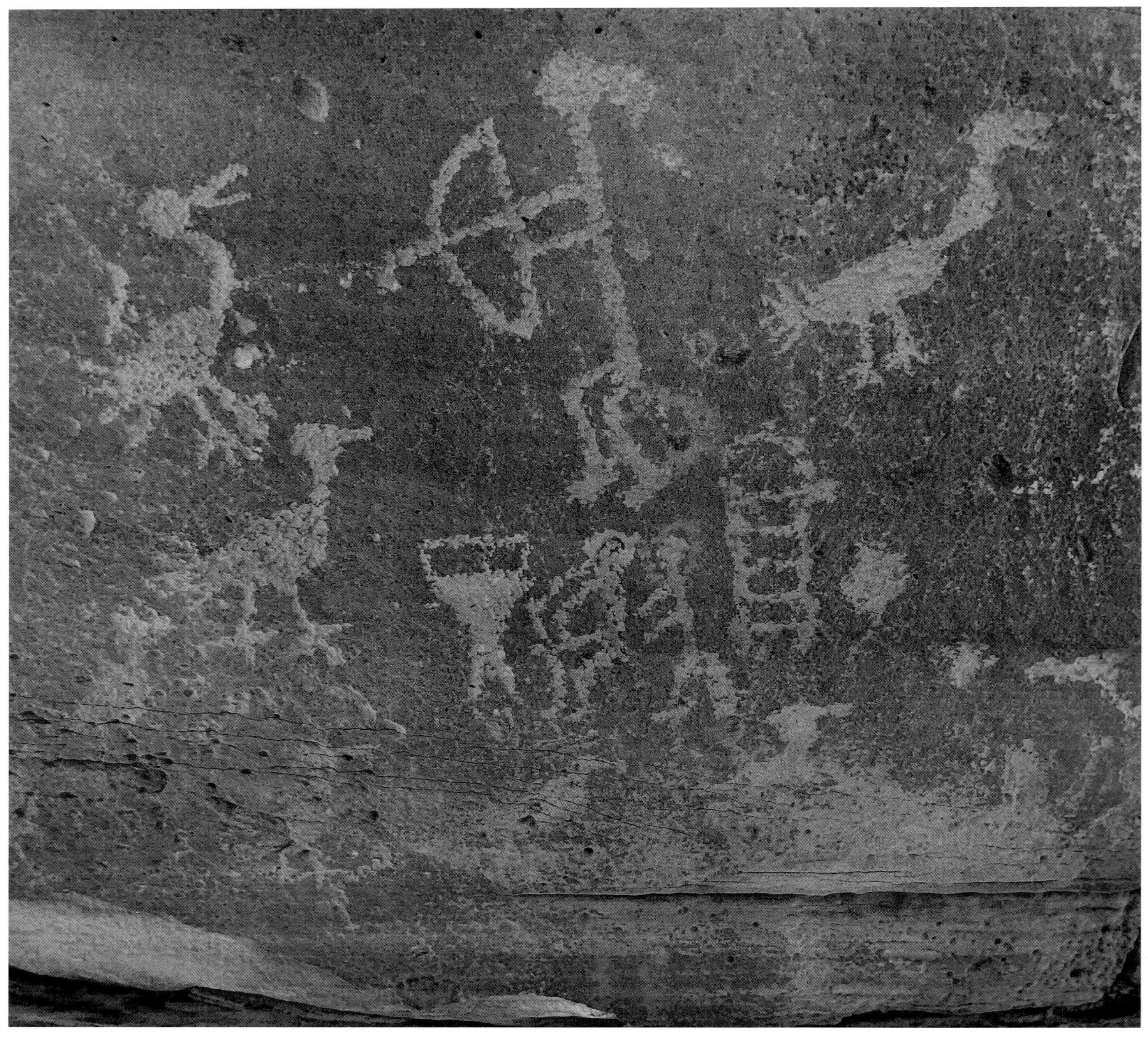



PETROGLYPHS DEPICTING BIRDS IN WUPATKI NATIONAL MONUMENT.

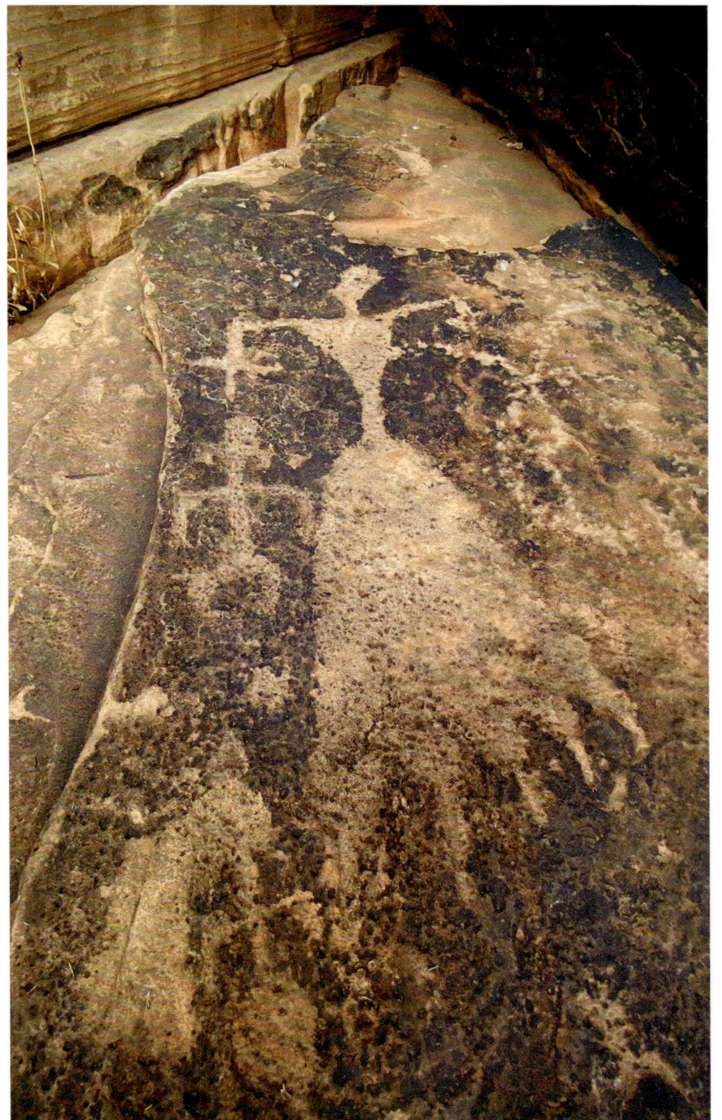



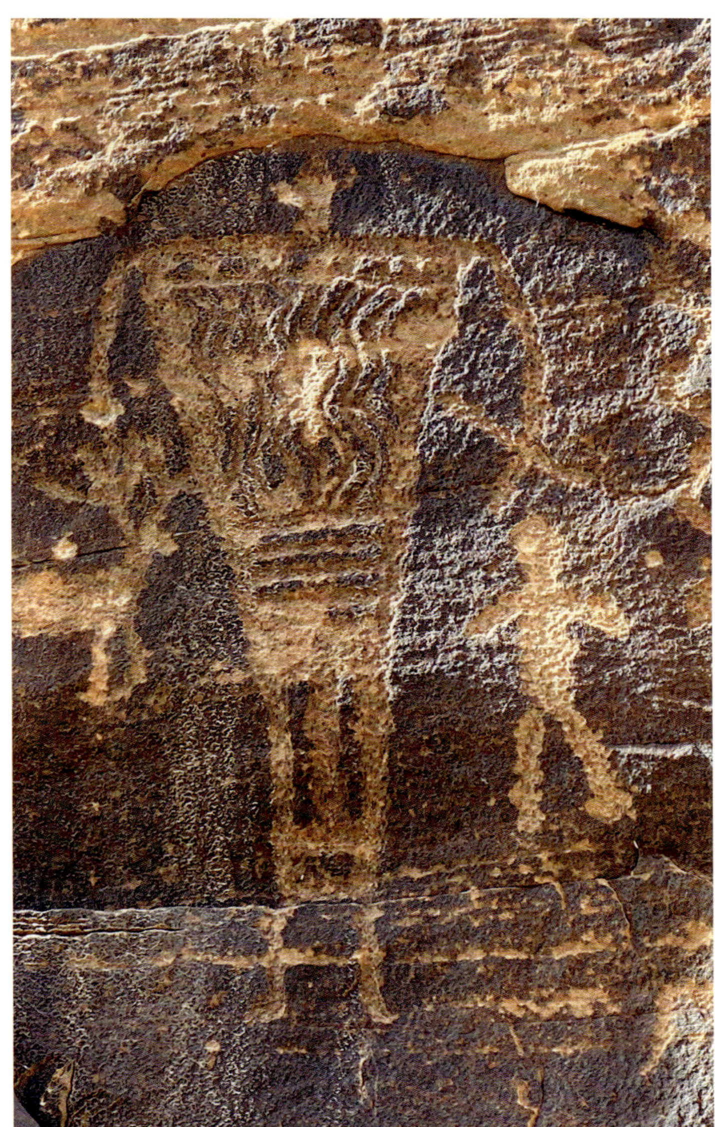

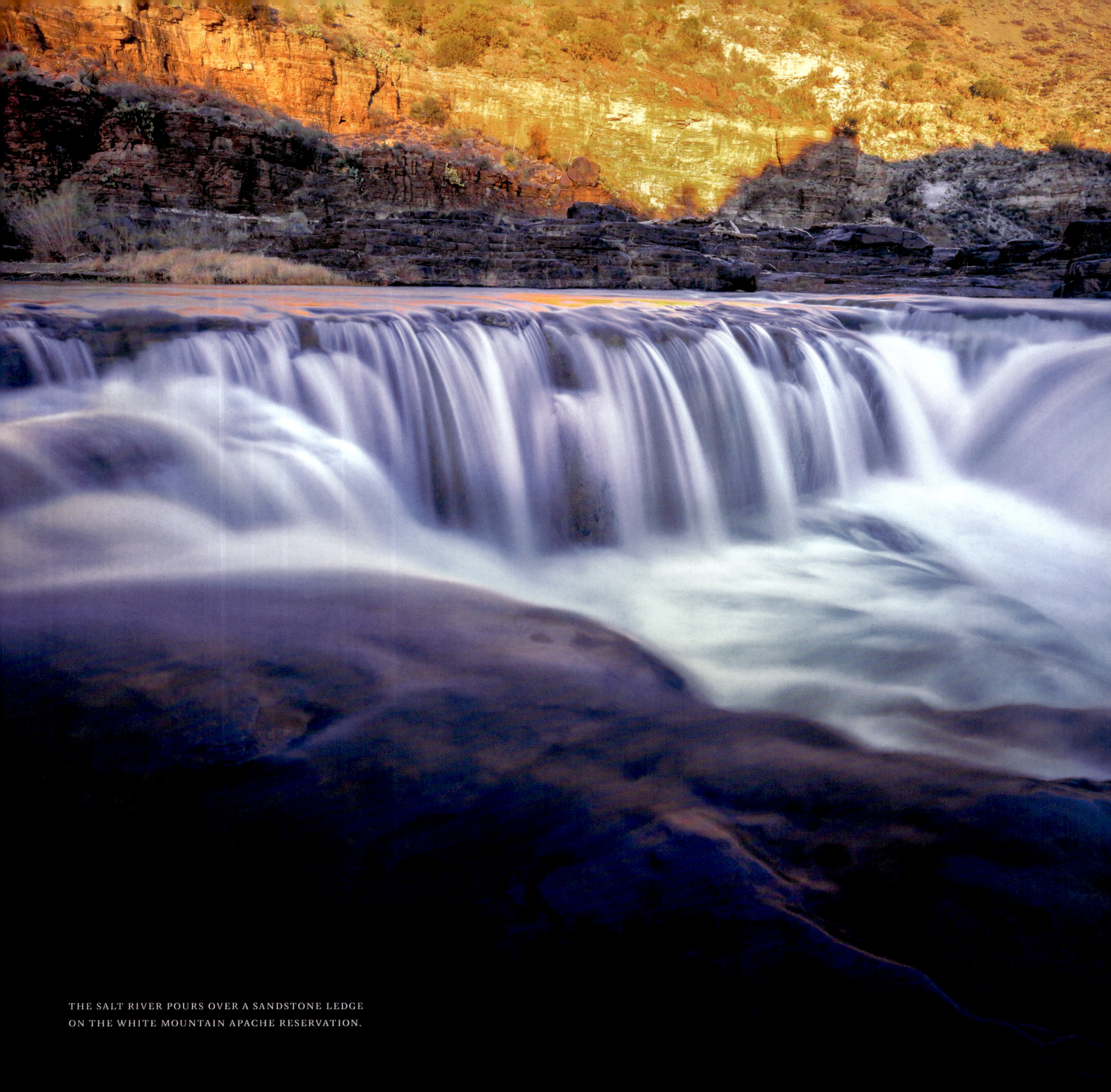

THE SALT RIVER POURS OVER A SANDSTONE LEDGE
ON THE WHITE MOUNTAIN APACHE RESERVATION.

# MOGOLLON RIM — TRANSITION

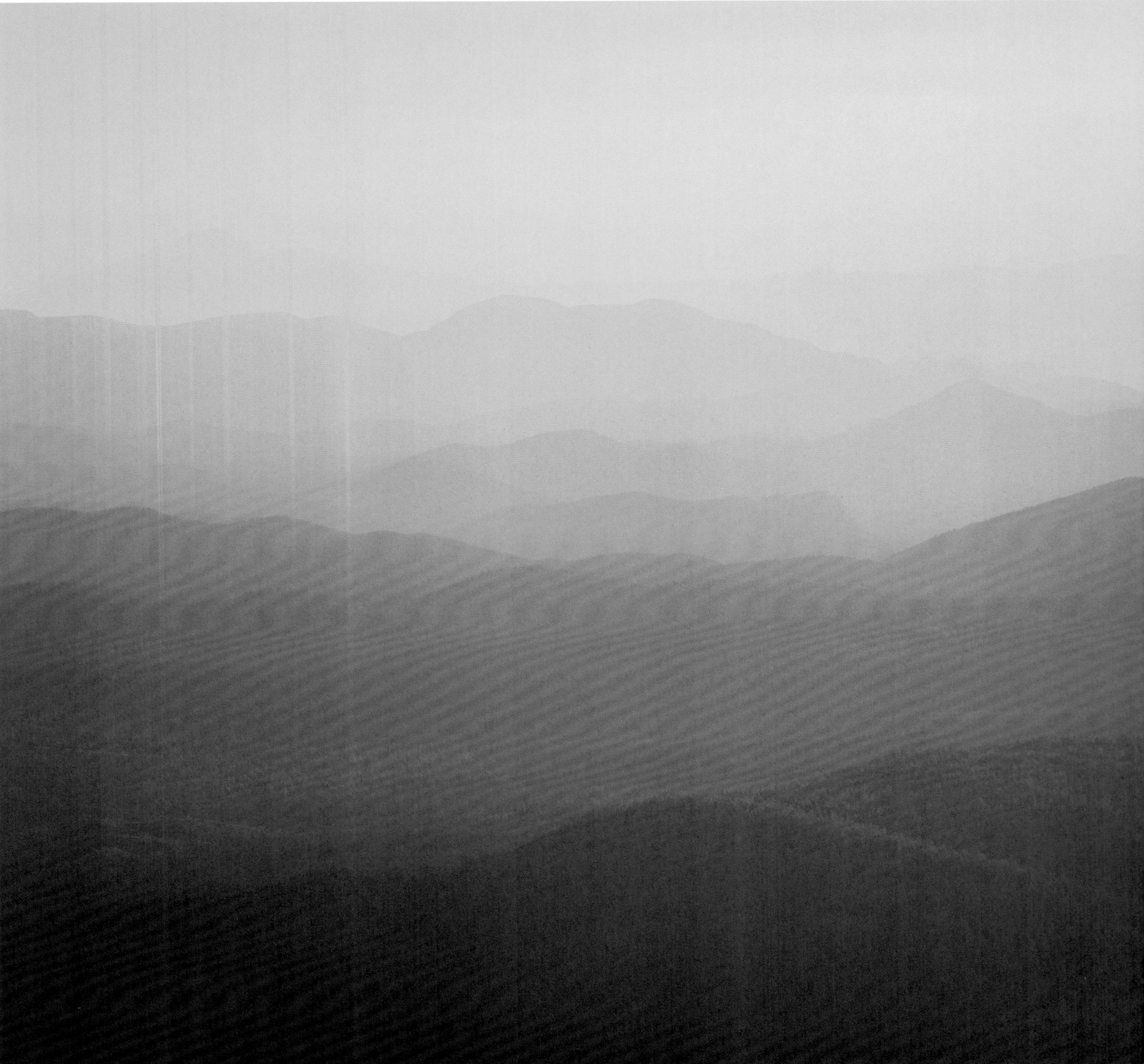

◀

SMOKE FILLS THE
VALLEYS BELOW THE
MOGOLLON RIM.

▶

CIBECUE CREEK, A
TRIBUTARY TO THE SALT
RIVER, ON THE WHITE
MOUNTAIN APACHE
RESERVATION.

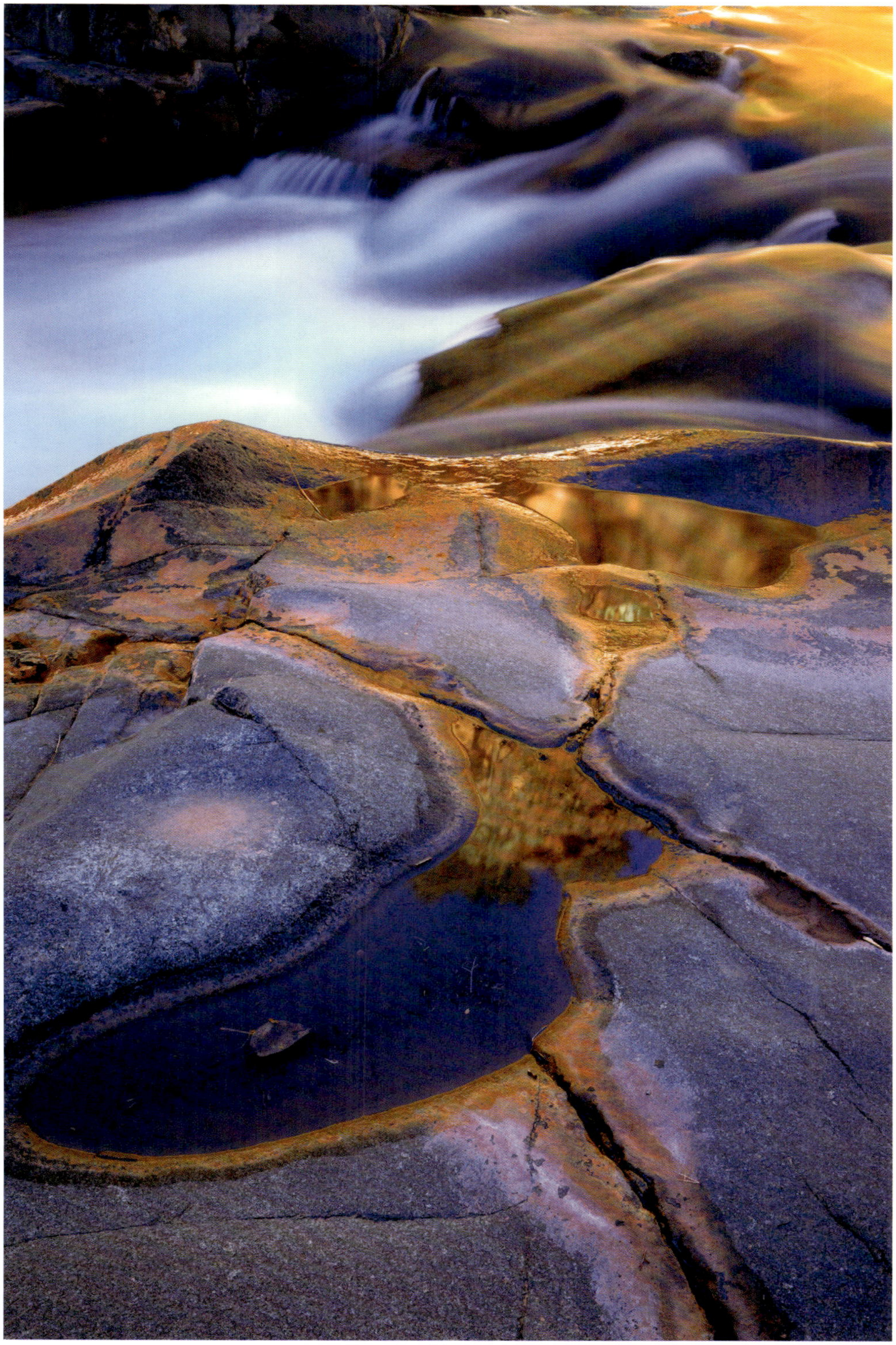

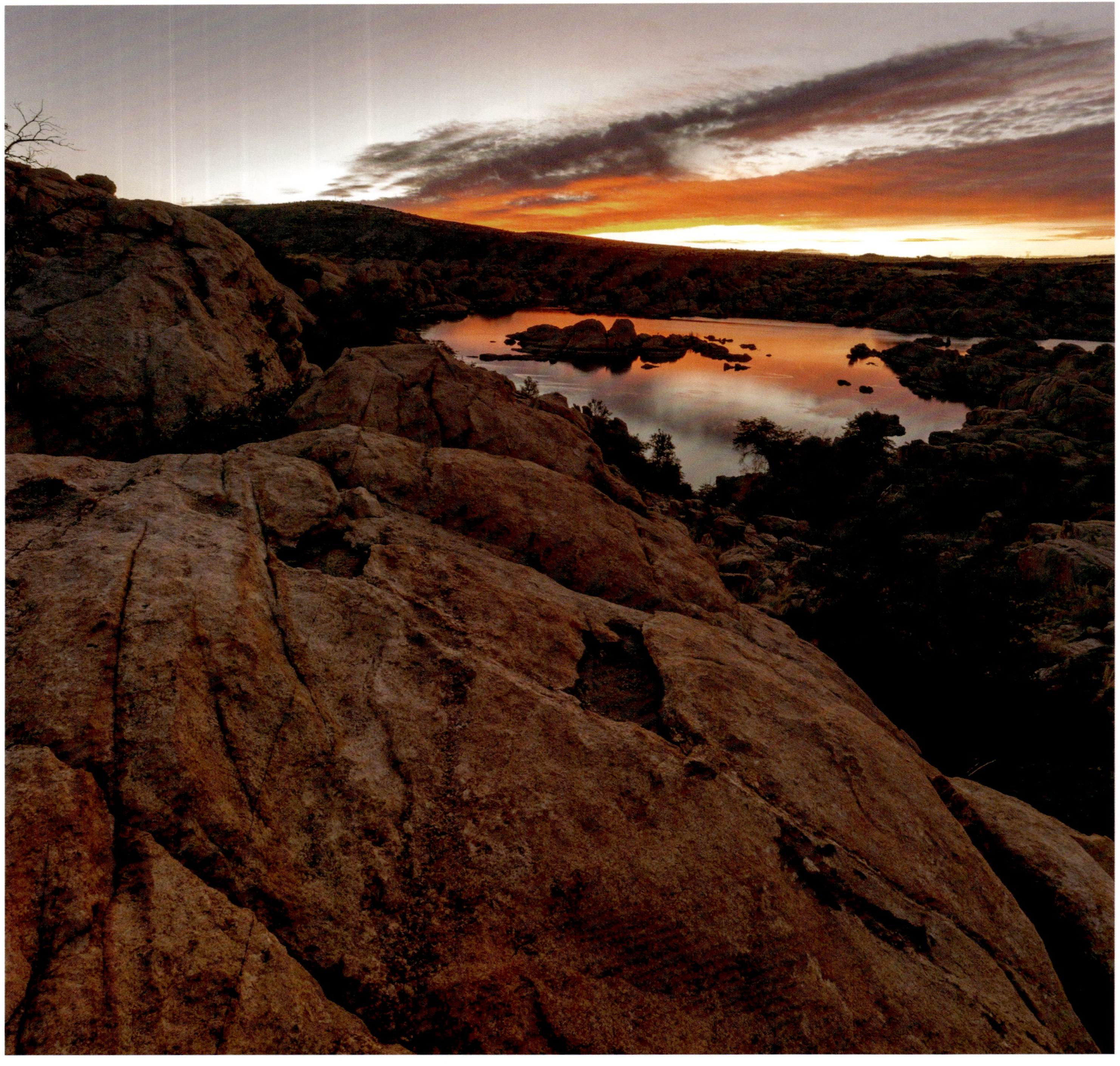



SUNRISE AT WATSON LAKE IN THE GRANITE DELLS.

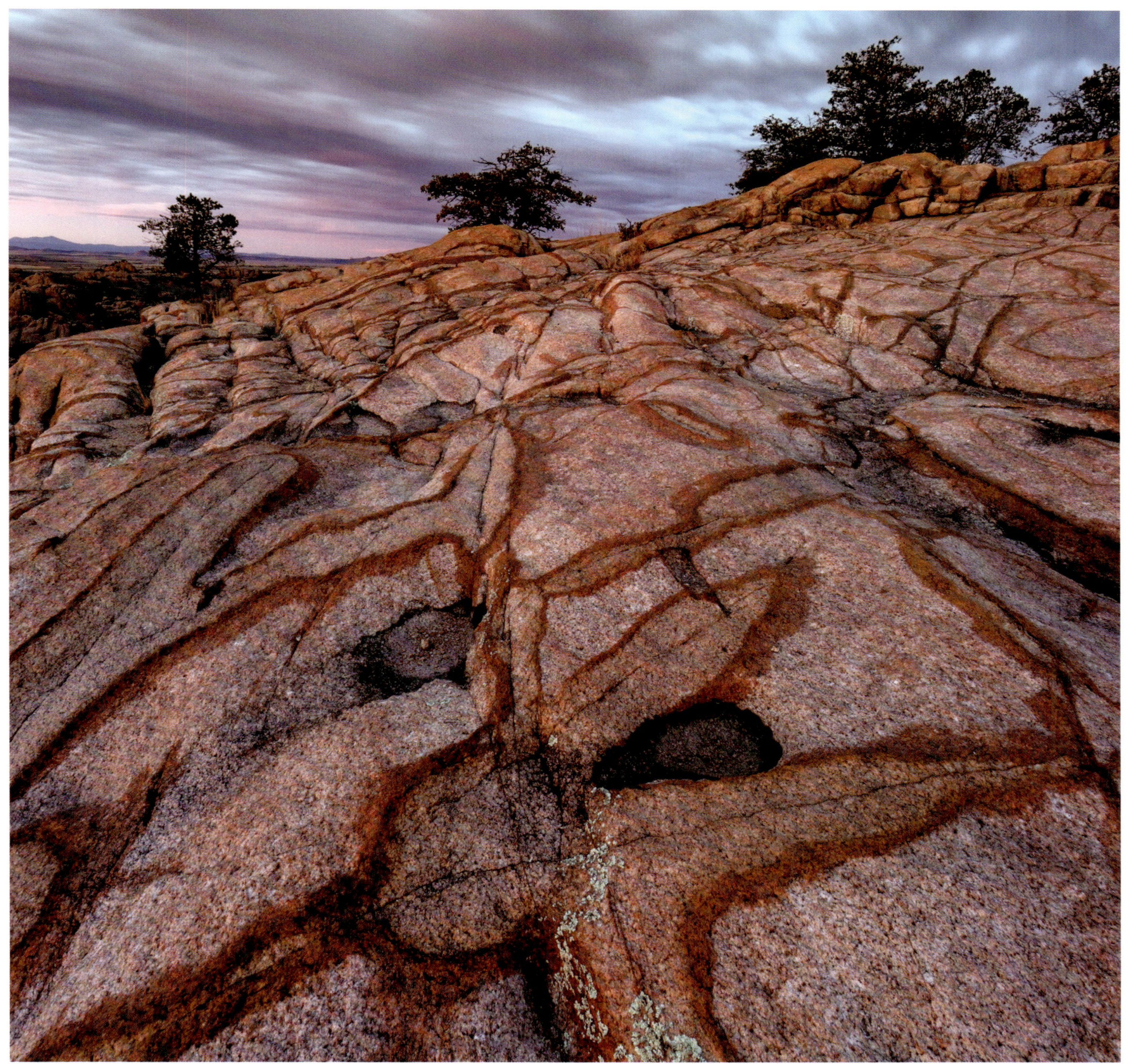

GRAPHIC PATTERNS IN THE WEATHERED ROCKS AT THE GRANITE DELLS IN PRESCOTT.

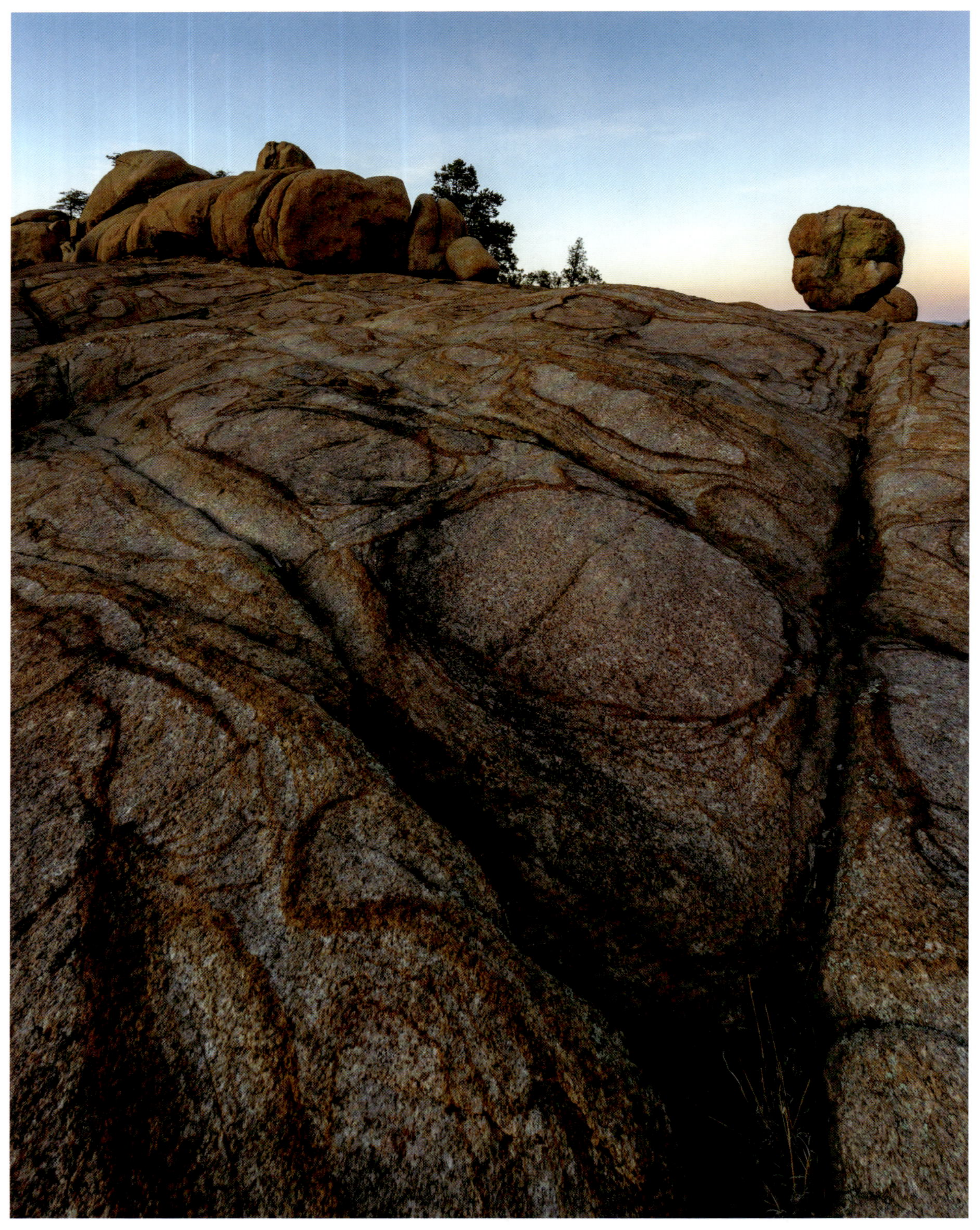

GRAPHIC PATTERNS AND
SHAPES IN THE ROCKS OF
THE GRANITE DELLS.

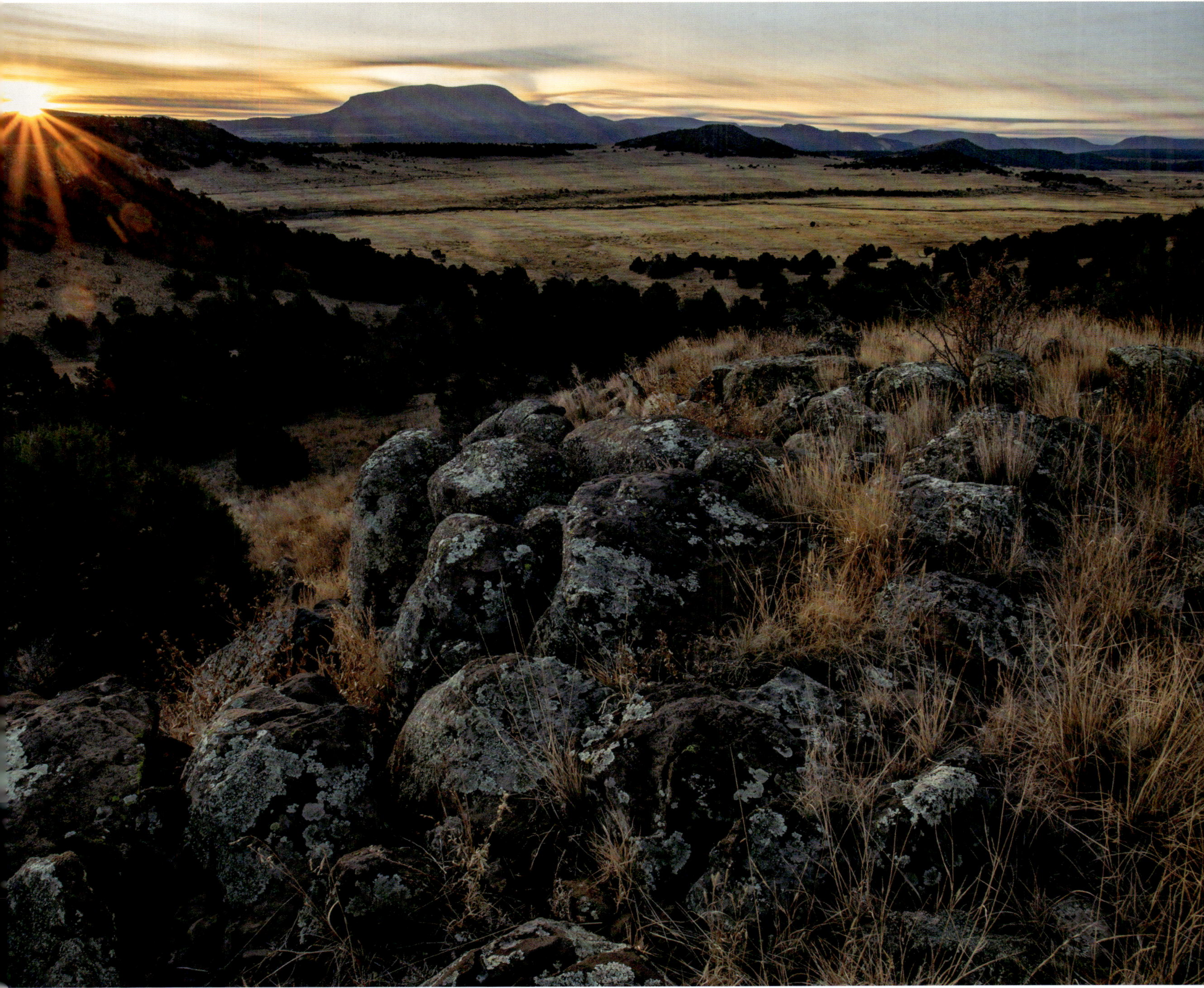



SUNRISE ON A LATE FALL DAY AT THE SIPE WHITE MOUNTAIN WILDLIFE AREA IN THE WHITE MOUNTAINS.

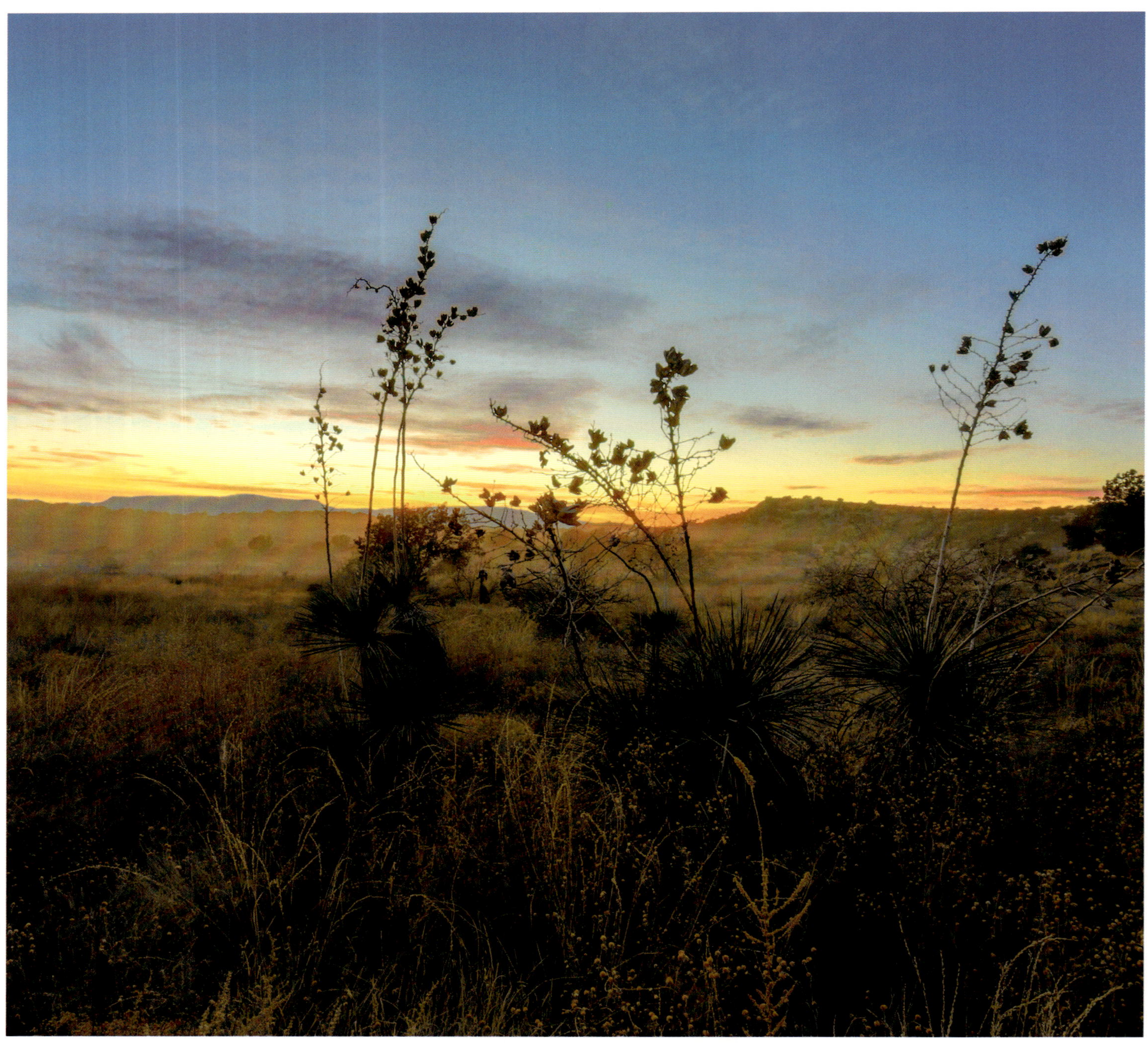

A MISTY MORNING IN THE DRY BEAVER
CREEK AREA NEAR SEDONA, ARIZONA.

THE SUN WARMS THE BOULDERS OF THE
GRANITE DELLS AND BEAUTIFUL WATSON LAKE.

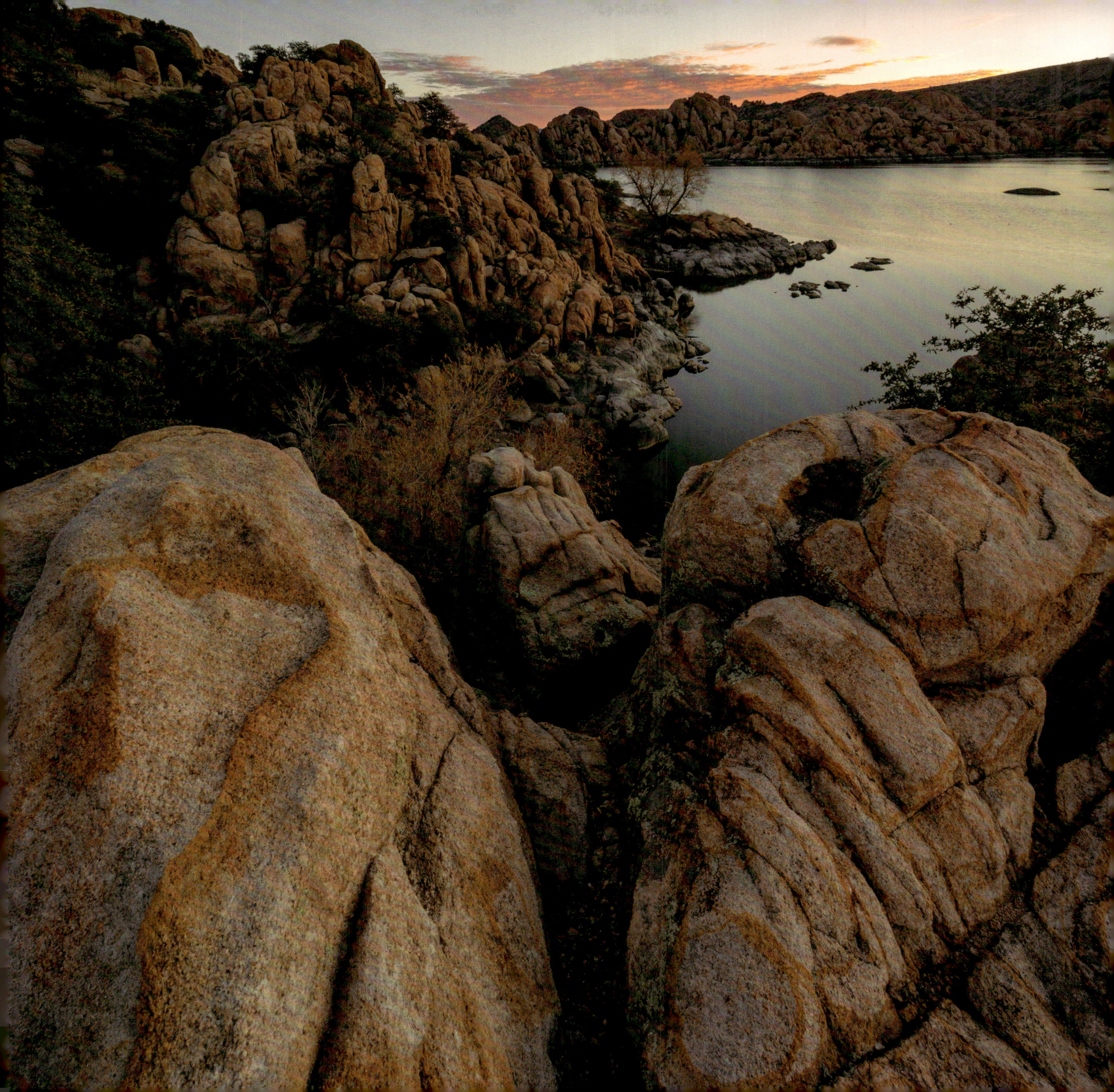

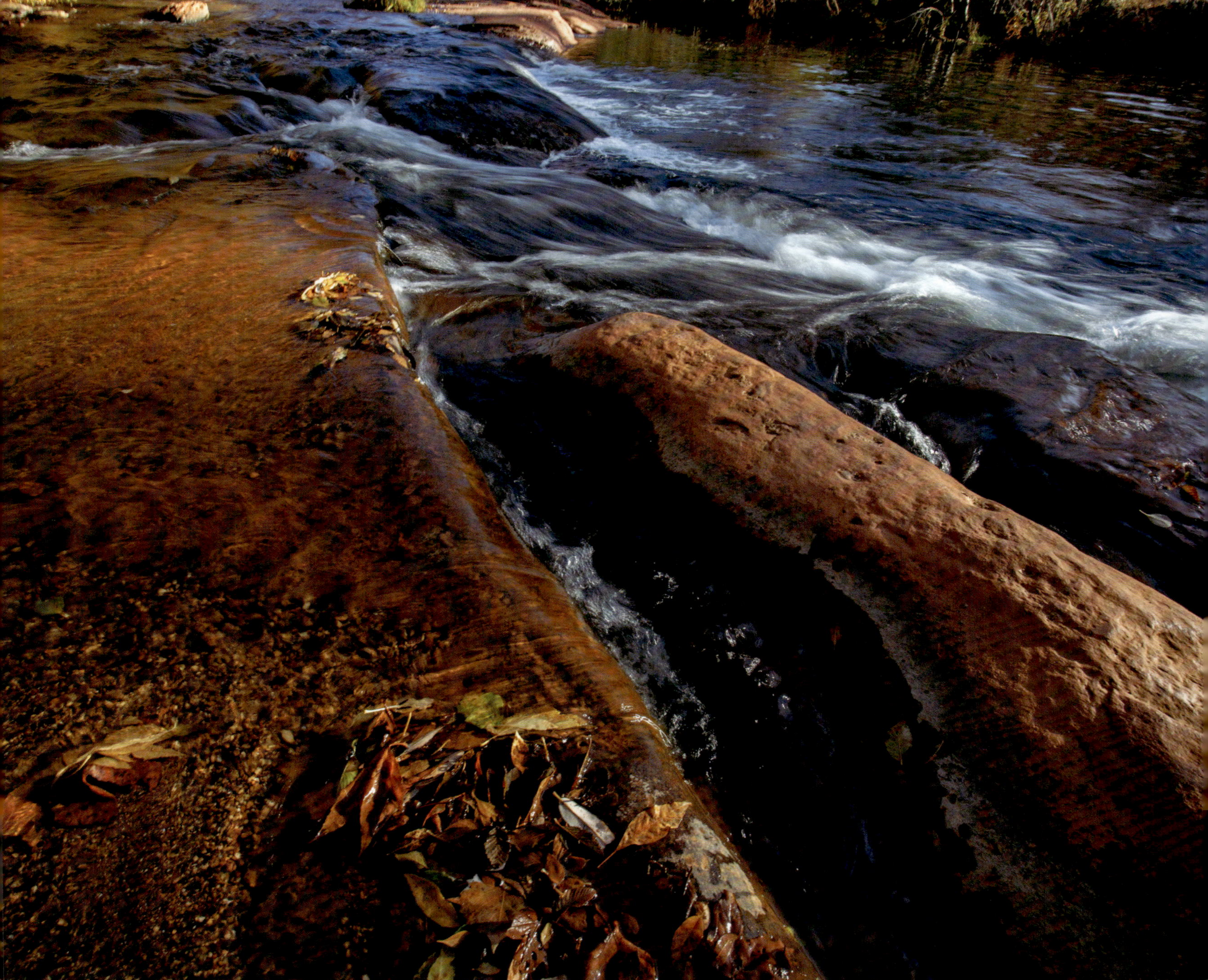



OAK CREEK CARVES INTO THE SANDSTONE RIVER BOTTOM AT RED ROCK CROSSING STATE PARK.

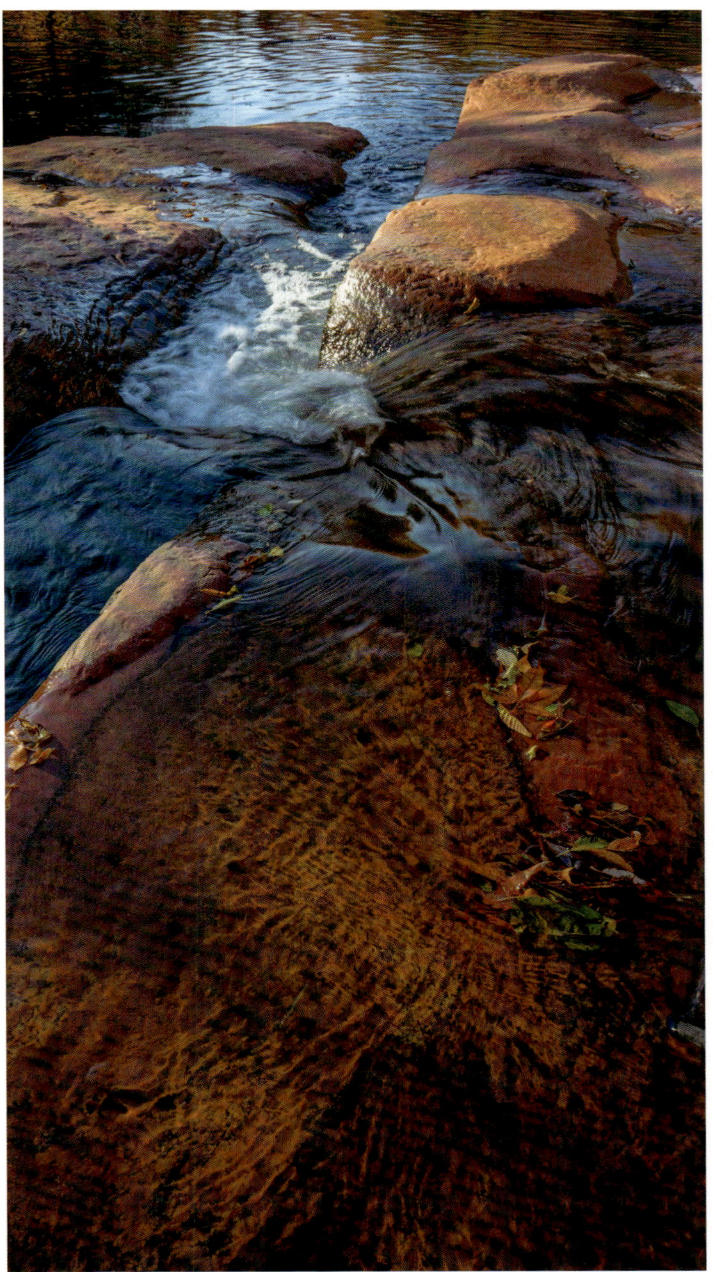

THE CONTINUAL FLOW OF OAK CREEK SHAPES THE SANDSTONE
RIVER BOTTOM AT RED ROCK CROSSING STATE PARK.

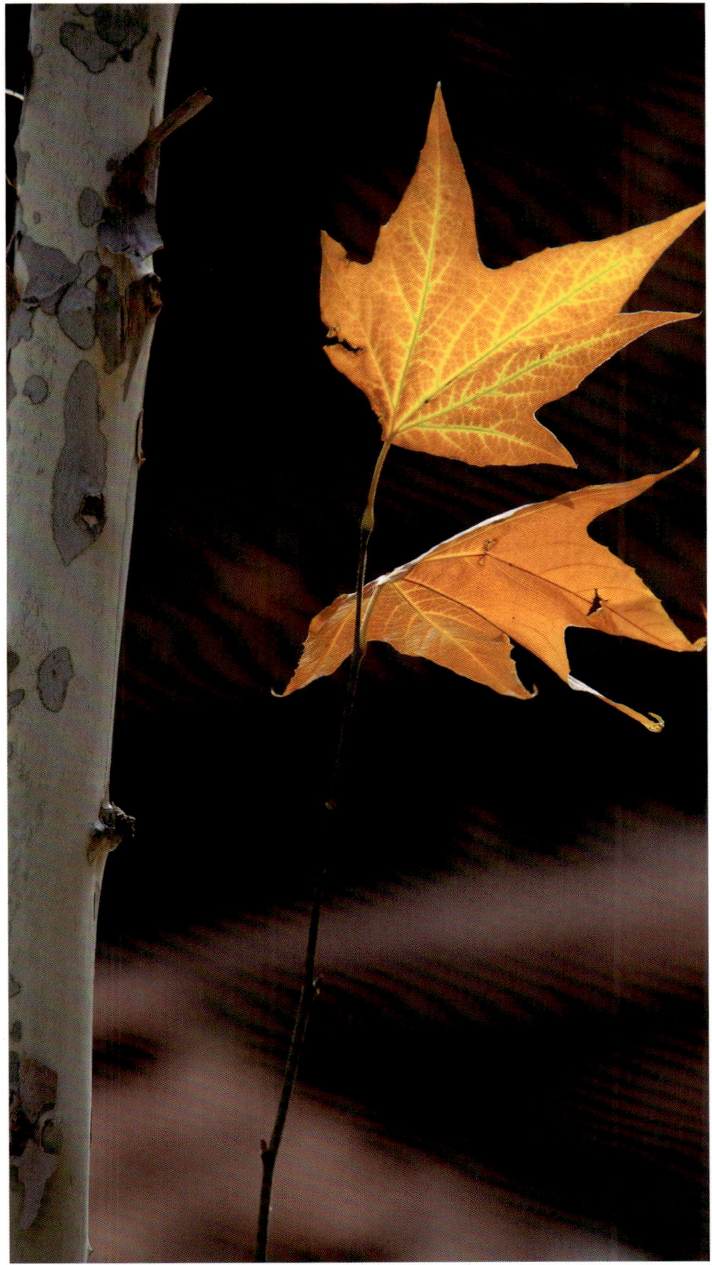

WHITE SYCAMORE LEAVES HANG ON IN
THE LATE FALL OF OAK CREEK CANYON.

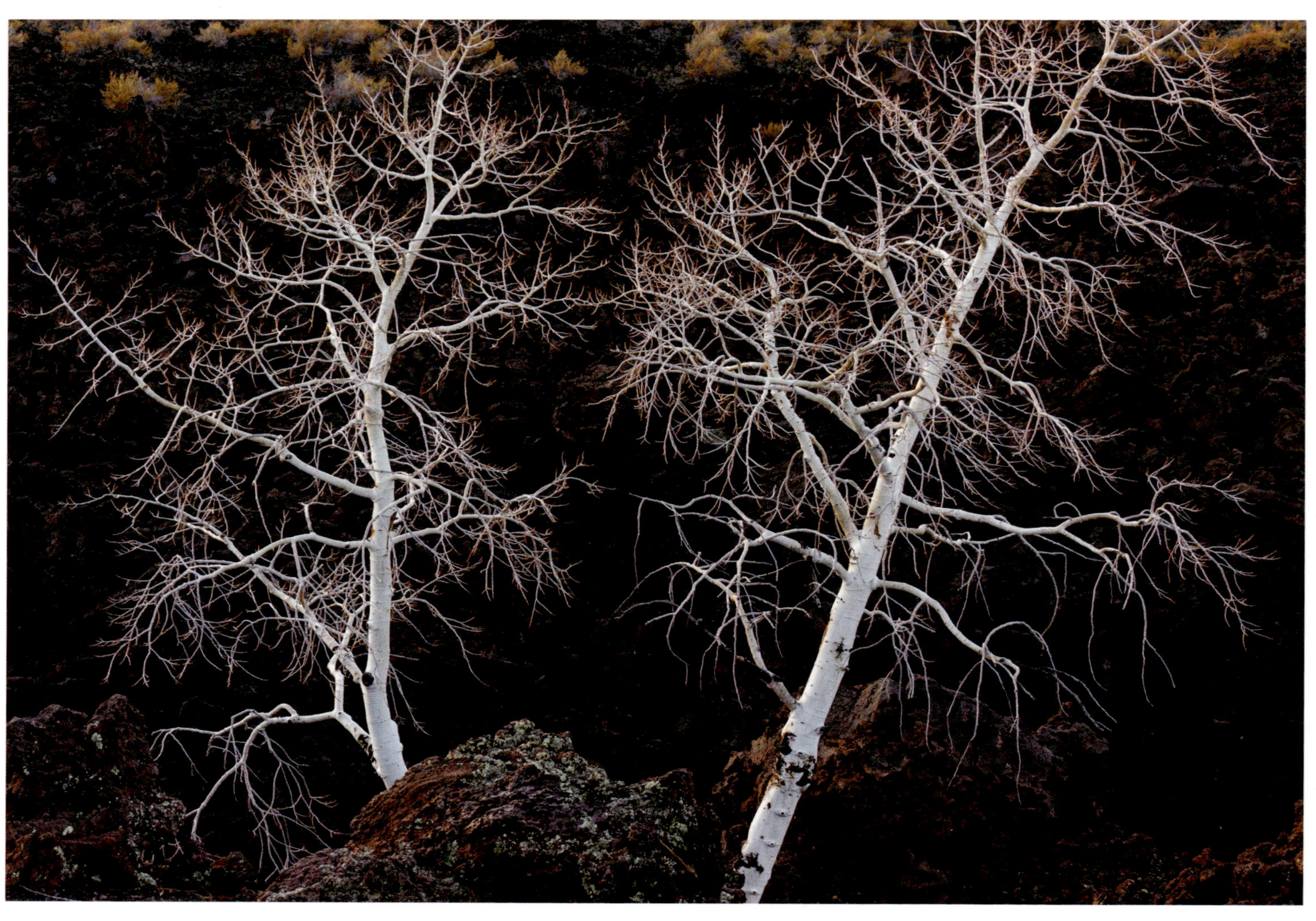

▲
BARE ASPEN TREES AGAINST DARK LAVA
ROCK CREATE A STARK CONTRAST AT THE
SUNSET CRATER NATIONAL MONUMENT.

▶
PINE CREEK FLOWS THROUGH TONTO
NATURAL BRIDGE, 183 FEET TALL.

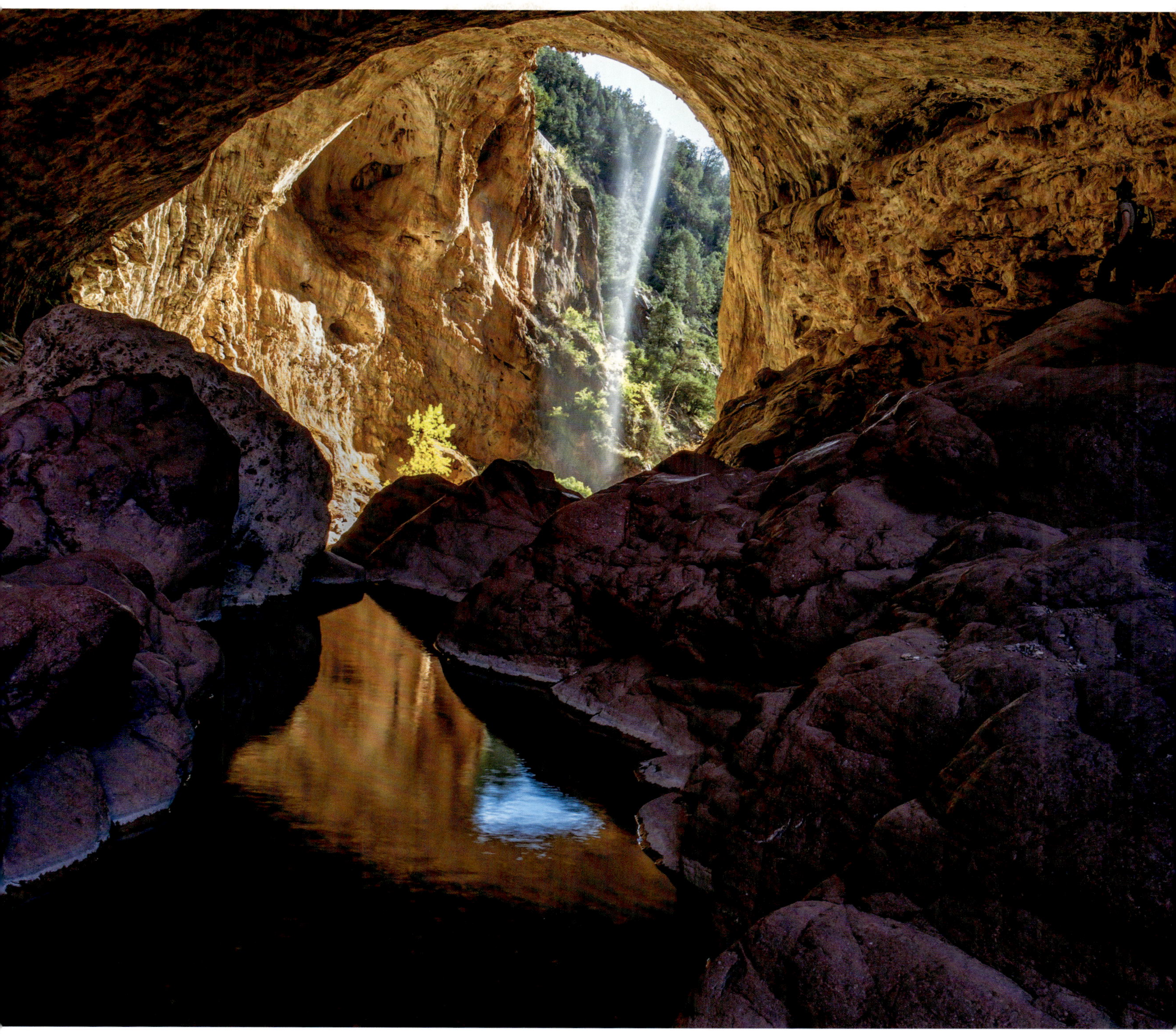

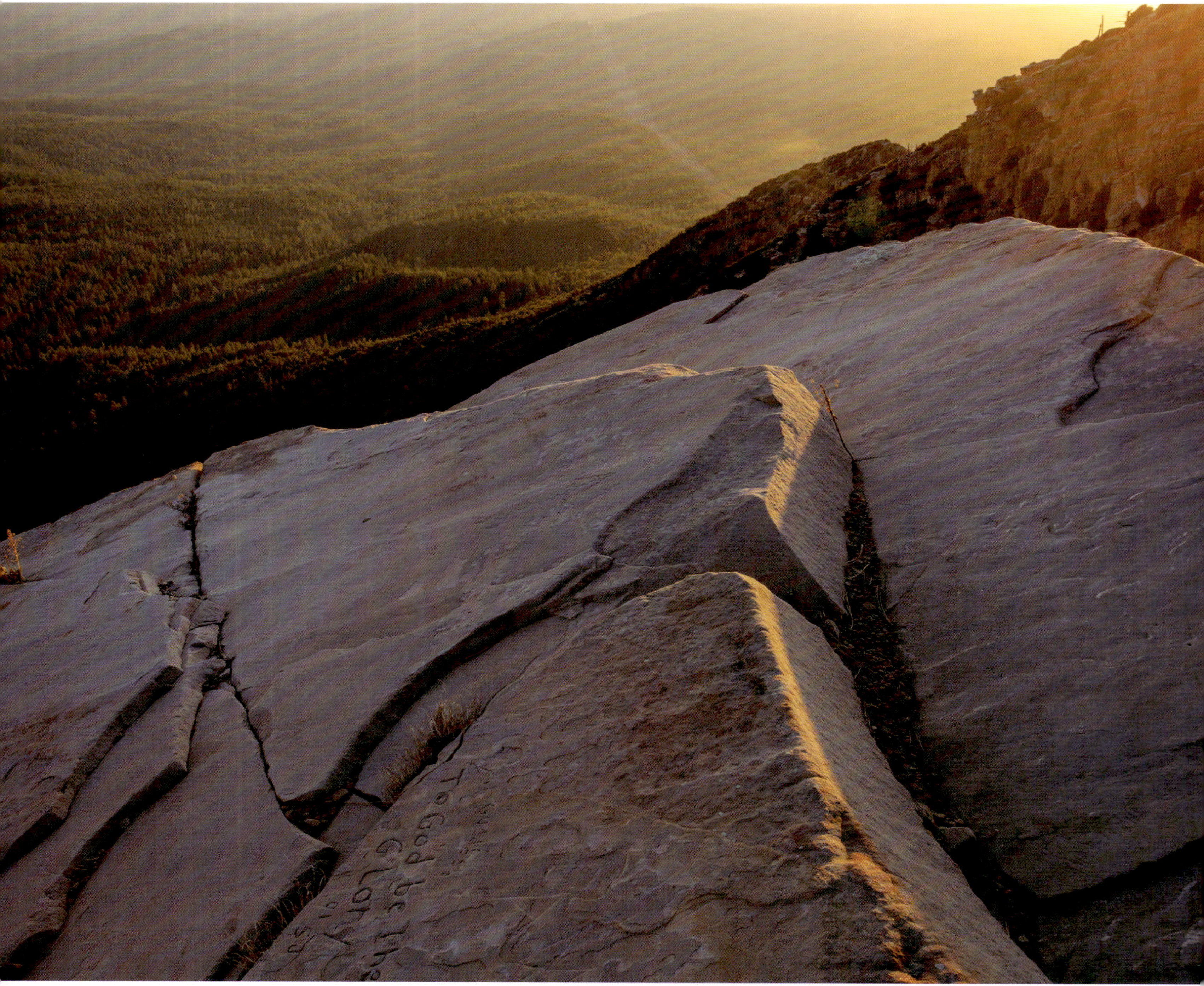



THE WINTER SUN SETS LOW AT THE MOGOLLON RIM NEAR FOREST ROAD 300.

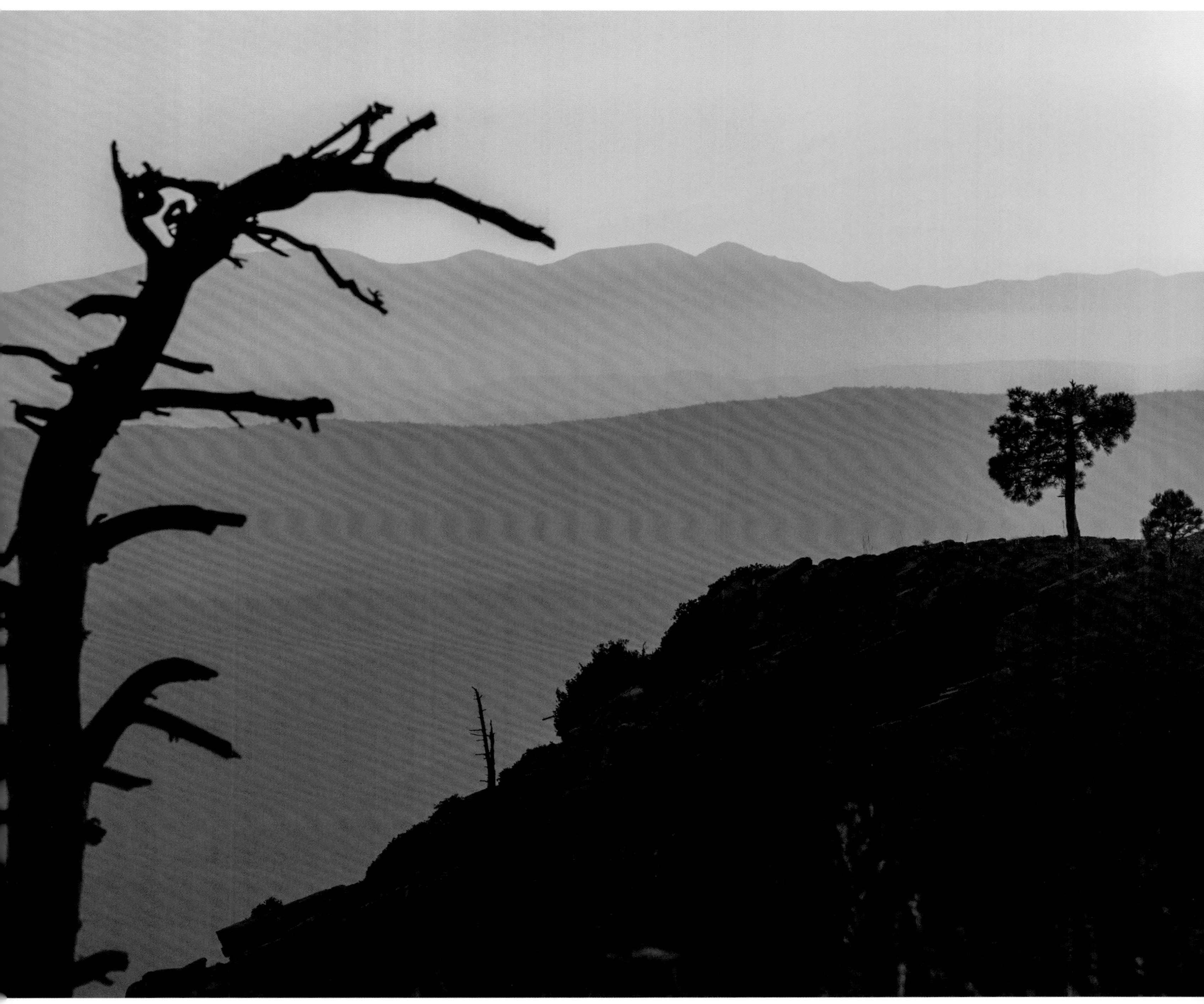

PINES HIGH ON THE MOGOLLON RIM SILHOUETTED BY A WARM FALL SUNSET.

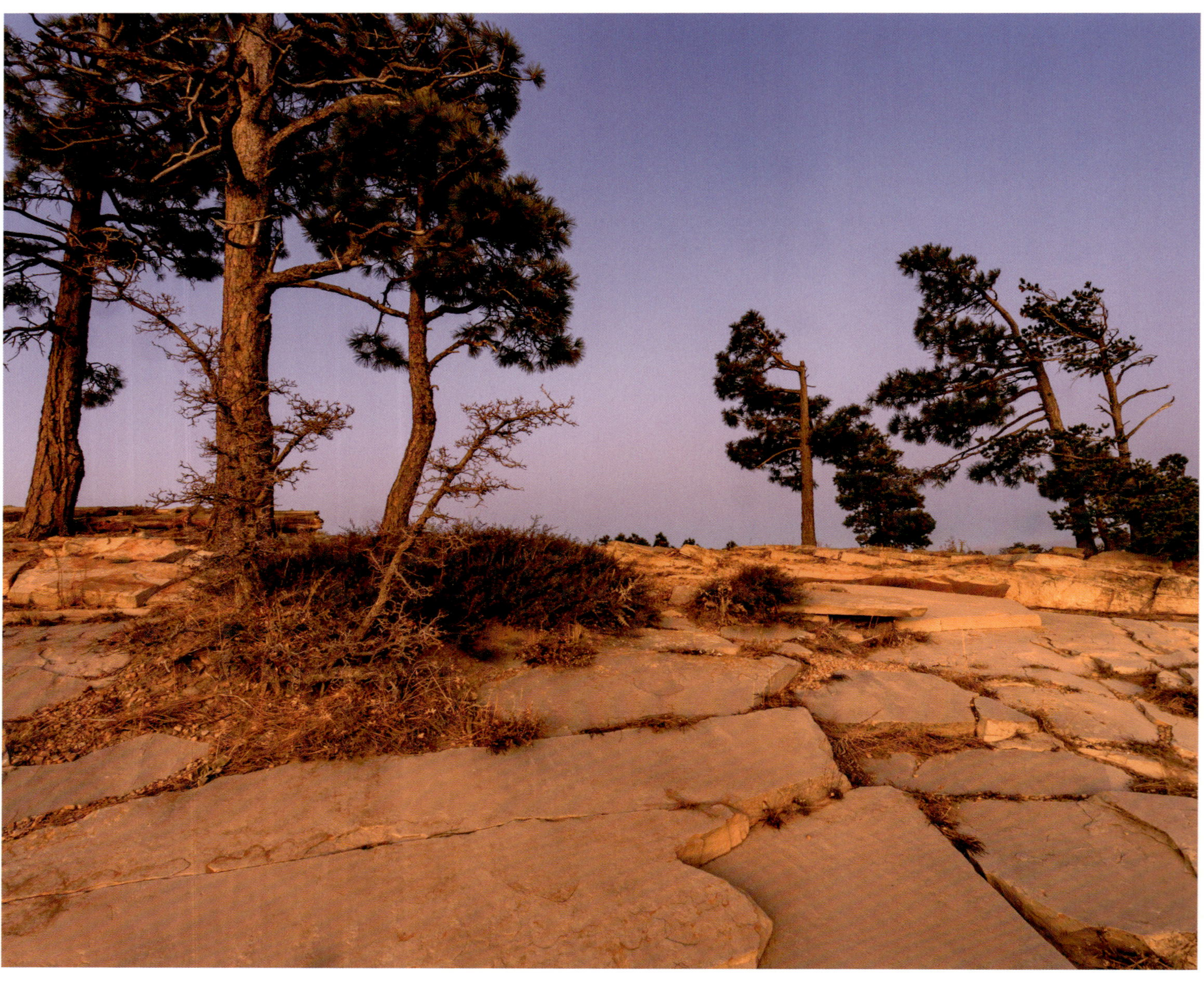

PINES WEATHERED BY DESERT WINDS SIT HIGH ON THE MOGOLLON RIM.

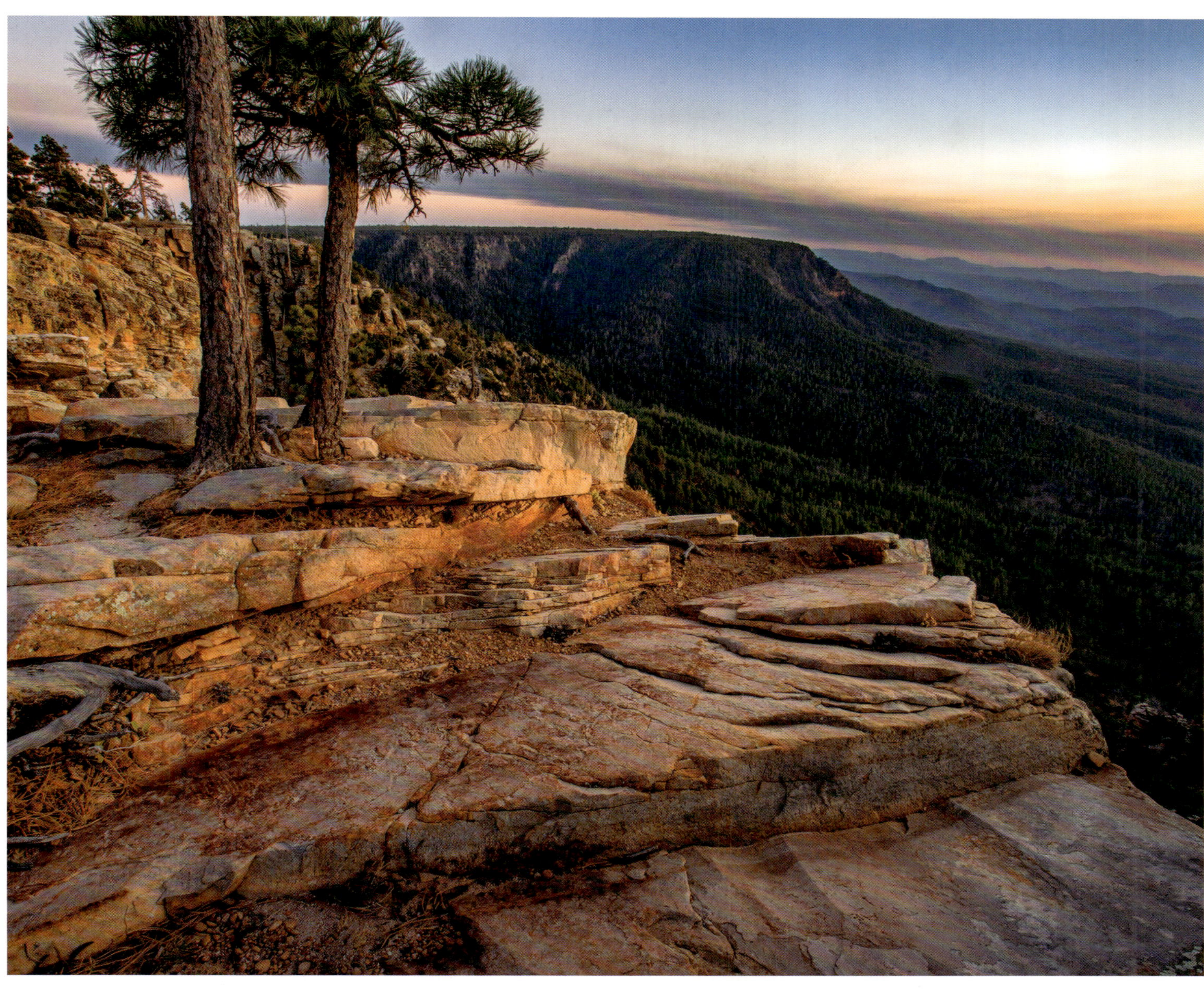

THE DENSE PINE FOREST ALONG THE MOGOLLON RIM STRETCHES 200 MILES TO THE NEW MEXICO BORDER.

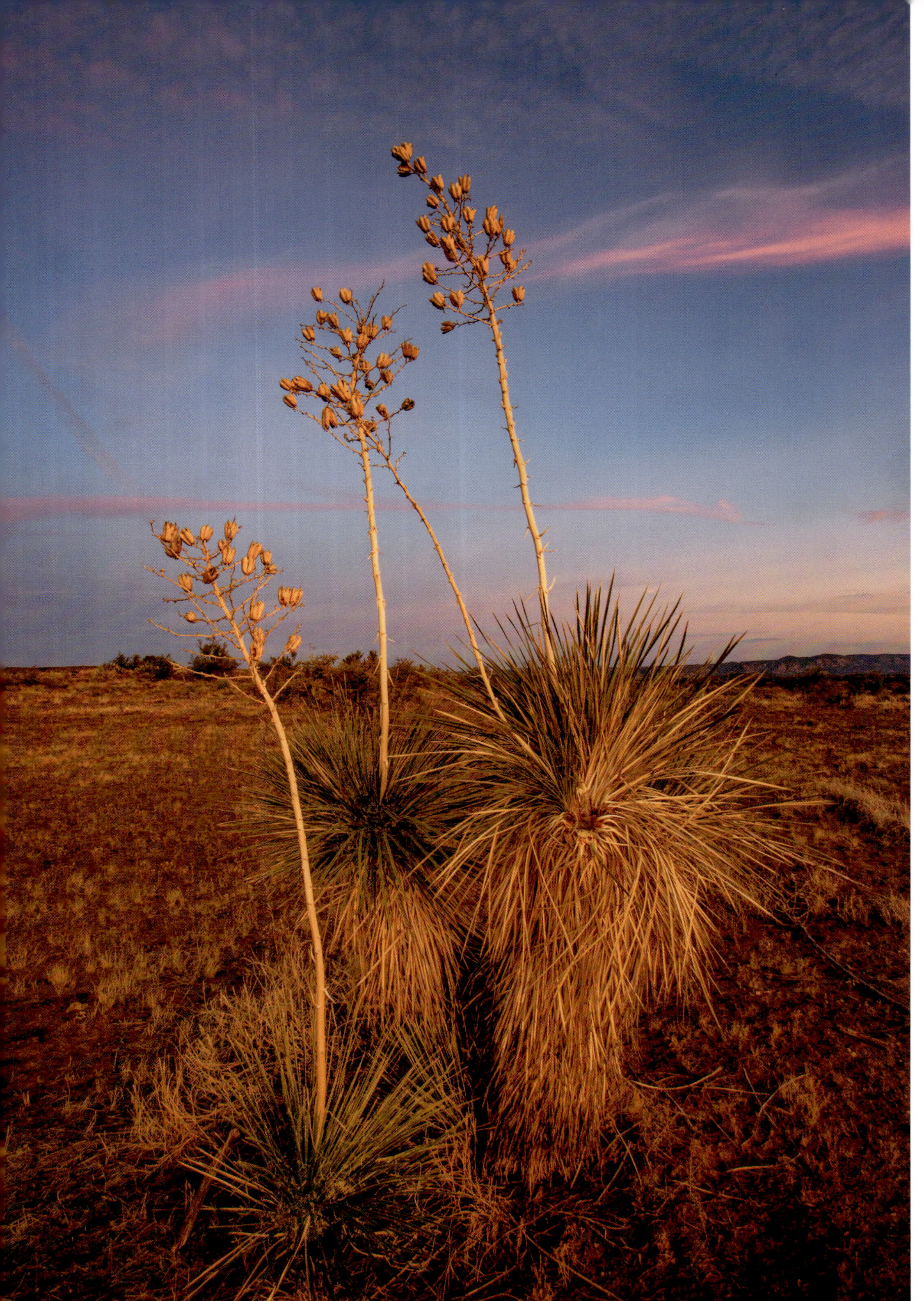

A WARM GLOW IS CAST ONTO
SOAPTREE YUCCAS IN THE WET
BEAVER WILDERNESS.

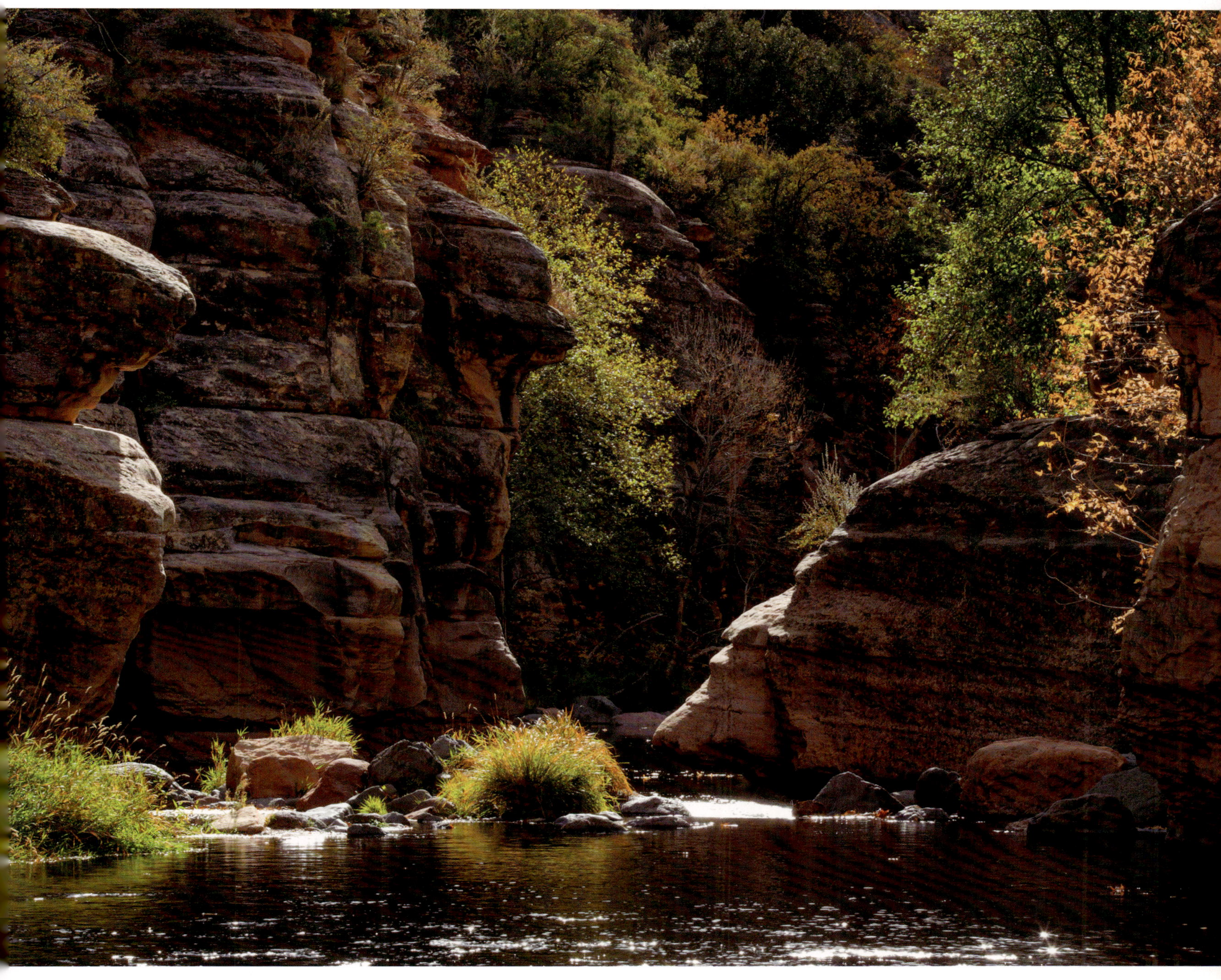

FALL BEGINS TO SHOW ITSELF IN LATE NOVEMBER IN OAK CREEK CANYON.

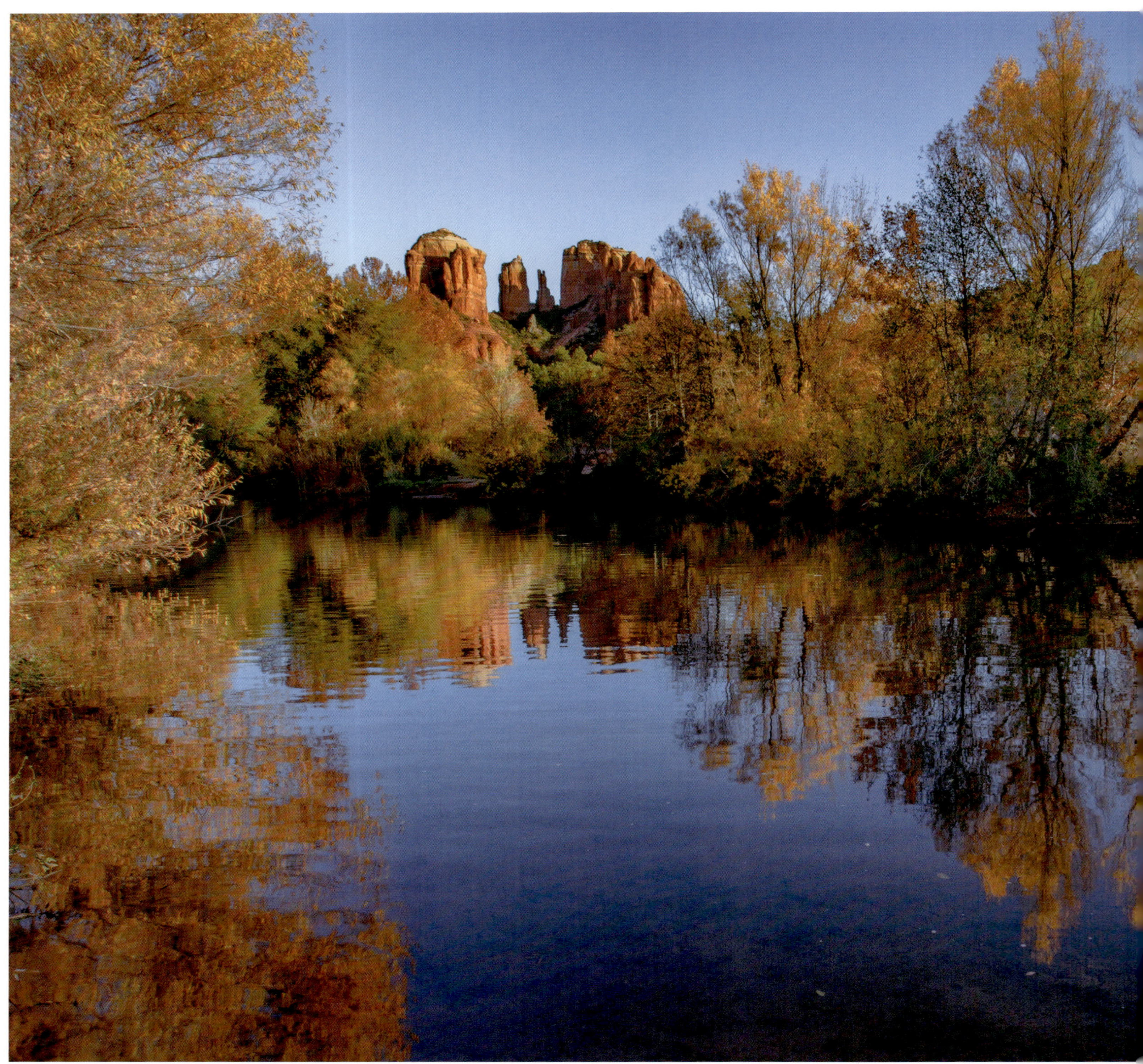

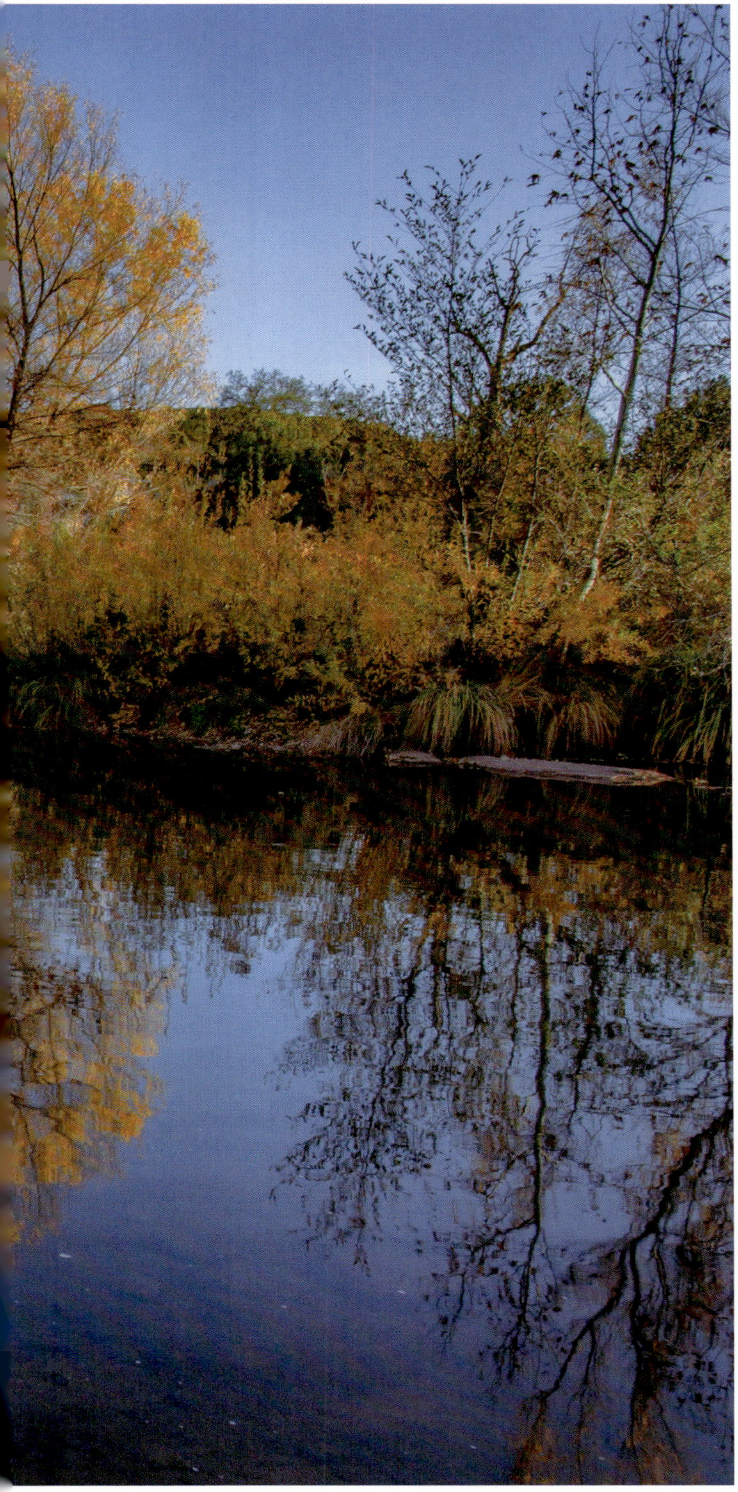

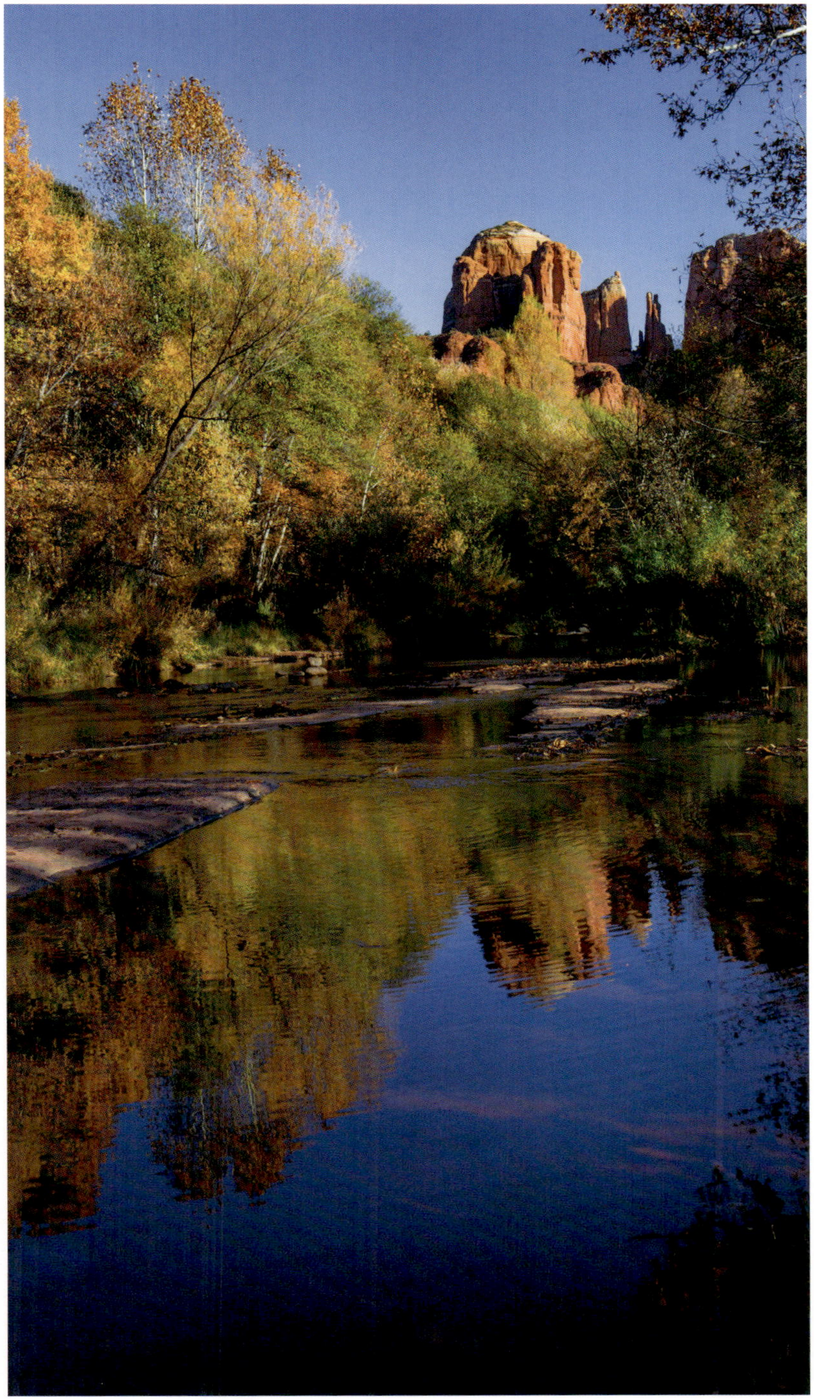

CATHEDRAL PEAKS AND FALL FOLIAGE ARE REFLECTED IN
THE TRANQUIL WATERS OF OAK CREEK.

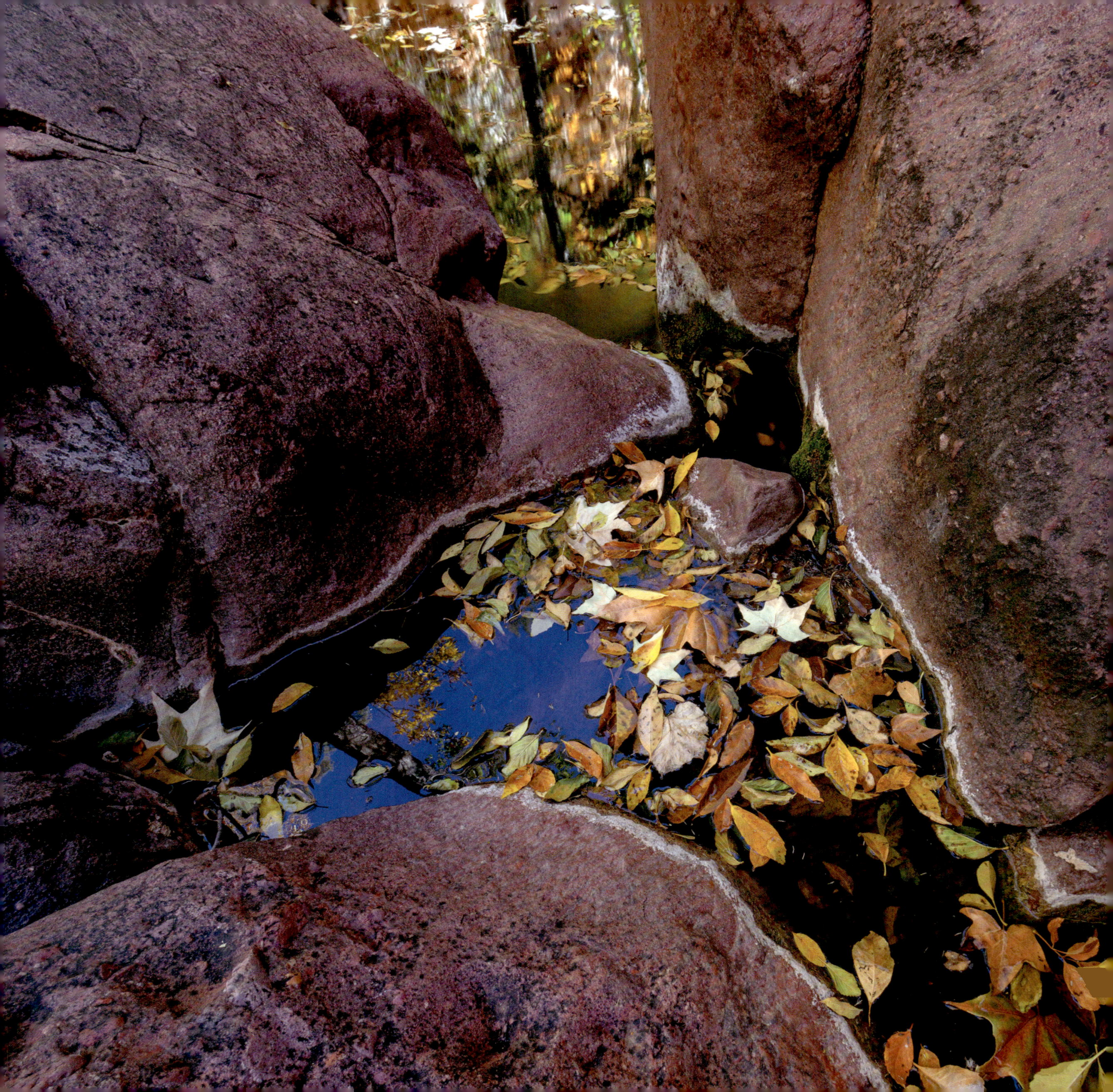

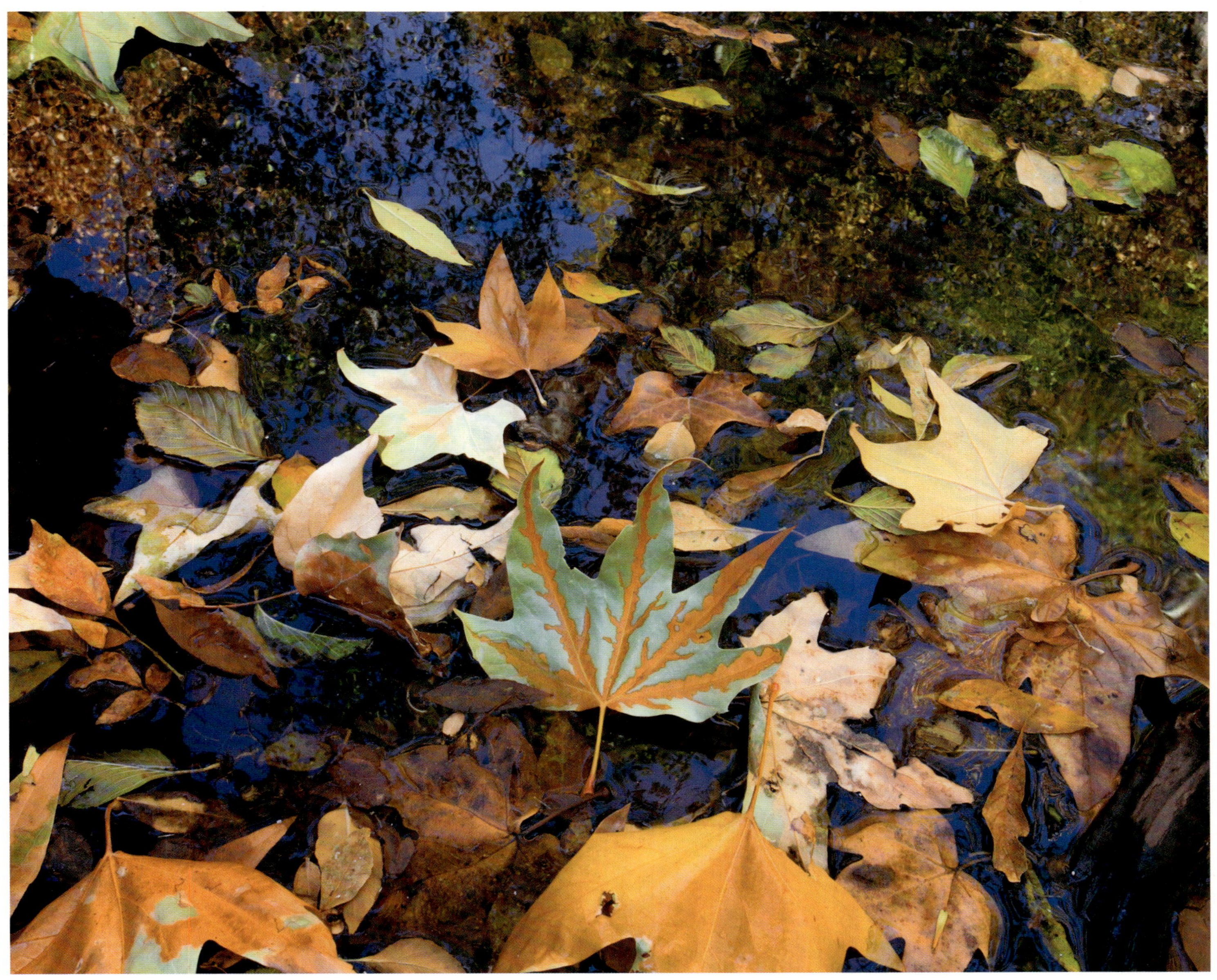

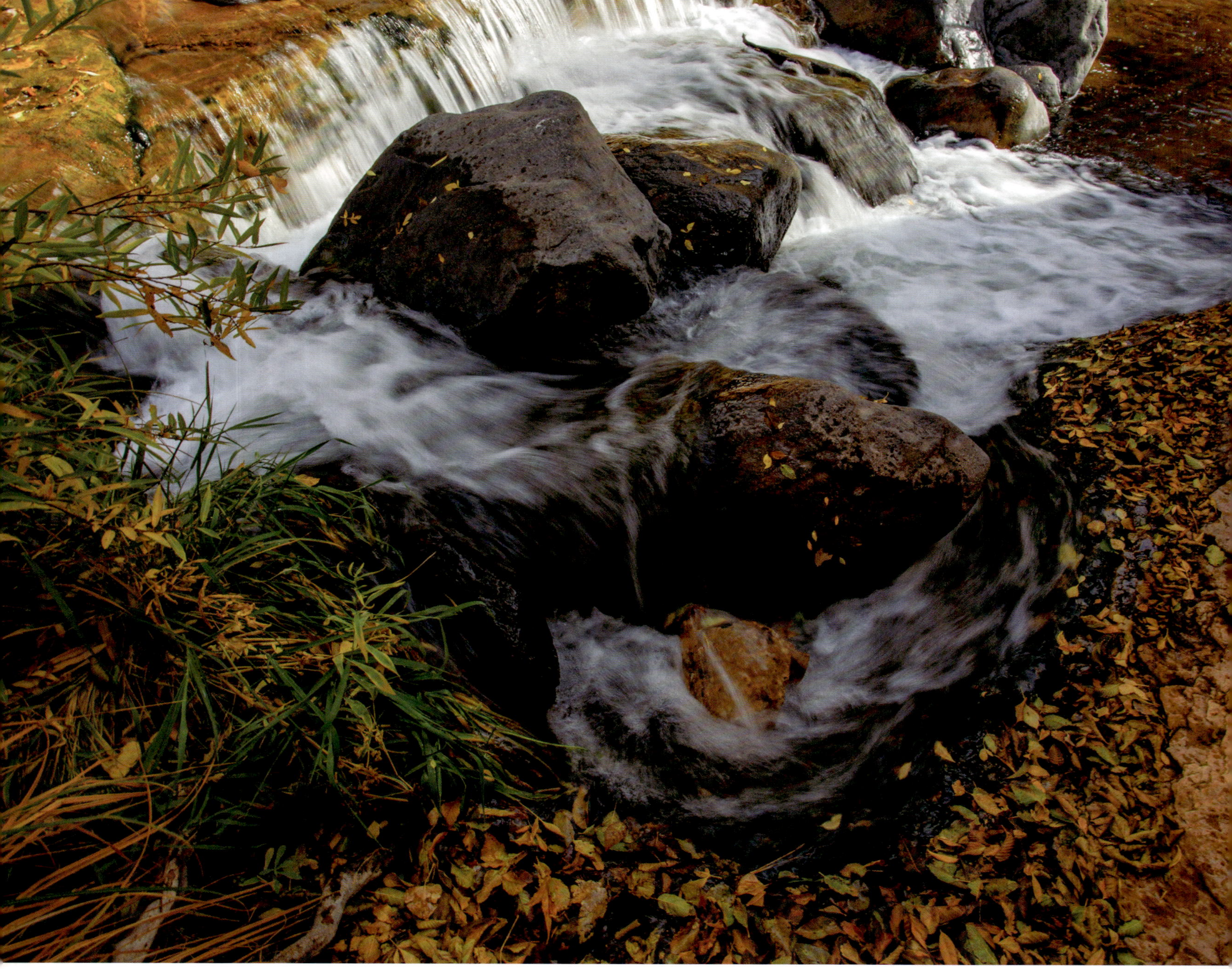



FALL LEAVES SWIRL IN POOLS ALONG OAK CREEK NEAR SEDONA.

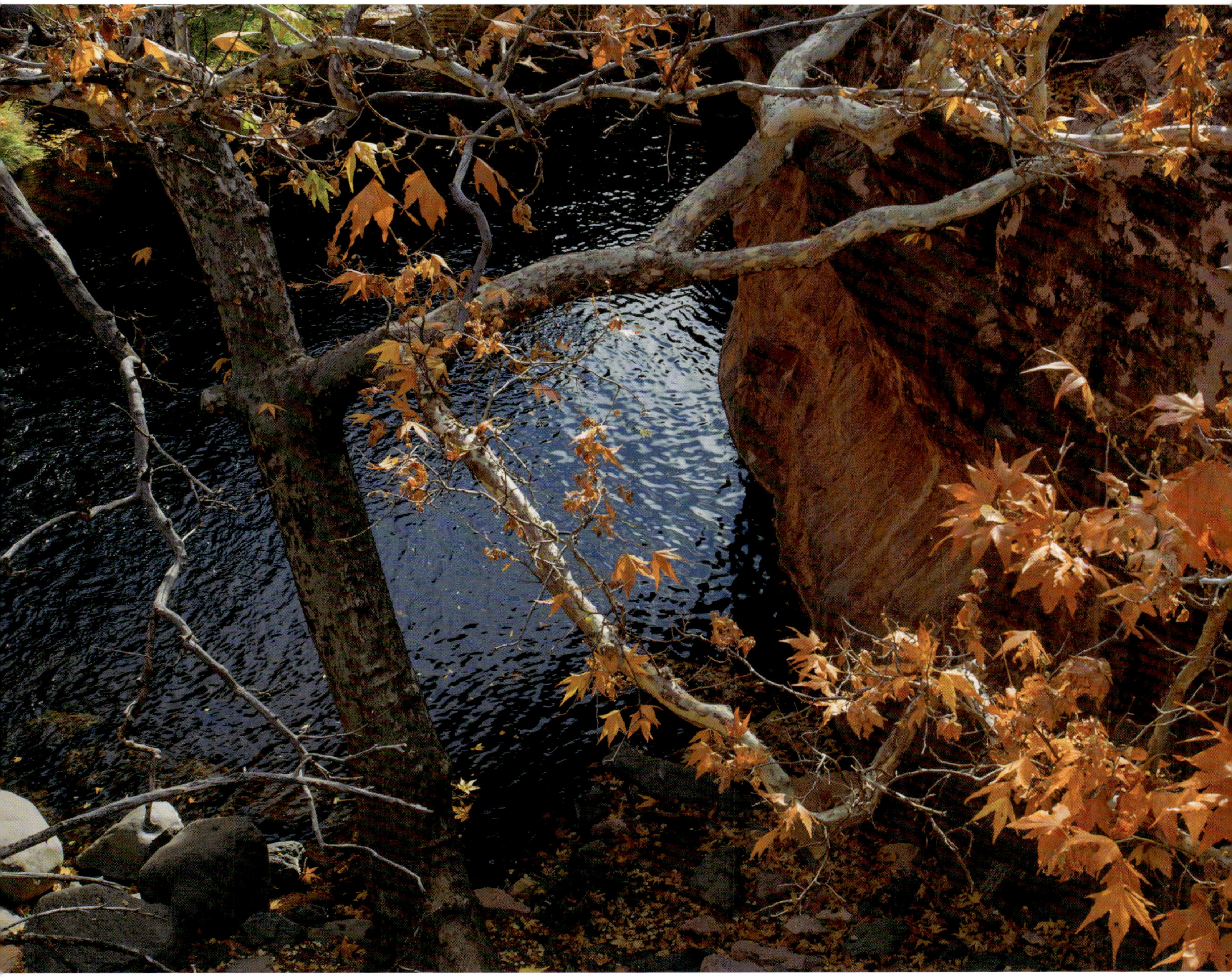

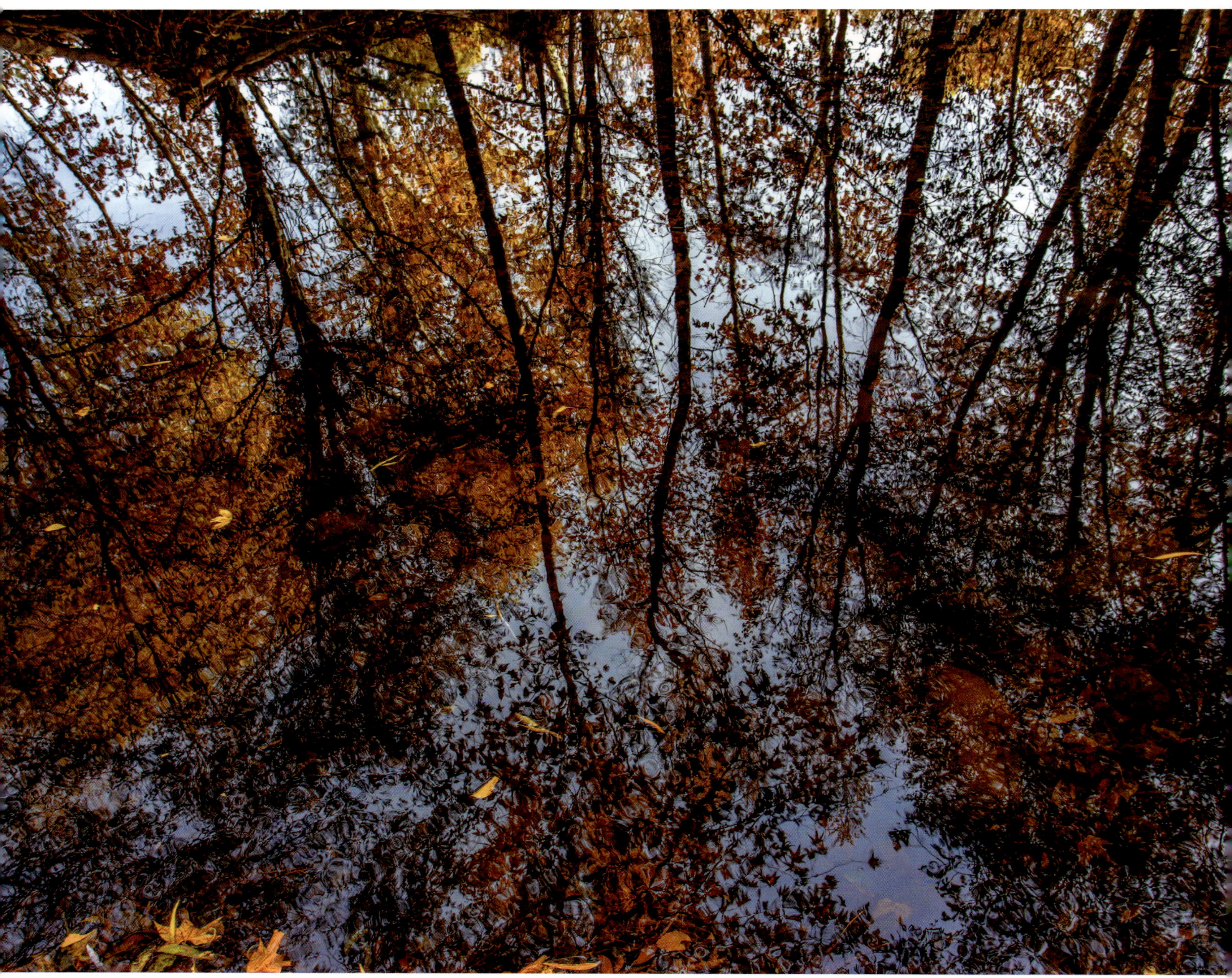

▲
WHITE SYCAMORES LINE THE BANKS OF THE
VERDE RIVER AT HISTORIC CAMP VERDE.

▶
OAKS AND PINES ALONG FOREST
ROAD 300 ON THE MOGOLLON RIM.

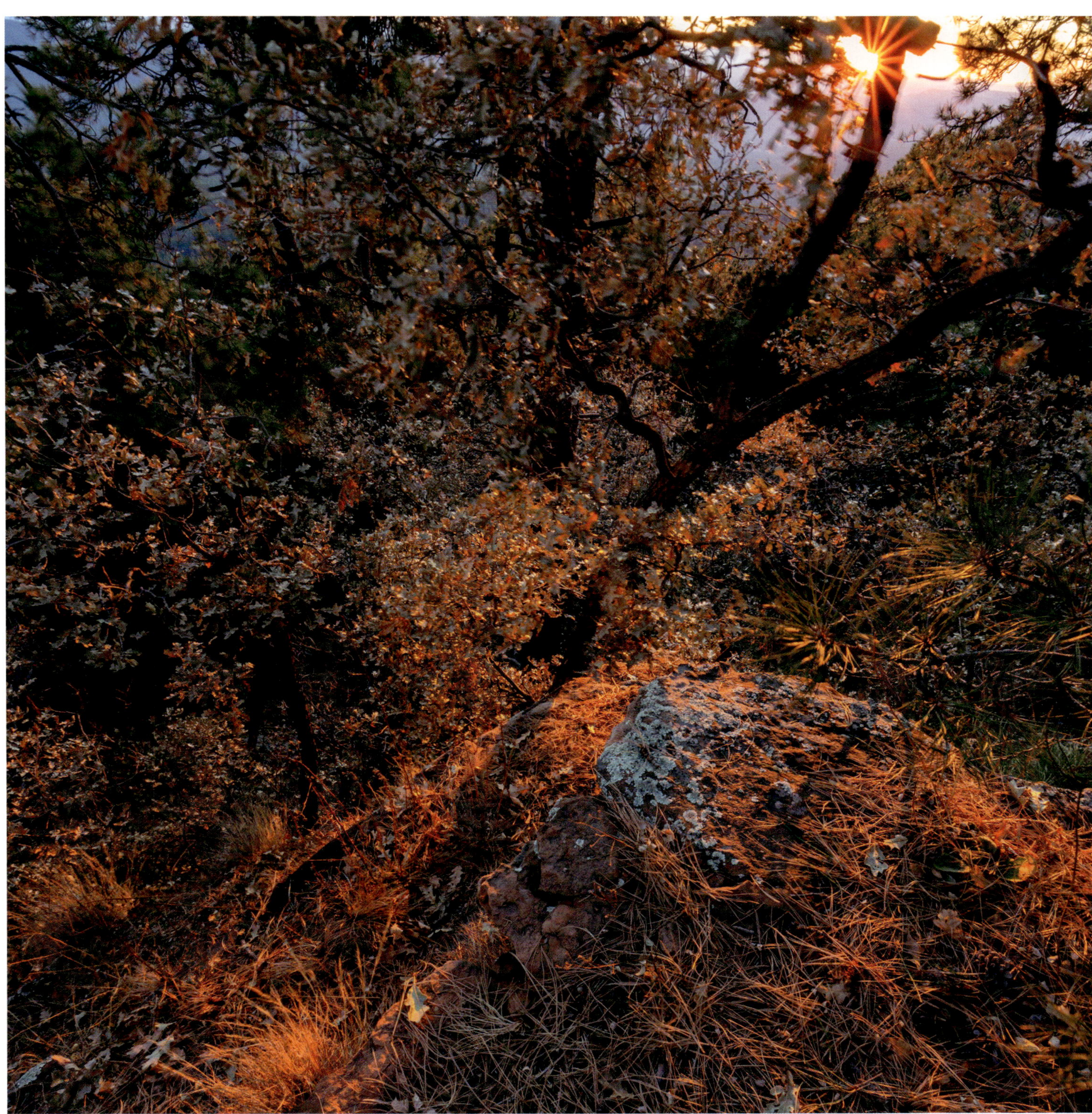

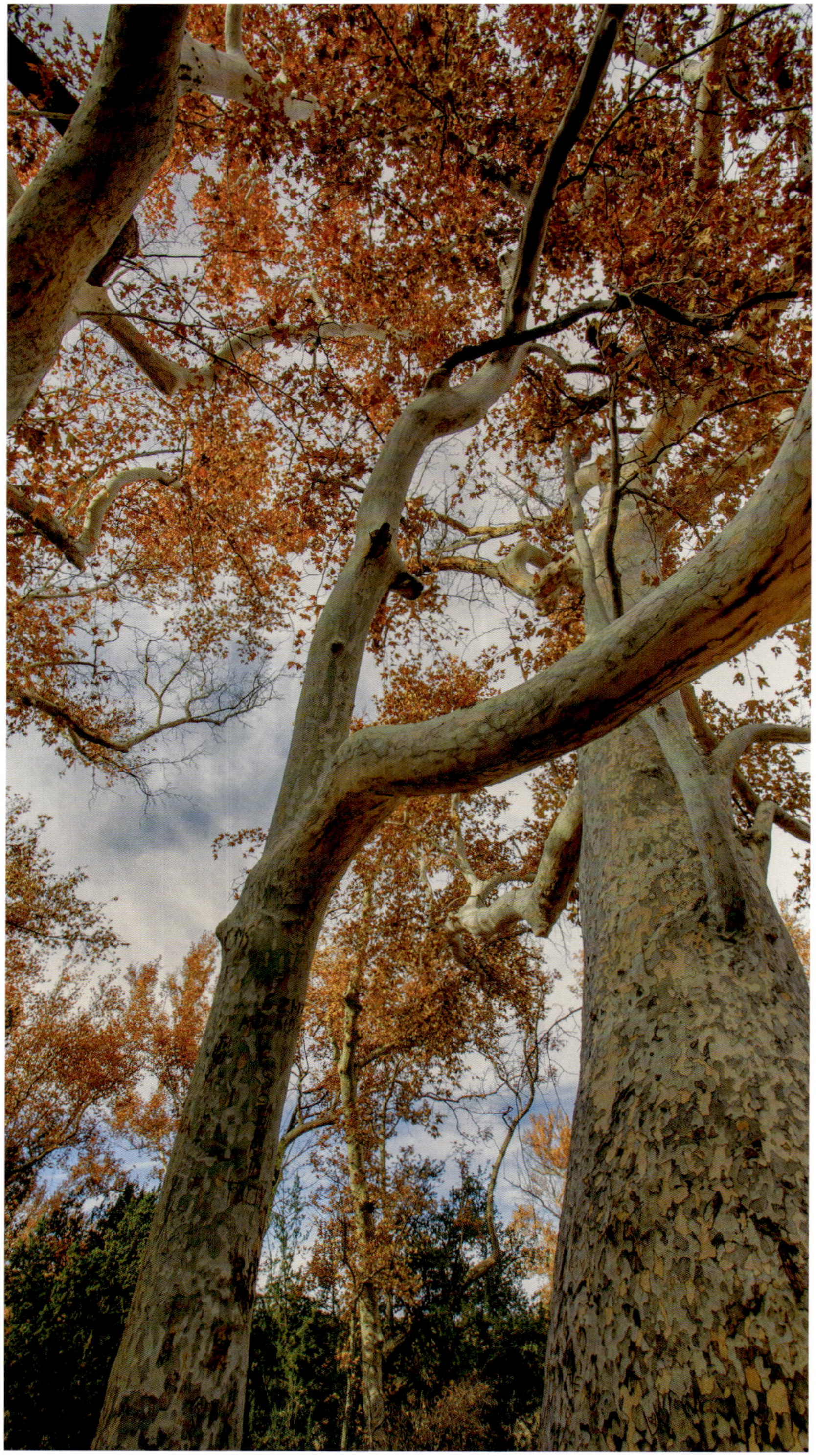

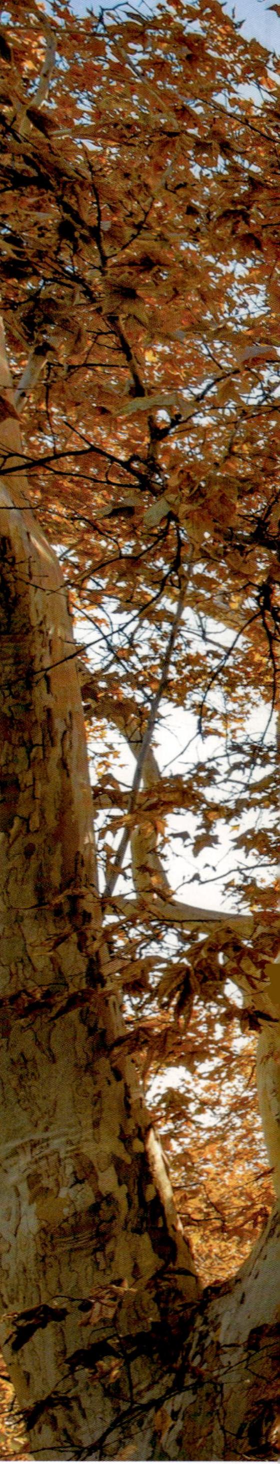


◄

LONG WHITE SYCAMORE
BRANCHES CREATE GRAPHIC
PATTERNS AGAINST A STORMY SKY.

►

GOLDEN COLORS OF FALL POP
IN CONTRAST WITH WHITE
SYCAMORE BRANCHES IN THE
VERDE RIVER VALLEY.

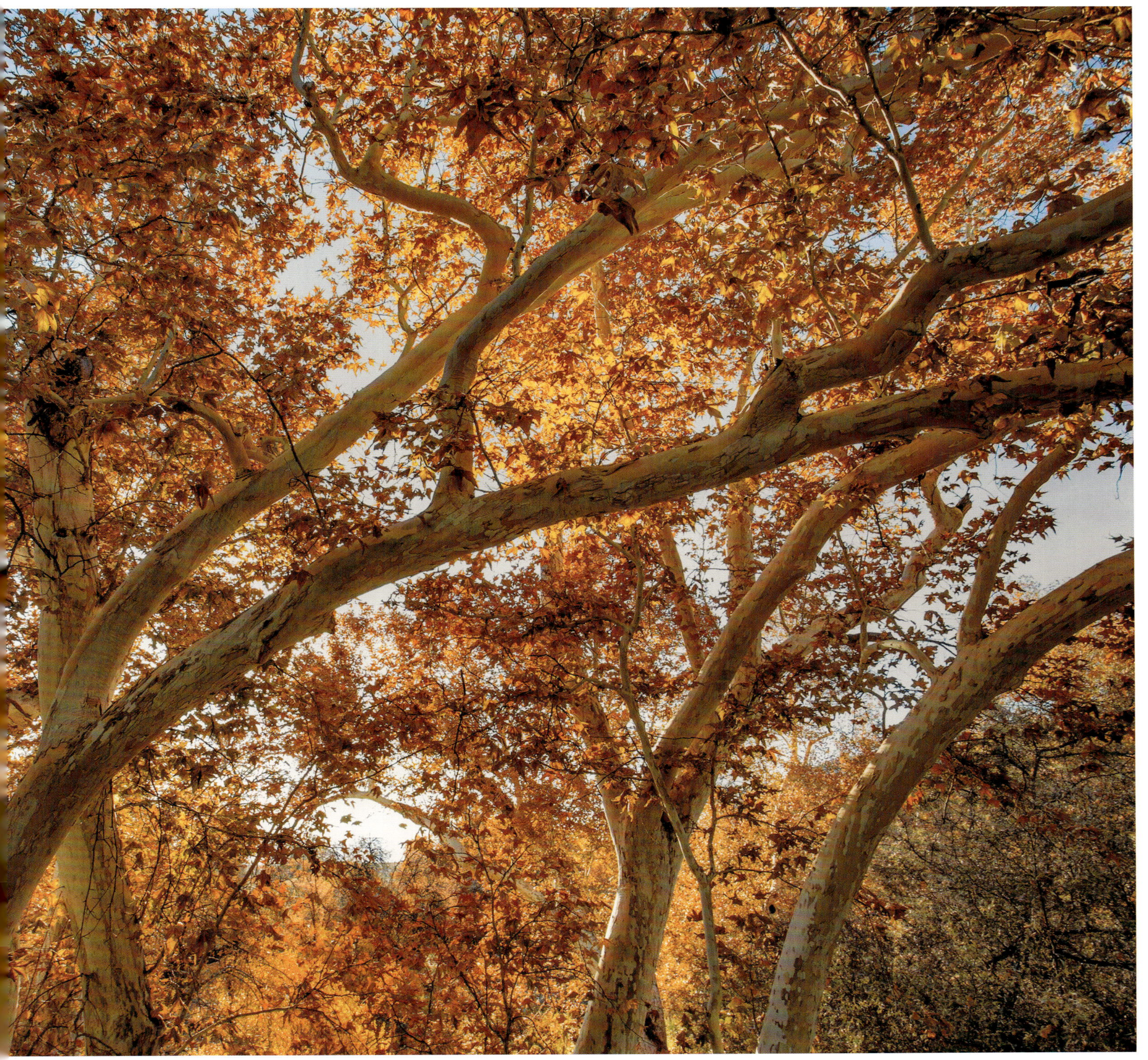

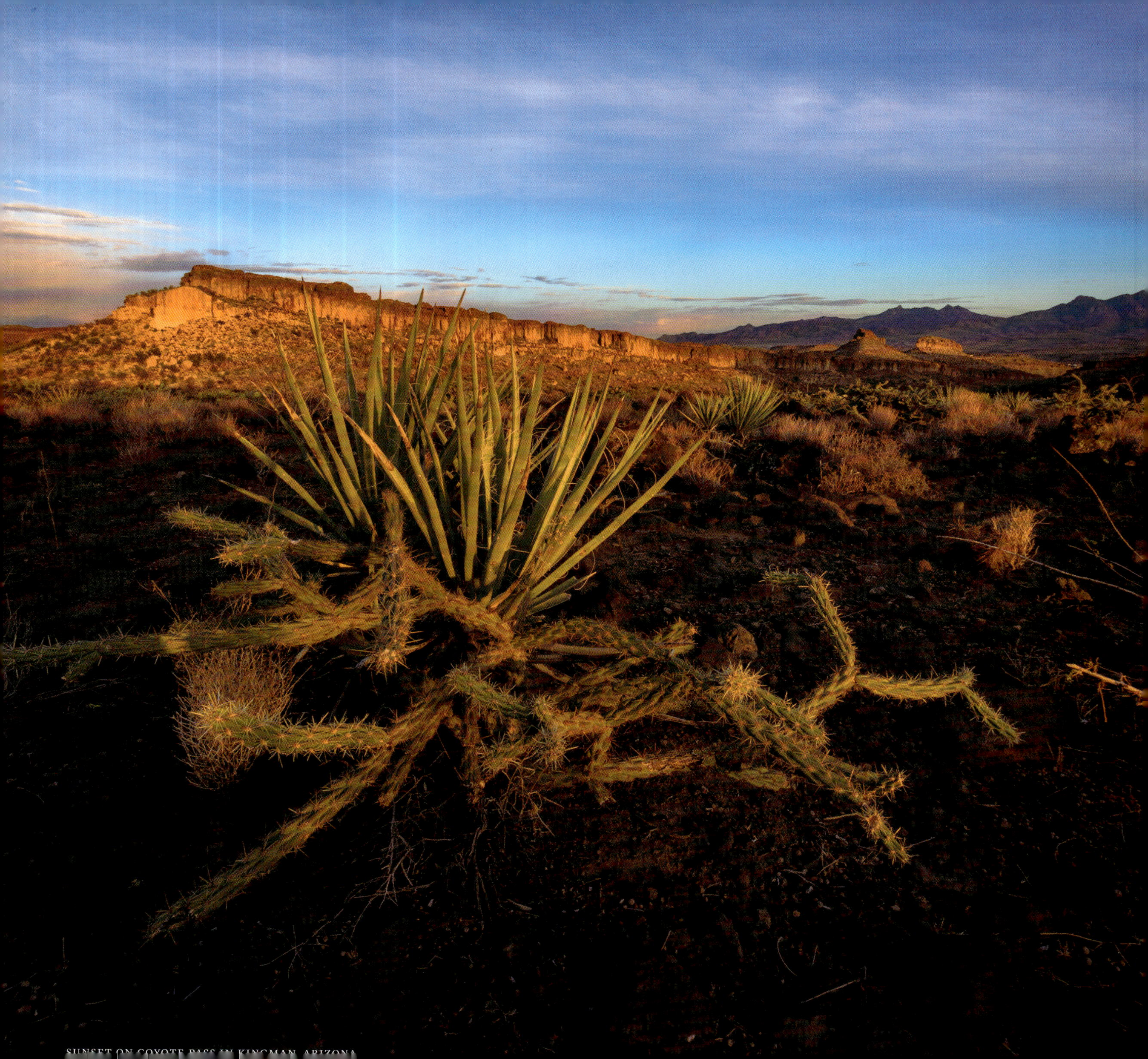

SUNSET ON COYOTE PASS IN KINGMAN, ARIZONA

MOJAVE DESERT

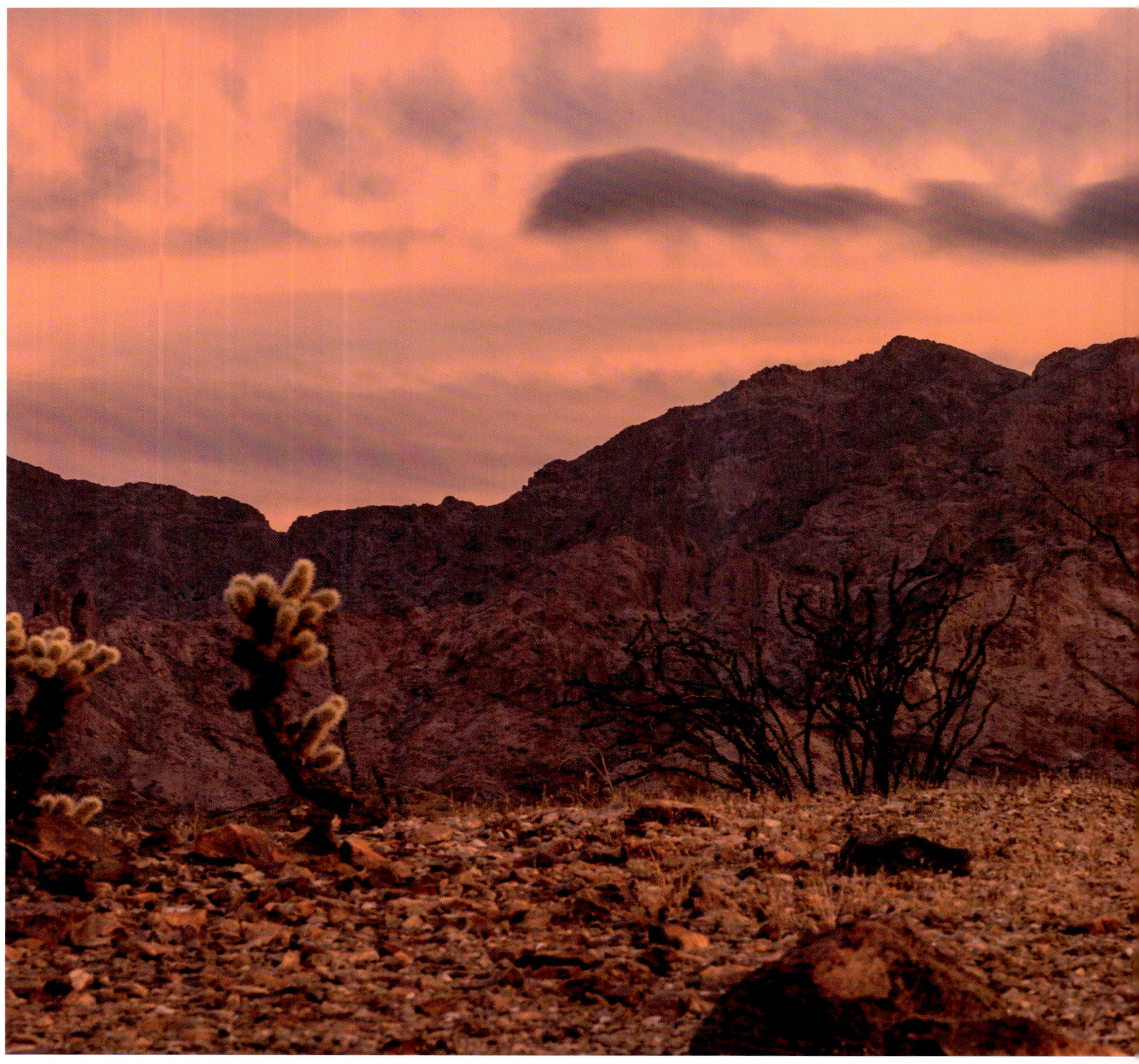

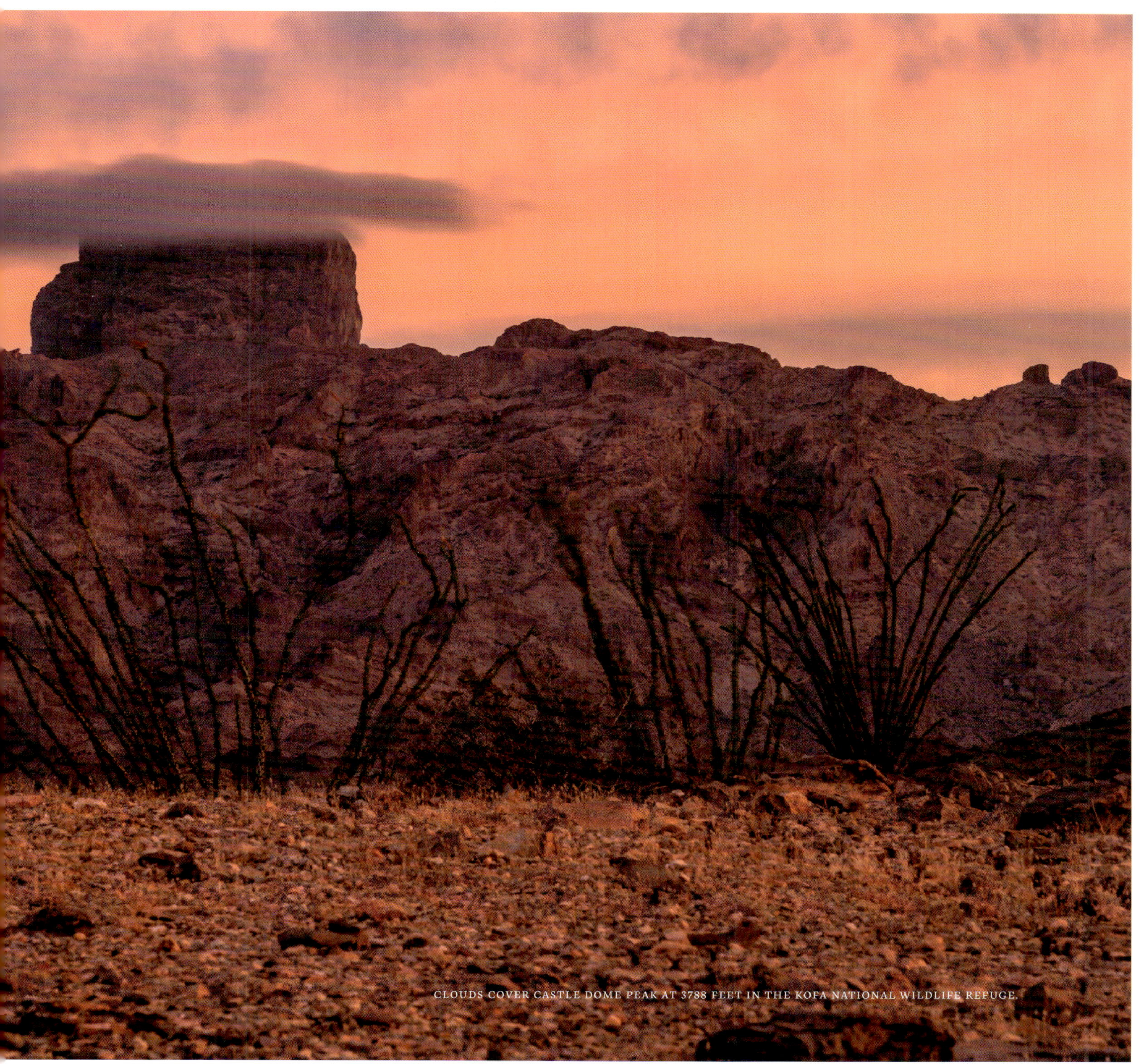

CLOUDS COVER CASTLE DOME PEAK AT 3788 FEET IN THE KOFA NATIONAL WILDLIFE REFUGE.

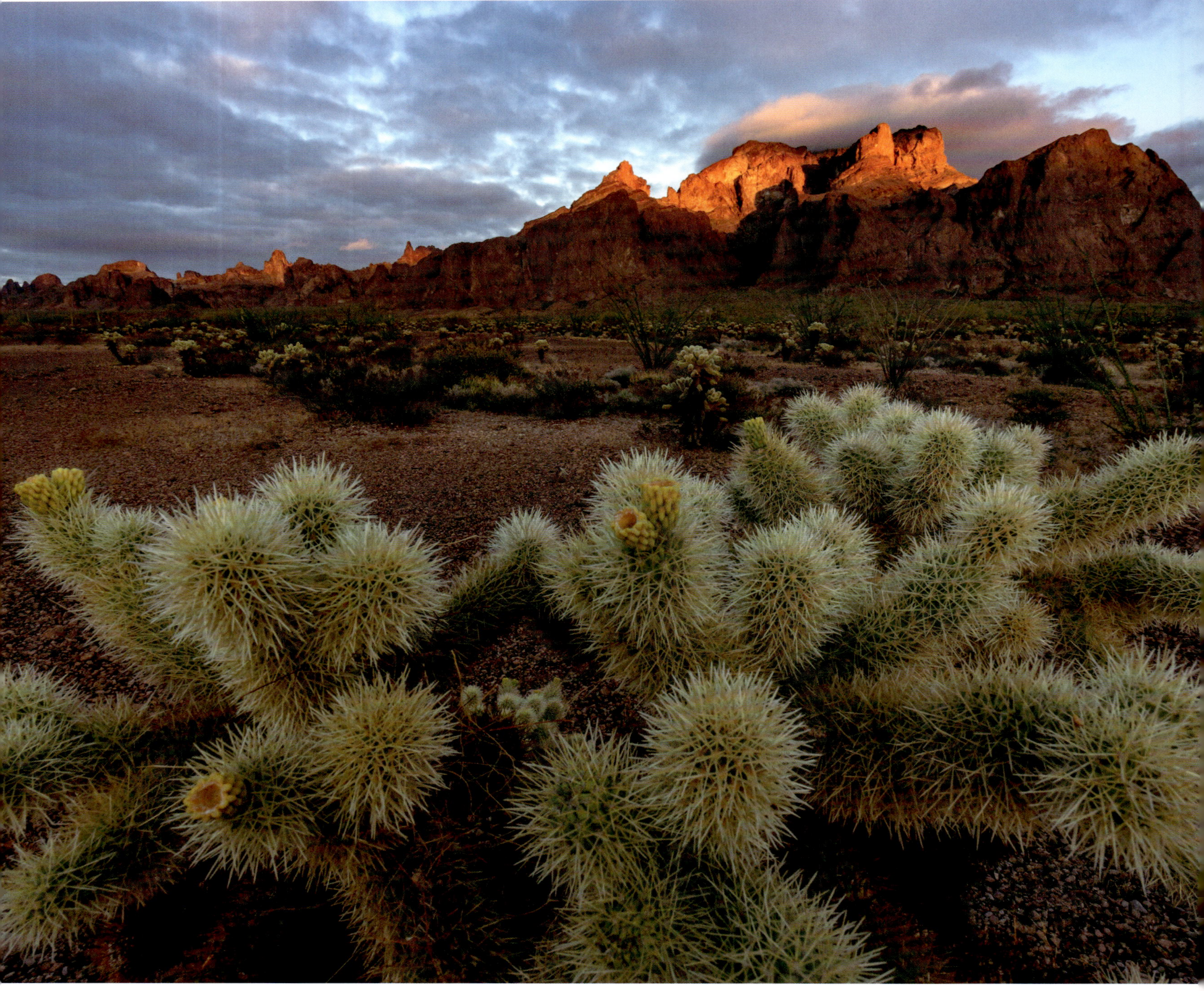



THE PEAKS OF THE KOFA RANGE RISE ABOVE THE FLAT DESERT PLAYA BELOW.

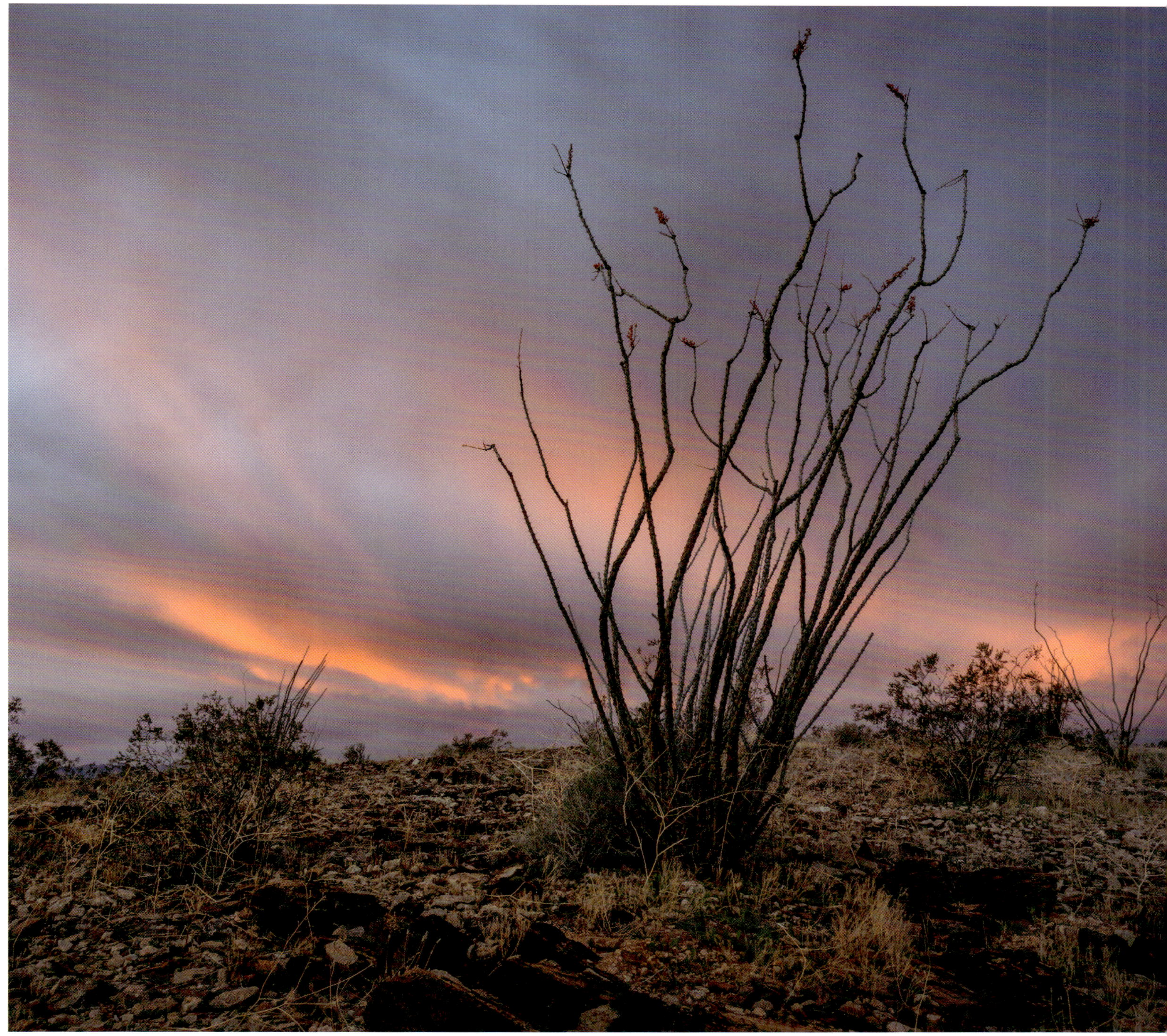

AN OCOTILLO BLOOMS IN THE HARSH CLIMATE OF THE EAST CACTUS PLAIN WILDERNESS.

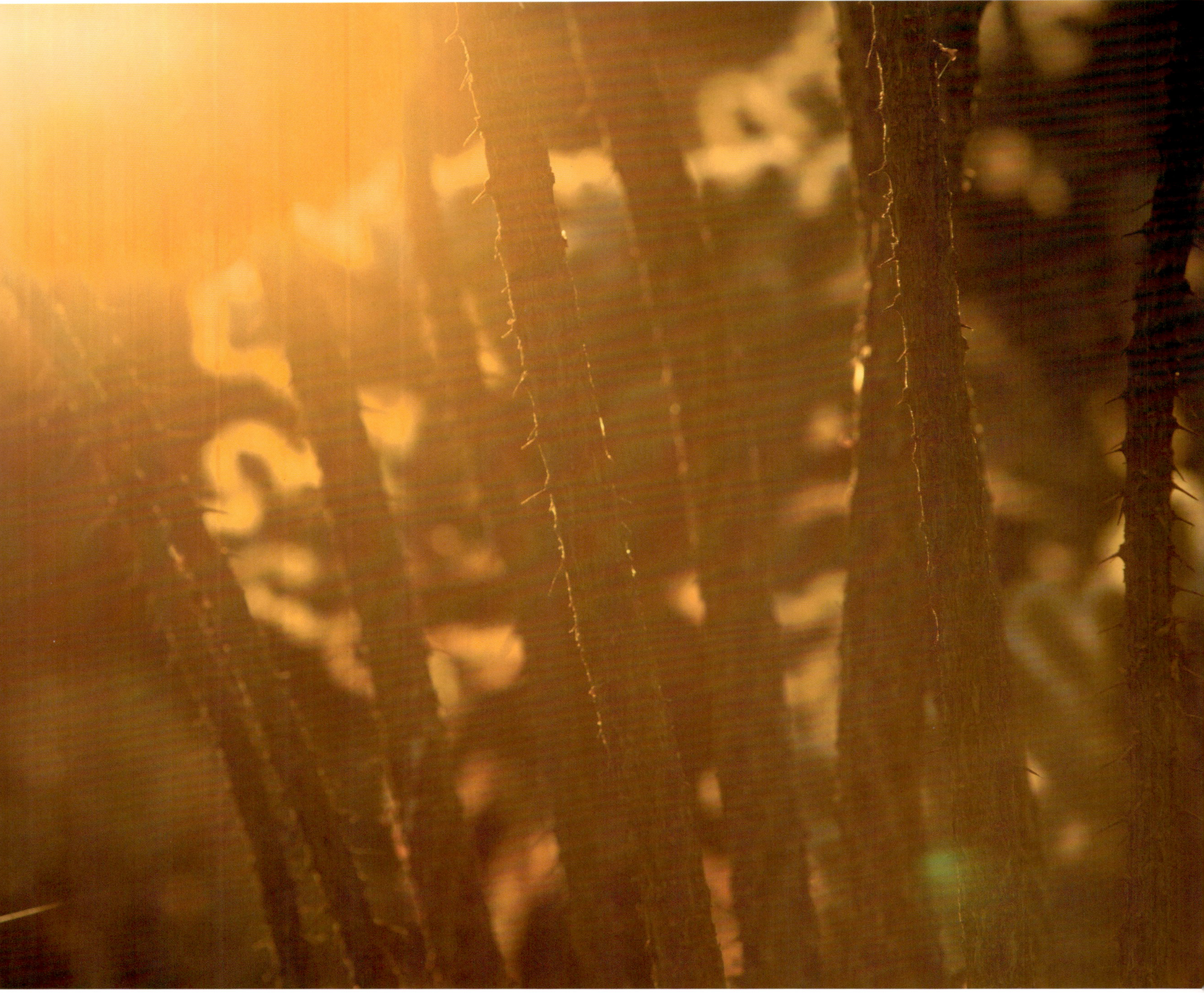

A GOLDEN GLOW SPILLS ACROSS CHOLLA IN THE PLOMOSA MOUNTAINS.

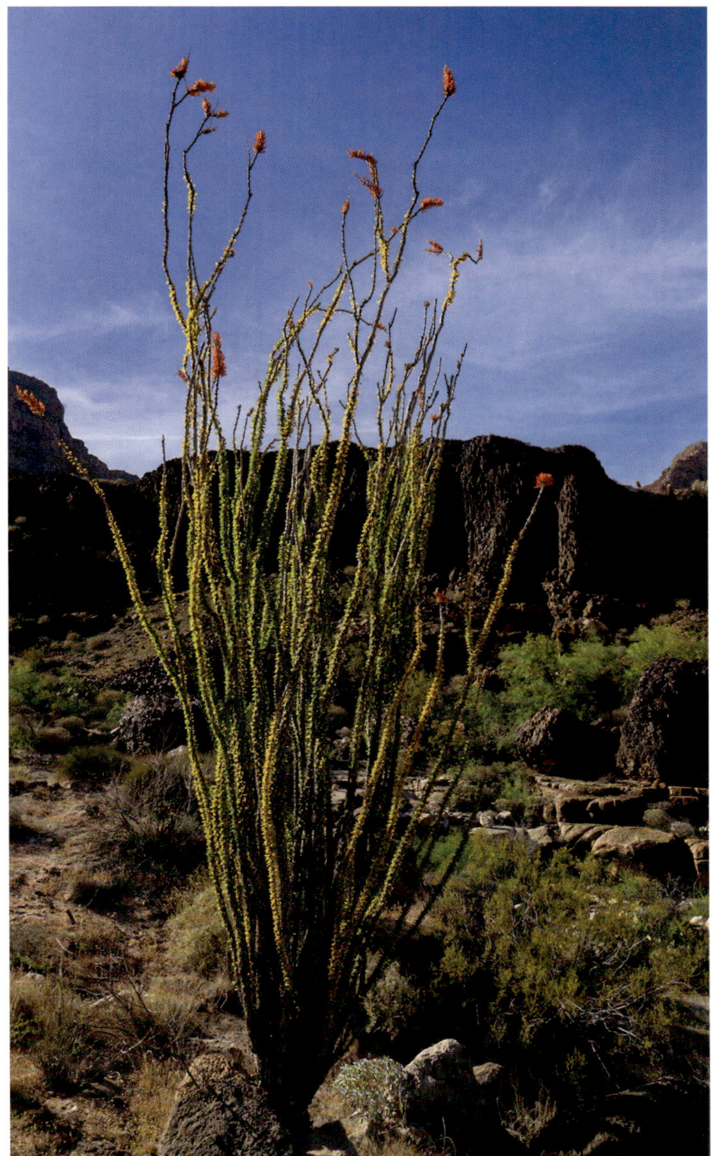

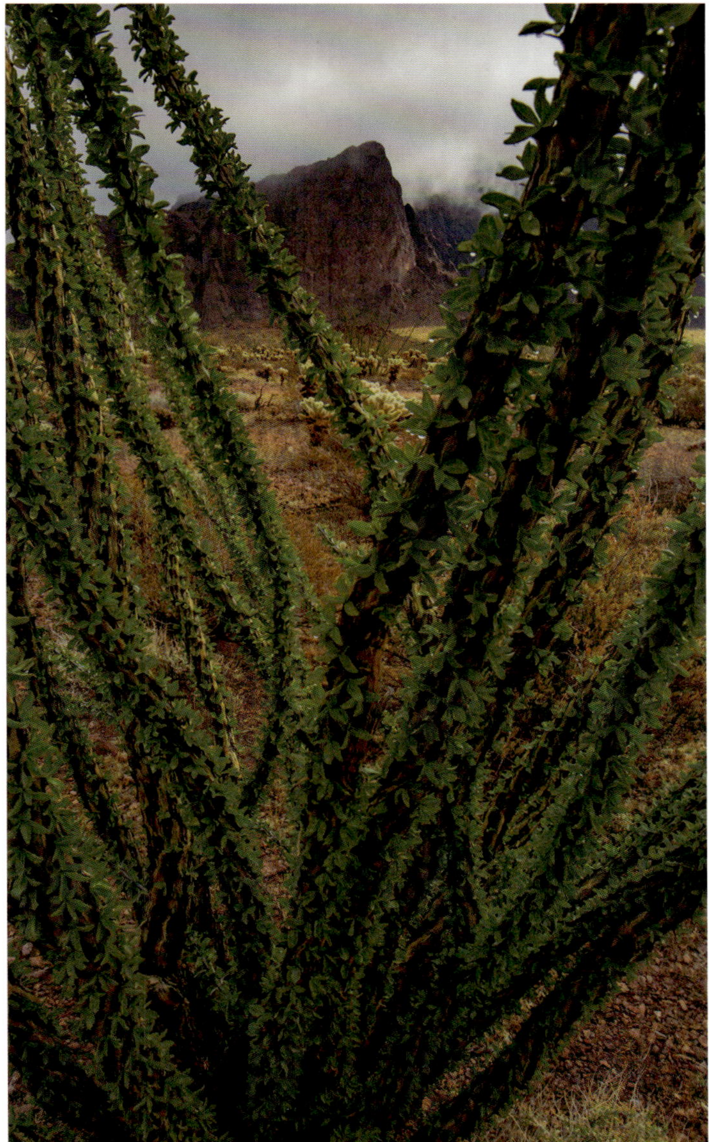

OCOTILLO BLOOM ALONG THE COLORADO RIVER IN THE TRANSITION
ZONE OF THE COLORADO PLATEAU AND MOJAVE DESERT.

AN OCOTILLO LEAFS OUT WITH THE WINTER
RAINS IN THE MOJAVE DESERT NEAR YUMA.

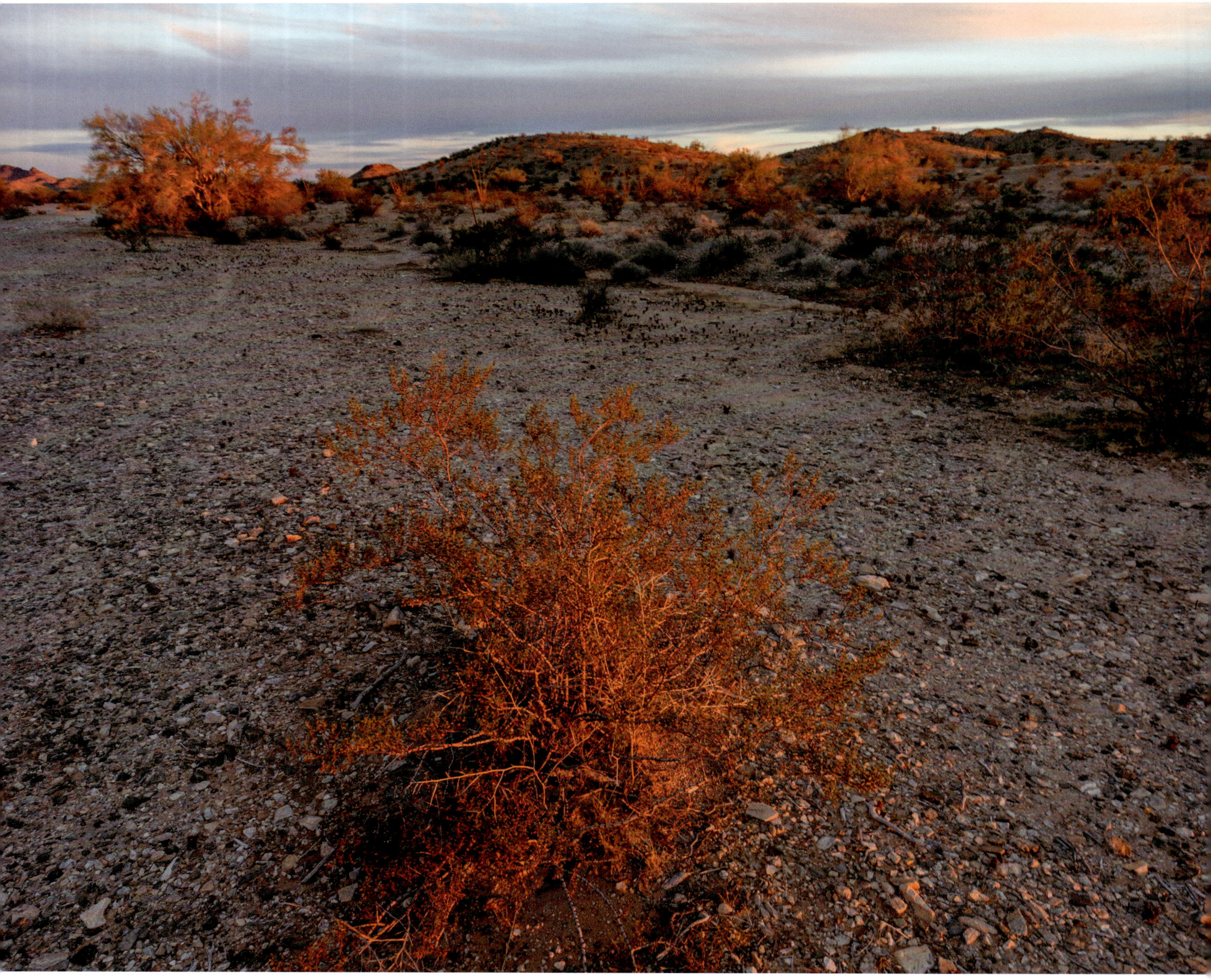



CREOSOTE AND PALO VERDE MAKE GOOD USE OF THE DESERT SOIL ON THE EAST CACTUS PLAIN WILDERNESS.

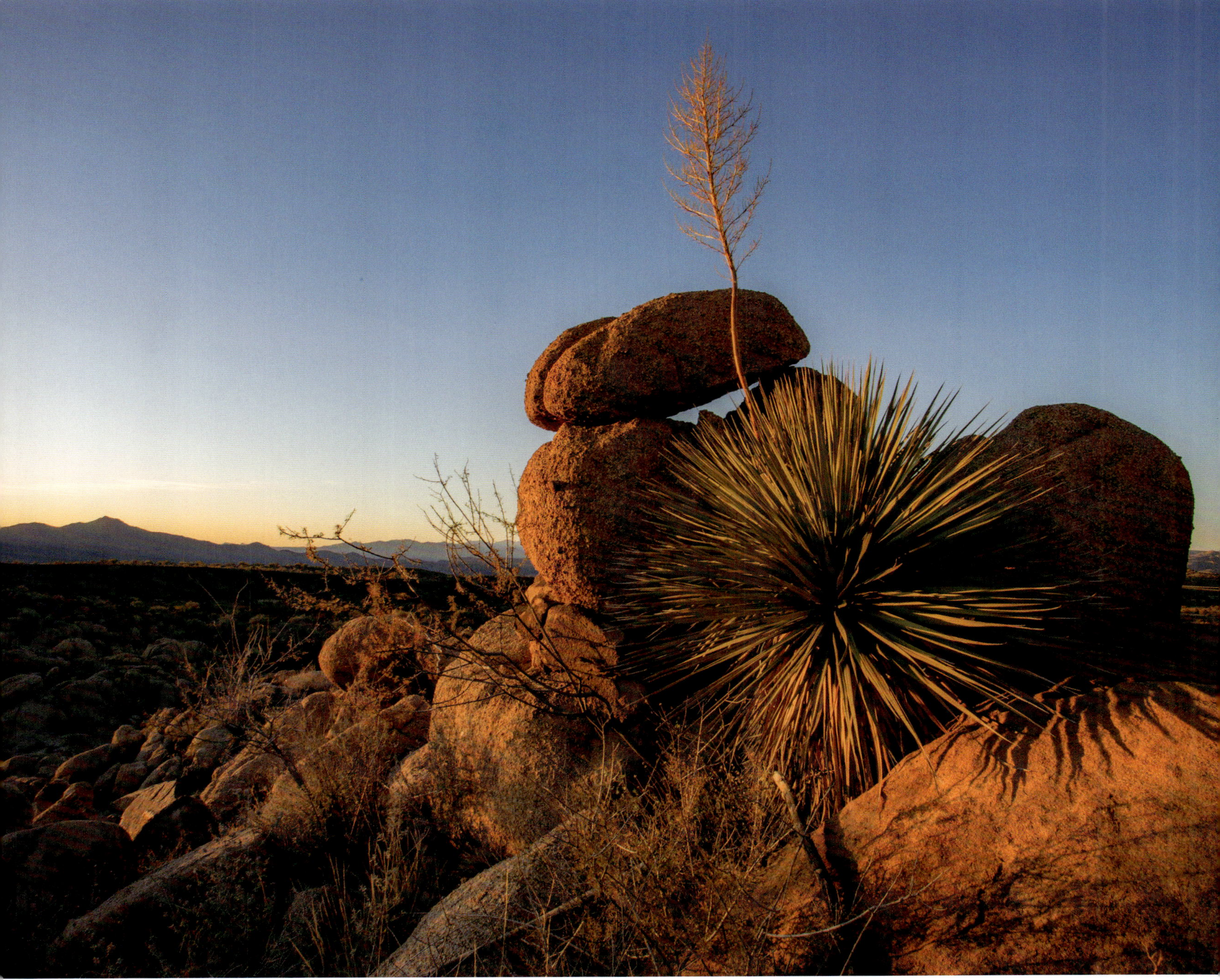

ROUND GRANITE BOULDERS IN THE BURRO CREEK WILDERNESS.

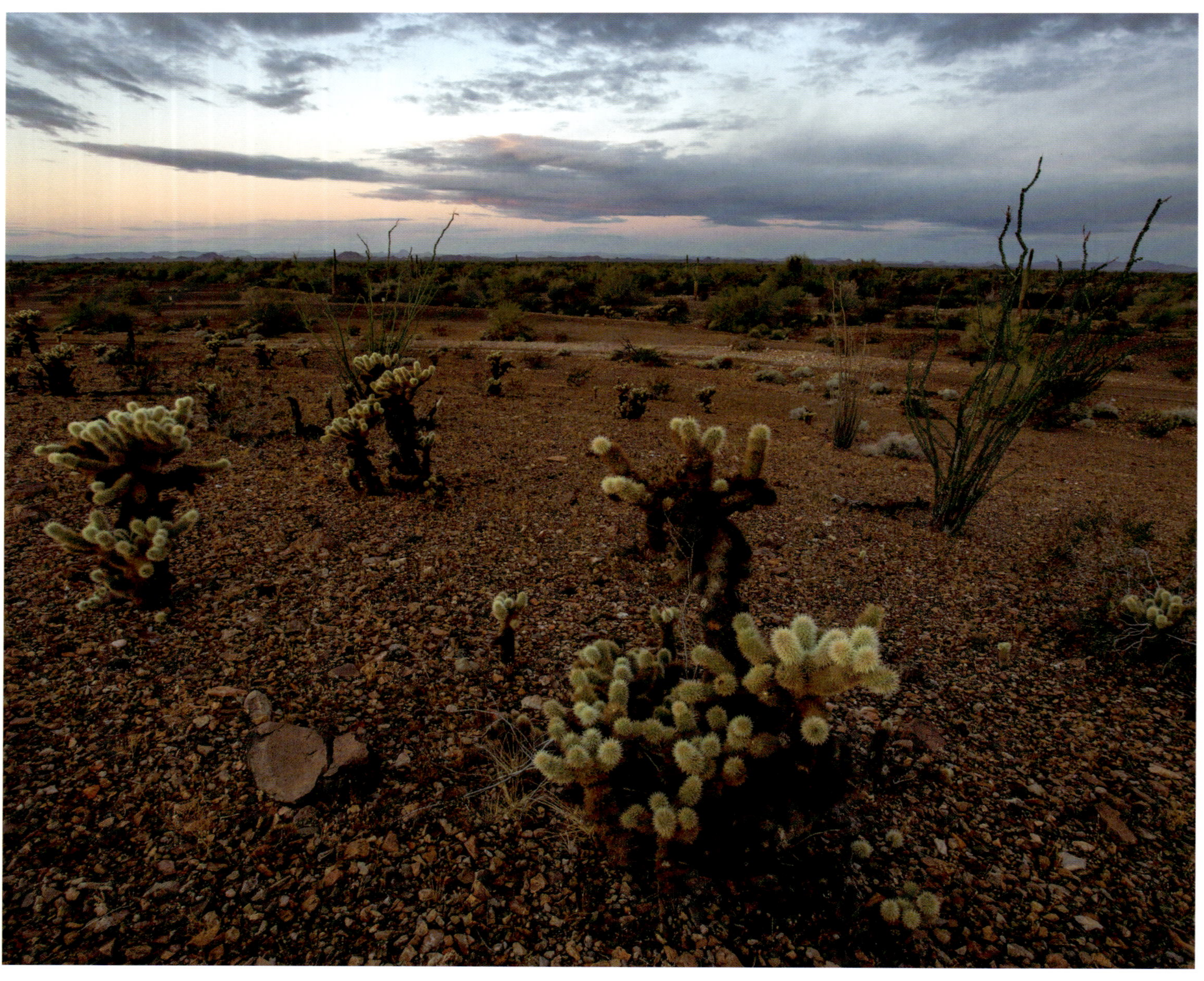



THIS FLAT RED DESERT FLOOR IS TYPICAL OF THE CASTLE DOME PLAIN.

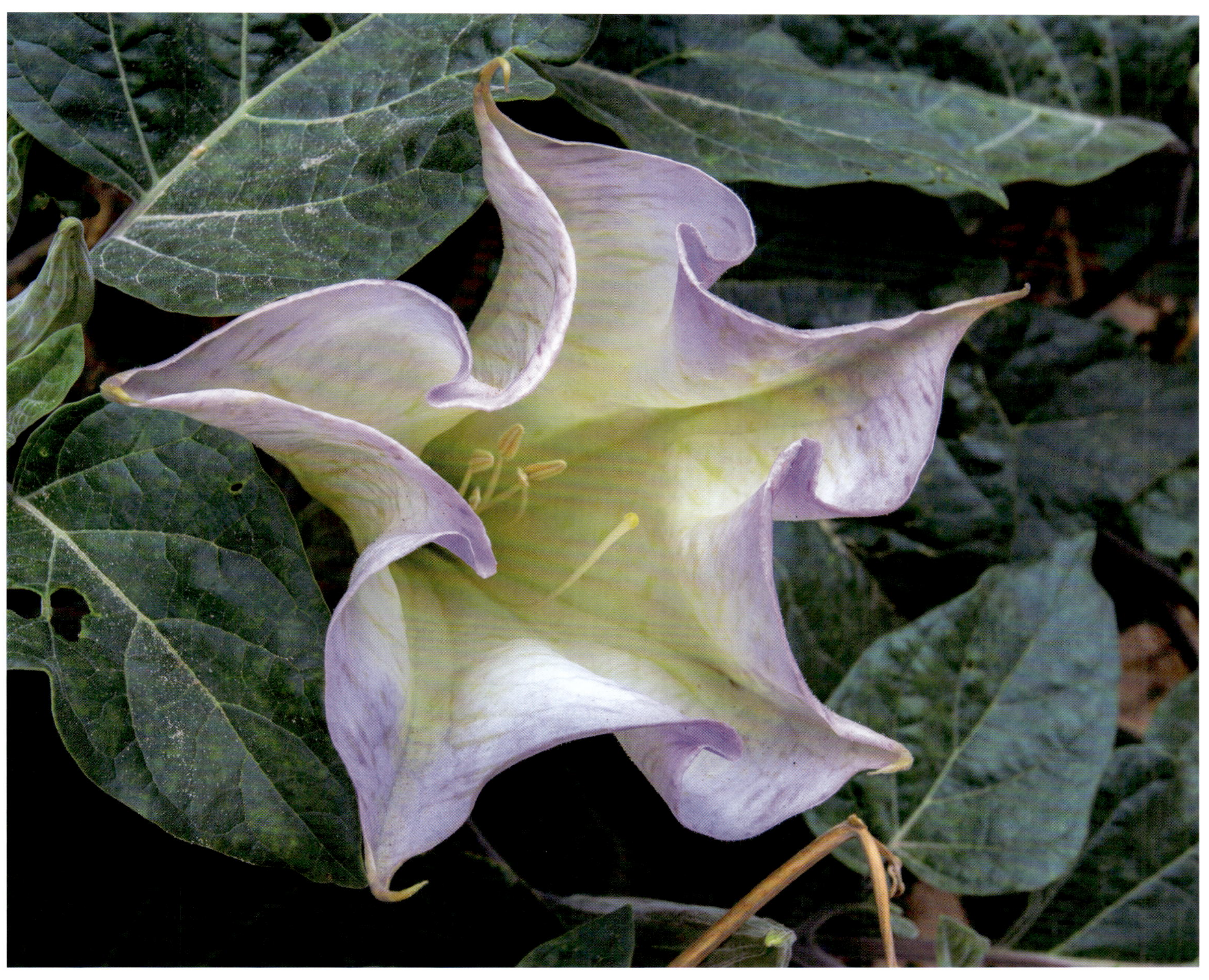

SPRING TEMPS AND MOISTURE ALLOW A DATURA TO UNFOLD IN THE DRY MOJAVE DESERT NEAR BLACK CANYON.

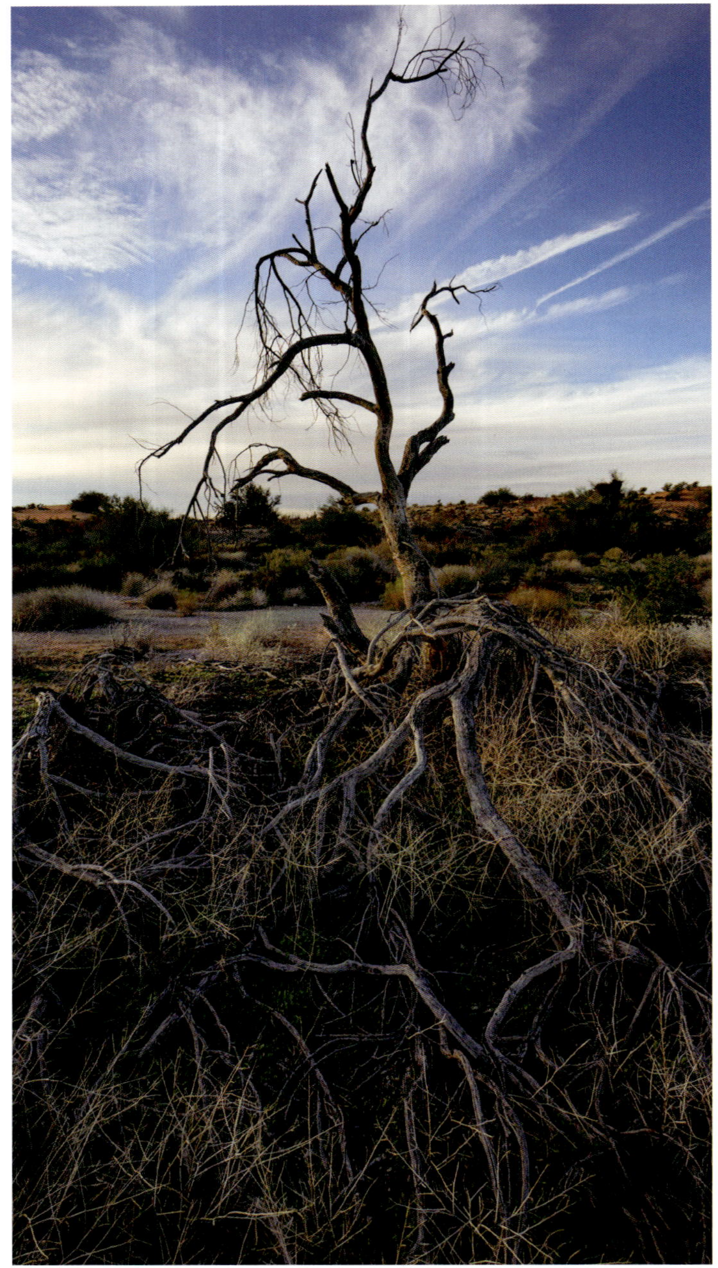



THIS PALO VERDE WAS UNABLE TO SURVIVE IN
THE HARSH EAST CACTUS PLAIN WILDERNESS.

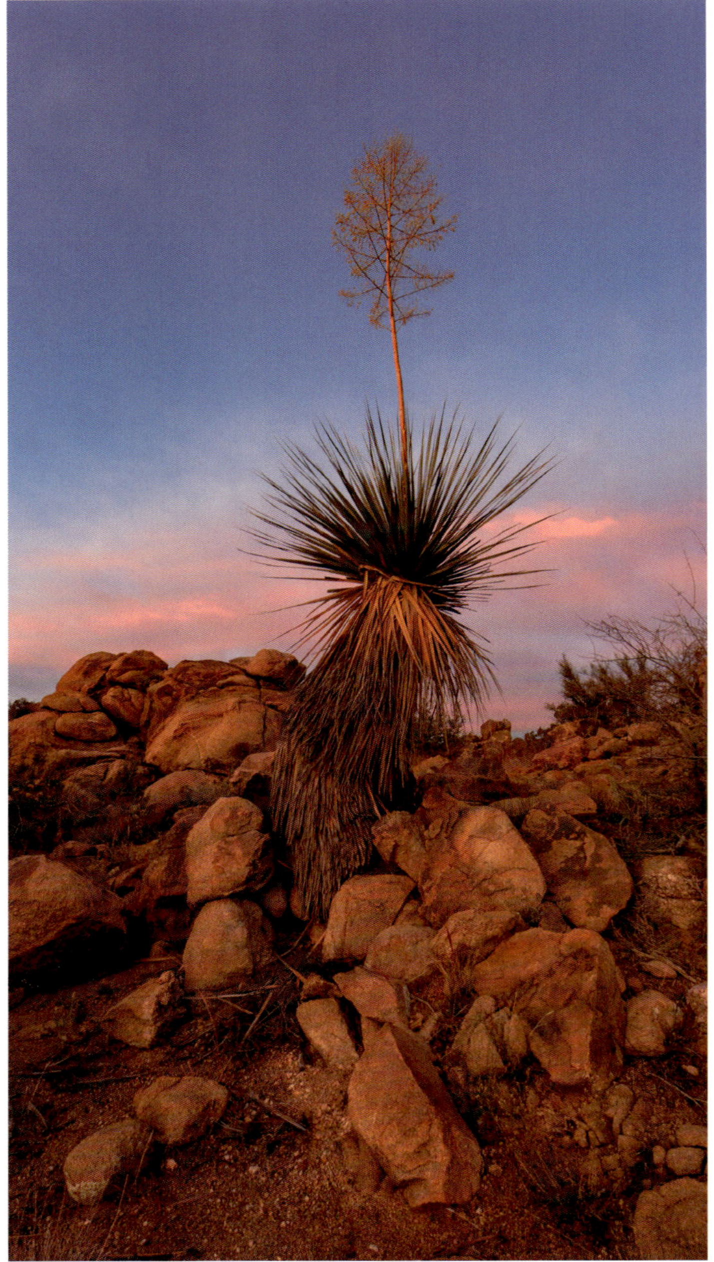

SOAPTREE YUCCA AND GRANITE IN THE BURRO CREEK WILDERNESS.

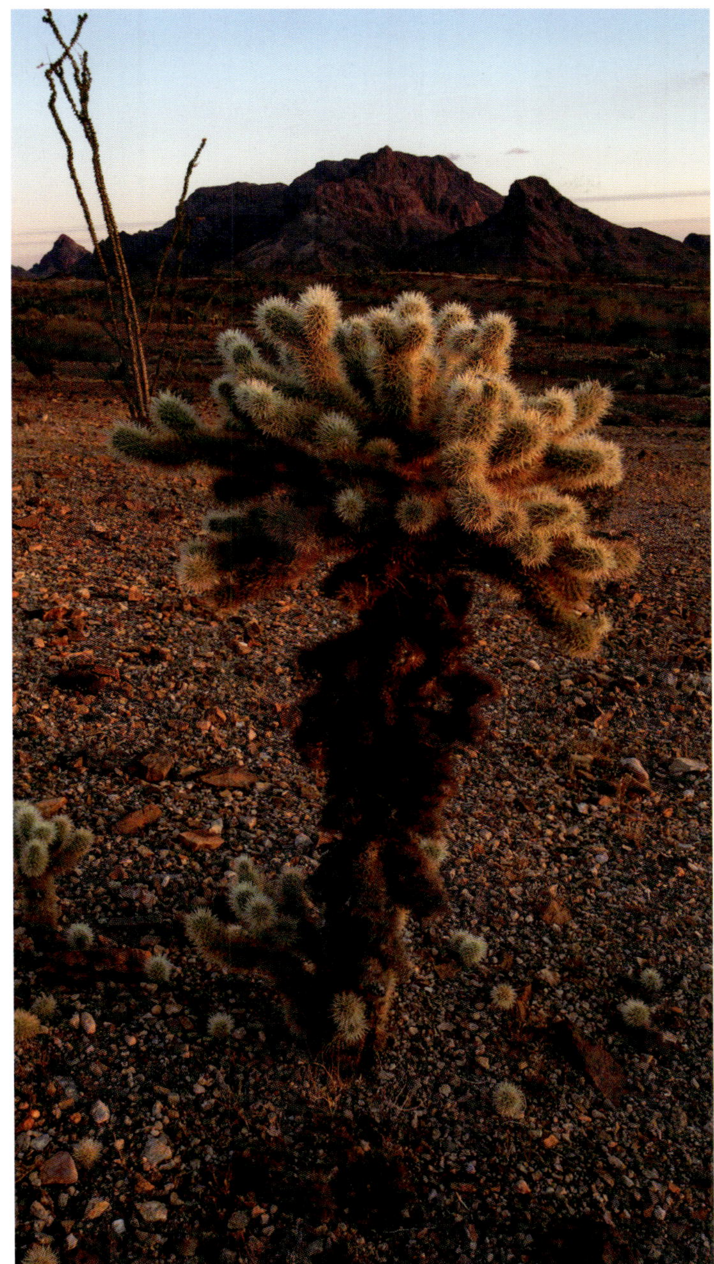

A CHOLLA CACTUS STANDS TALL AT THUMB
PEAK IN THE CASTLE DOME MOUNTAINS.

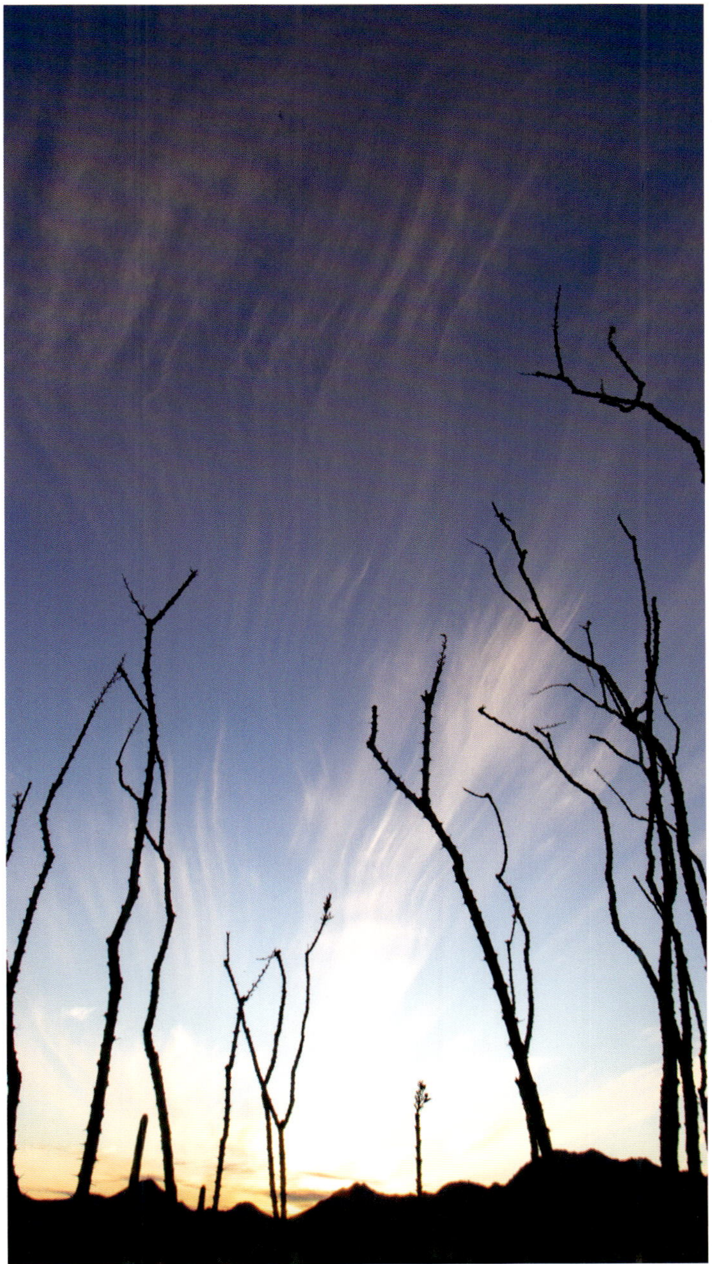

OCOTILLO ON THE HILLSIDES ALONG DIAMOND CREEK ROAD.

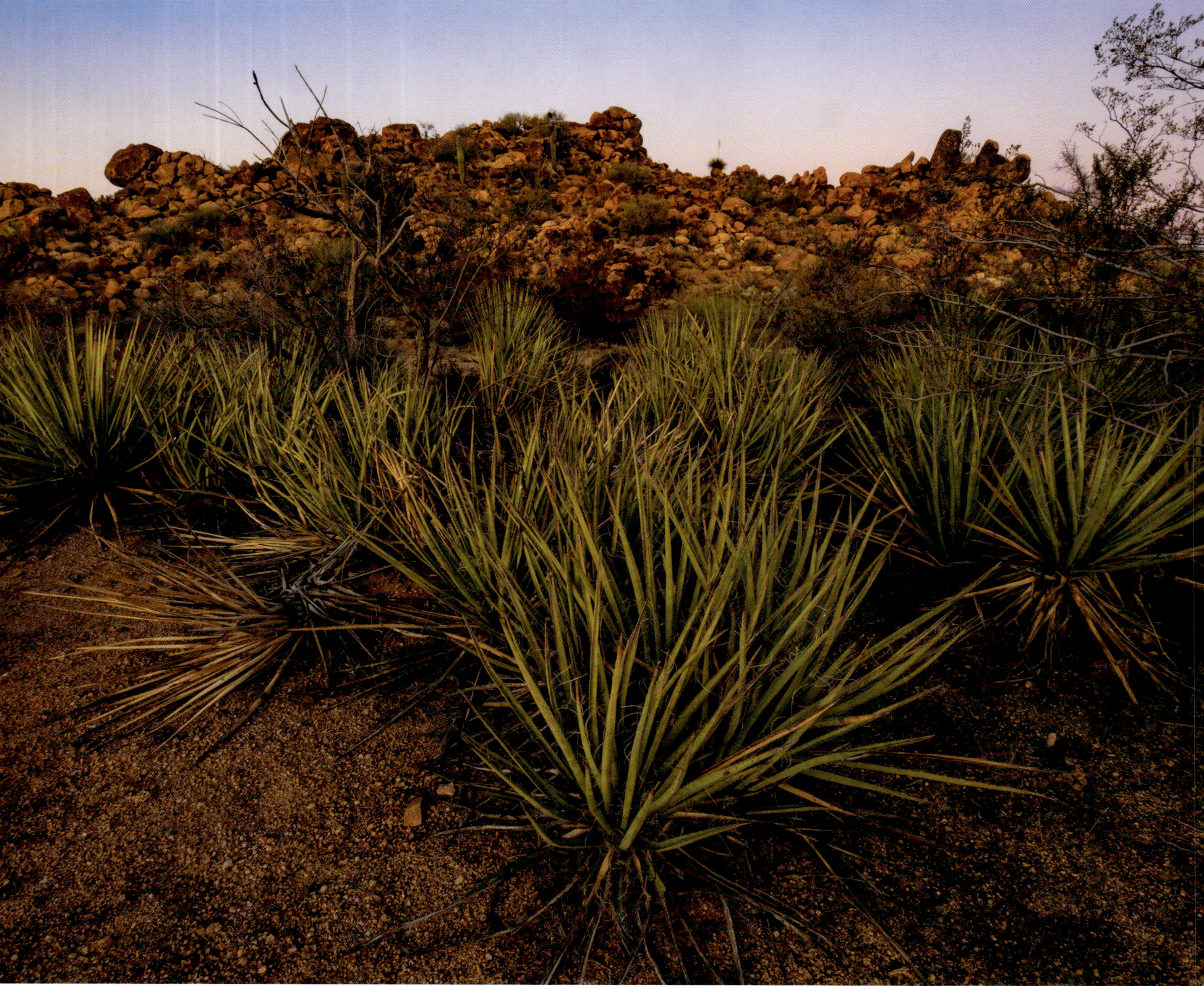



THE ARRASTRA MOUNTAIN WILDERNESS AREA FROM 17 MILE ROAD, NEAR BURRO CREEK.

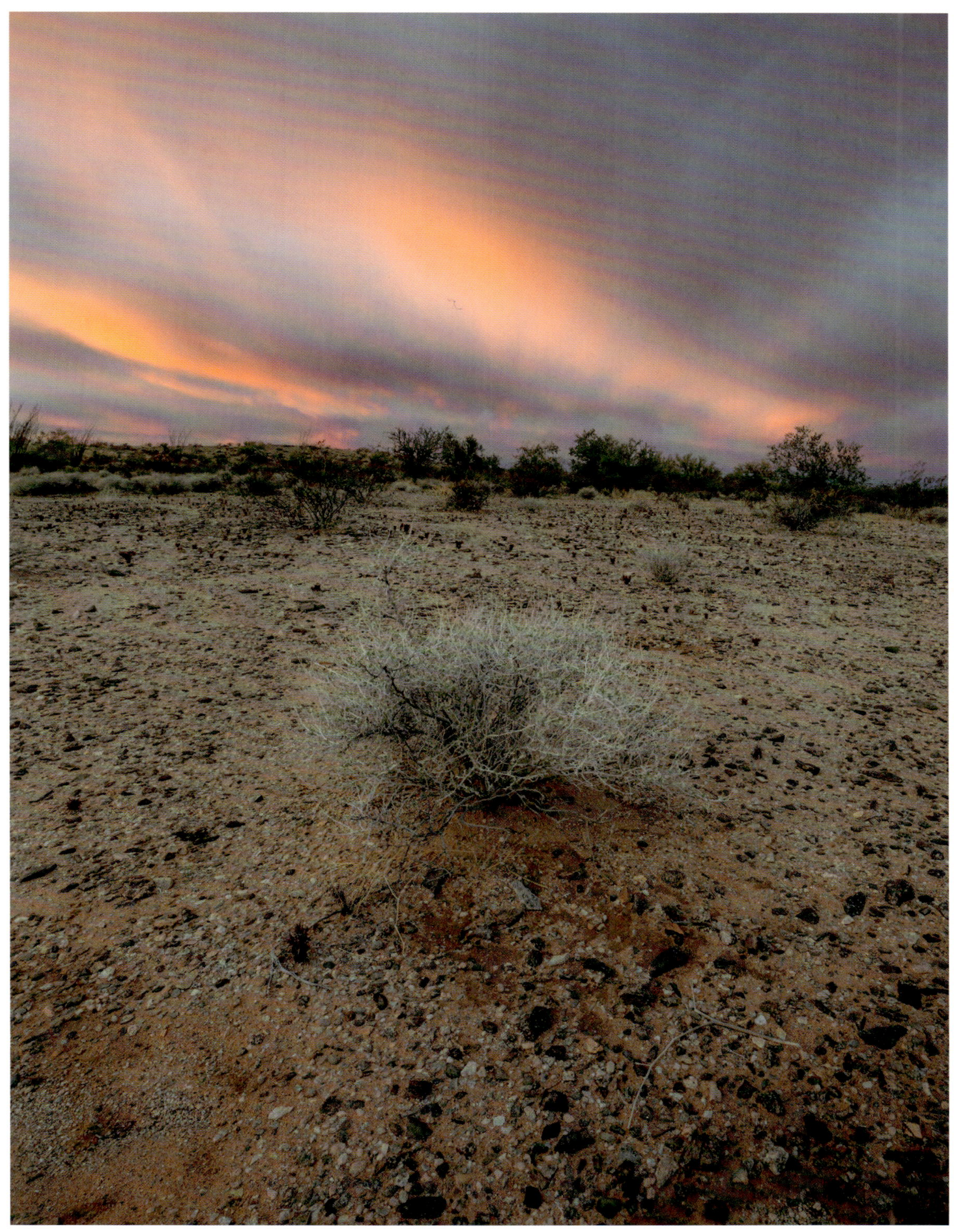

A WINTER STORM BLOWS ACROSS THE DESOLATE EAST CACTUS PLAIN WILDERNESS.

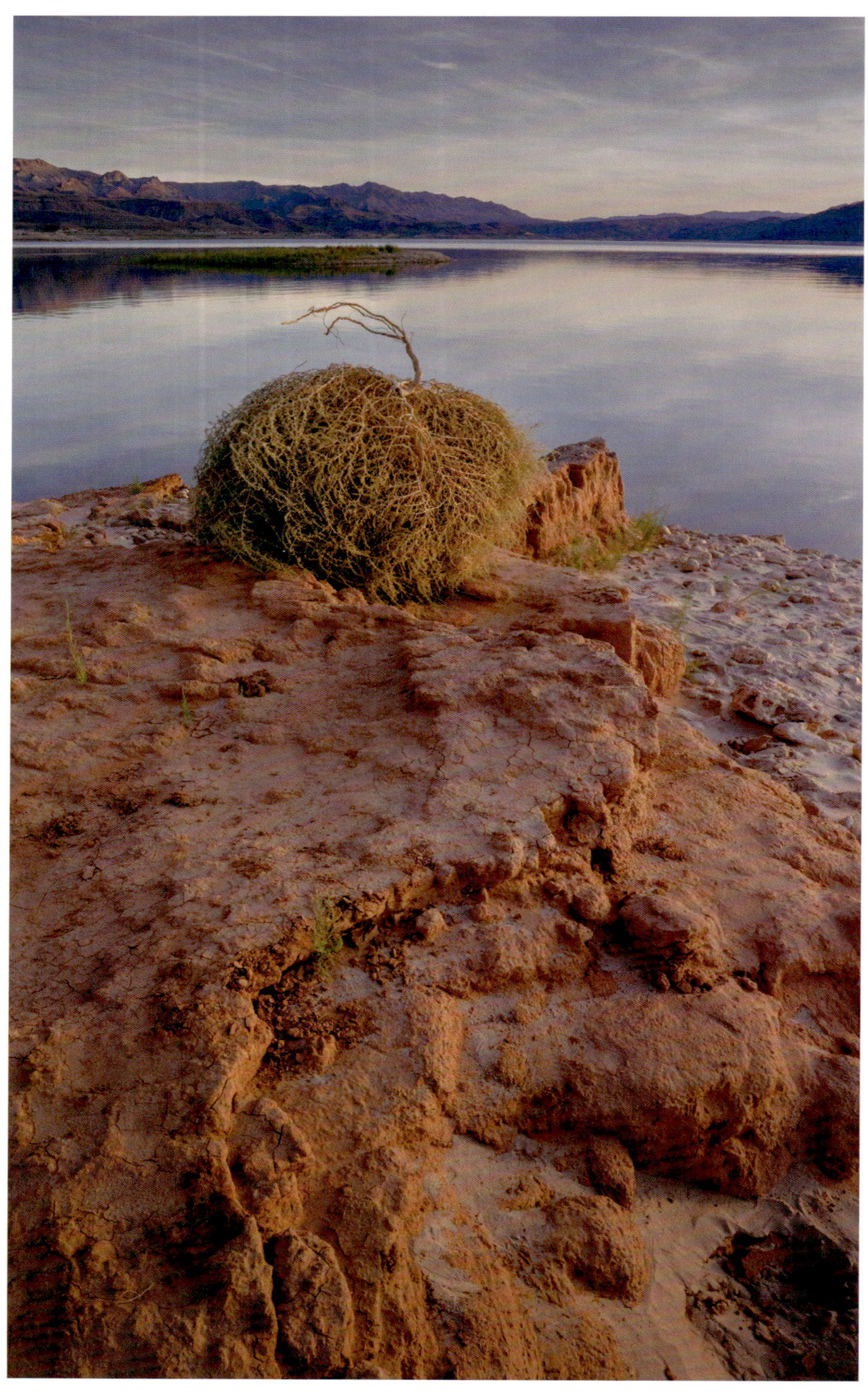

TUMBLEWEEDS ON THE SHORELINE OF
LAKE MEAD NEAR THE SOUTH COVE TAKEOUT.

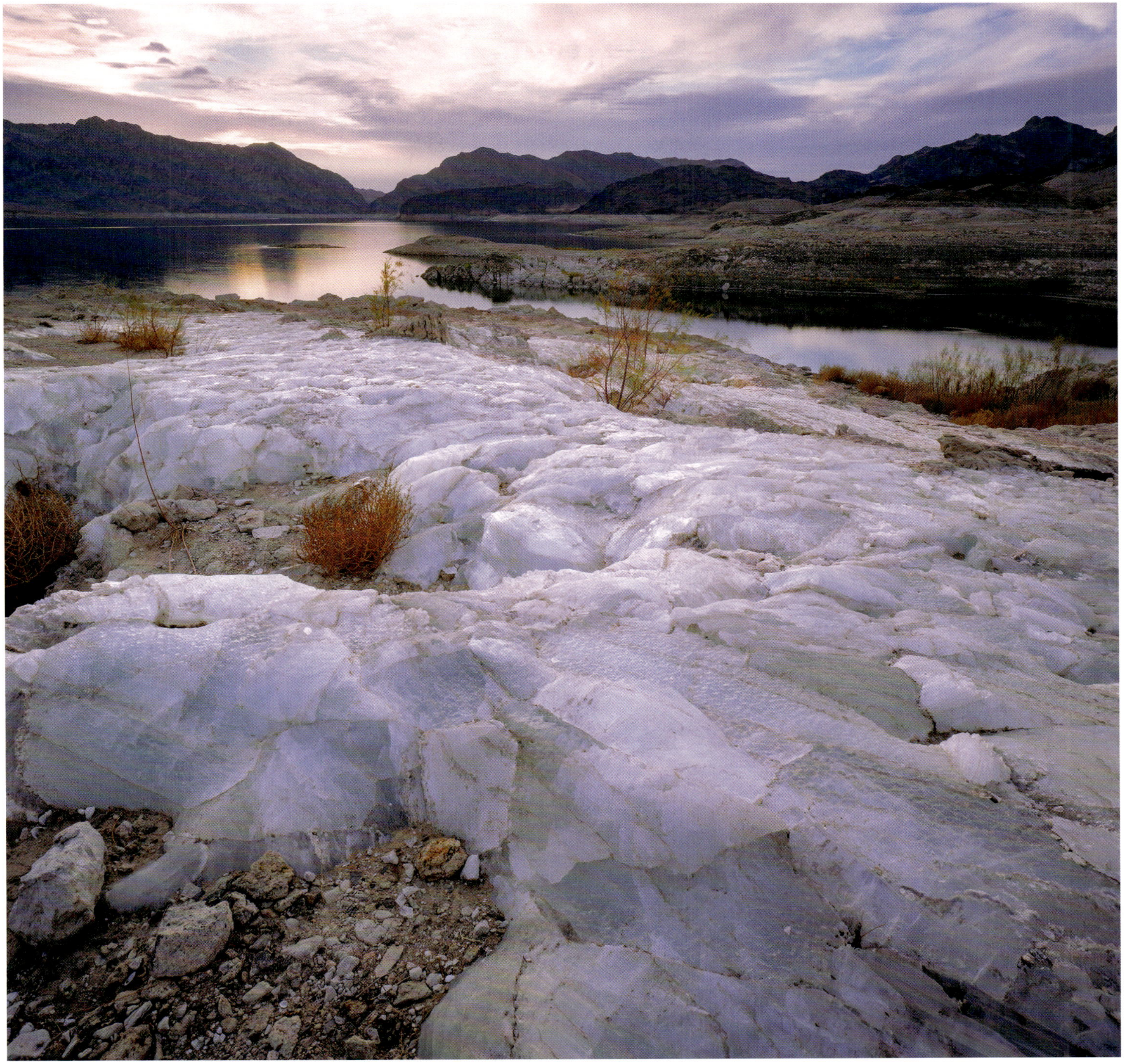

CRYSTALLIZED GYPSUM EXPOSED BY THE RECEDING WATERS OF LAKE MEAD ON THE ARIZONA/NEVADA BORDER.

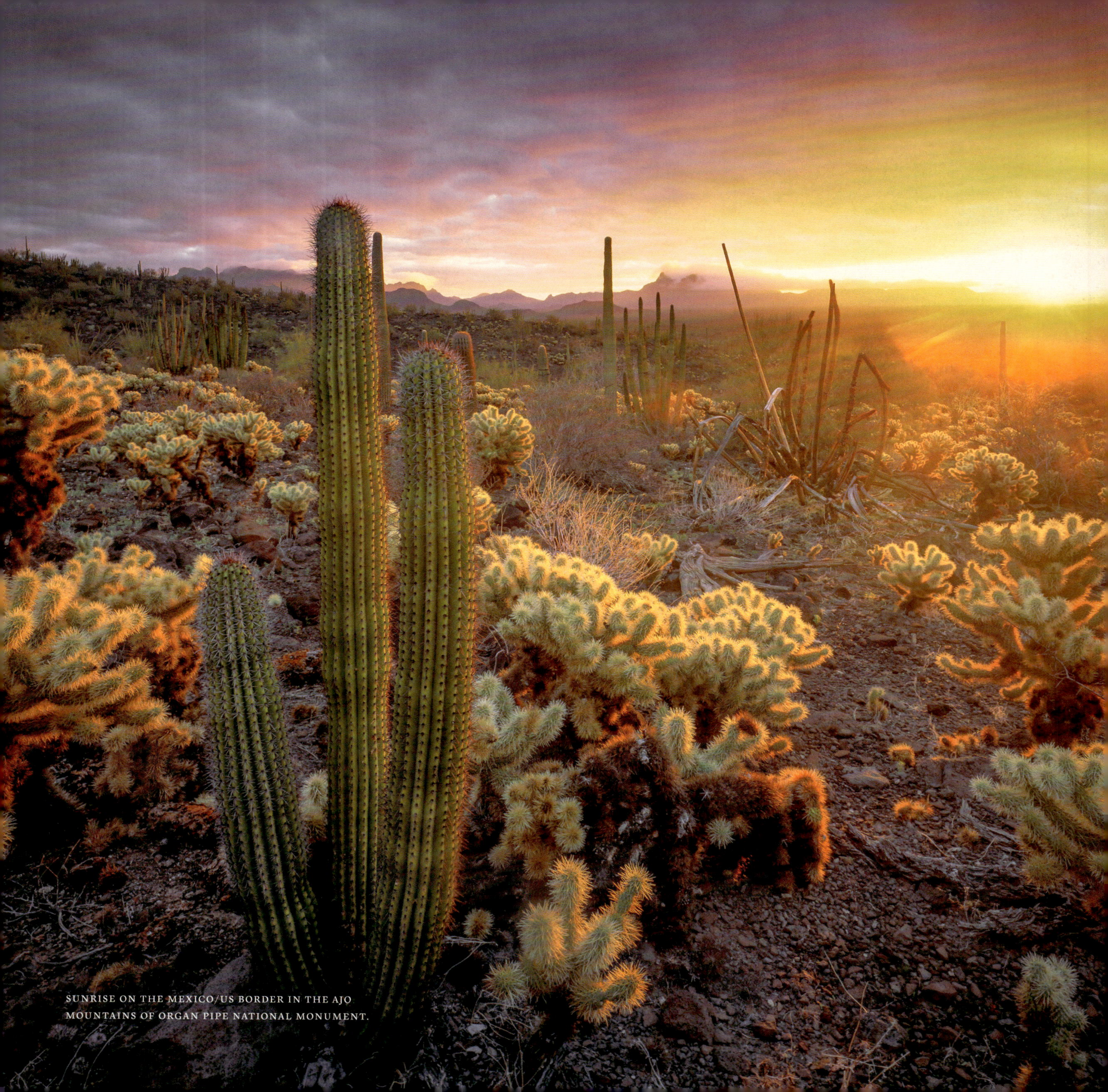


SUNRISE ON THE MEXICO/US BORDER IN THE AJO
MOUNTAINS OF ORGAN PIPE NATIONAL MONUMENT.

SONORAN DESERT

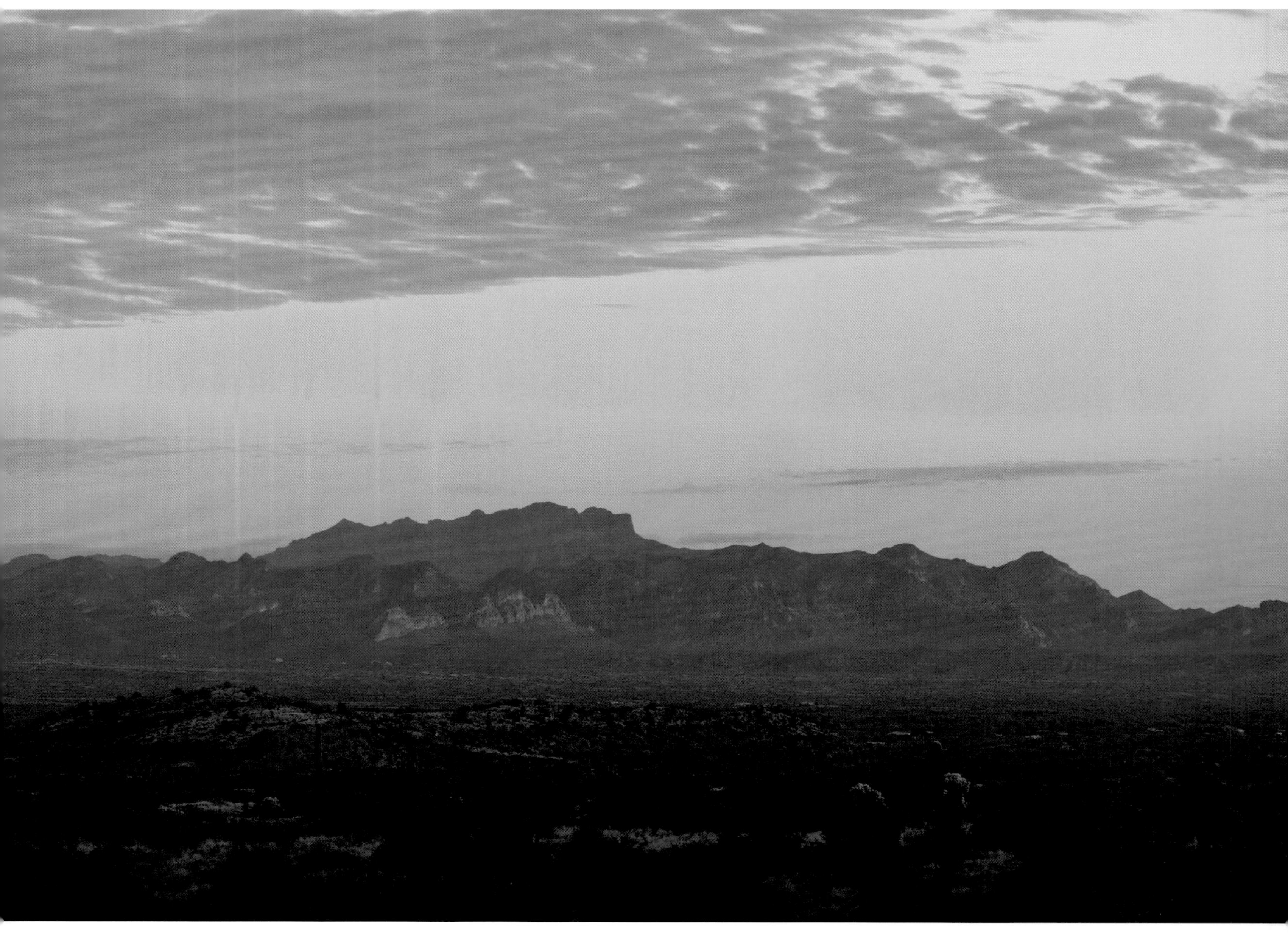

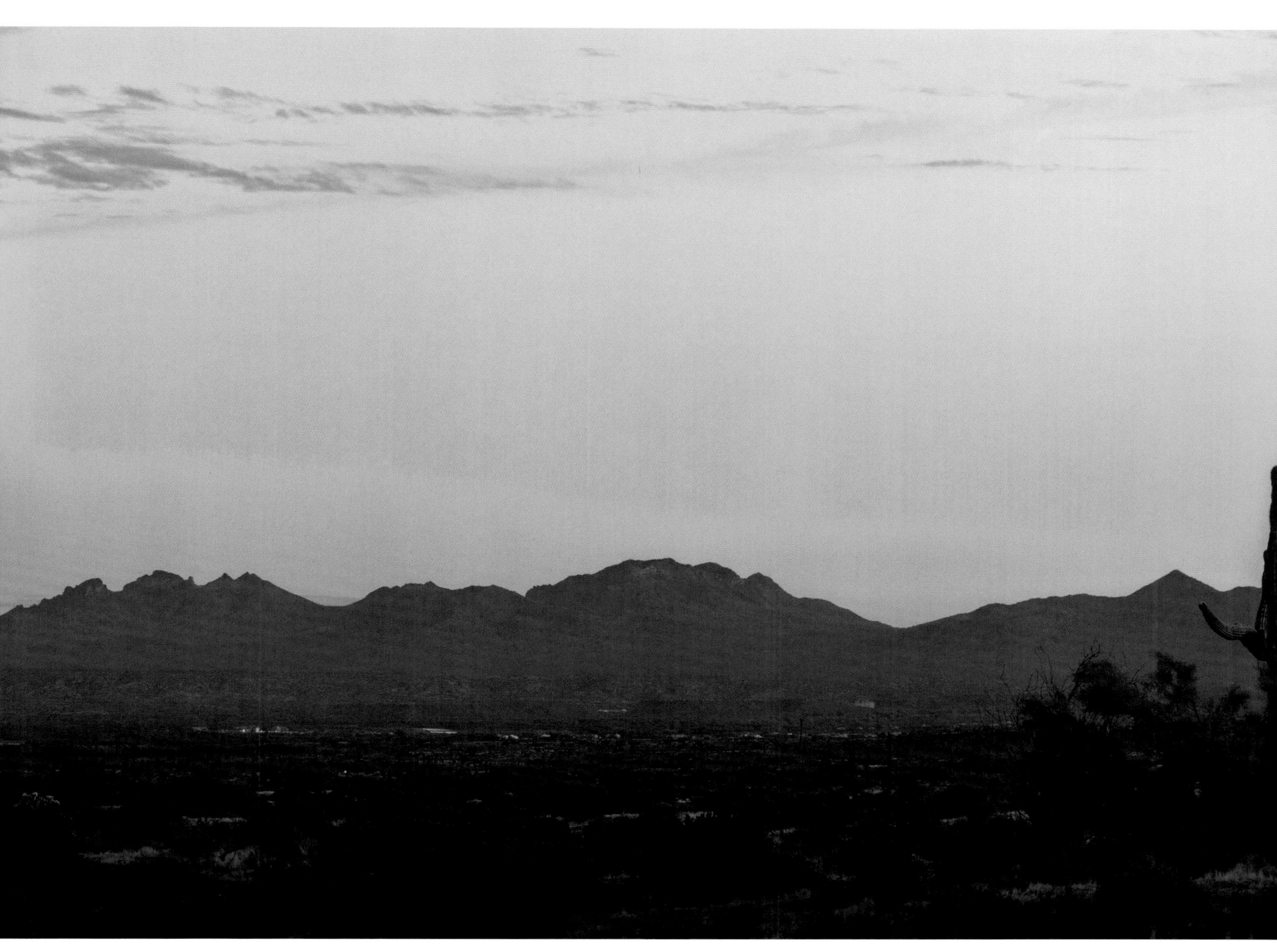

A VIEW OF THE SUPERSTITION MOUNTAINS FROM FOUNTAIN HILLS.

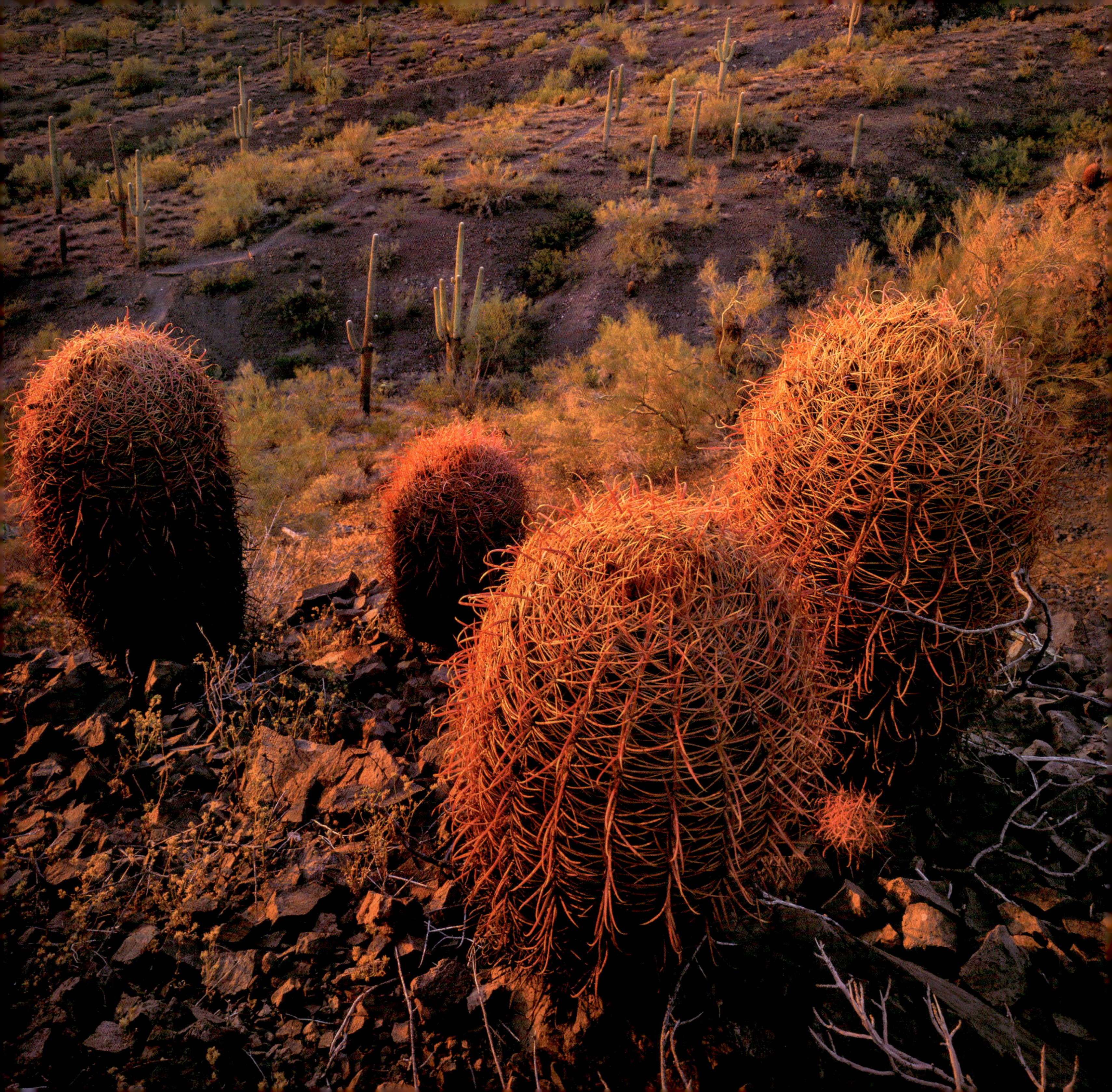

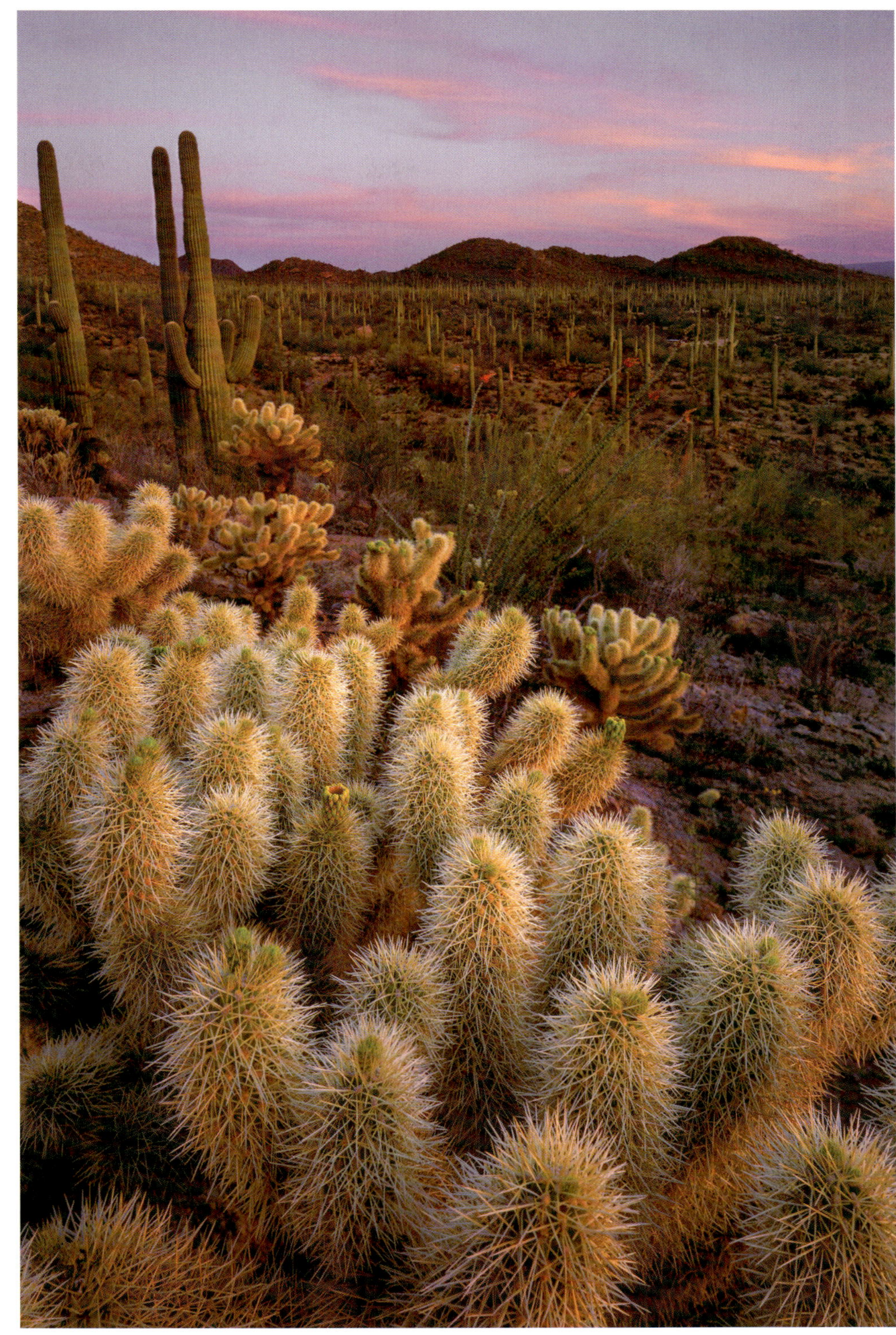



TEDDY BEAR CHOLLA IN THE SIGNAL HILL
AREA OF SAGUARO NATIONAL PARK.

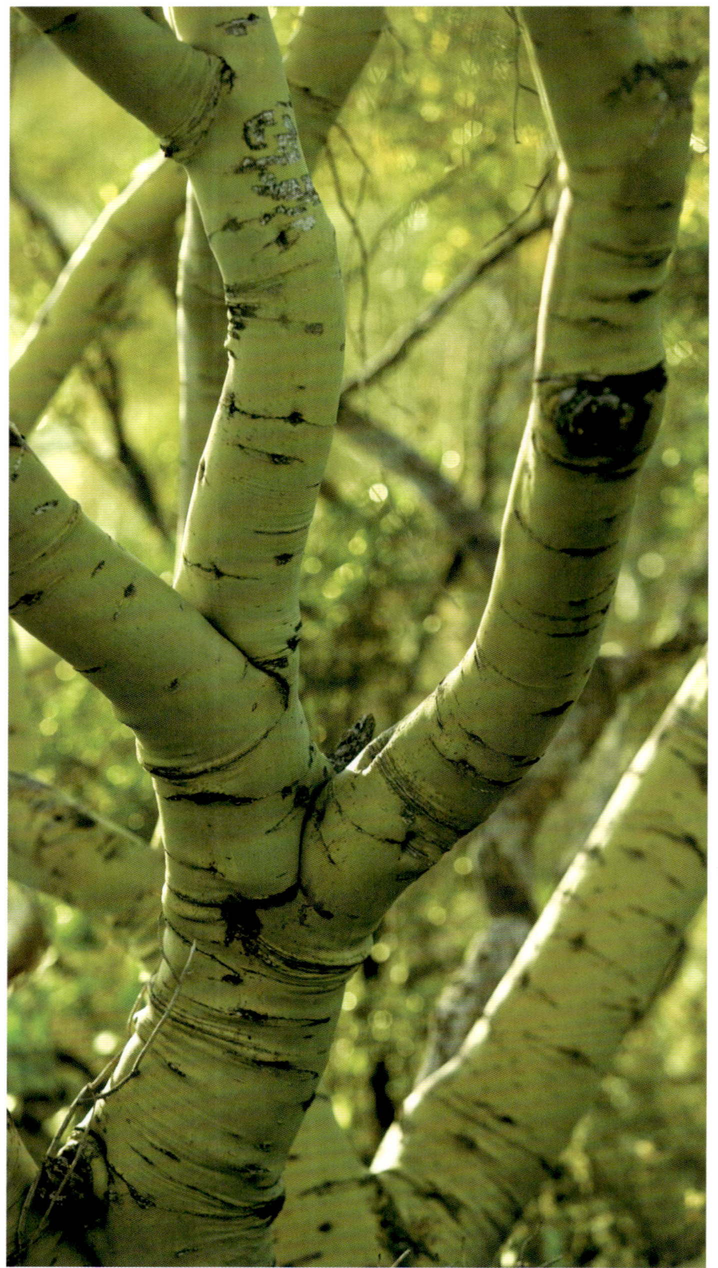



THE TWISTED BRANCHES AND BRILLIANT GREEN BARK OF THE
PALO VERDE MAKES FOR AN INTERESTING GRAPHIC PATTERN.

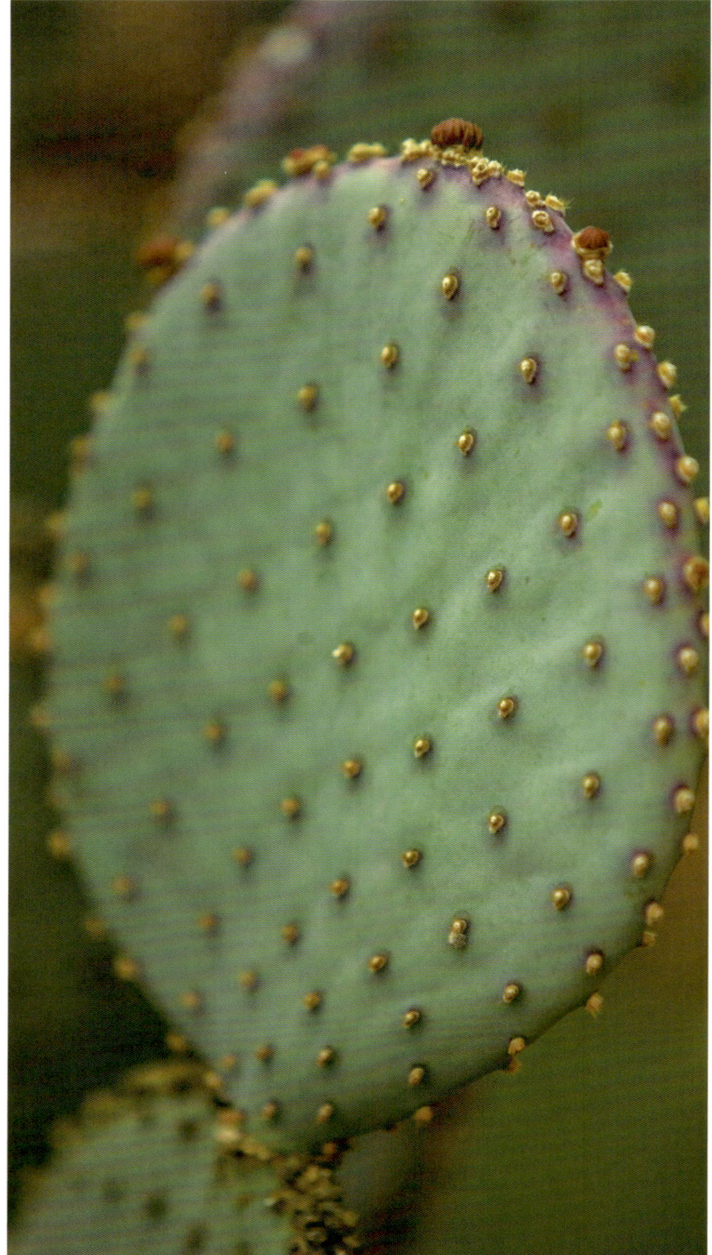

SYSTEMICALLY PLACED NEEDLES GIVE THIS
CACTUS A WELL-DESIGNED GRAPHIC PATTERN.

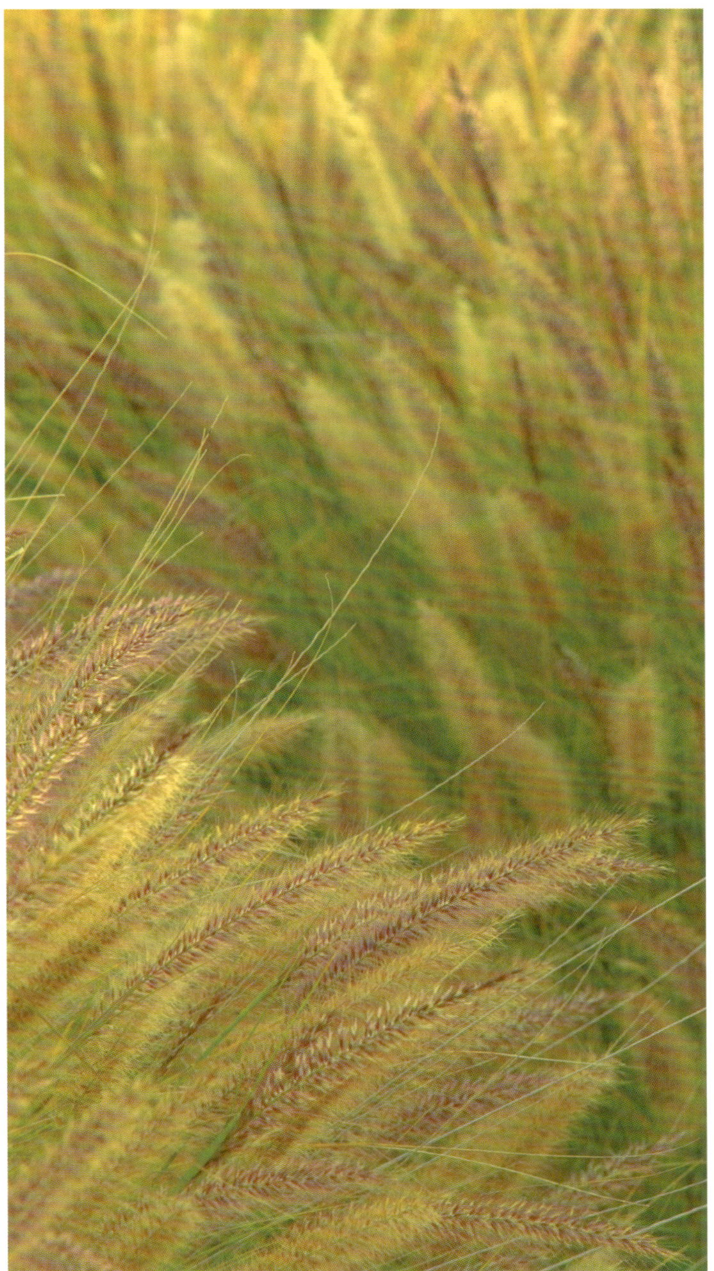

BEARDED GRASSES AND BRITTLEBUSH FILL
A WASH IN THE SUPERSTITION WILDERNESS.

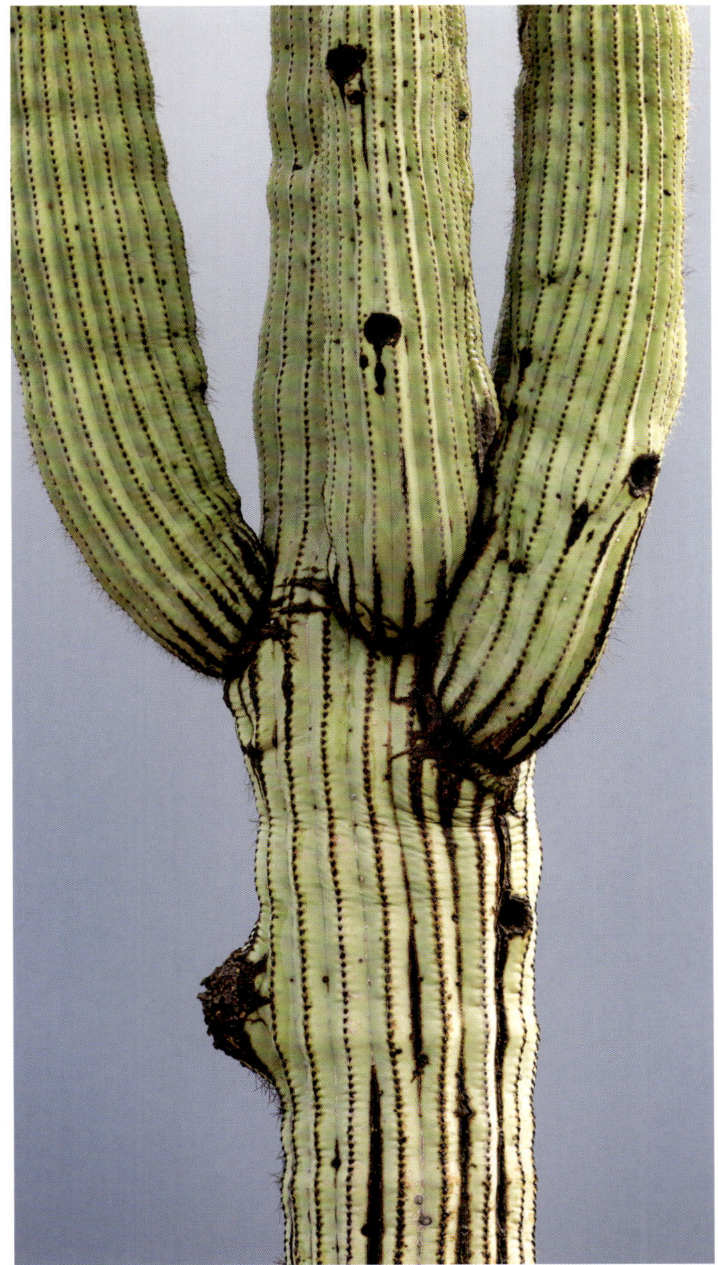

A COLD WINTER DAY PRODUCES COOL DESERT TONES ON A
SAGUARO IN McDOWELL MOUNTAIN REGIONAL PARK.

151

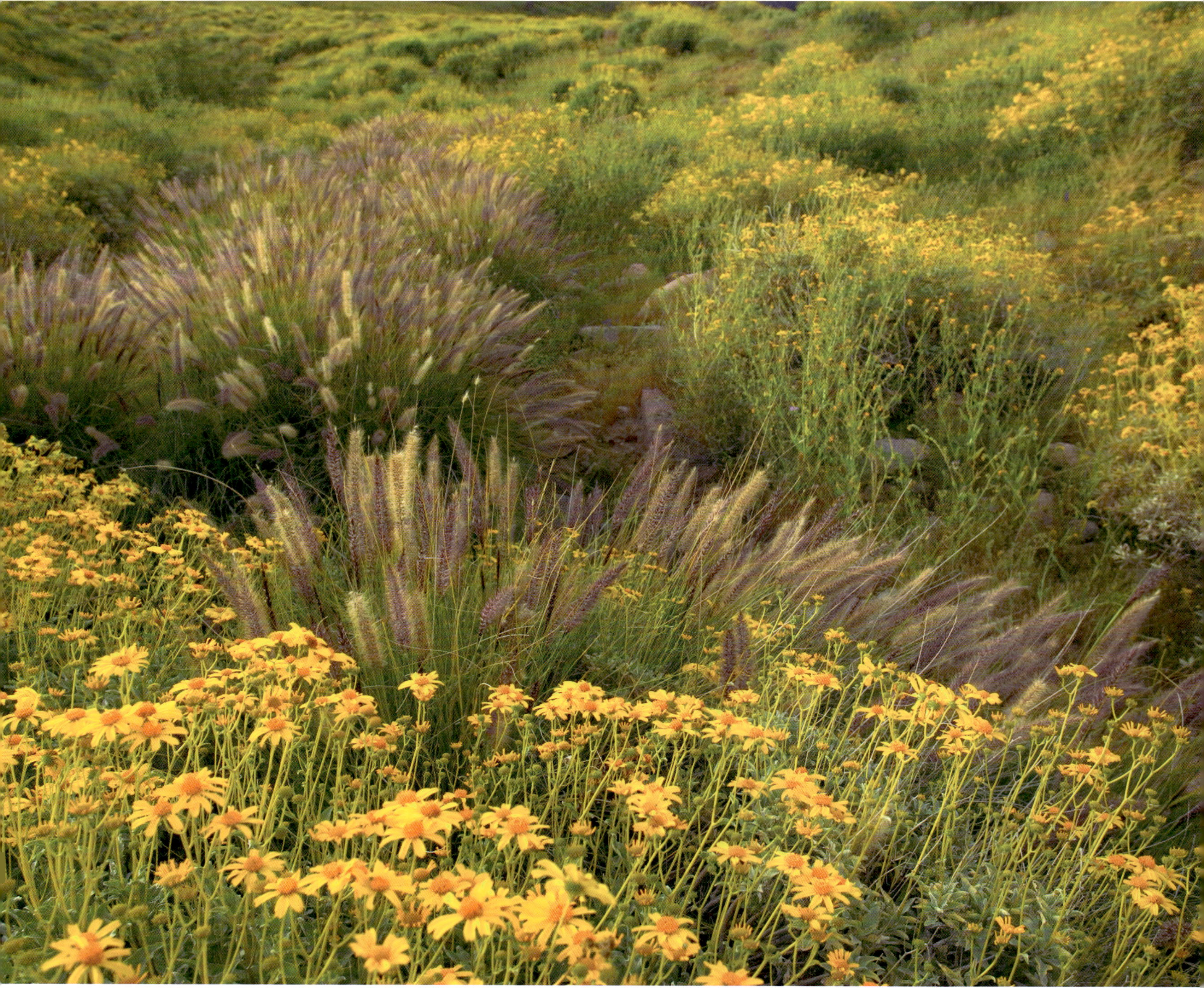



BRITTLEBUSH BLOOMS IN EARLY SPRING IN THE FOOTHILLS OF THE SUPERSTITION MOUNTAINS.

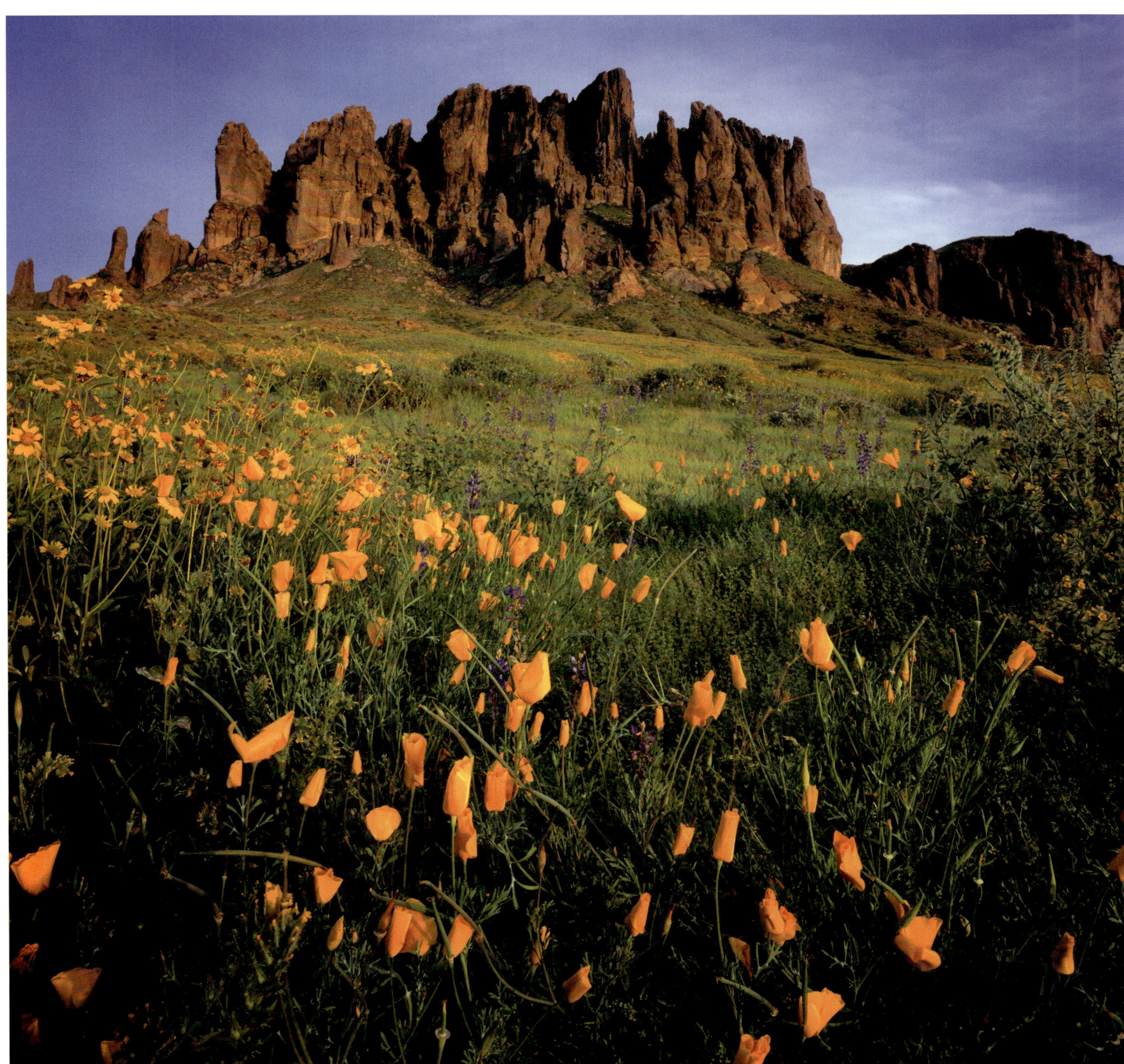

BRITTLEBUSH, LUPINE, AND POPPIES BLANKET THE BASE OF ARIZONA'S SUPERSTITION MOUNTAINS WITH AN ARRAY OF COLOR.

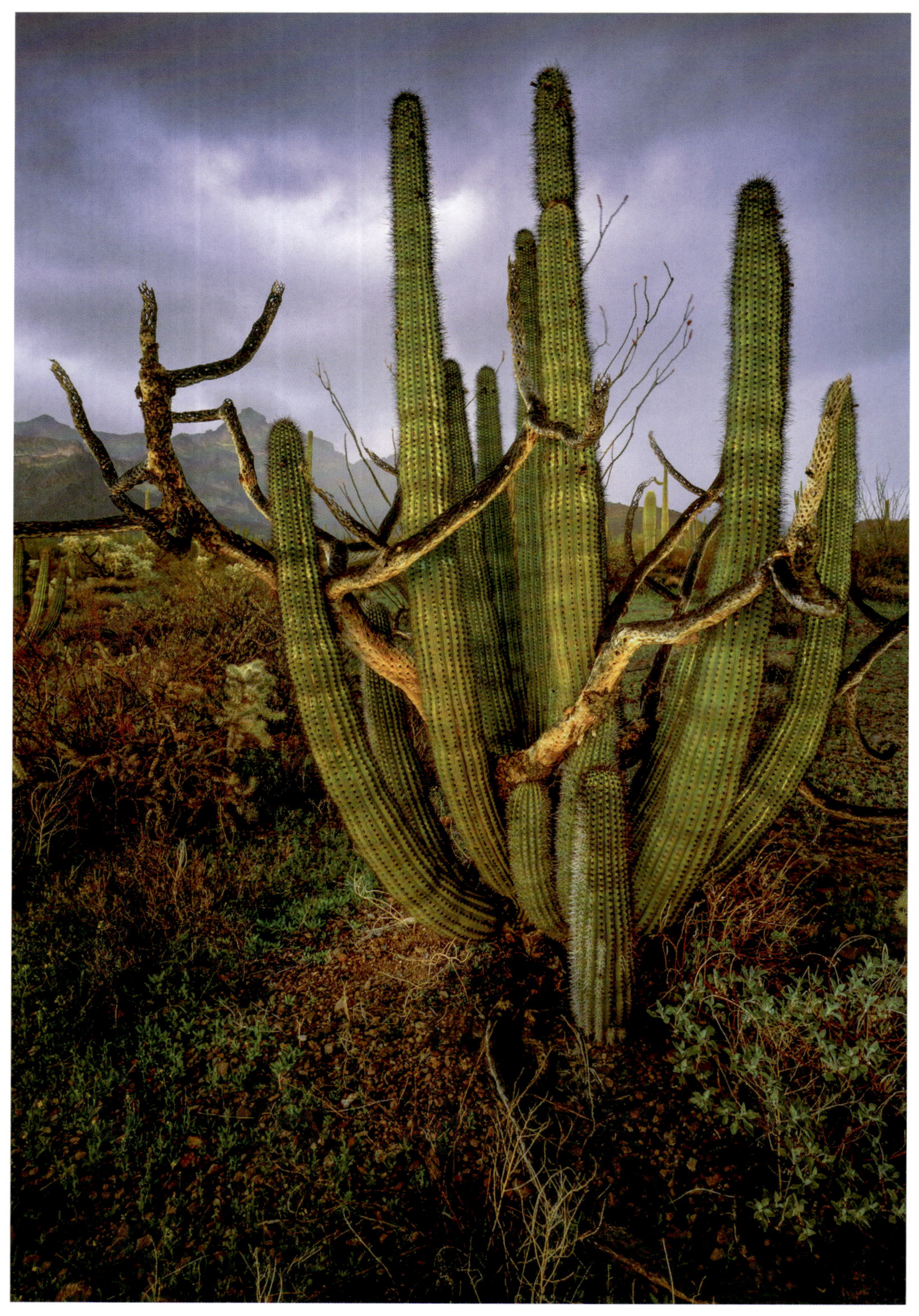

THIS ORGAN PIPE CACTUS USES
A CHOLLA SKELETON FOR SUPPORT
IN THE HARSH CLIMATE OF THE
SONORAN DESERT.

RAINS IN THE AJO MOUNTAIN RANGE
NEAR THE MEXICAN BORDER.

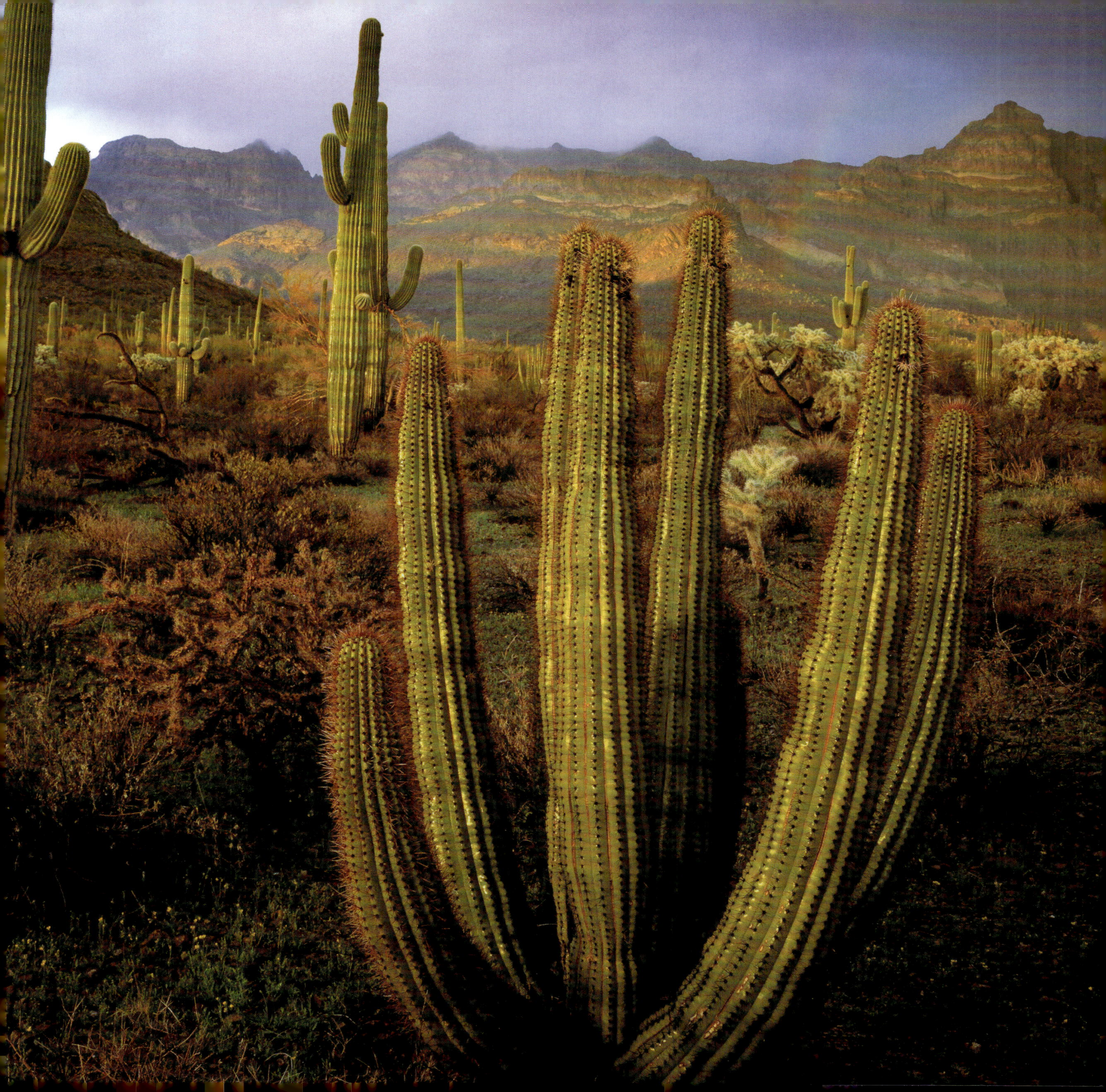

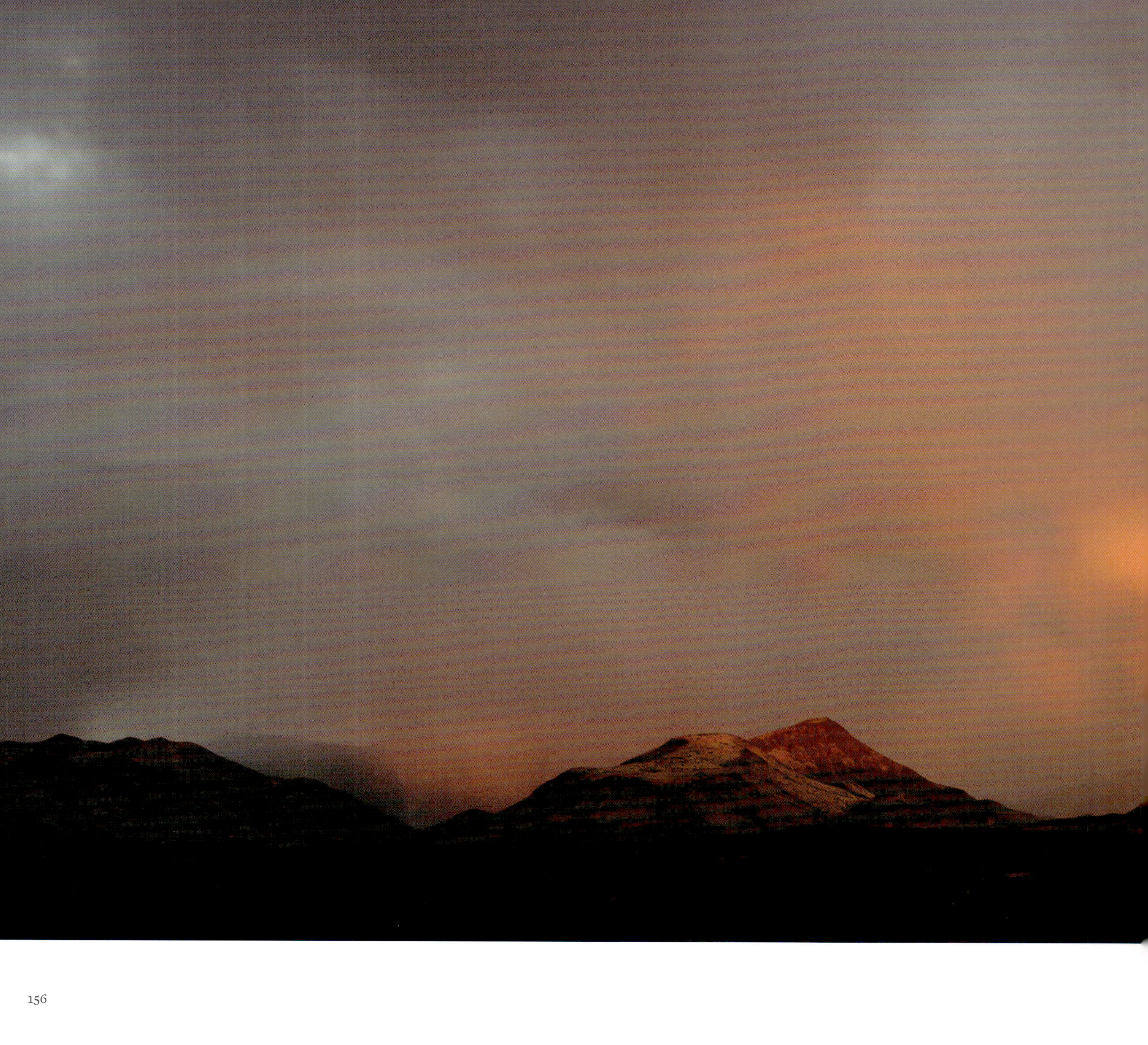

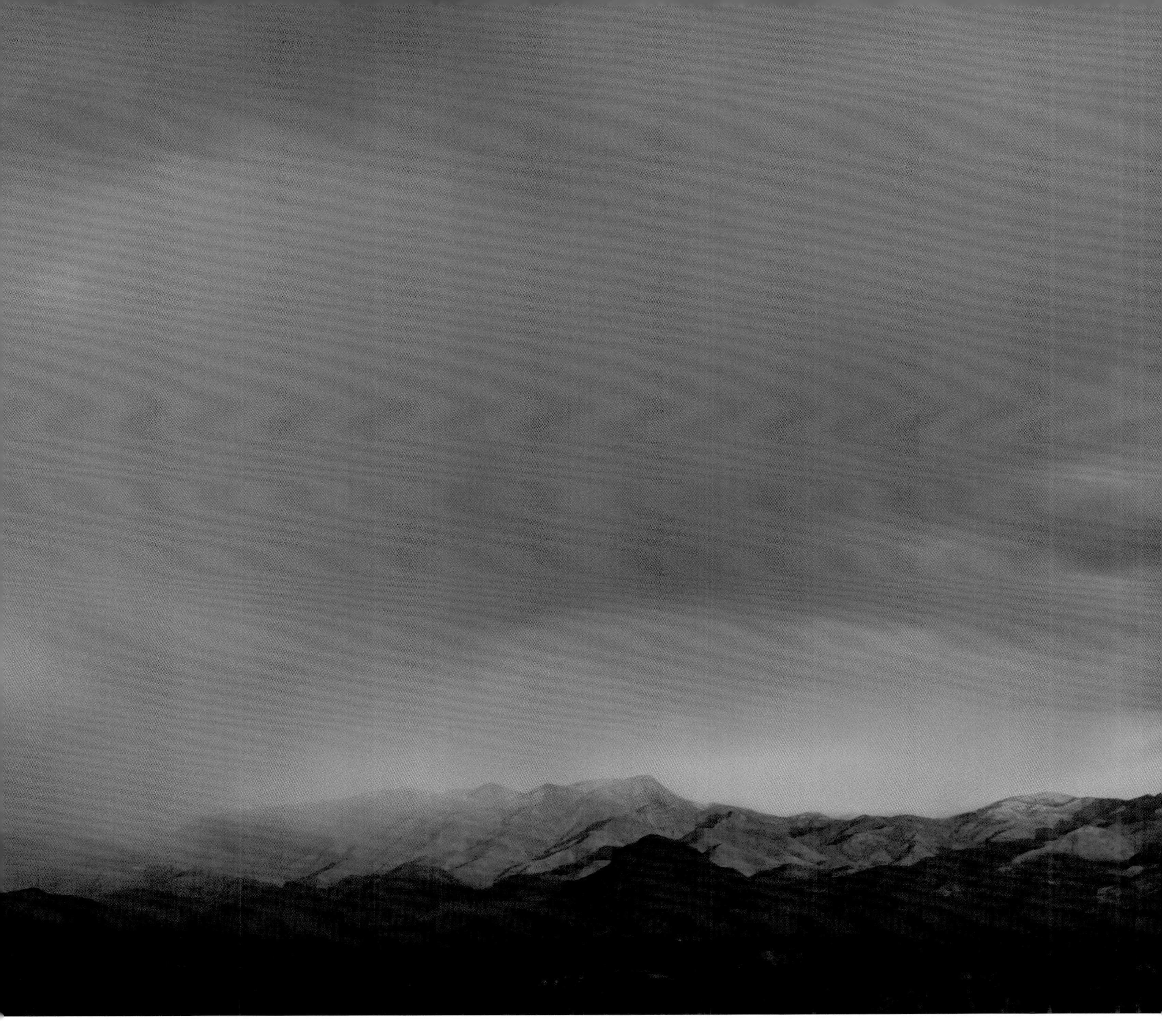

BEAUTIFUL LIGHT IN THE MAZATZAL RANGE NEAR DAVENPORT WASH.

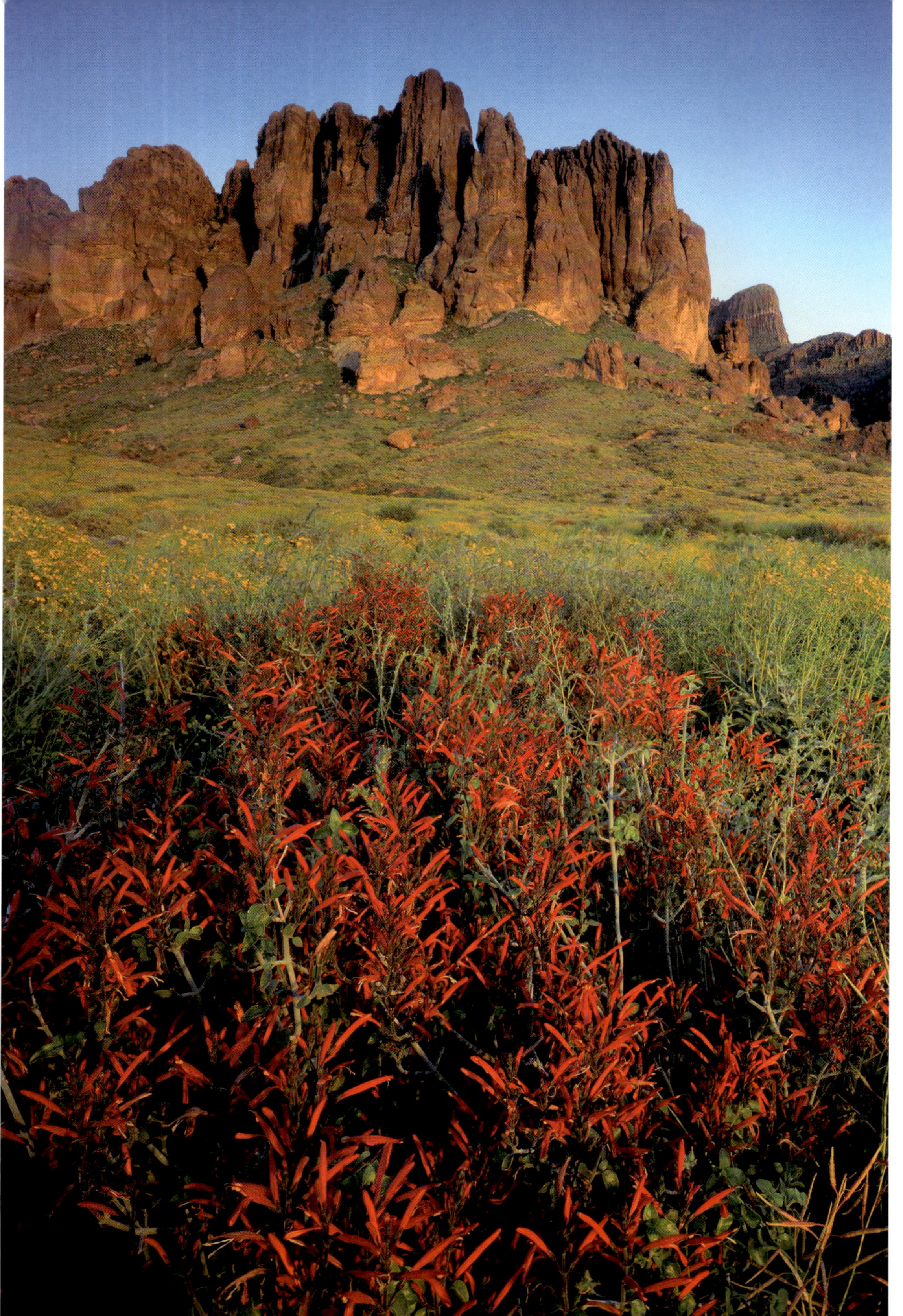

CRIMSON WOOLLY-POD
THRIVES AT THE BASE OF THE
SUPERSTITION MOUNTAINS.

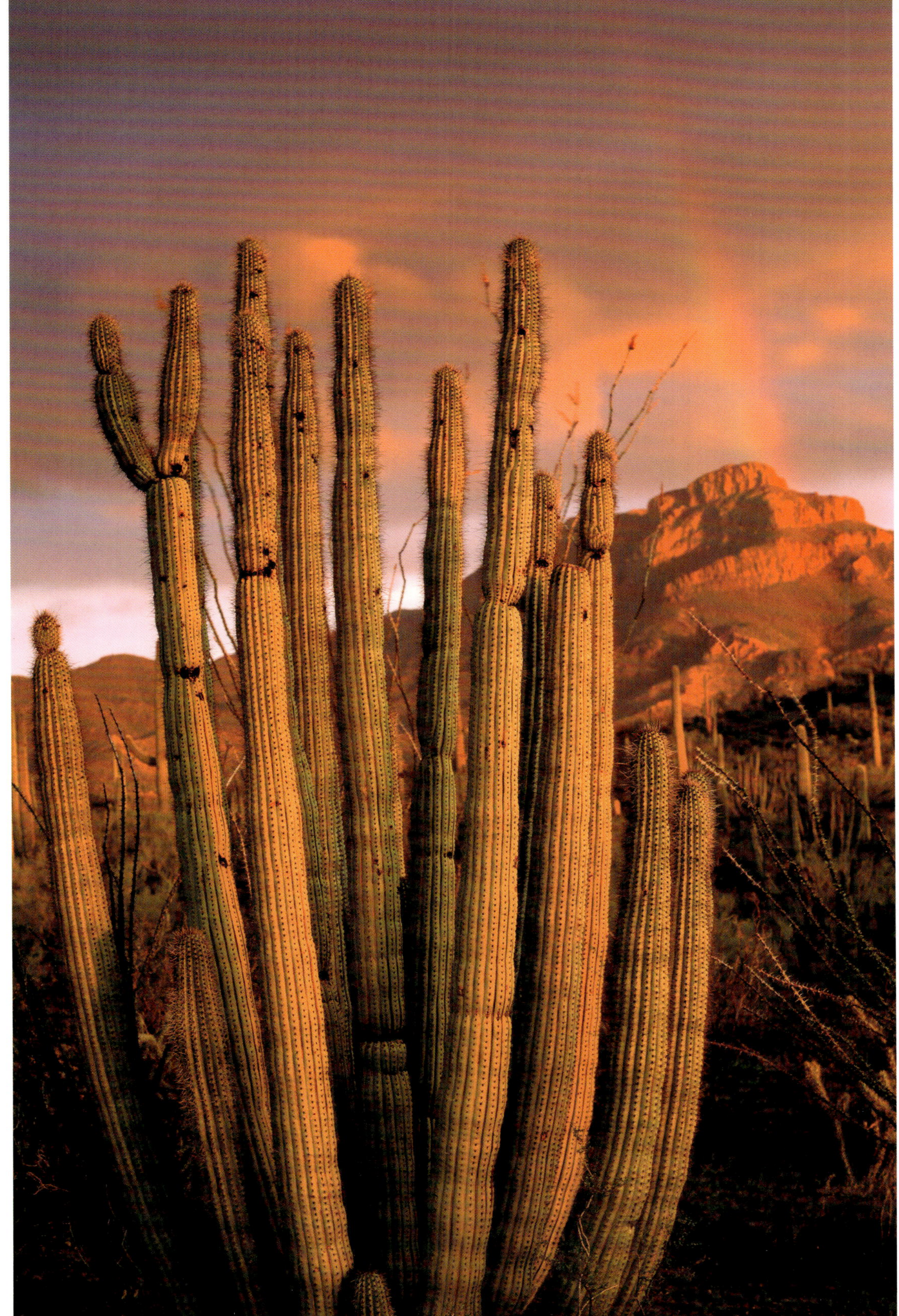

RAINBOW OVER MOUNT
AJO IN ORGAN PIPE
NATIONAL MONUMENT.

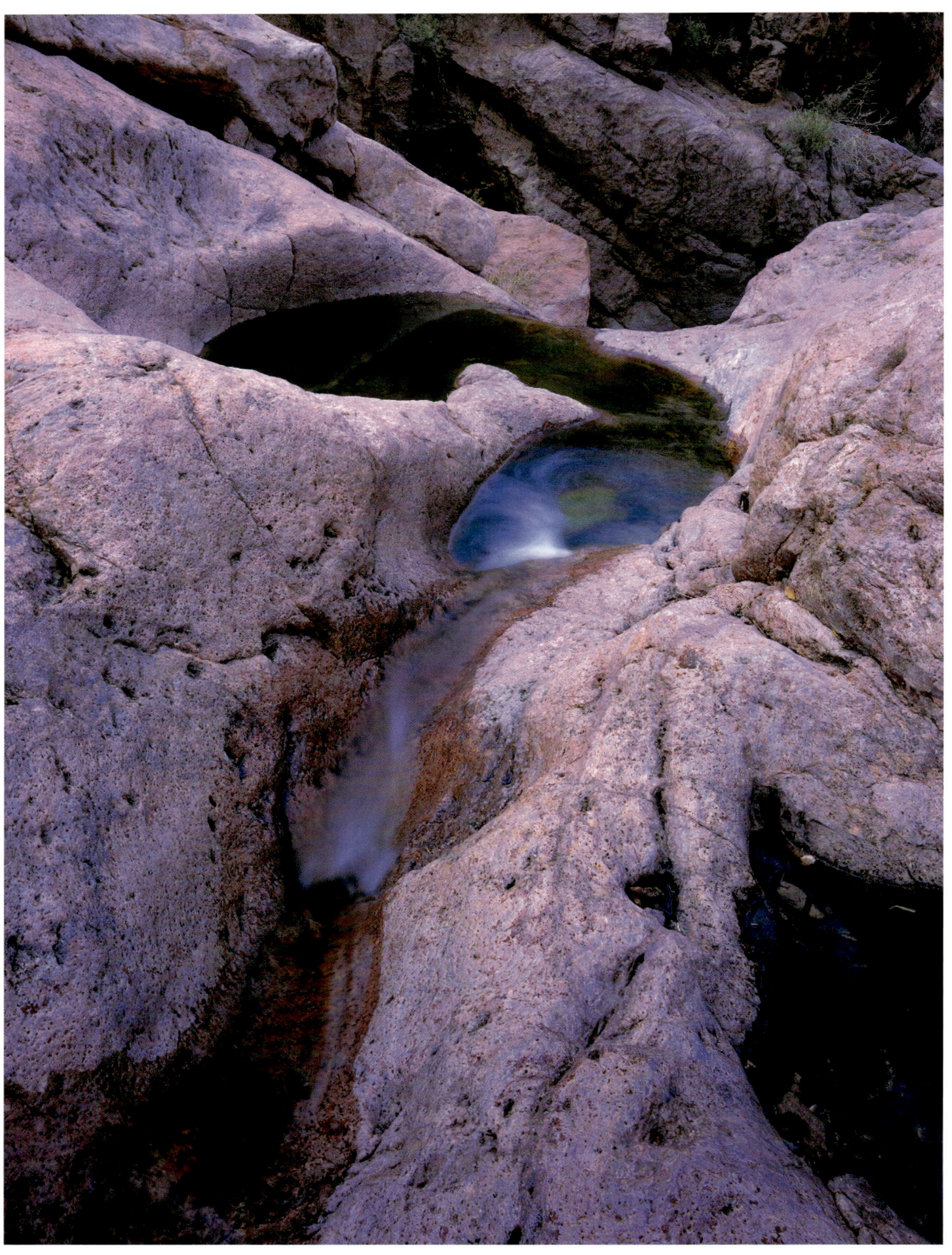

ALAMO CREEK CARVES A UNIQUE
DESIGN THROUGH SOLID
GRANITE ROCK IN ORGAN PIPE
NATIONAL MONUMENT.

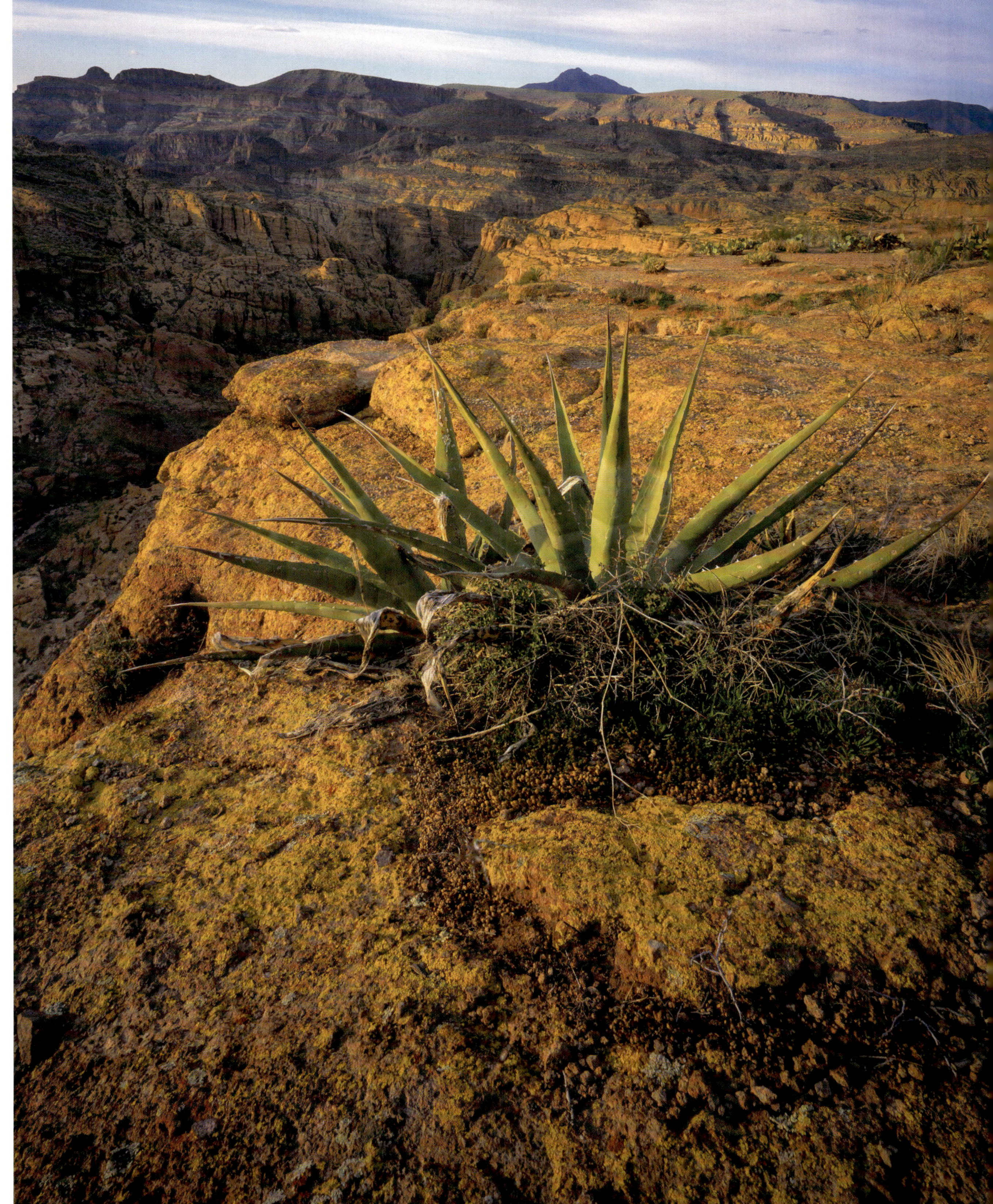

A CENTURY
PLANT SITS HIGH,
OVERLOOKING FISH
CREEK ON THE
APACHE TRAIL.

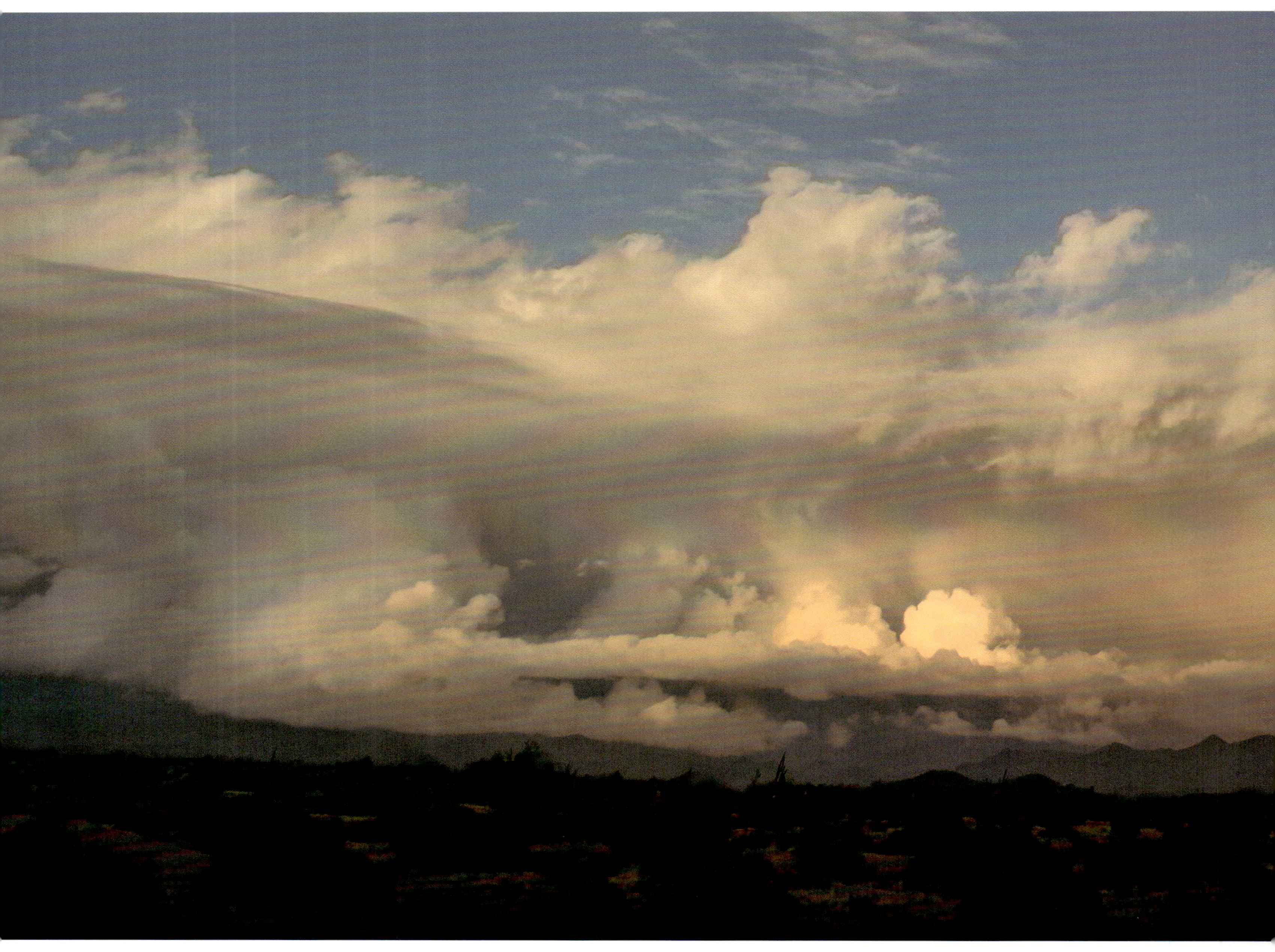

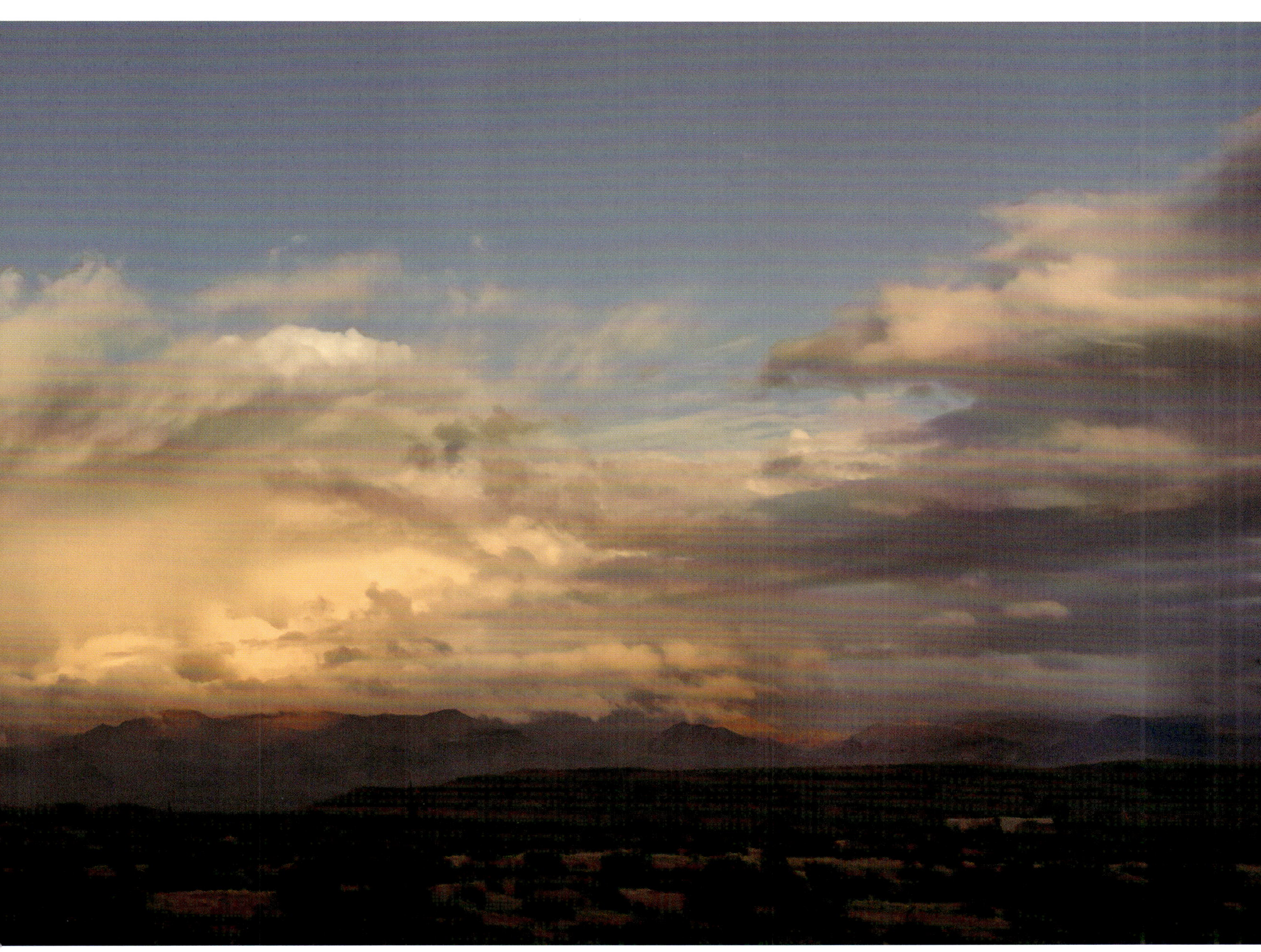

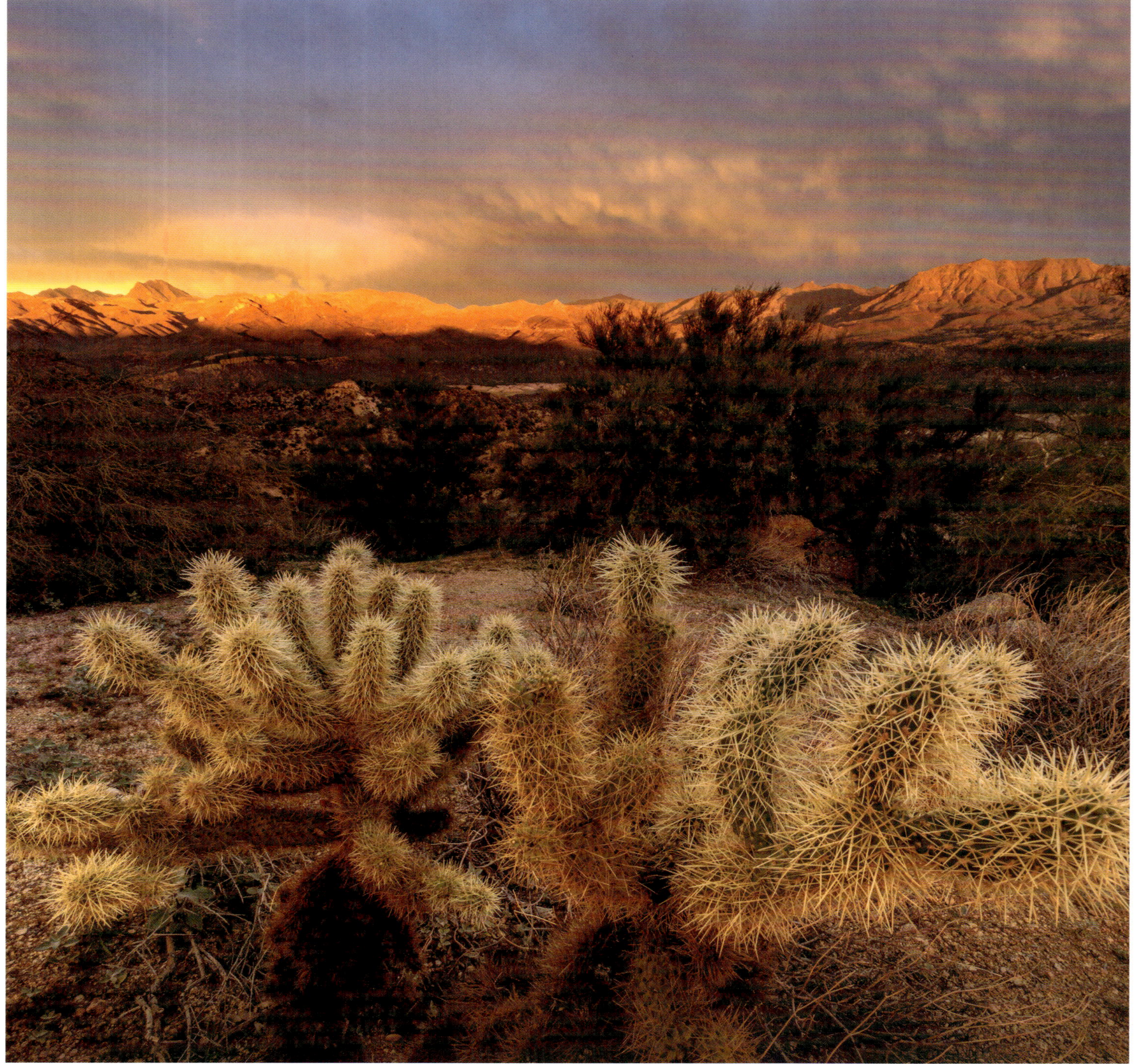



WONDERFUL STORM CLOUDS FORM OVER THE MAZATZAL WILDERNESS IN THE TONTO AND COCONINO NATIONAL FORESTS.

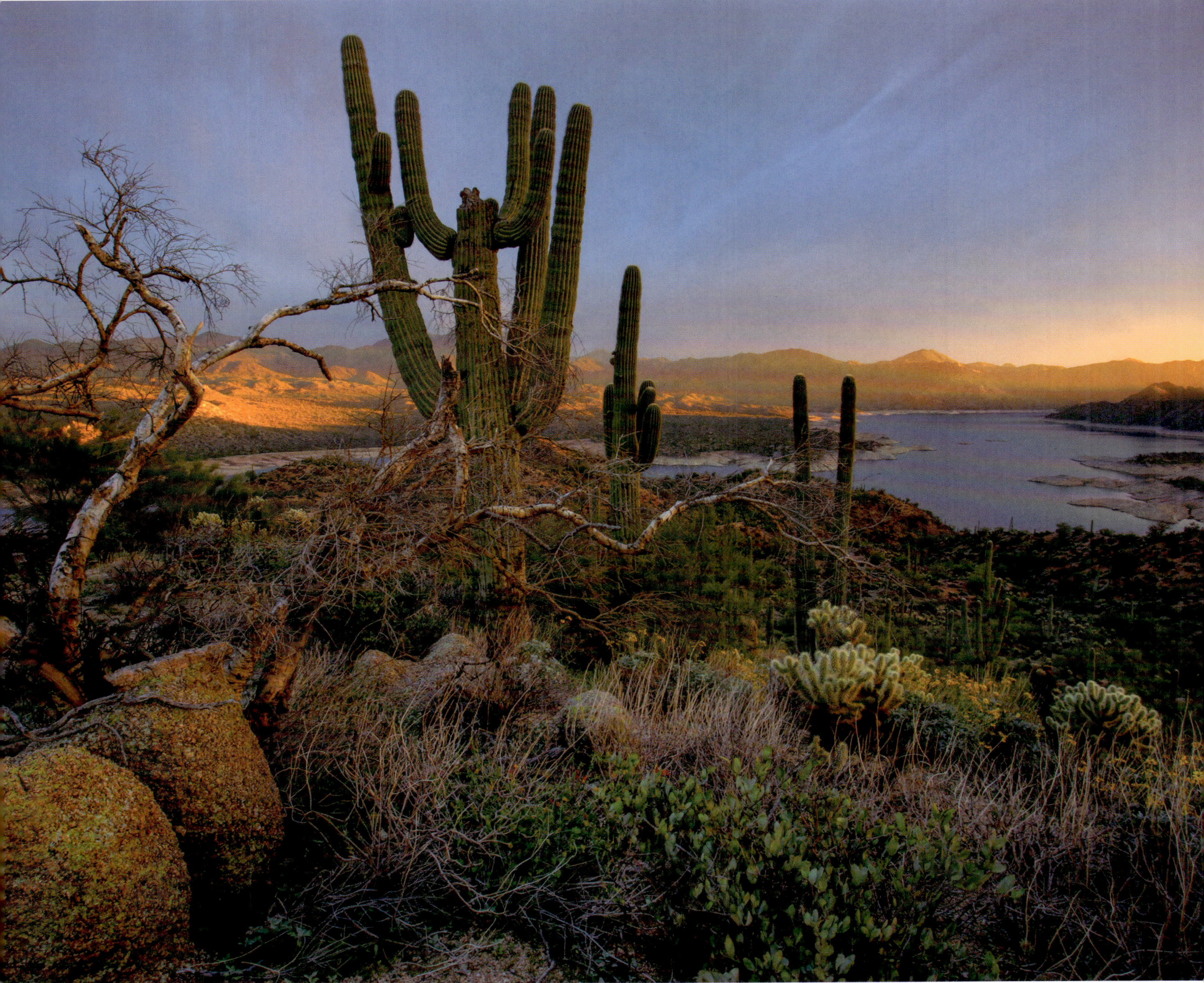

SUNSET SLIPS UNDER A STORMY SKY AT BARTLETT LAKE, A BEAUTIFUL LAKE IN THE VERDE RIVER VALLEY.

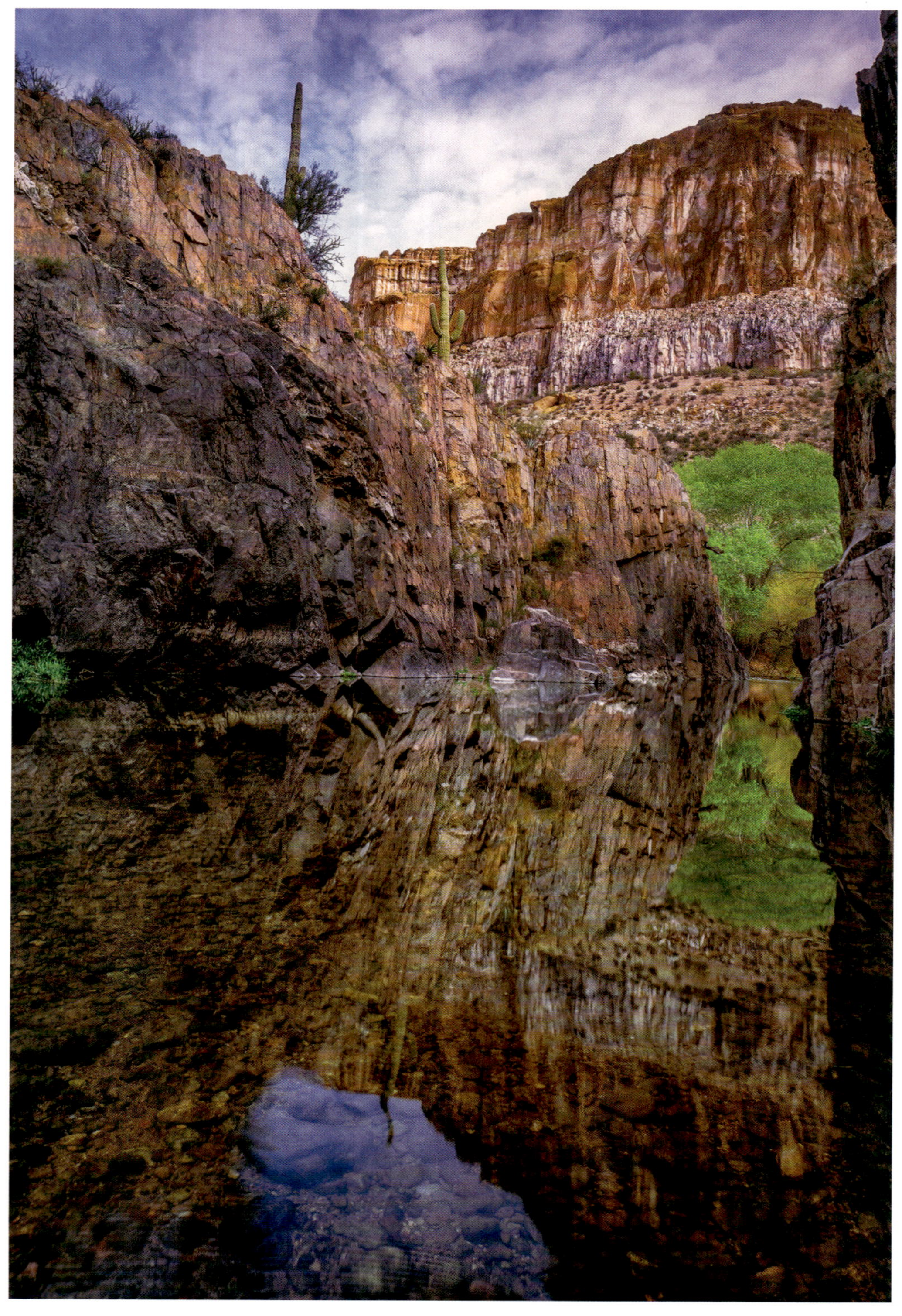

ARAVAIPA CREEK RUNS YEAR-ROUND
THROUGH A LUSH DESERT ECOSYSTEM.

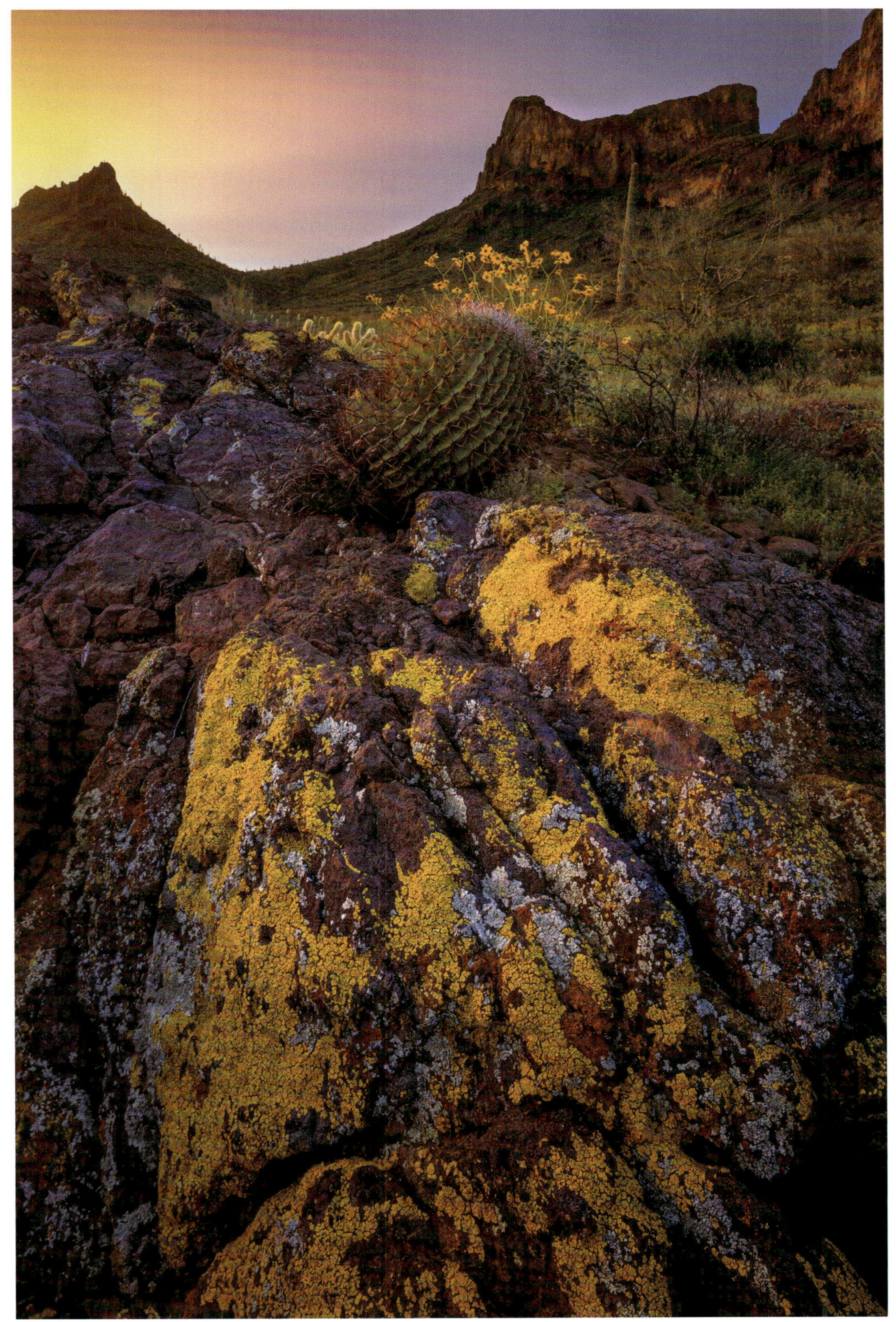

VIBRANT GREEN AND YELLOW LICHEN
GLOWS IN THE SUNRISE ON PICACHO PEAK
IN THE SONORAN DESERT.

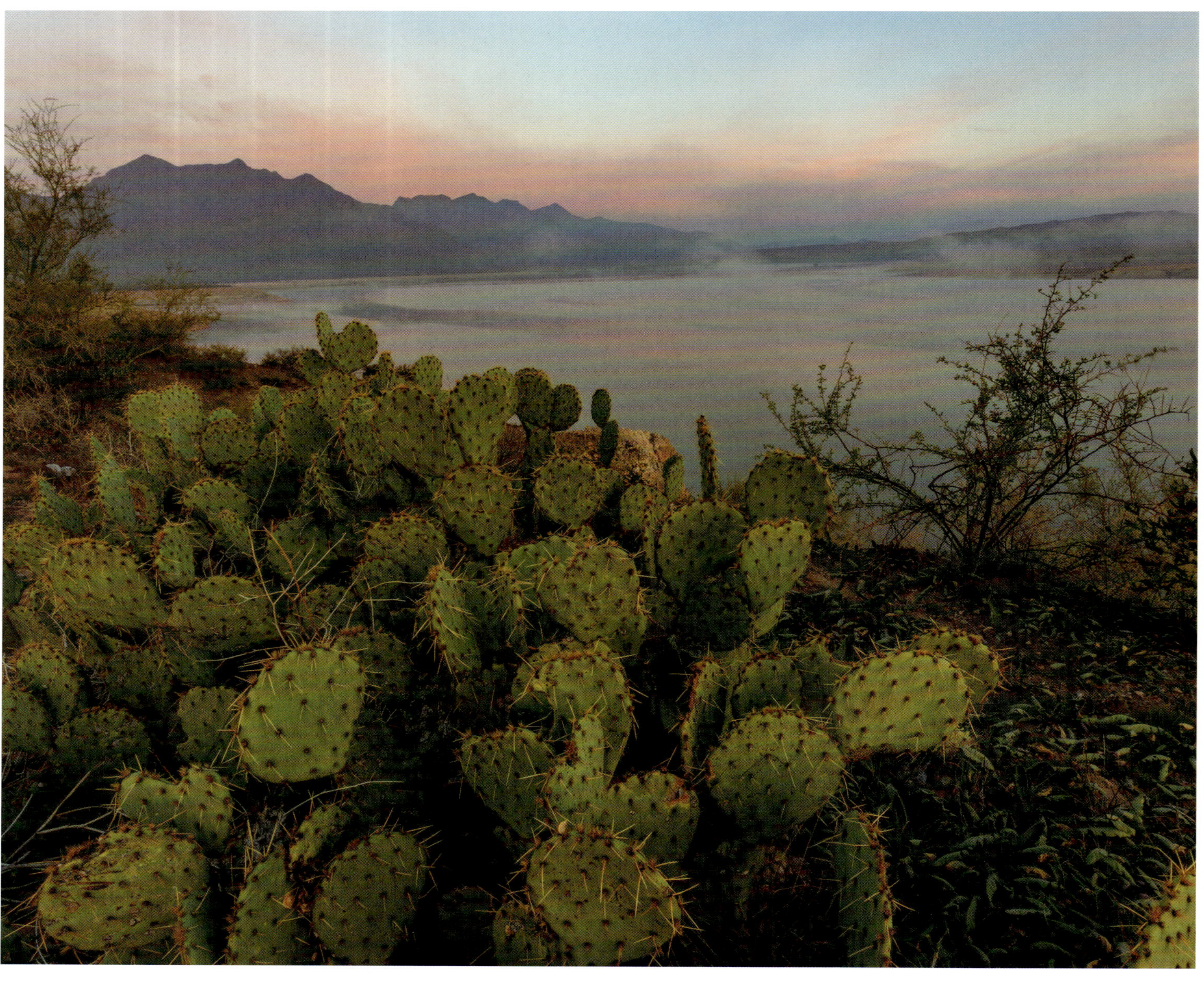



THE VERDE RIVER FILLS HORSESHOE RESERVOIR IN TONTO NATIONAL FOREST.

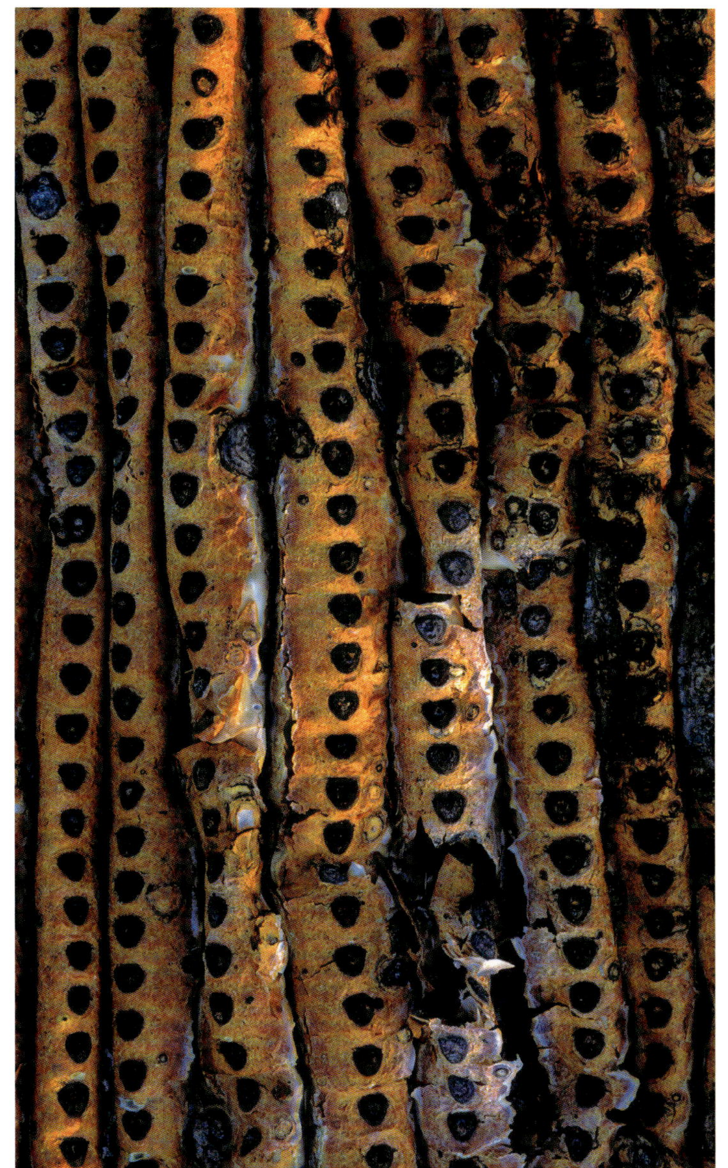

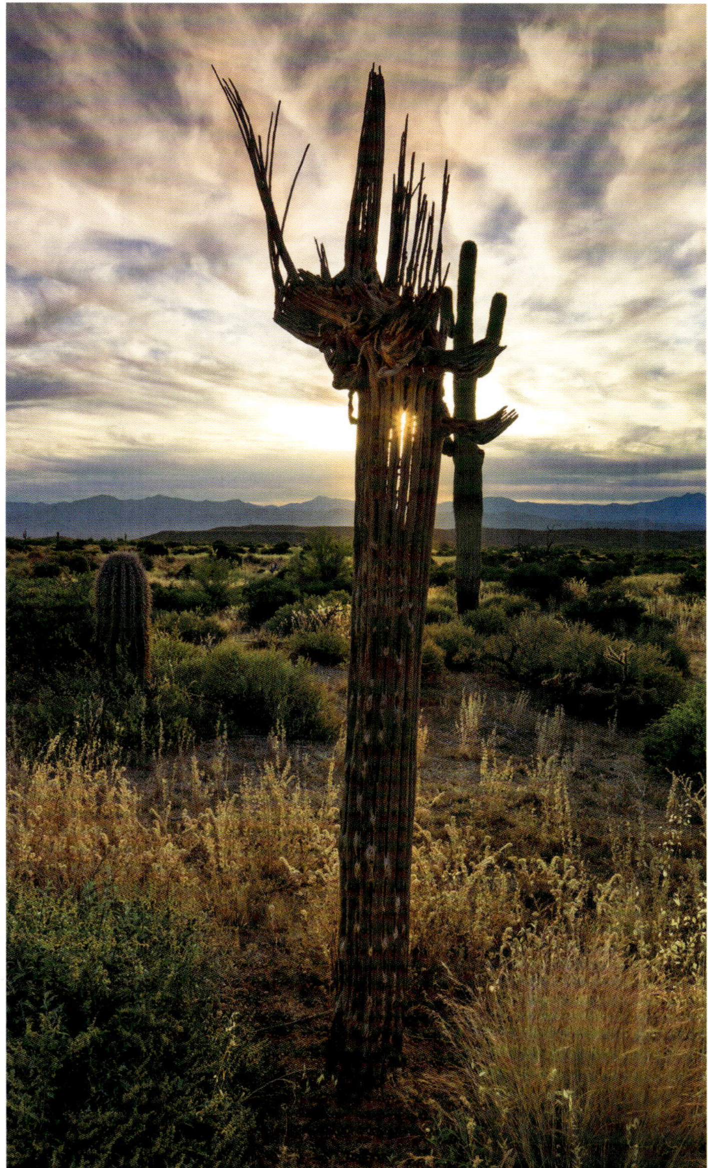

GRAPHIC PATTERNS ON A DYING SAGUARO CACTUS
IN SAGUARO NATIONAL PARK IN TUCSON, ARIZONA.

SKELETON OF SAGUARO CACTUS,
McDOWELL MOUNTAIN REGIONAL PARK.

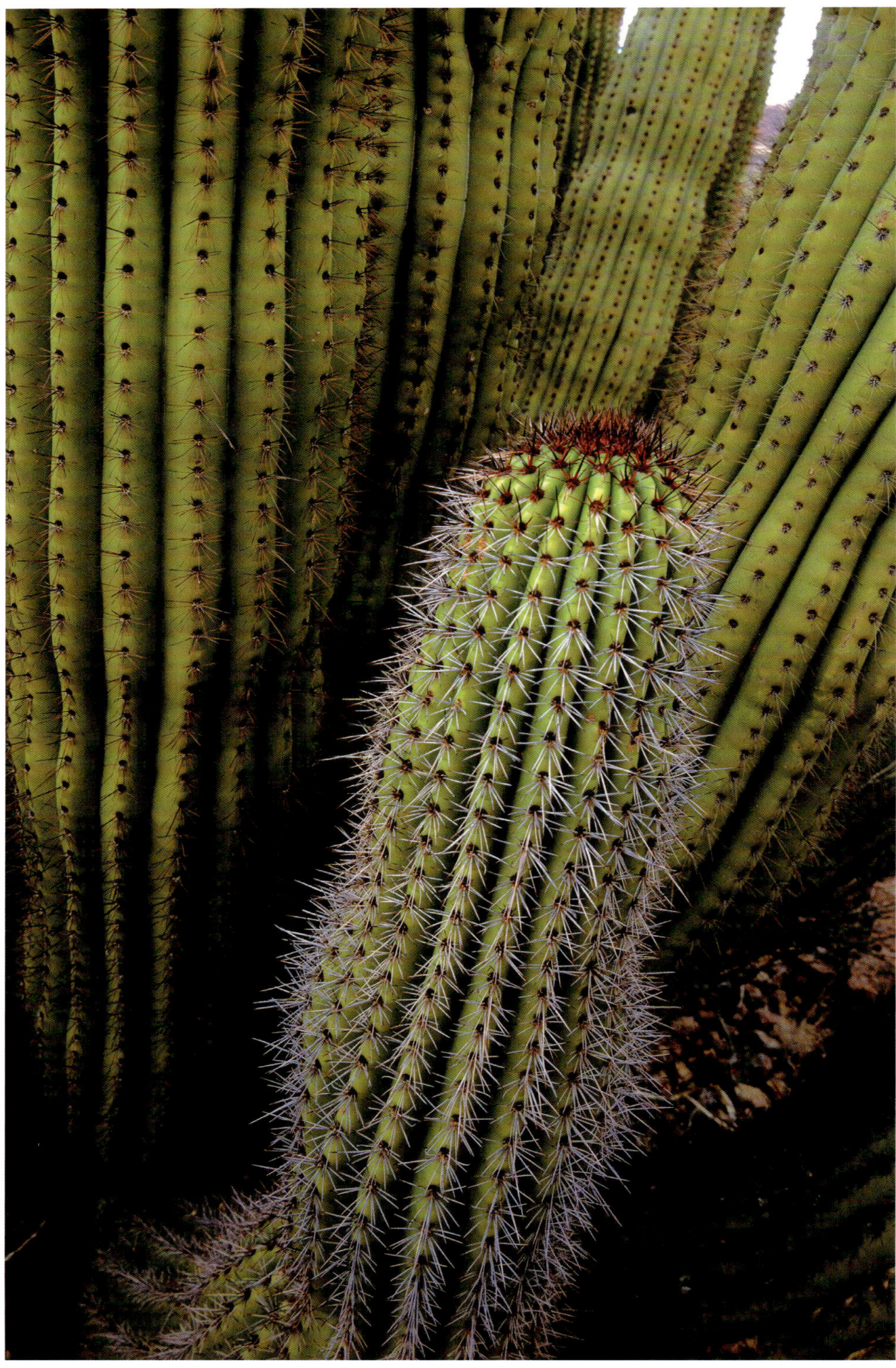

DETAIL OF THE SPINE PATTERN
ON AN ORGAN PIPE CACTUS.

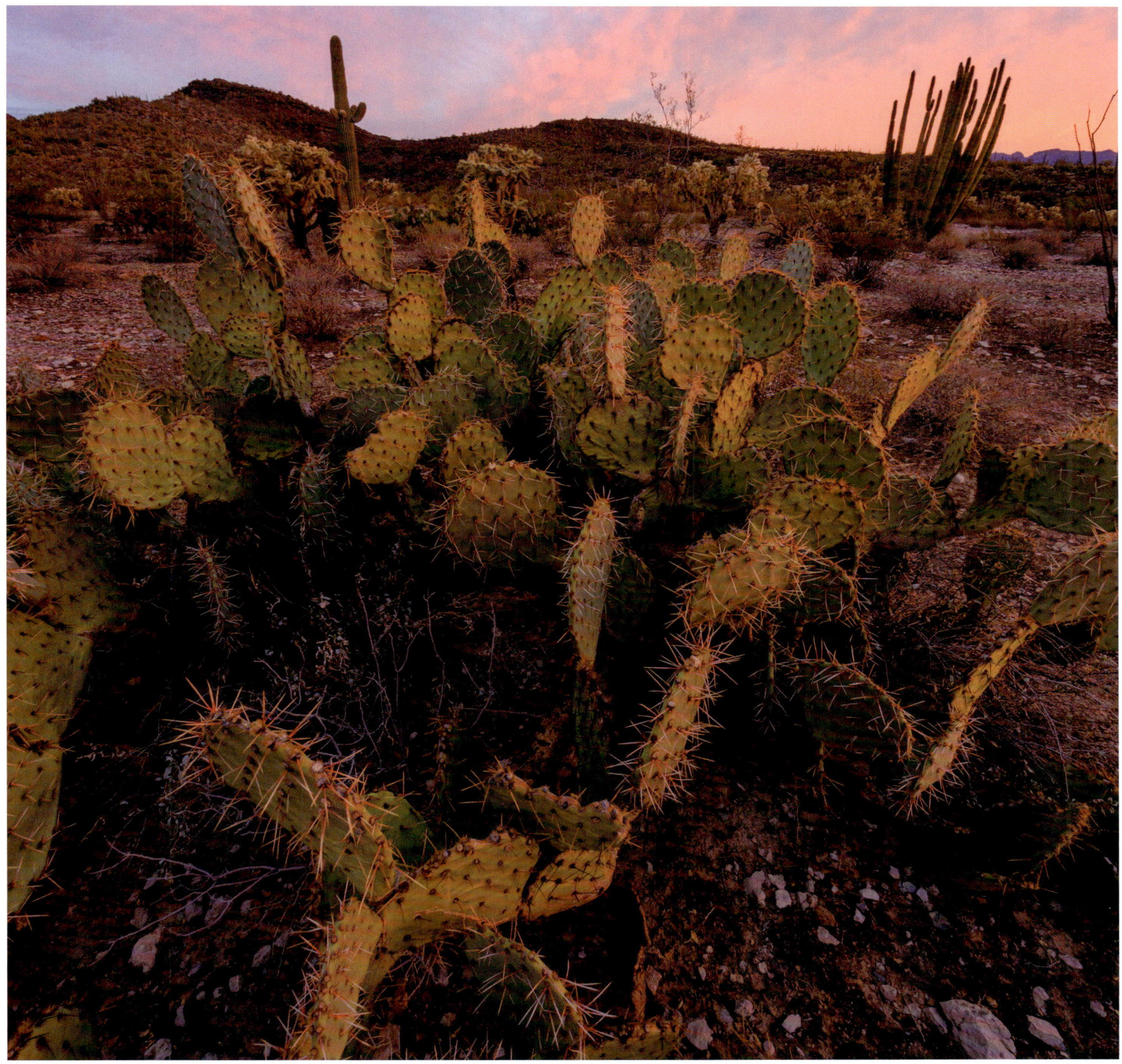

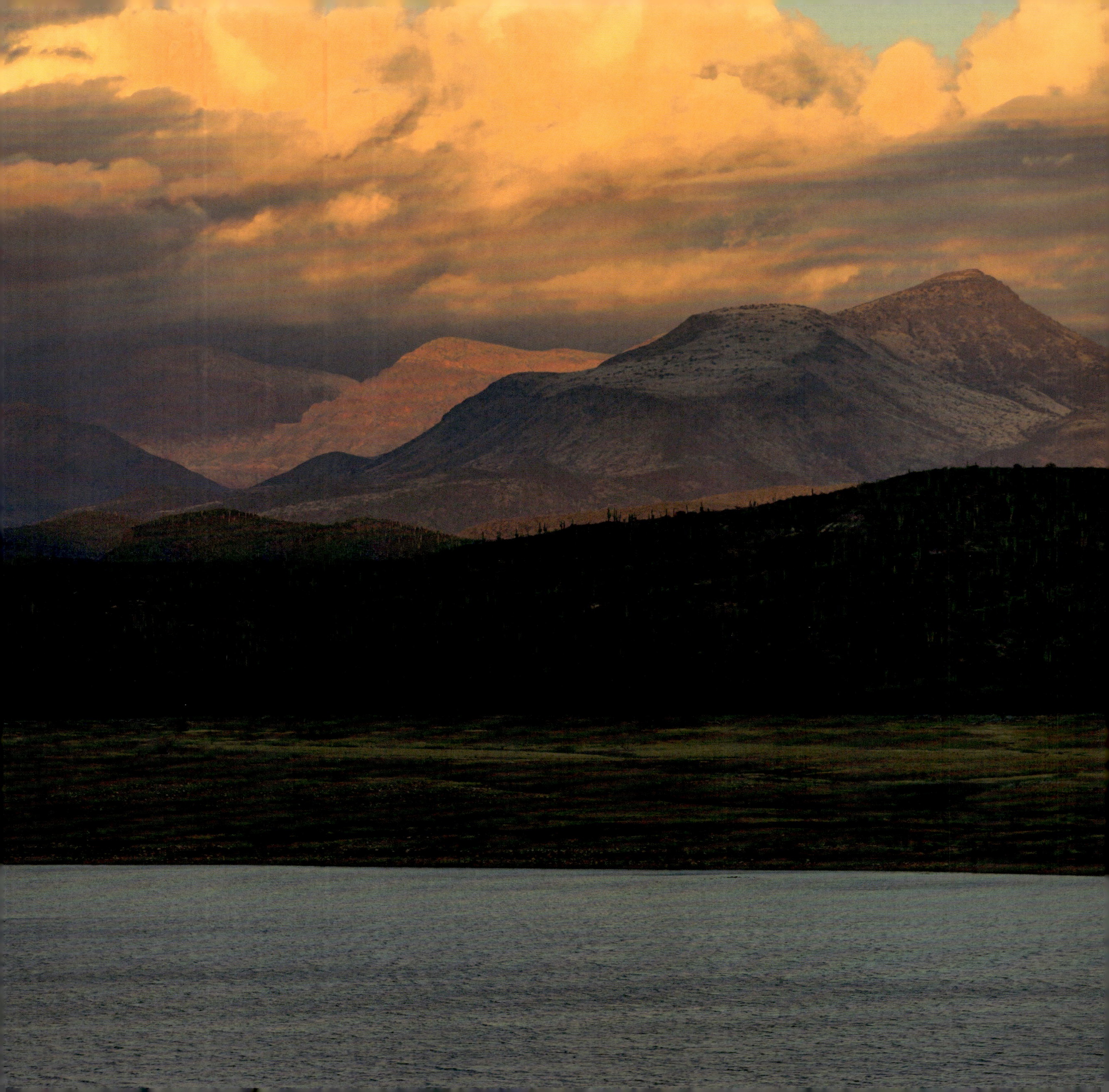

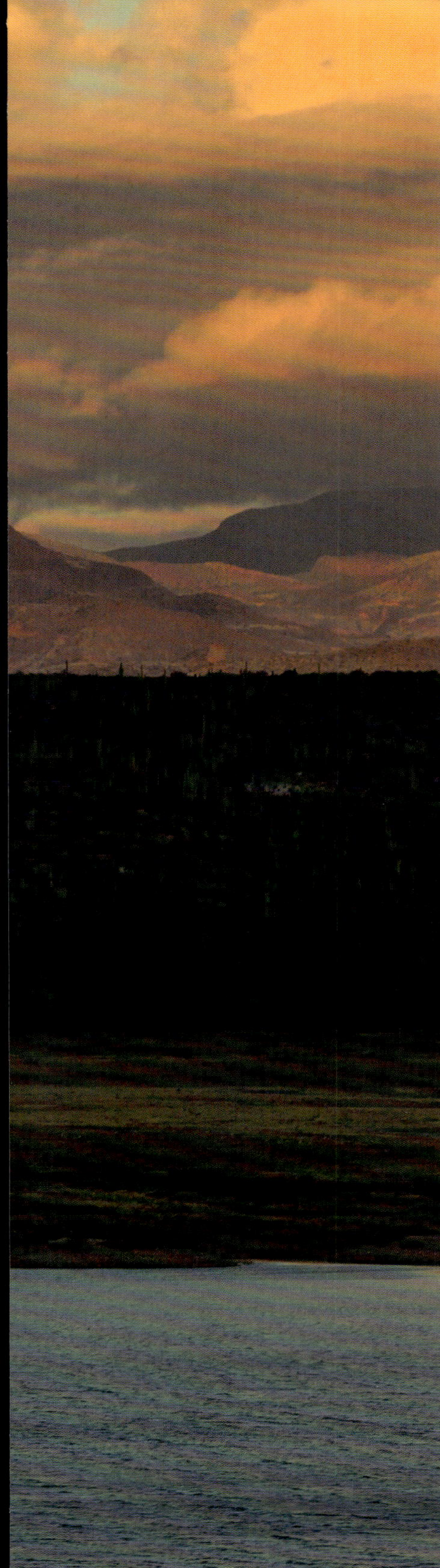

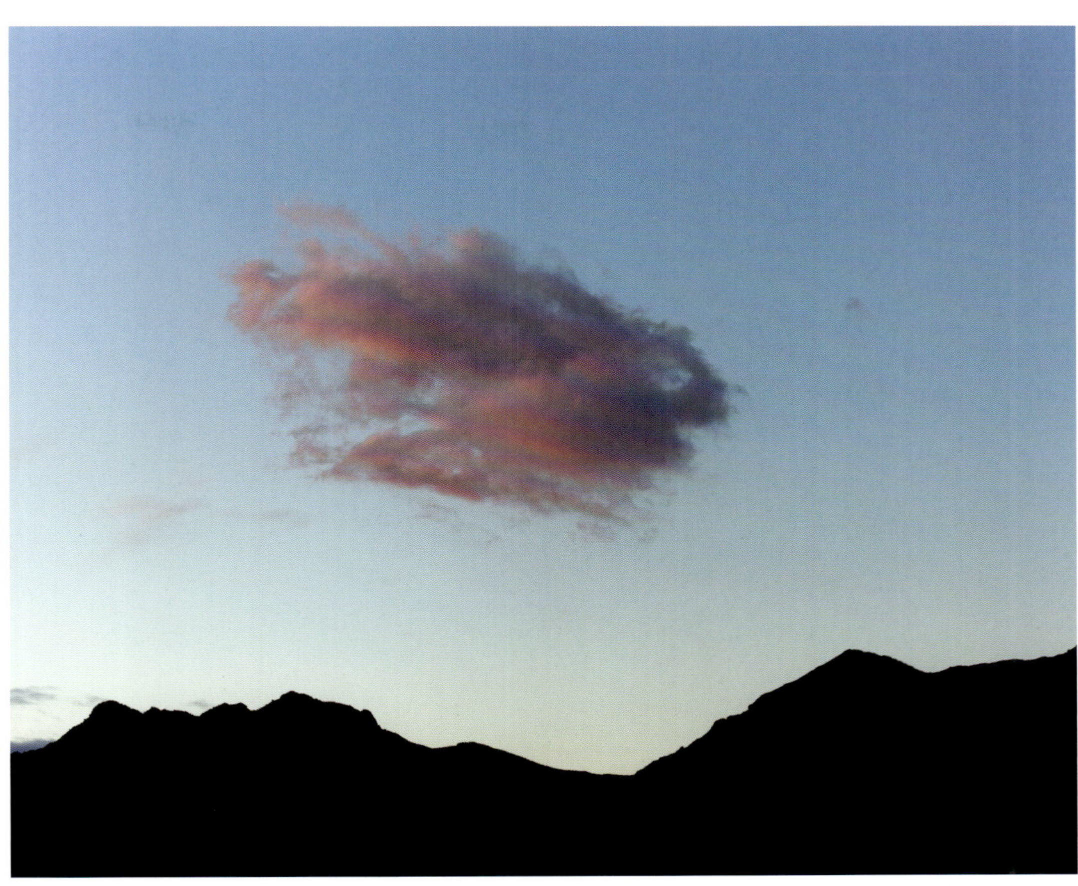

▲

A CLOUD FLOATS SOFTLY OVER WILLOW
SPRINGS MOUNTAIN.

◀

STORMS IN THE MAZATZAL MOUNTAINS
AT HORSESHOE RESERVOIR.

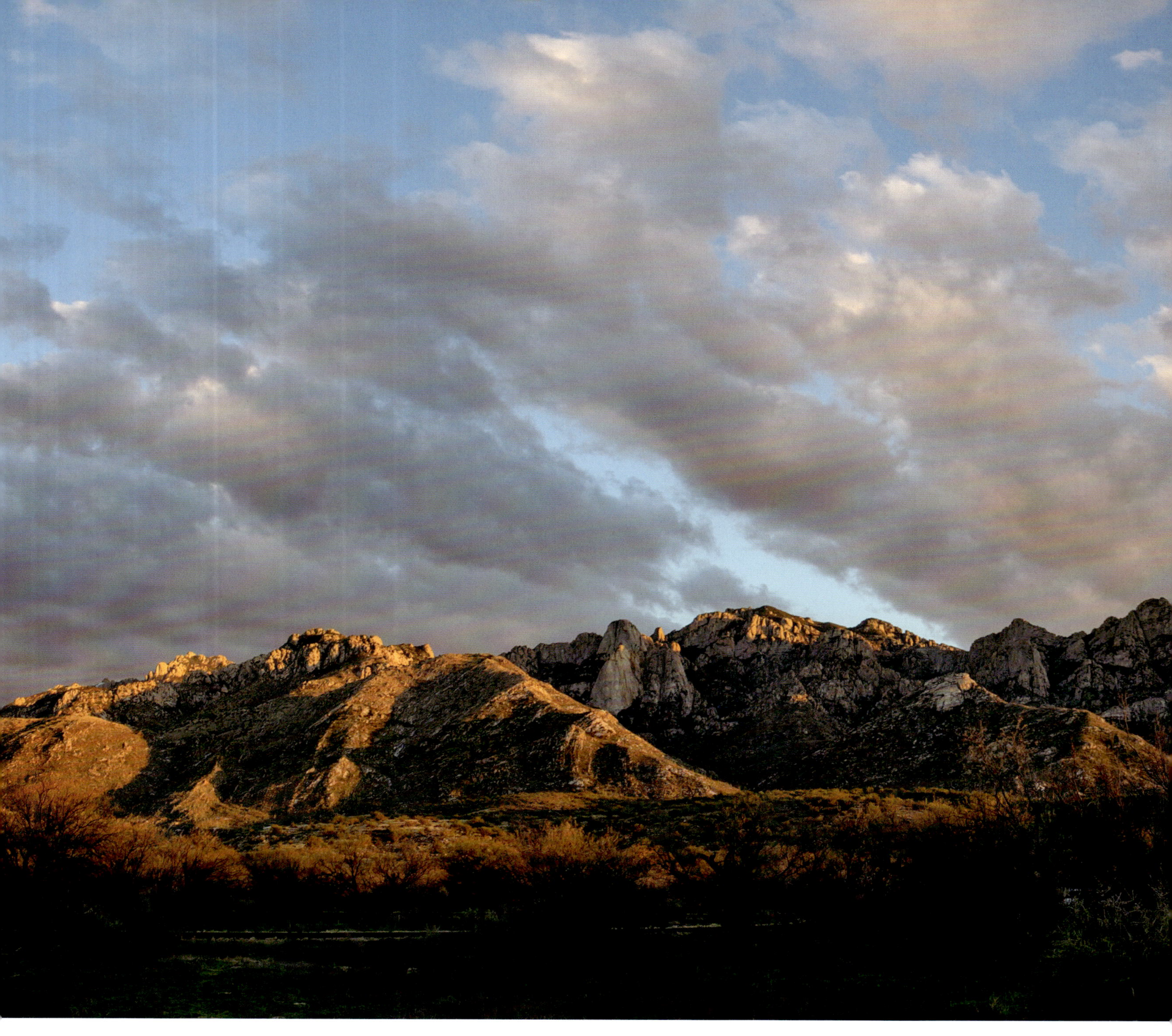

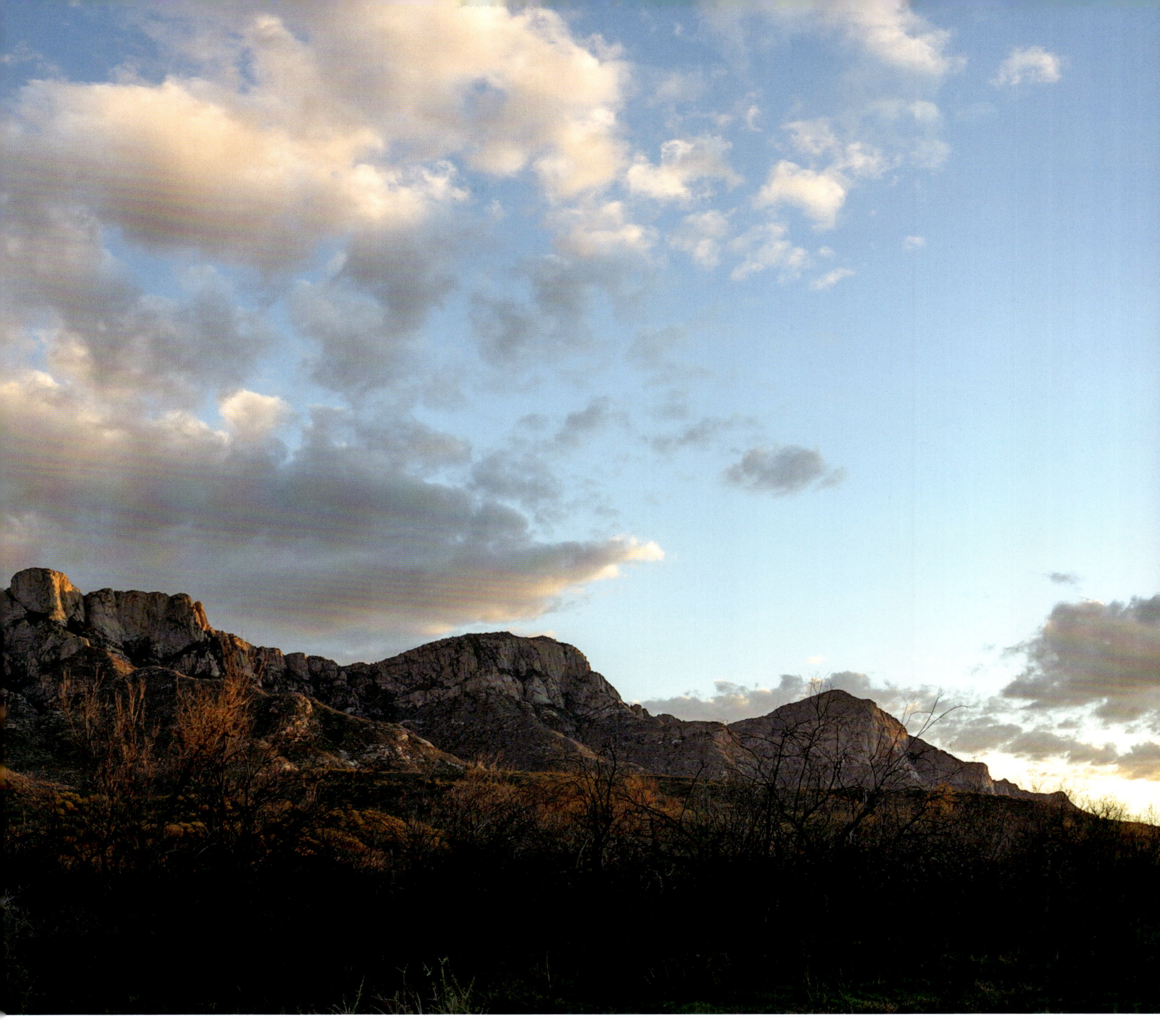

MESQUITE FILLS A WASH BELOW THE PEAKS CATALINA STATE PARK.

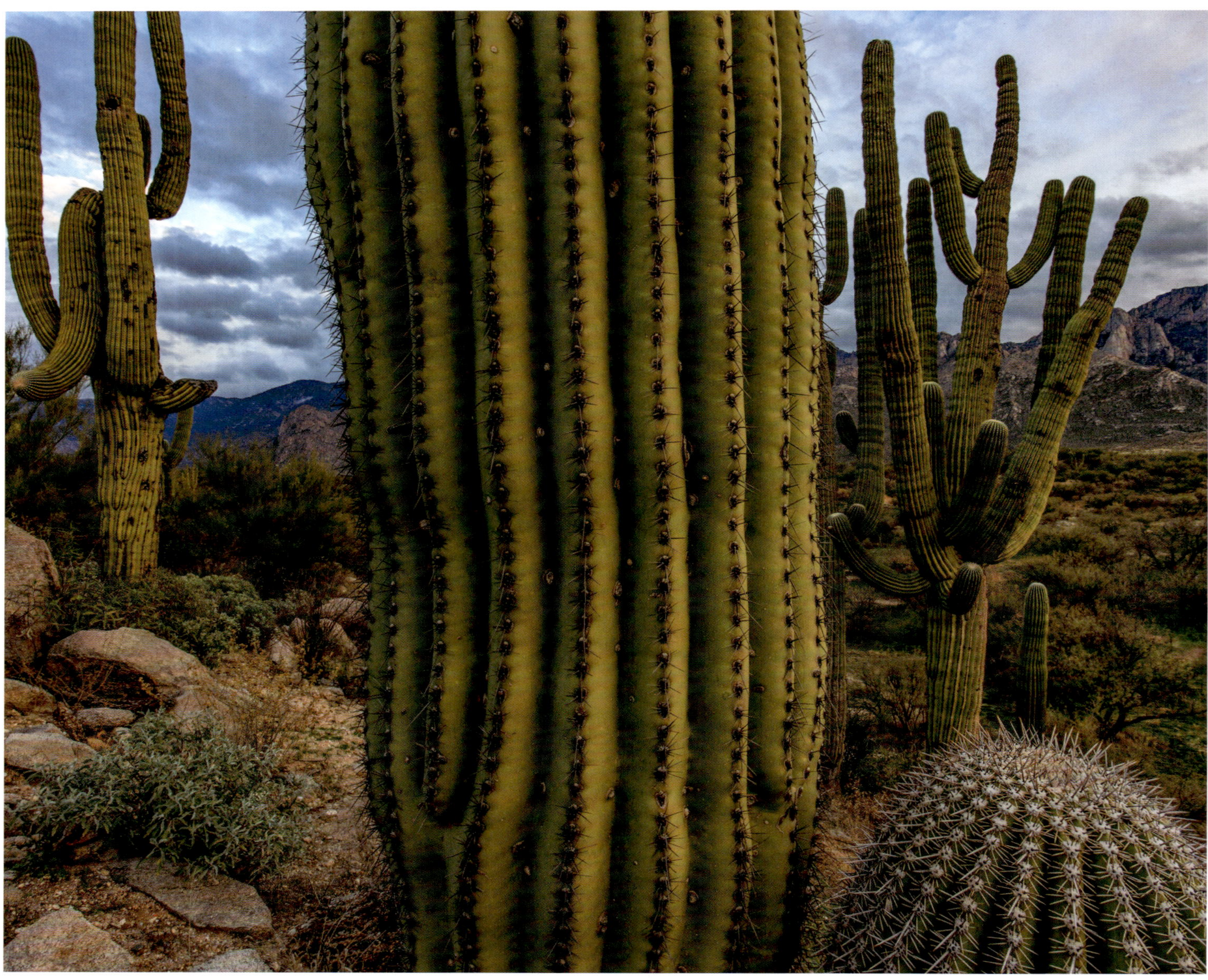

SAGUARO CACTI THRIVE ON THE HILLSIDES OF THE CATALINA MOUNTAINS.

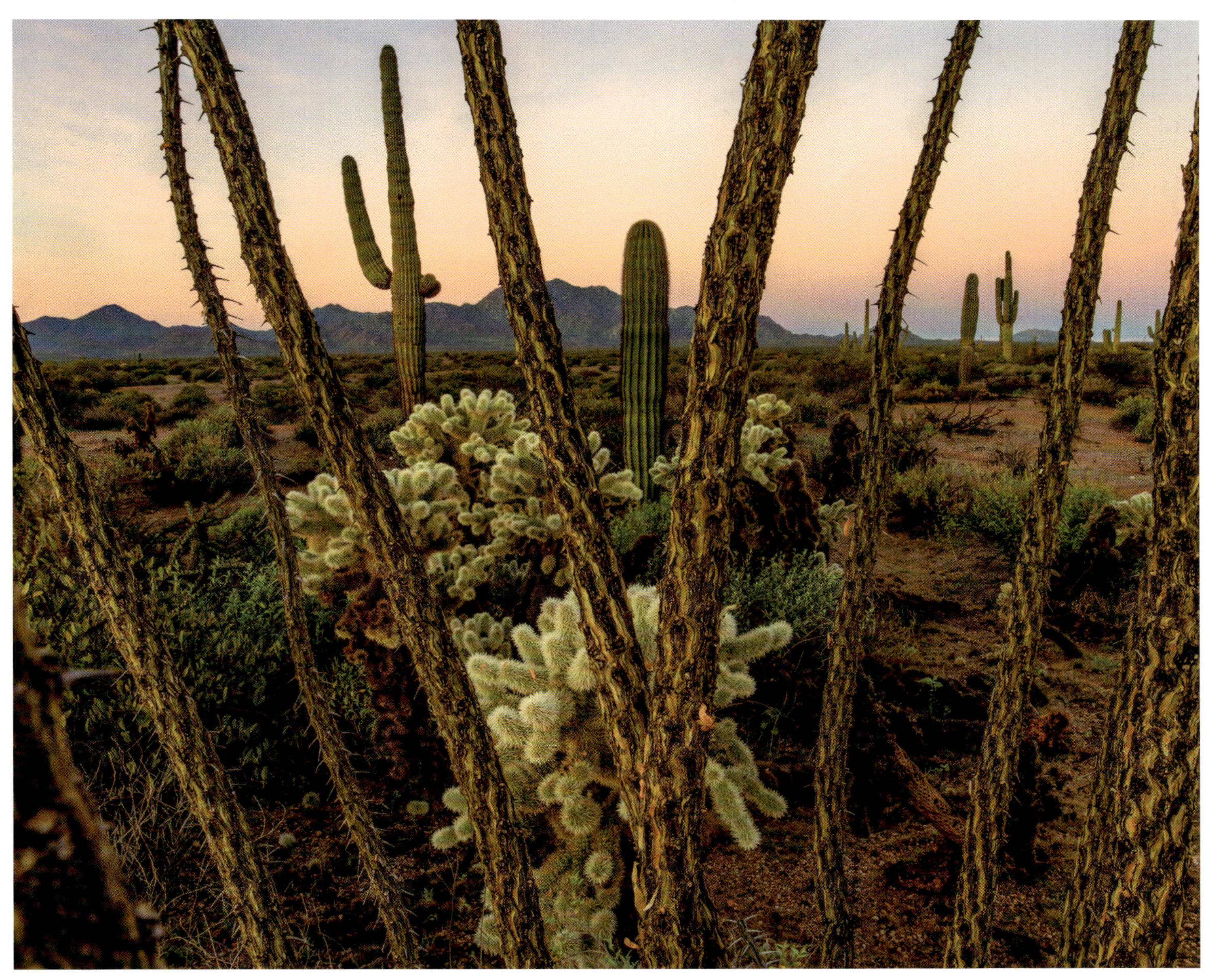

OCOTILLO, CHOLLA, AND SAGUARO COVER THE SONORAN DESERT IN THE VERDE RIVER VALLEY.

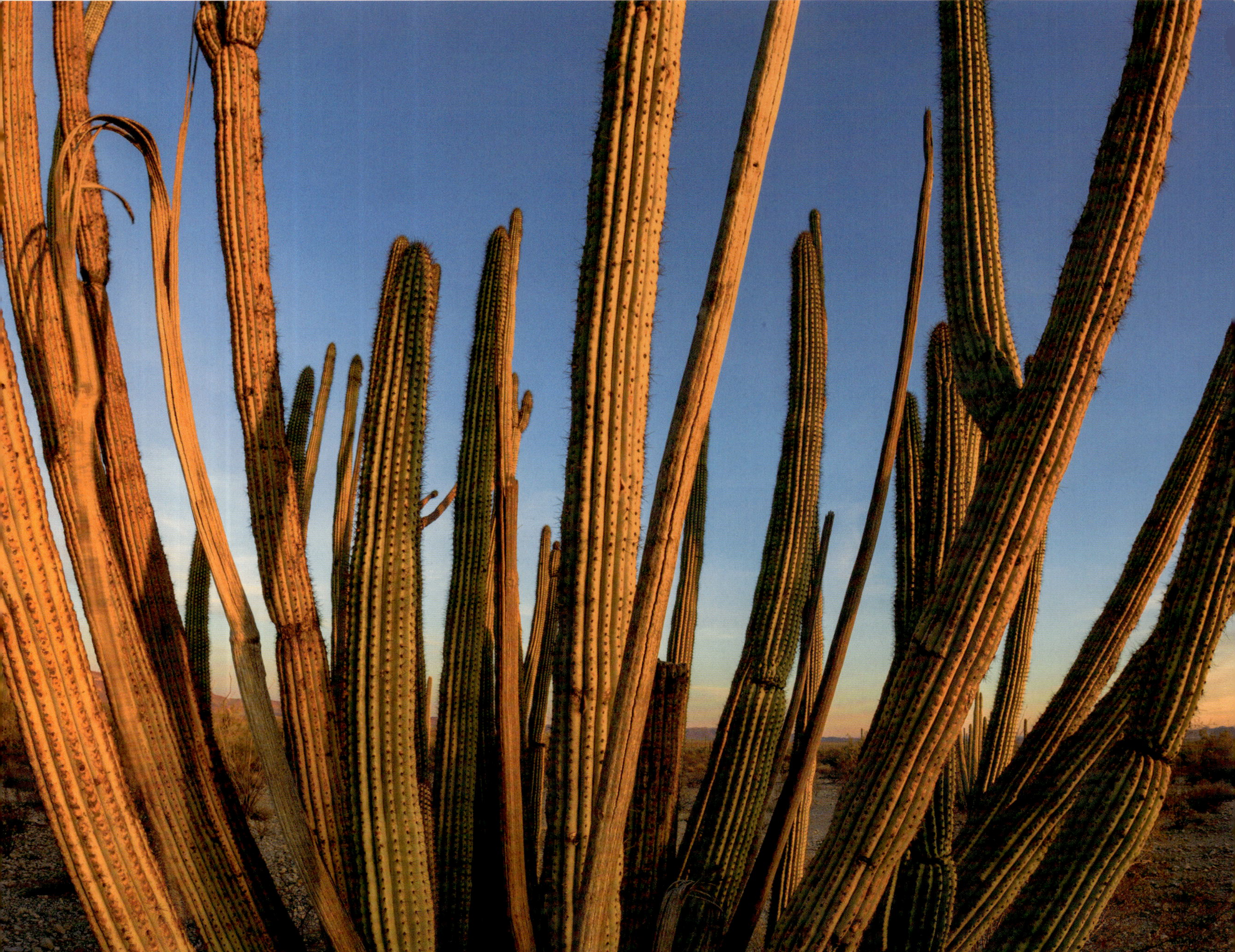



ORGAN PIPE CACTI DOMINATE THE SONORAN DESERT FLOOR IN ORGAN PIPE NATIONAL MONUMENT.

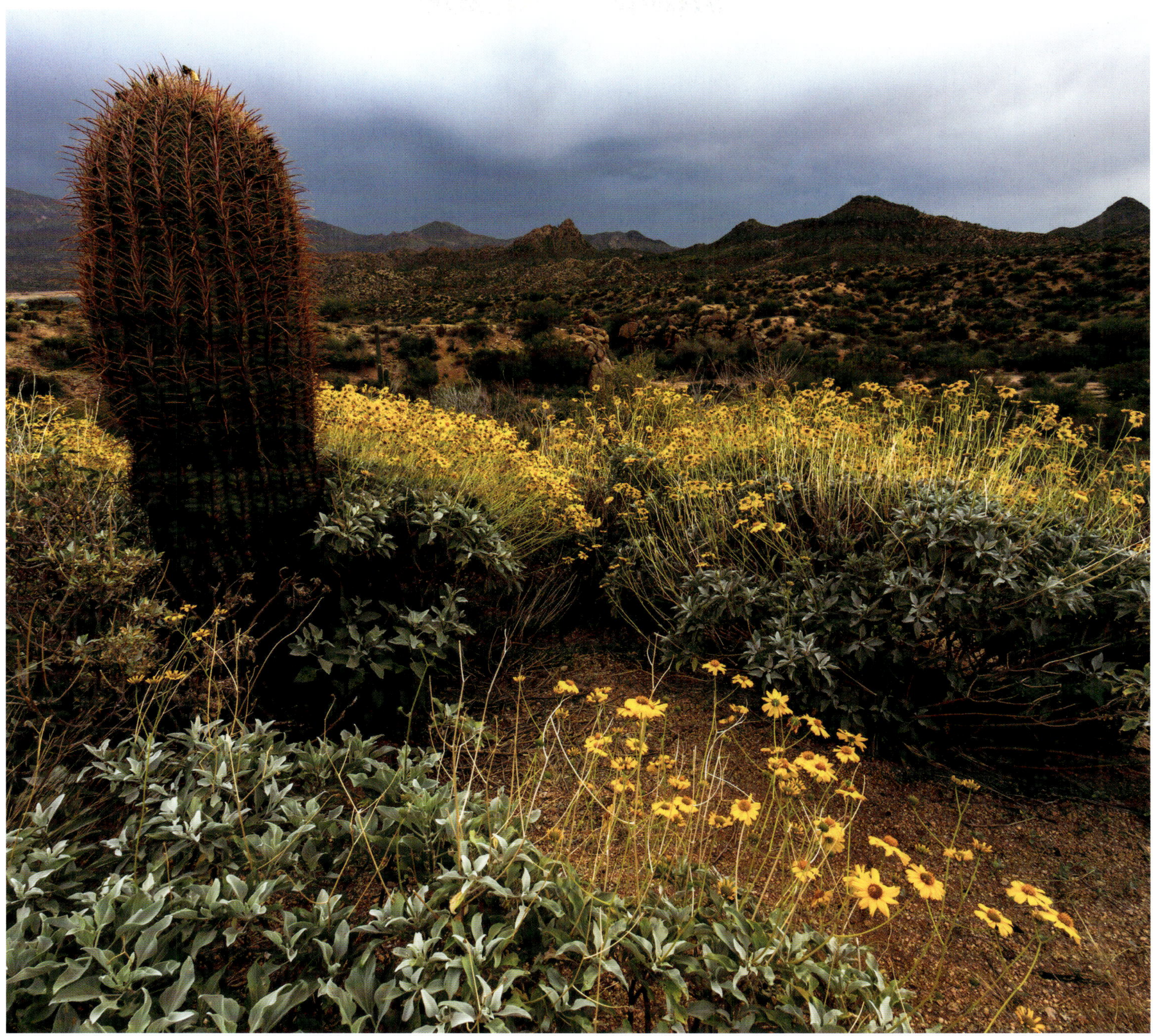

BRITTLEBUSH BLOOM IN LATE FEBRUARY ALONG BARTLETT DAM ROAD.

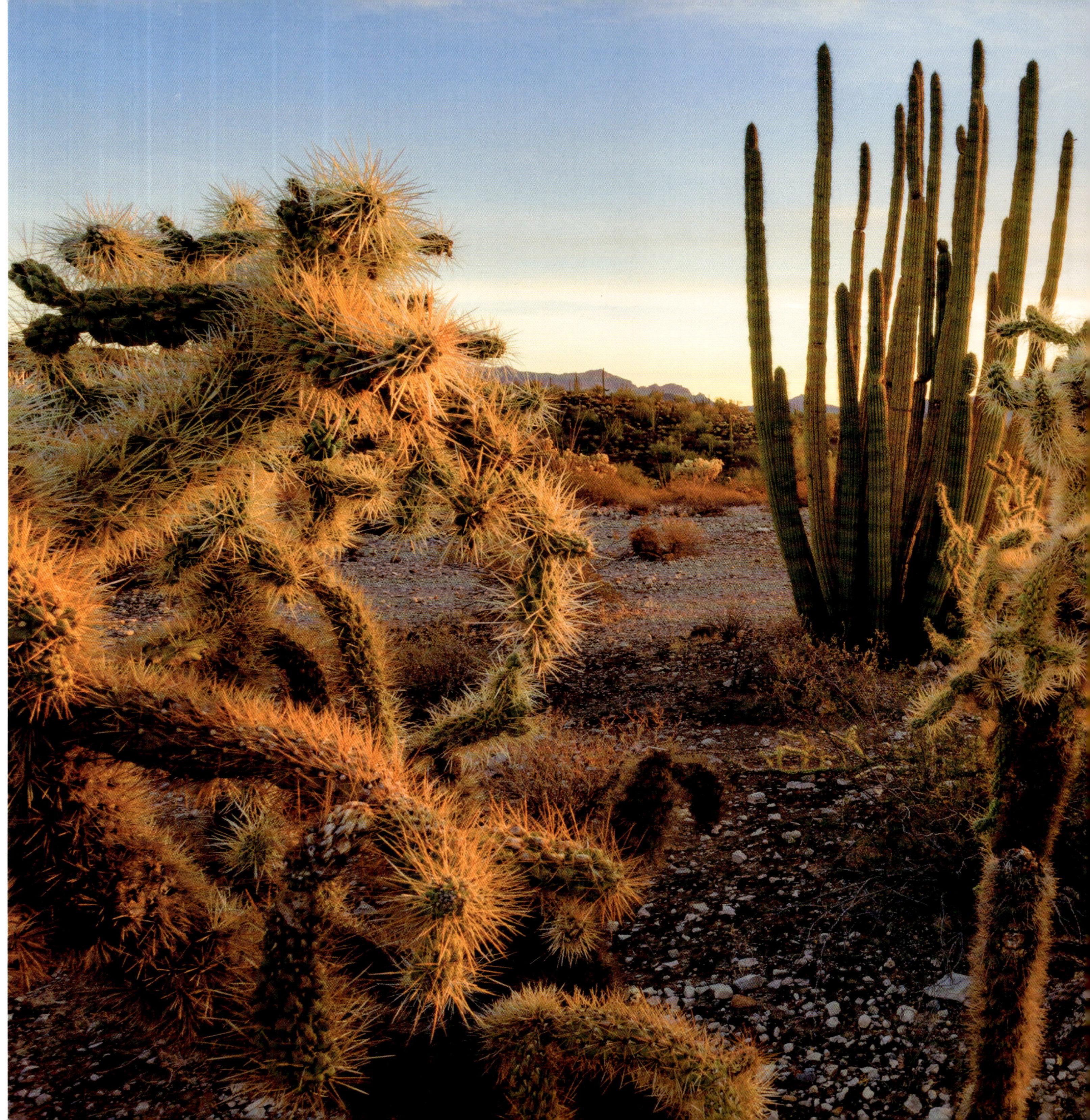

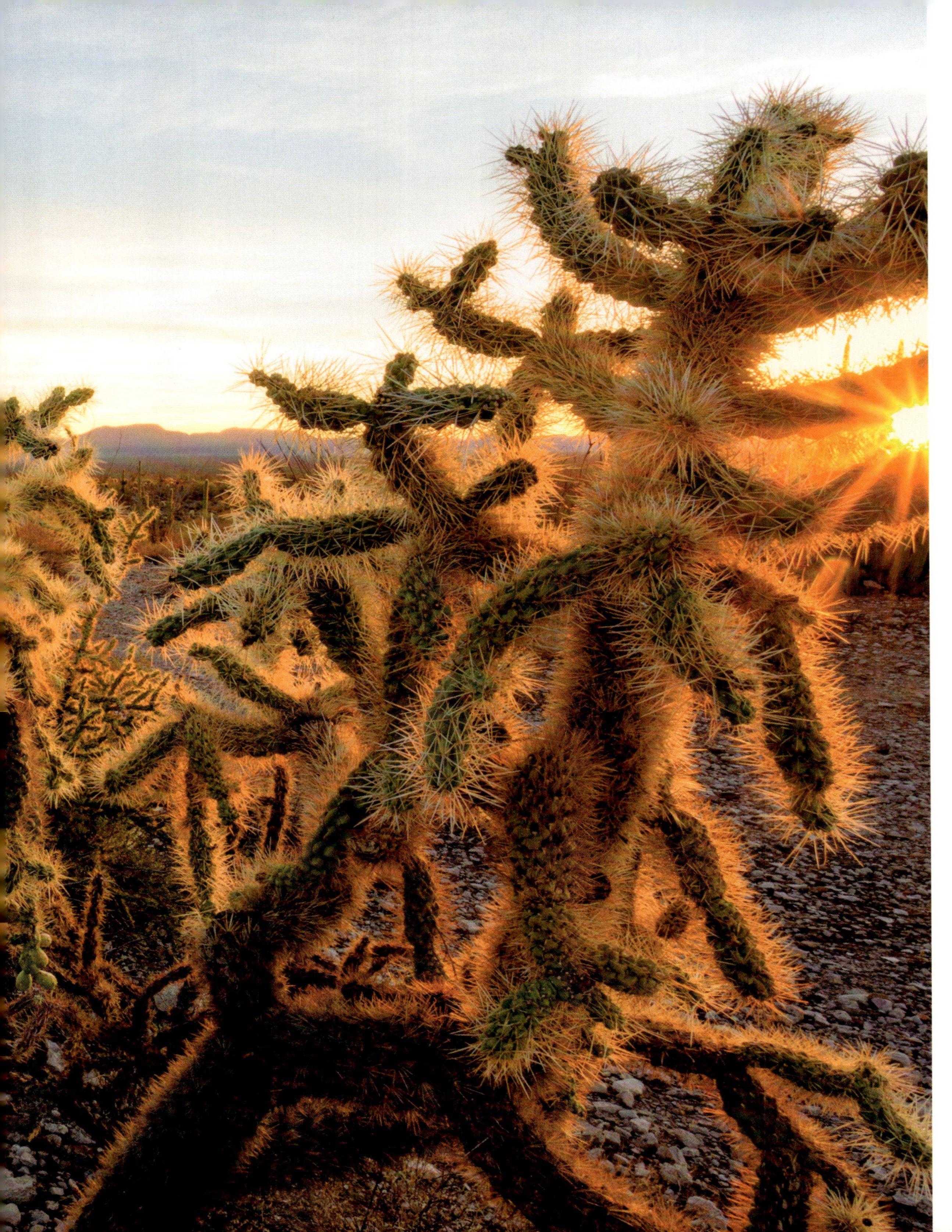

WARM MORNING LIGHT
BRINGS A SHARP CONTRAST
TO CHOLLA CACTI IN ORGAN
PIPE NATIONAL MONUMENT.

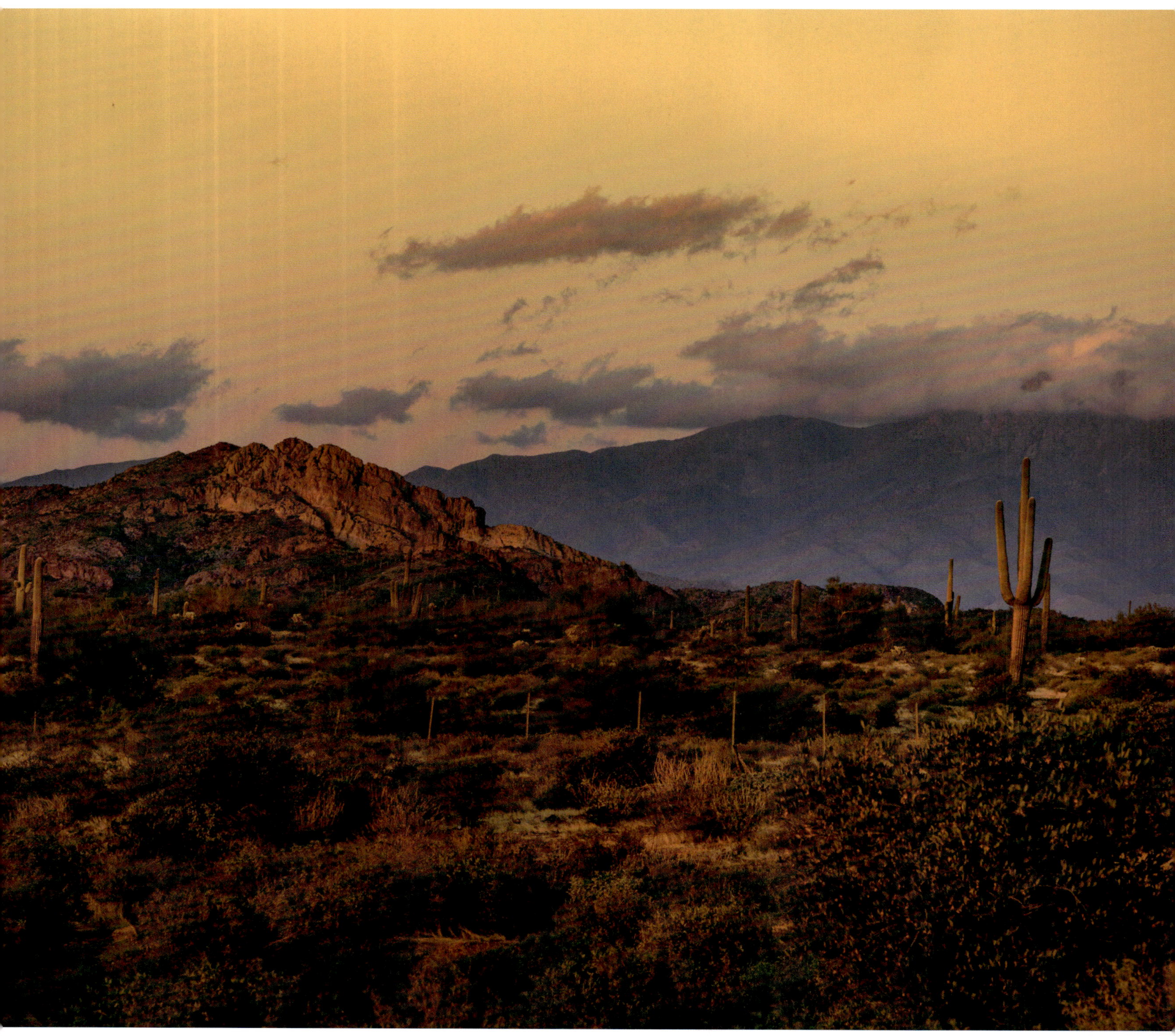

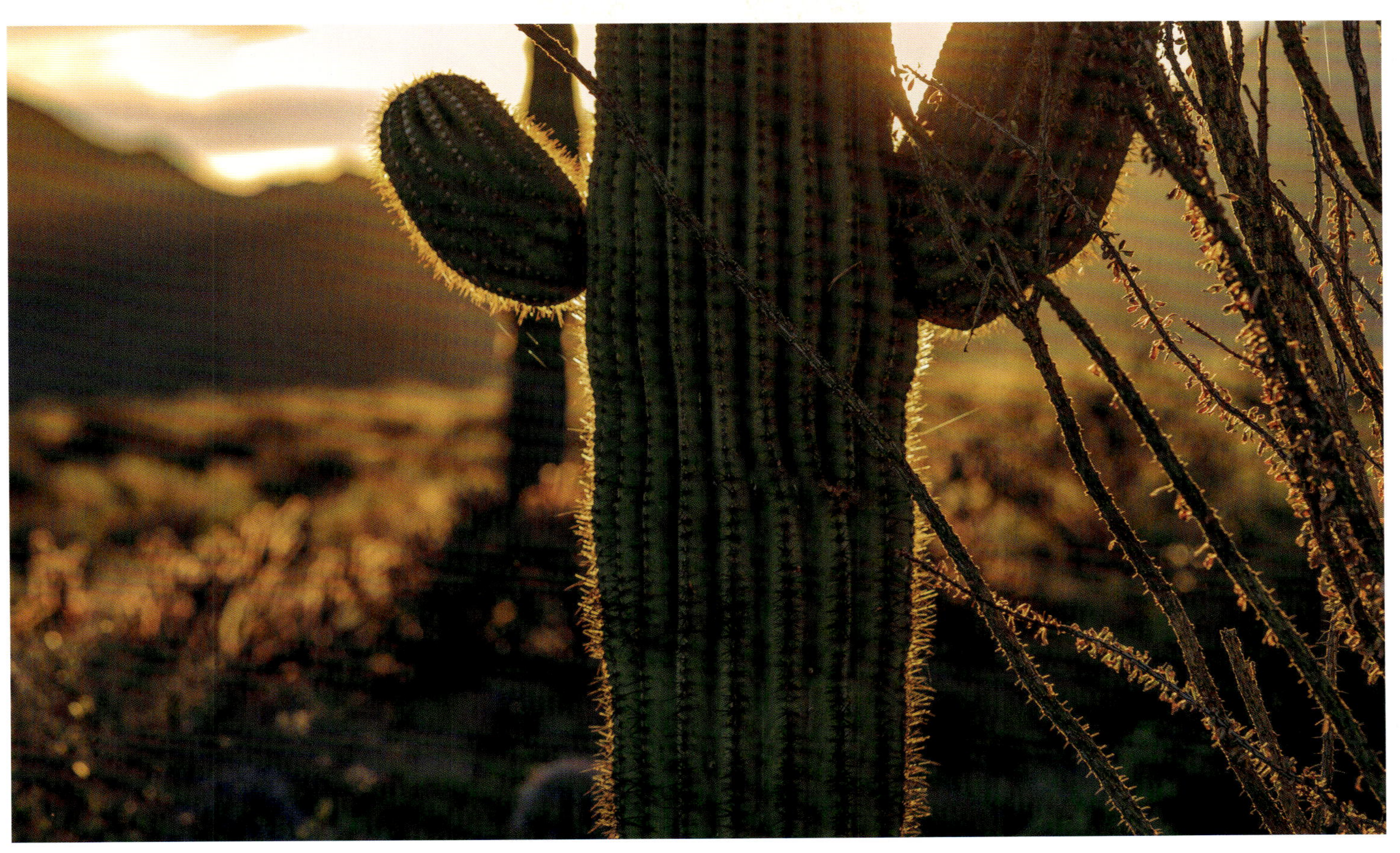

▲
DENSE DESERT FOLIAGE IN THE SONORAN
DESERT, McDOWELL MOUNTAIN REGIONAL PARK
NEAR FOUNTAIN HILLS.

◄

LOOKING TOWARD THE FOUR PEAKS WILDERNESS
FROM LOST DUTCHMAN STATE PARK.

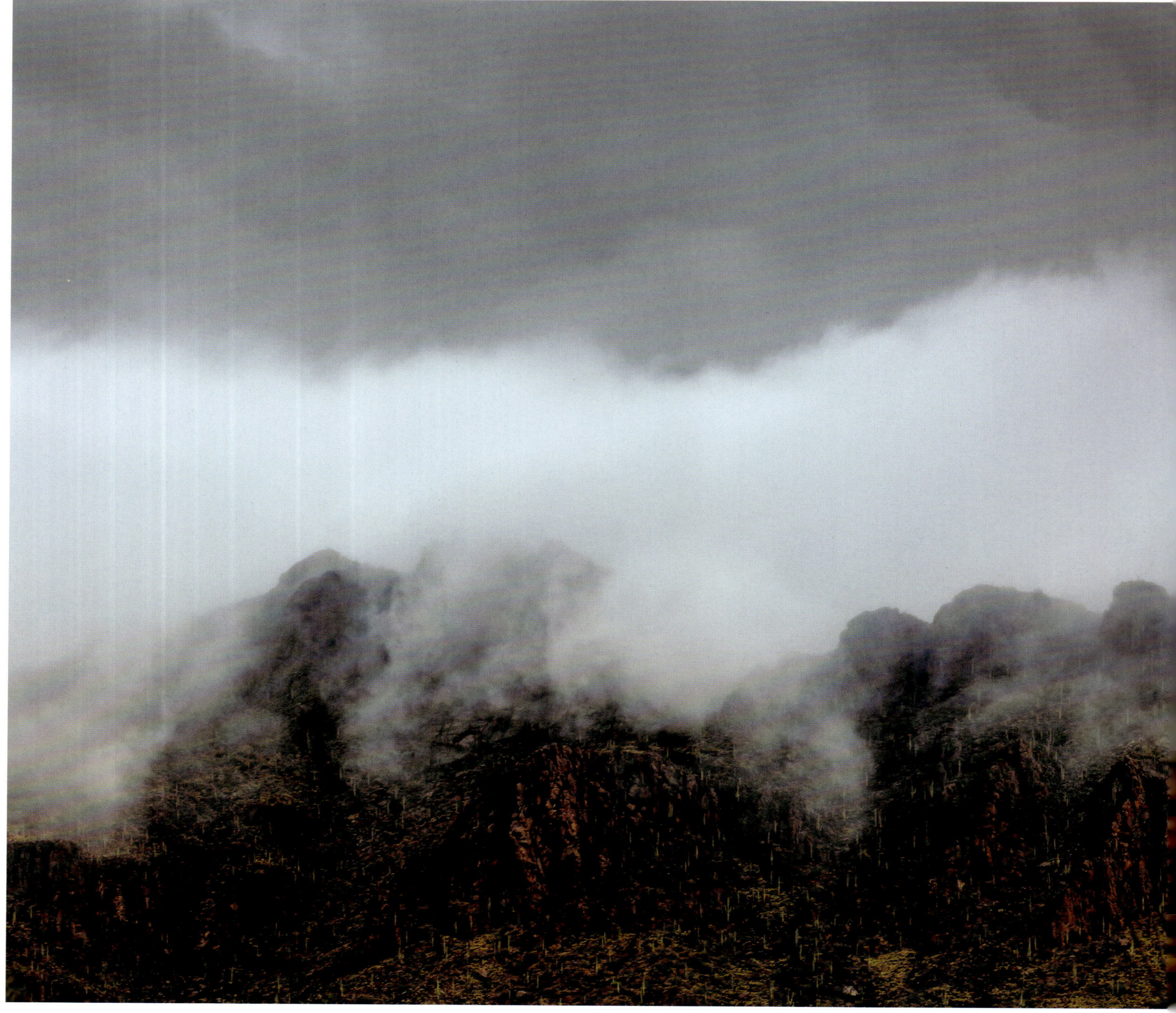

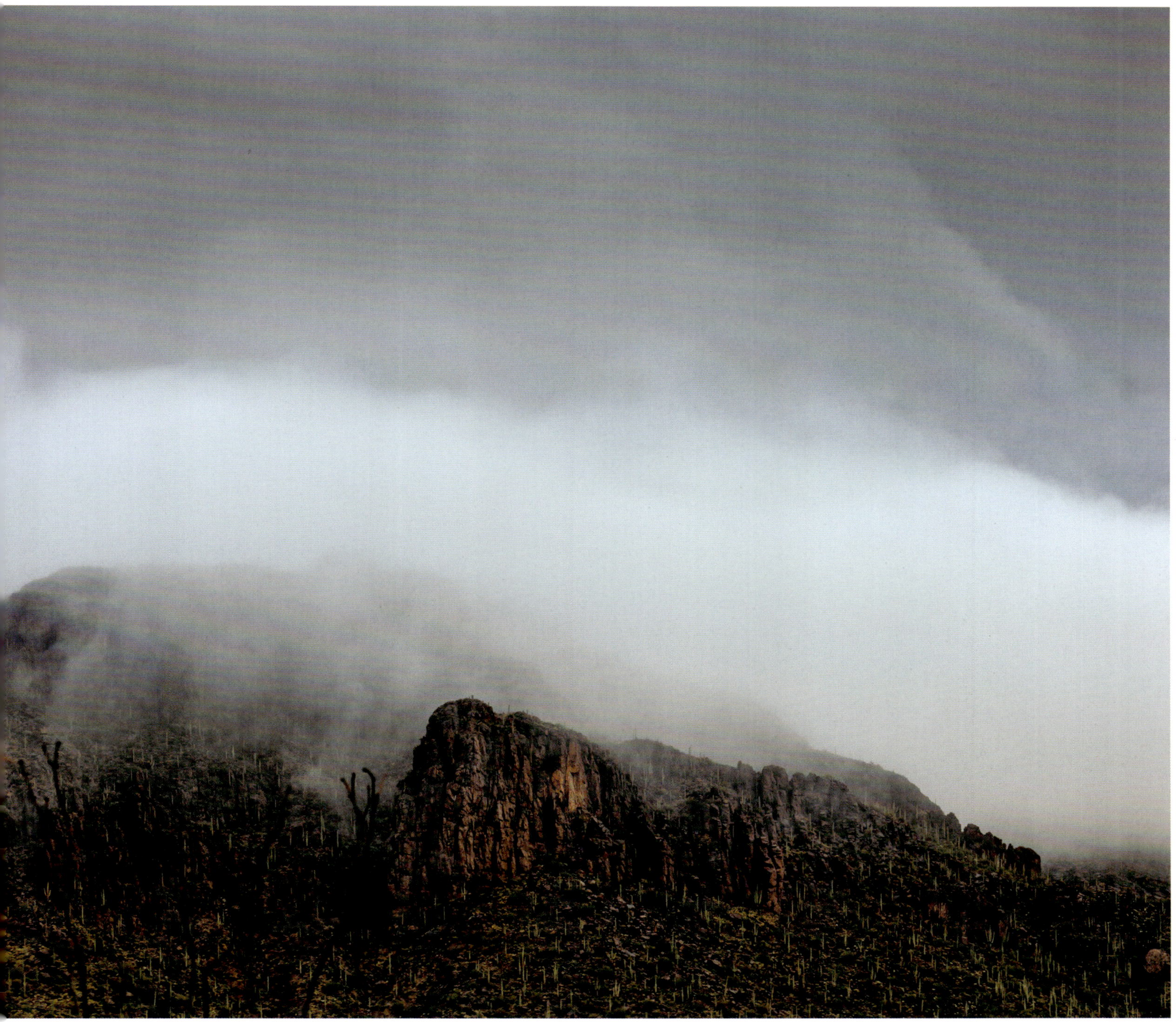

WINTER CLOUDS PILE UP ON THE PEAKS ABOVE TUCSON MOUNTAIN PARK.

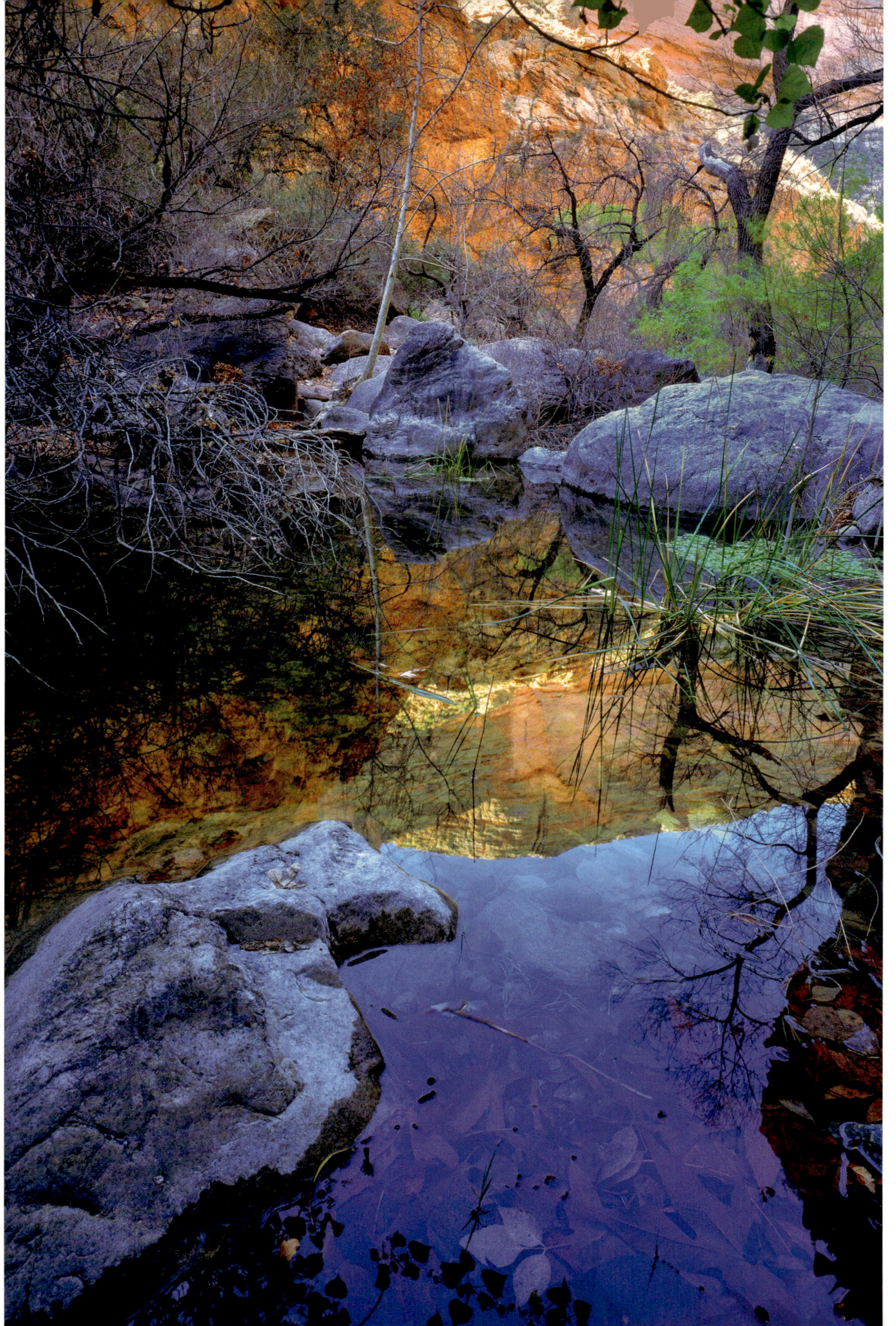

FISH CREEK OCCASIONALLY
SPRINGS UP FROM THE
ROCKY BOTTOM ALONG
THE APACHE TRAIL.

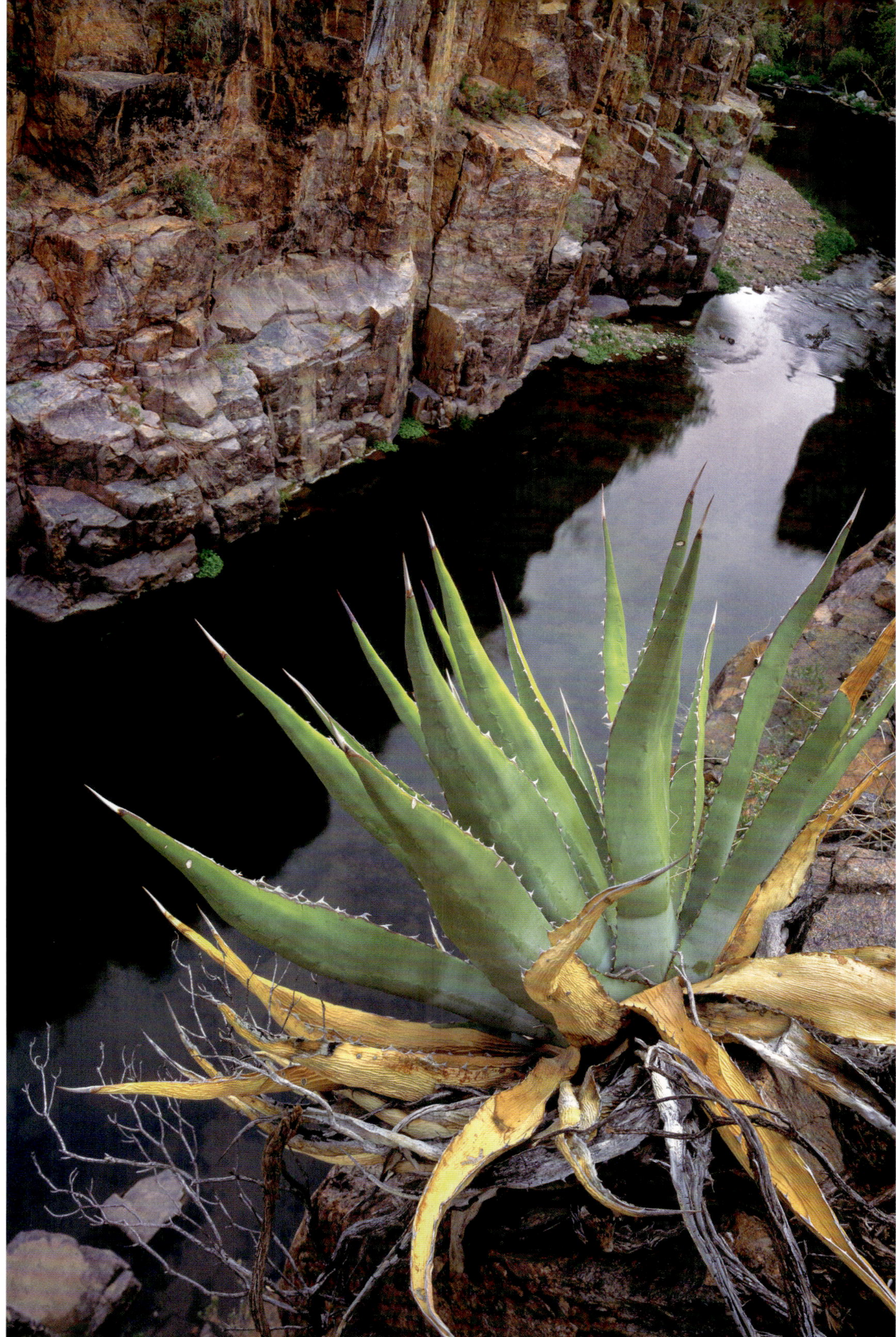

A CENTURY PLANT SITS ON
THE CLIFF EDGE ABOVE
ARAVAIPA CREEK, A STREAM
THAT FLOWS YEAR-ROUND.

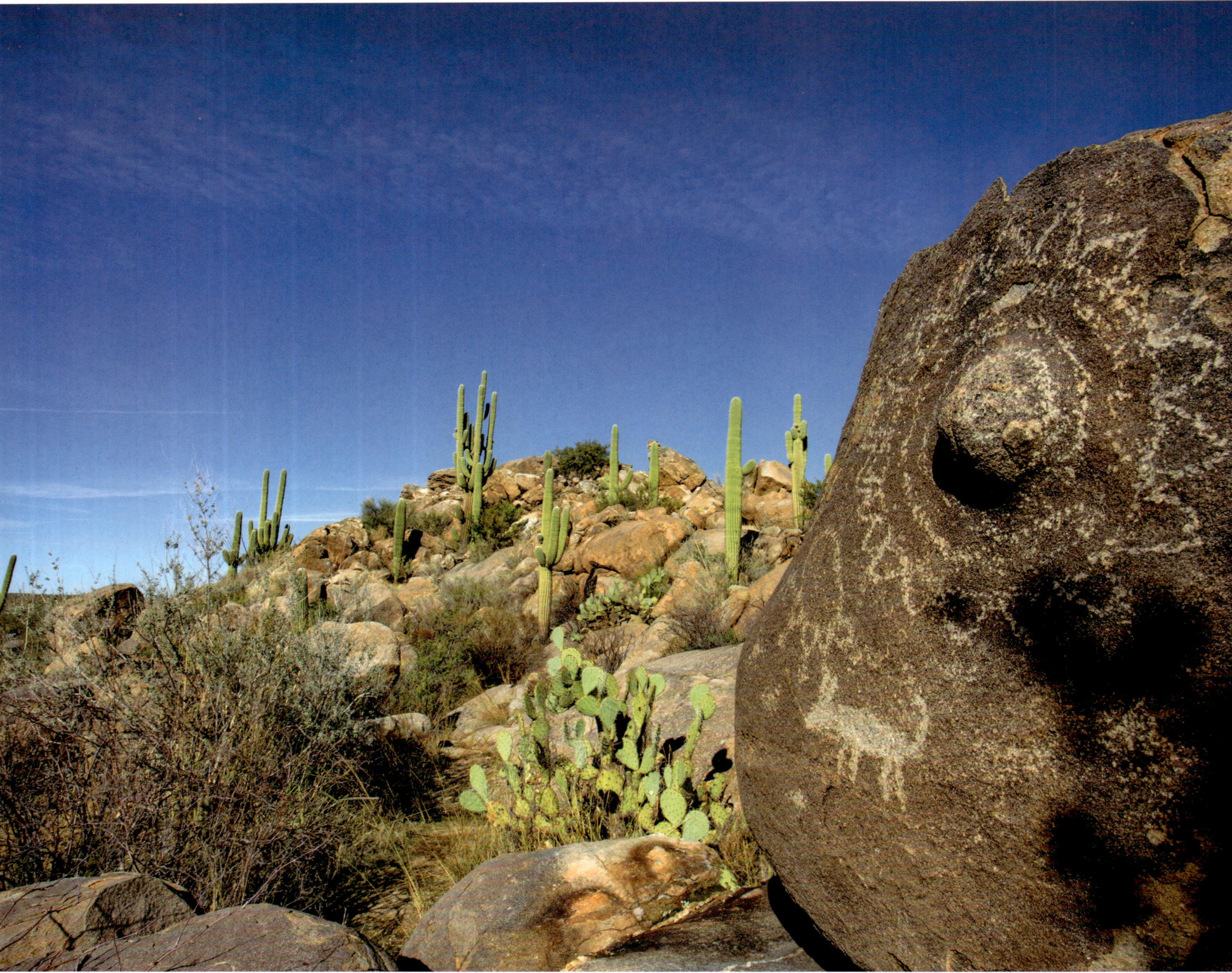



A SHIELD PATTERN PETROGLYPH IN THE CORONADO NATIONAL FOREST.

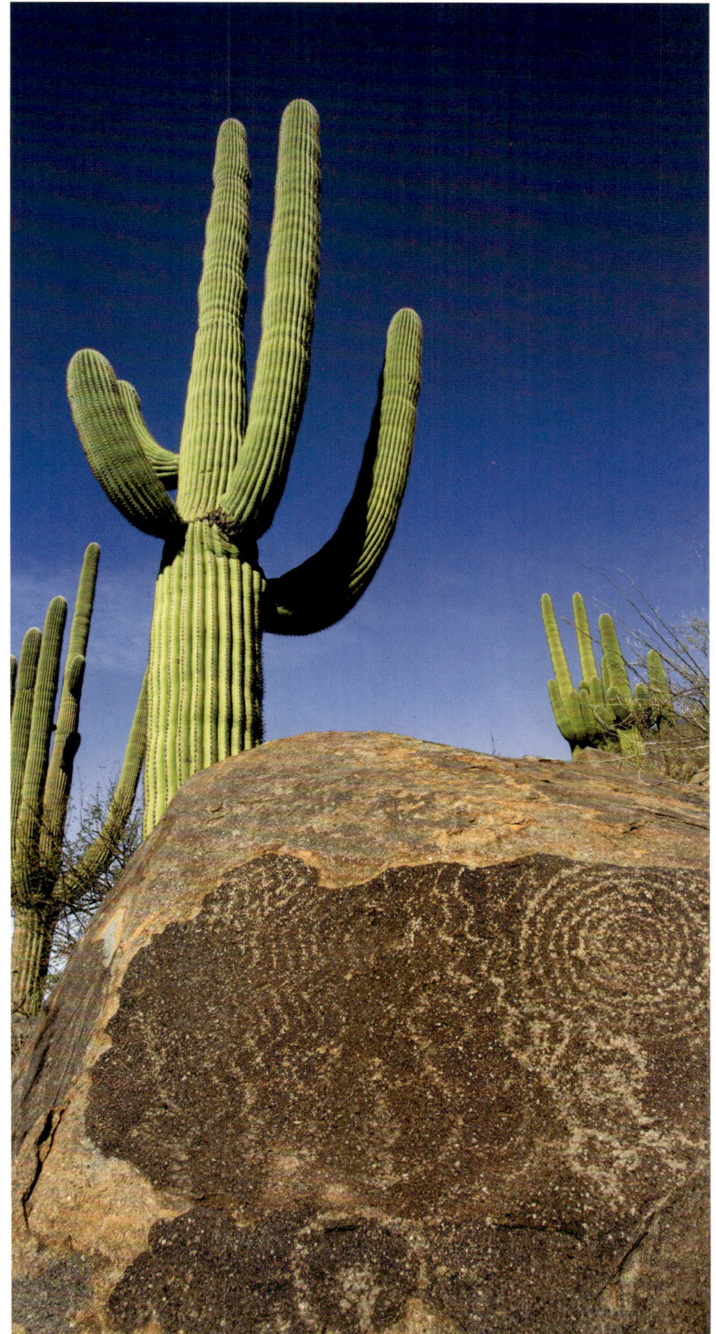

PETROGLYPHS IN THE CORONADO NATIONAL FOREST.

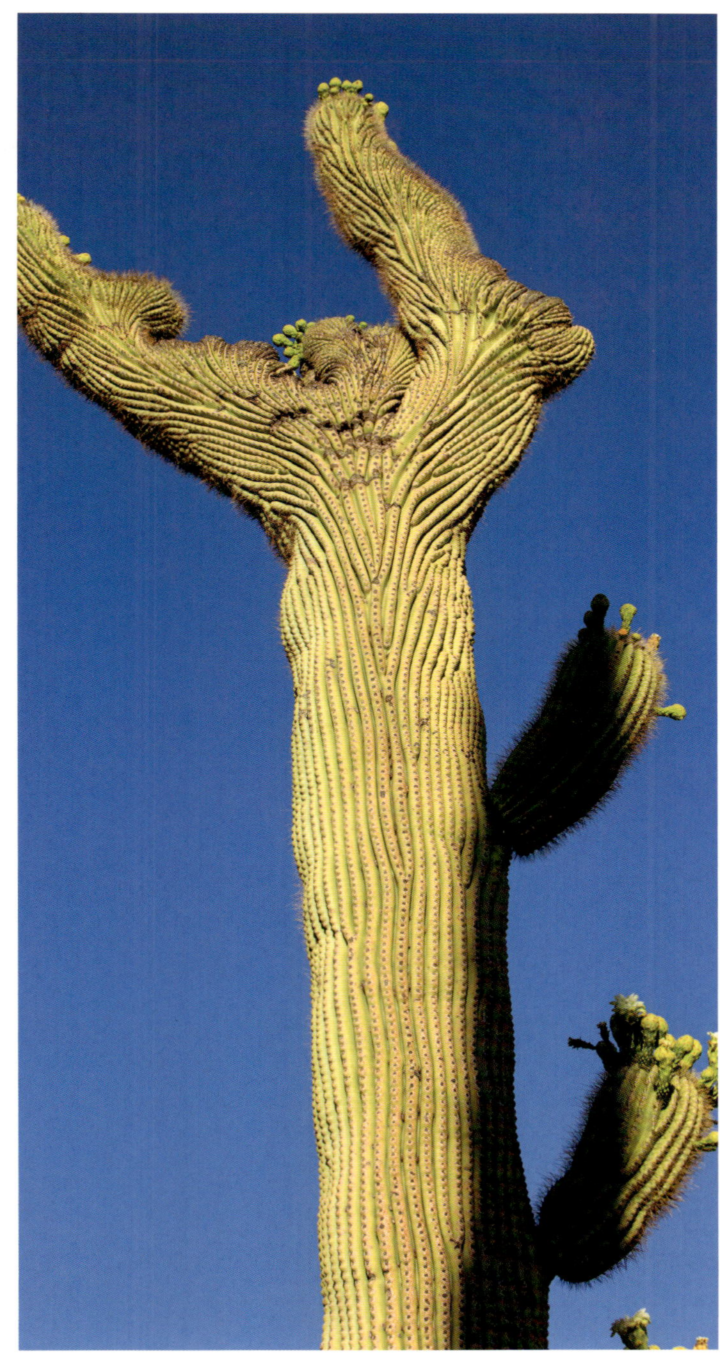

A CRESTED SAGUARO CACTUS LIKE THIS IS A RARE
FIND IN SWEETWATER PRESERVE.

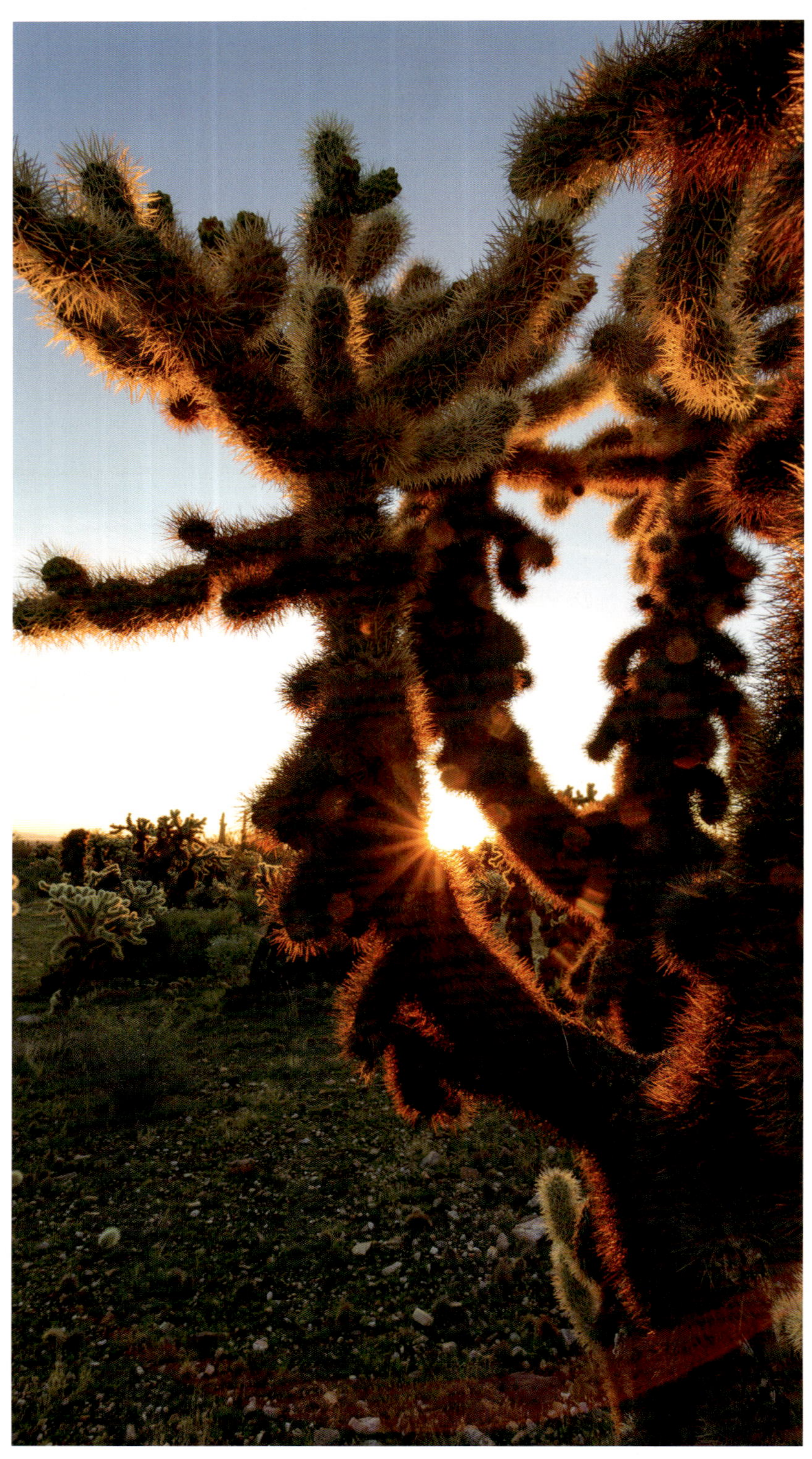

◀

A SUNBURST EMPHASIZES
THE NASTY NATURE OF THE
CHOLLA CACTUS IN WHITE TANK
MOUNTAIN REGIONAL PARK.

▶

DENSE CACTI ALONG
THE ARIZONA TRAIL IN THE
SUPERSTITION MOUNTAINS.

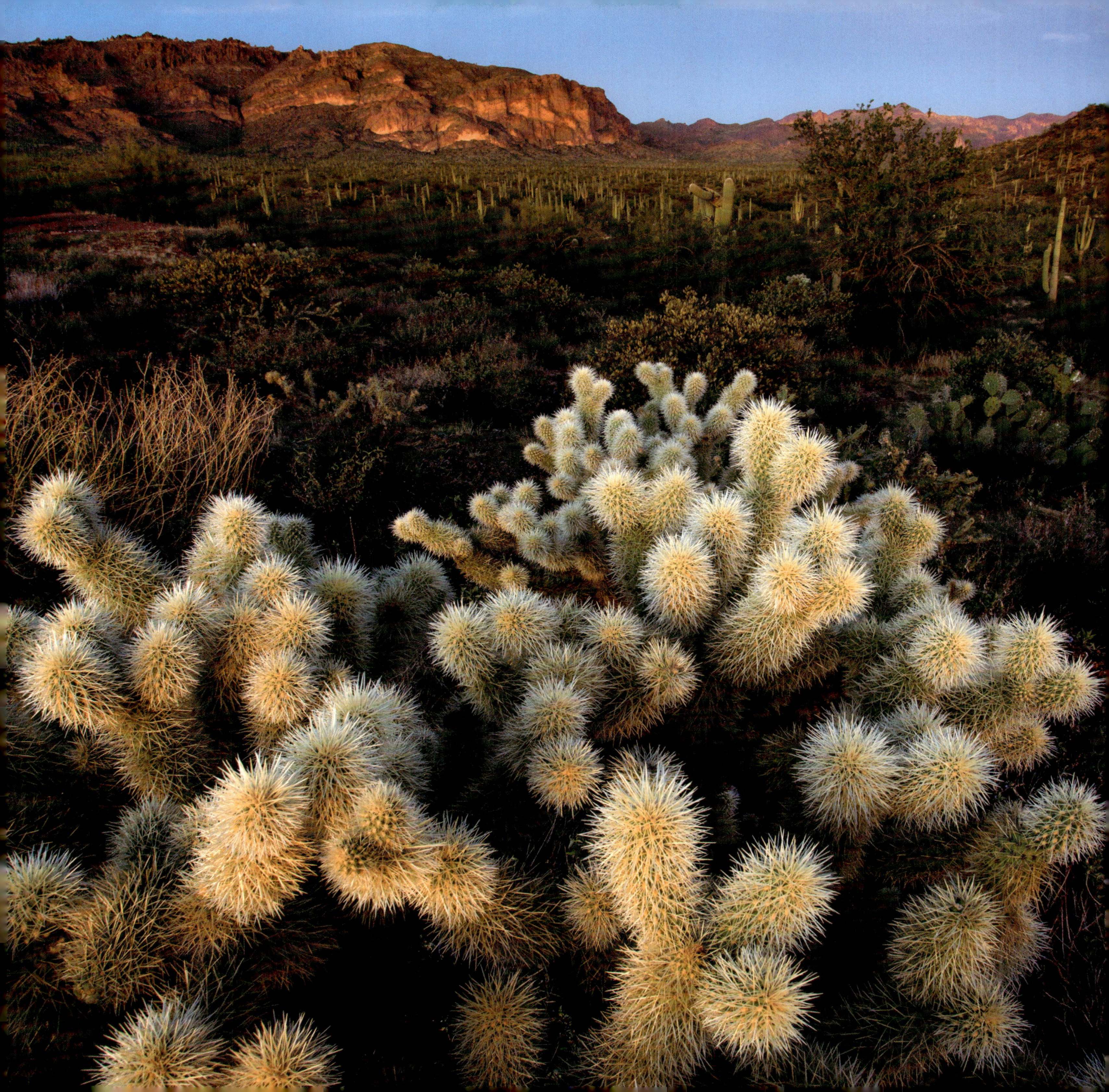

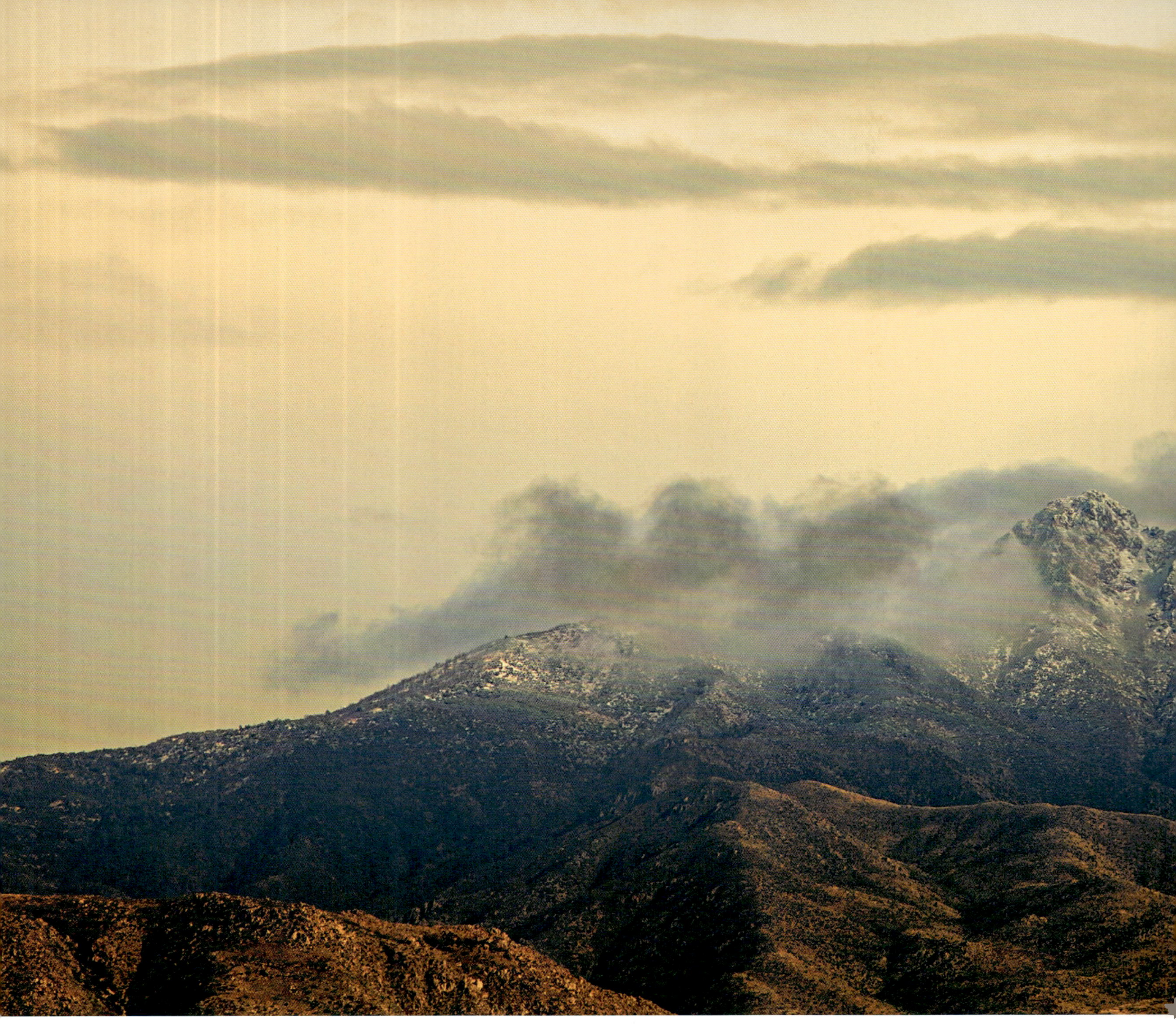

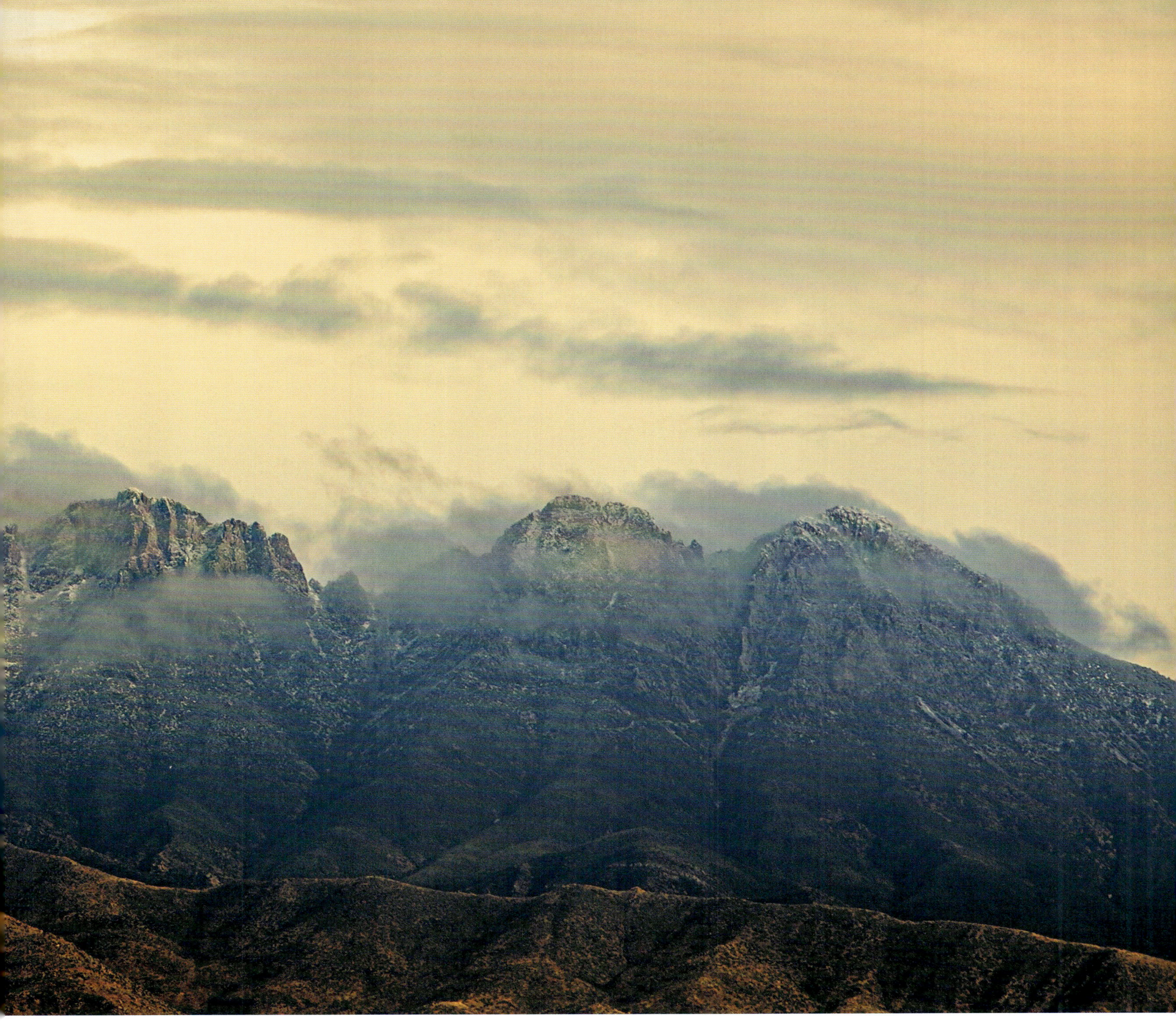

THE PEAKS OF THE FOUR PEAKS WILDERNESS BREAK THROUGH WINTER CLOUDS.

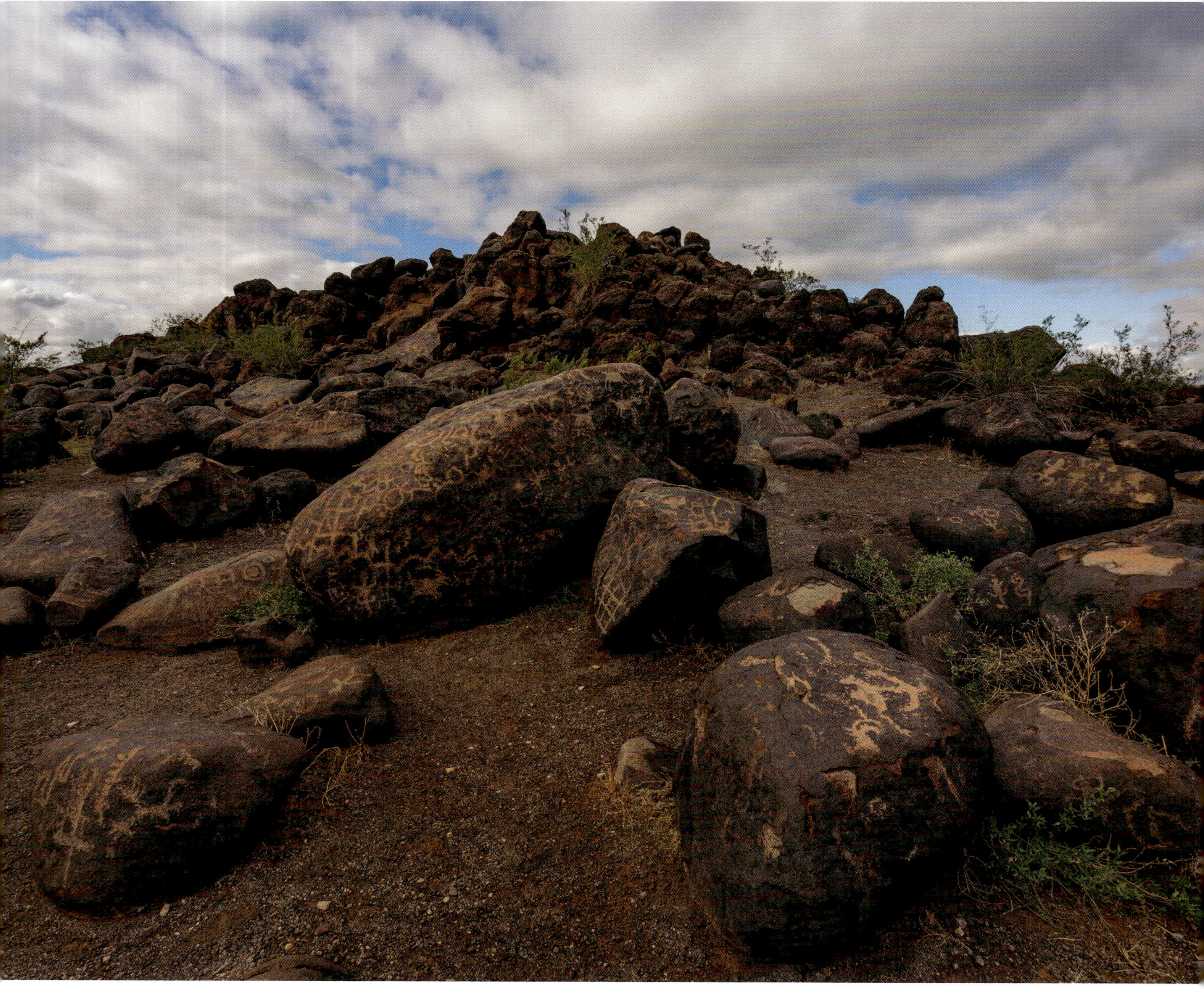



GILA STYLE PETROGLYPHS NEAR GILA BEND.

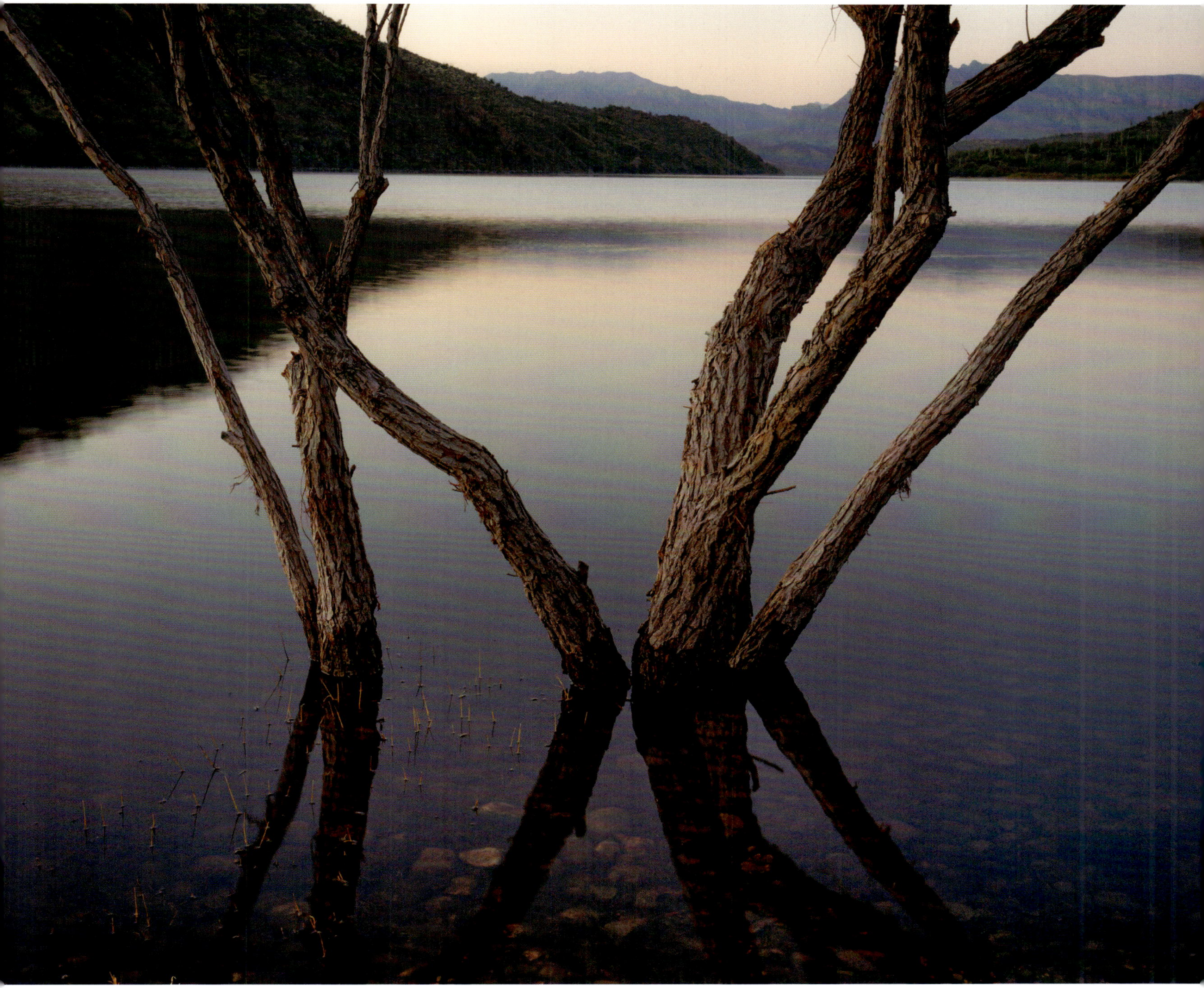

SUBTLE DESERT LIGHT SWIRLS AROUND SUBMERGED TREES ON THE SHORE OF APACHE LAKE.

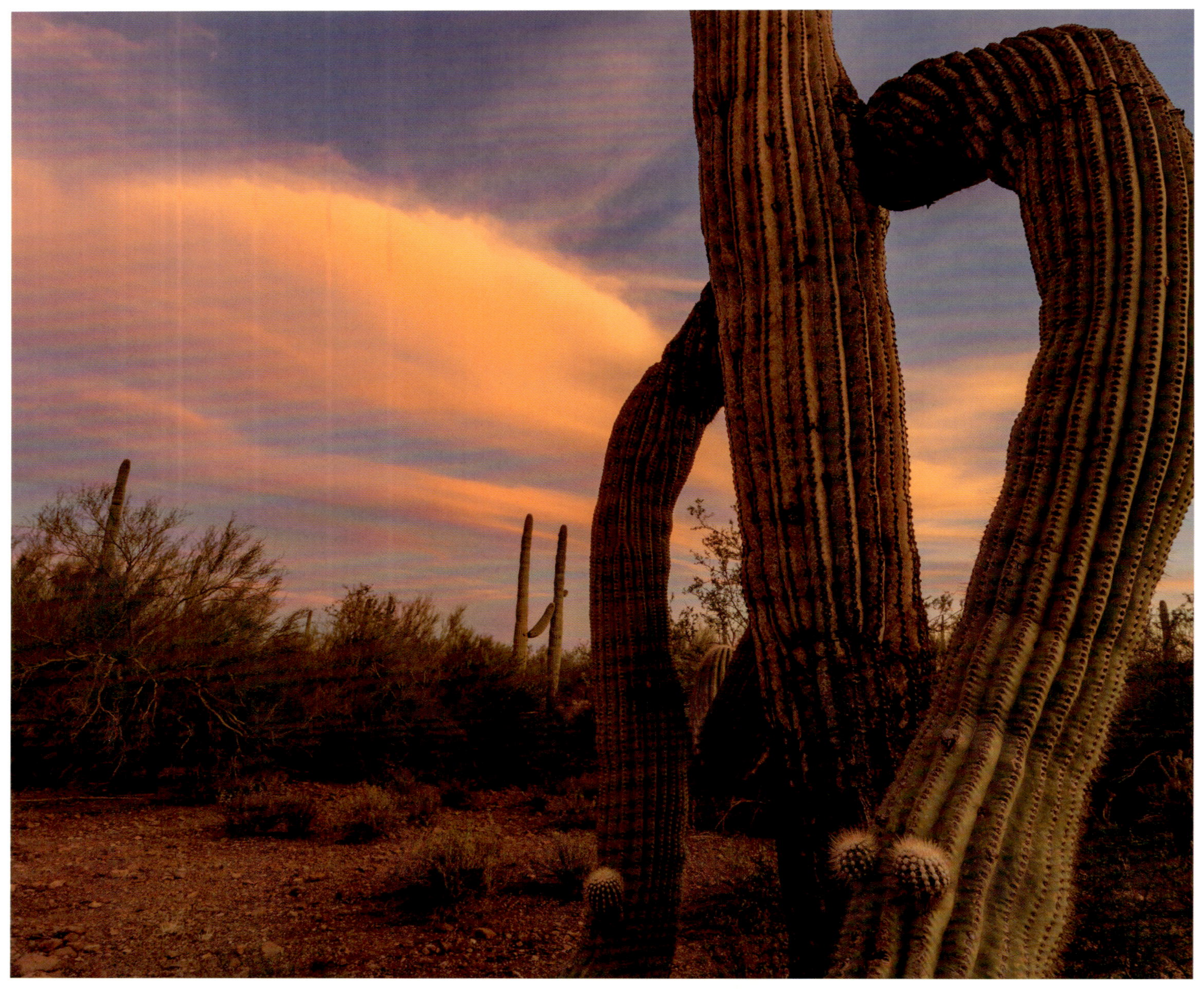

A DROOPING SAGUARO ILLUSTRATES THE HARSH ENVIRONMENT OF THE IRONWOOD FOREST NATIONAL MONUMENT.

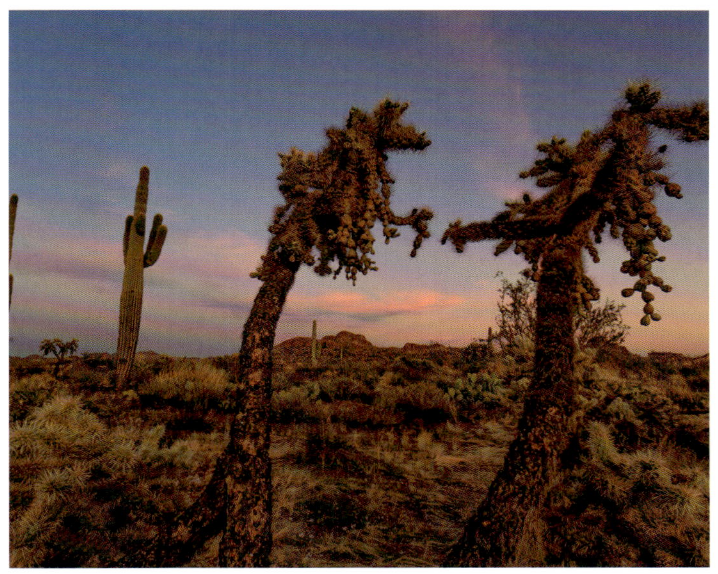

CHAIN FRUIT CHOLLA IN THE SUPERSTITION MOUNTAINS.

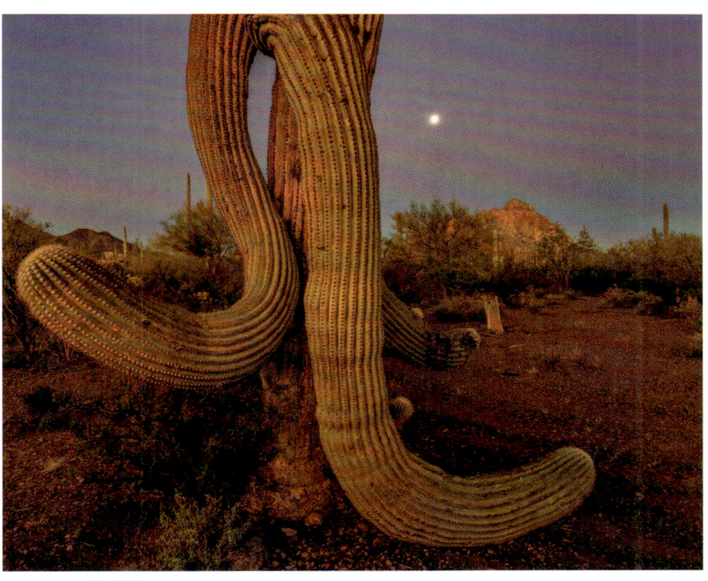

MOONRISE IN THE IRONWOOD FOREST NATIONAL MONUMENT.

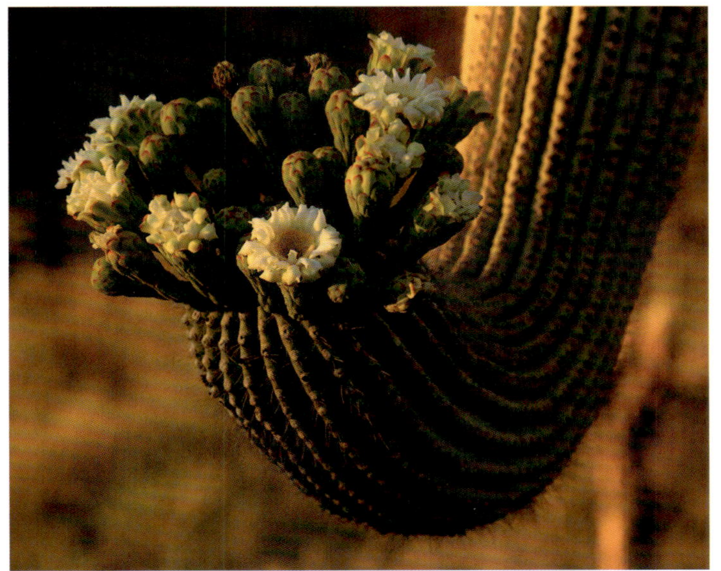

SAGUARO CACTUS BLOOMS IN TUCSON MOUNTAIN PARK.

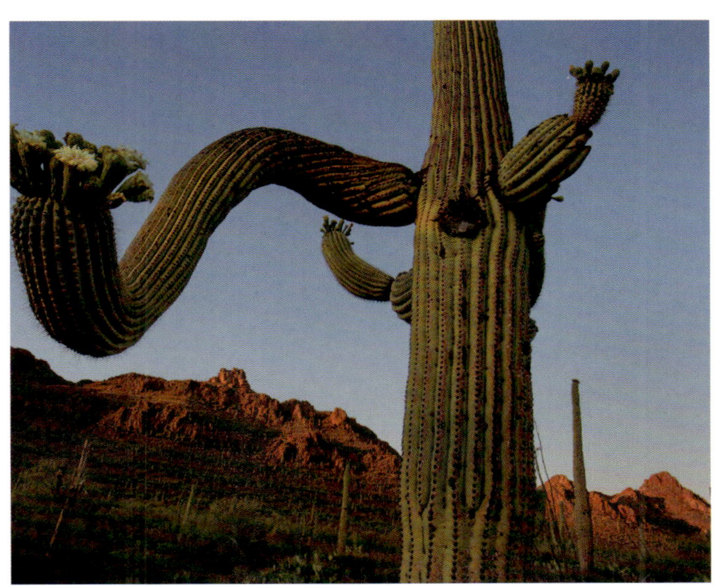

SAGUARO CACTUS BLOOMS ON THE WARM ROCKY
HILLSIDES OF TUCSON MOUNTAIN PARK.

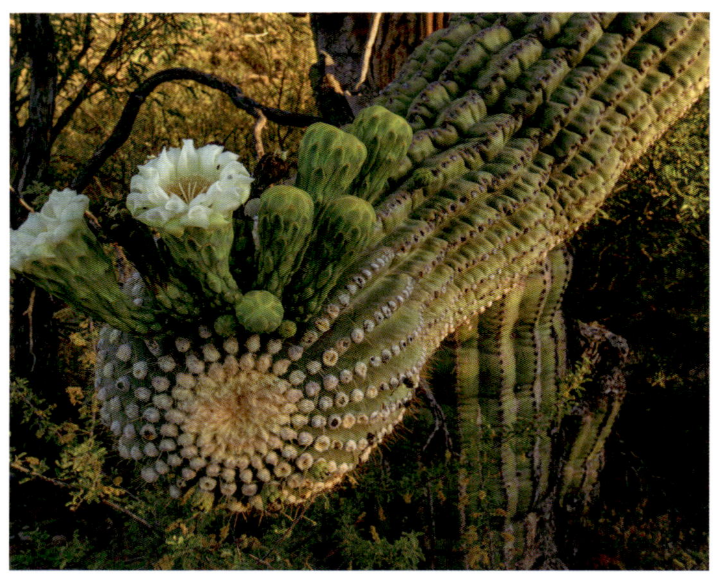

SAGUARO CACTUS BLOOMS IN SWEETWATER PRESERVE IN WEST TUCSON.

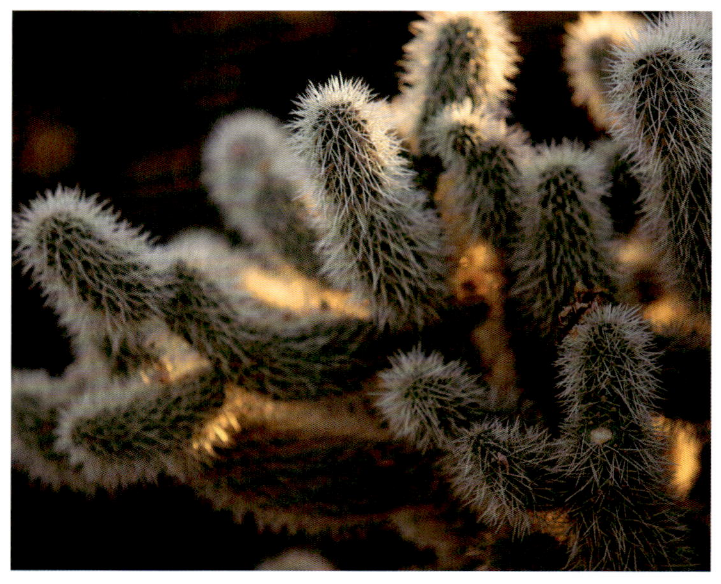

A GOLDEN GLOW SPILLS ACROSS CHOLLA AT
McDOWELL MOUNTAIN REGIONAL PARK.

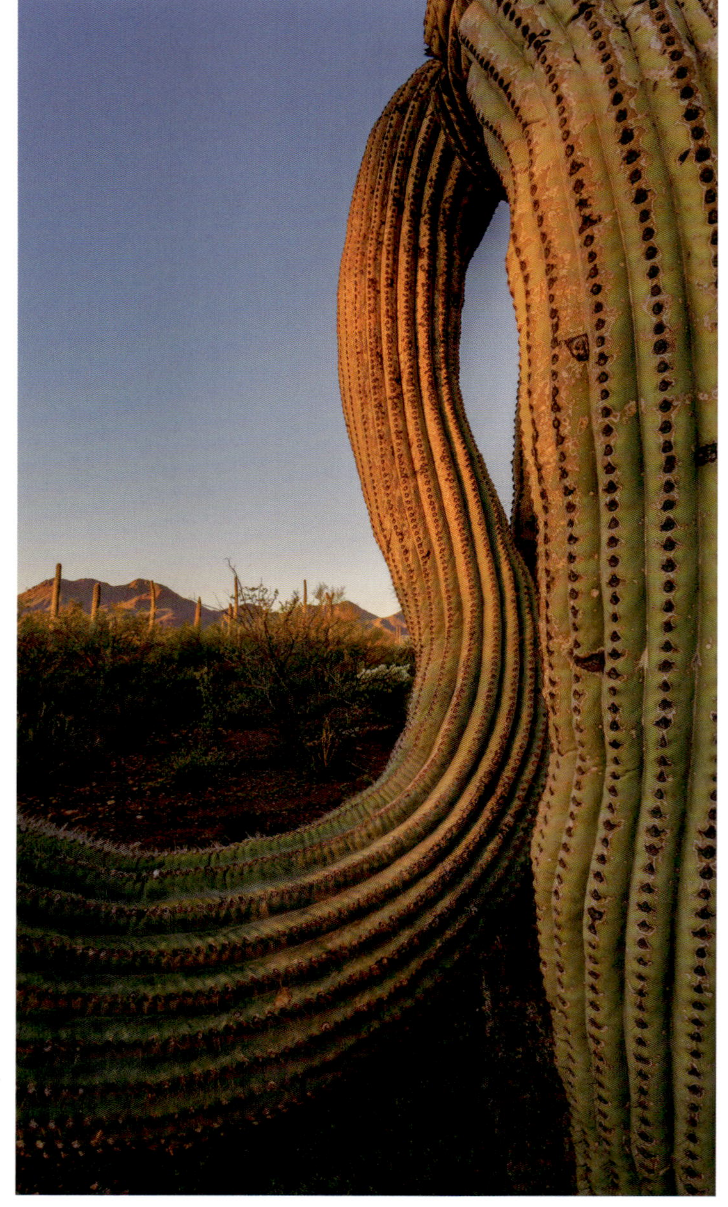

SILVER BELL MOUNTAINS CRADLED BY THE
TWISTED ARMS OF A GIANT SAGUARO CACTUS.

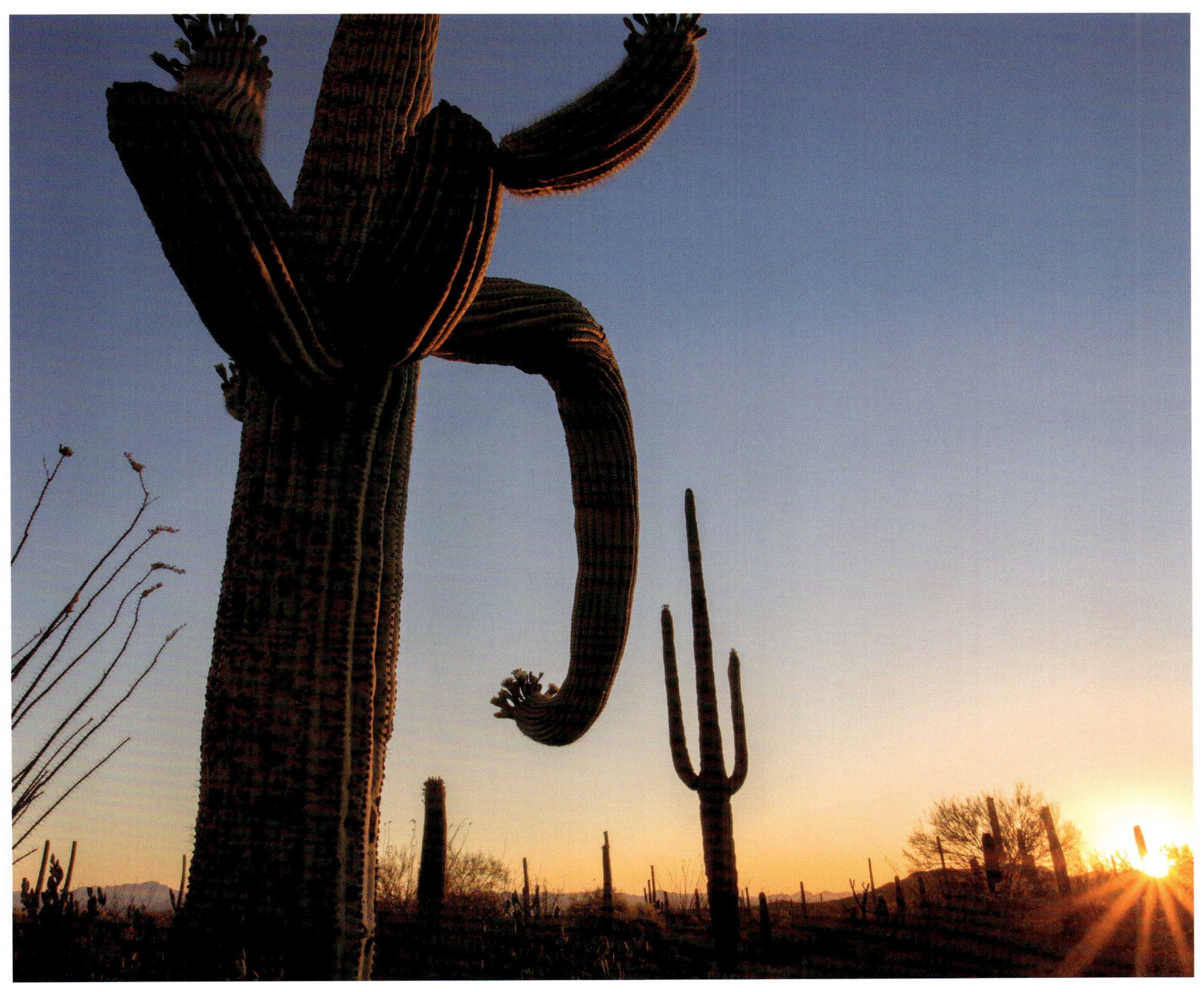

SAGUARO SILHOUETTED BY A BEAUTIFUL SUNSET IN TUCSON MOUNTAIN PARK.

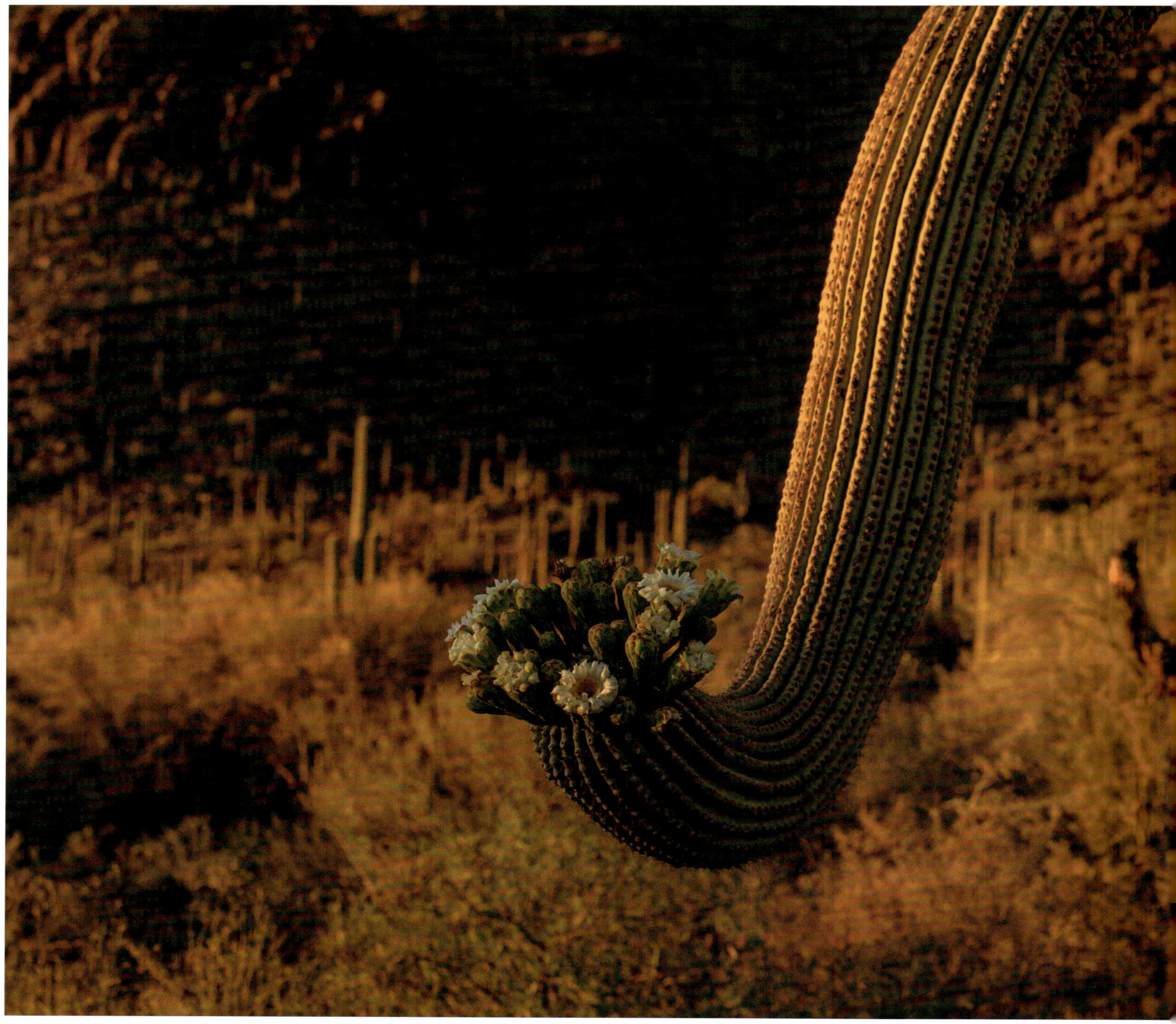

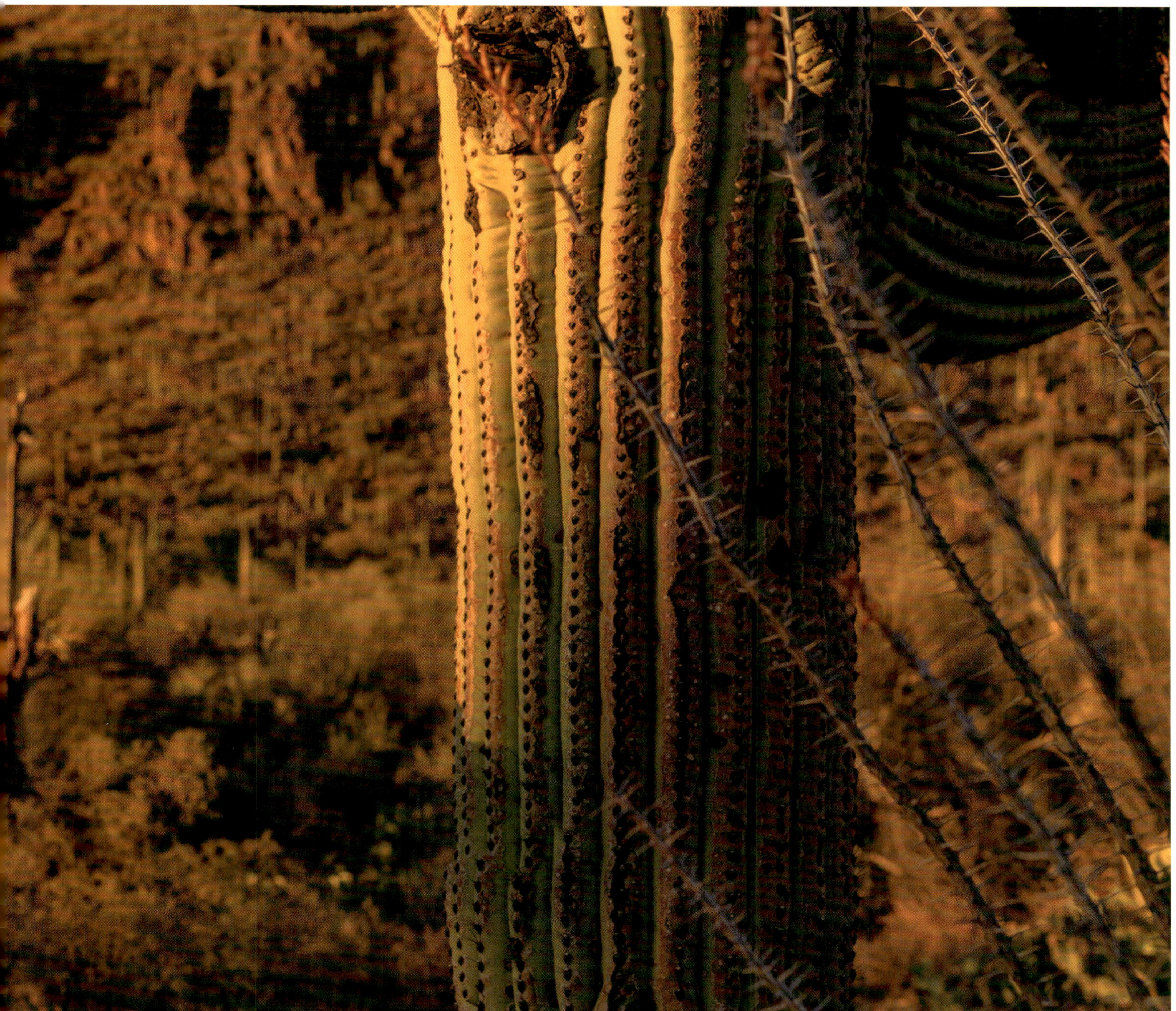

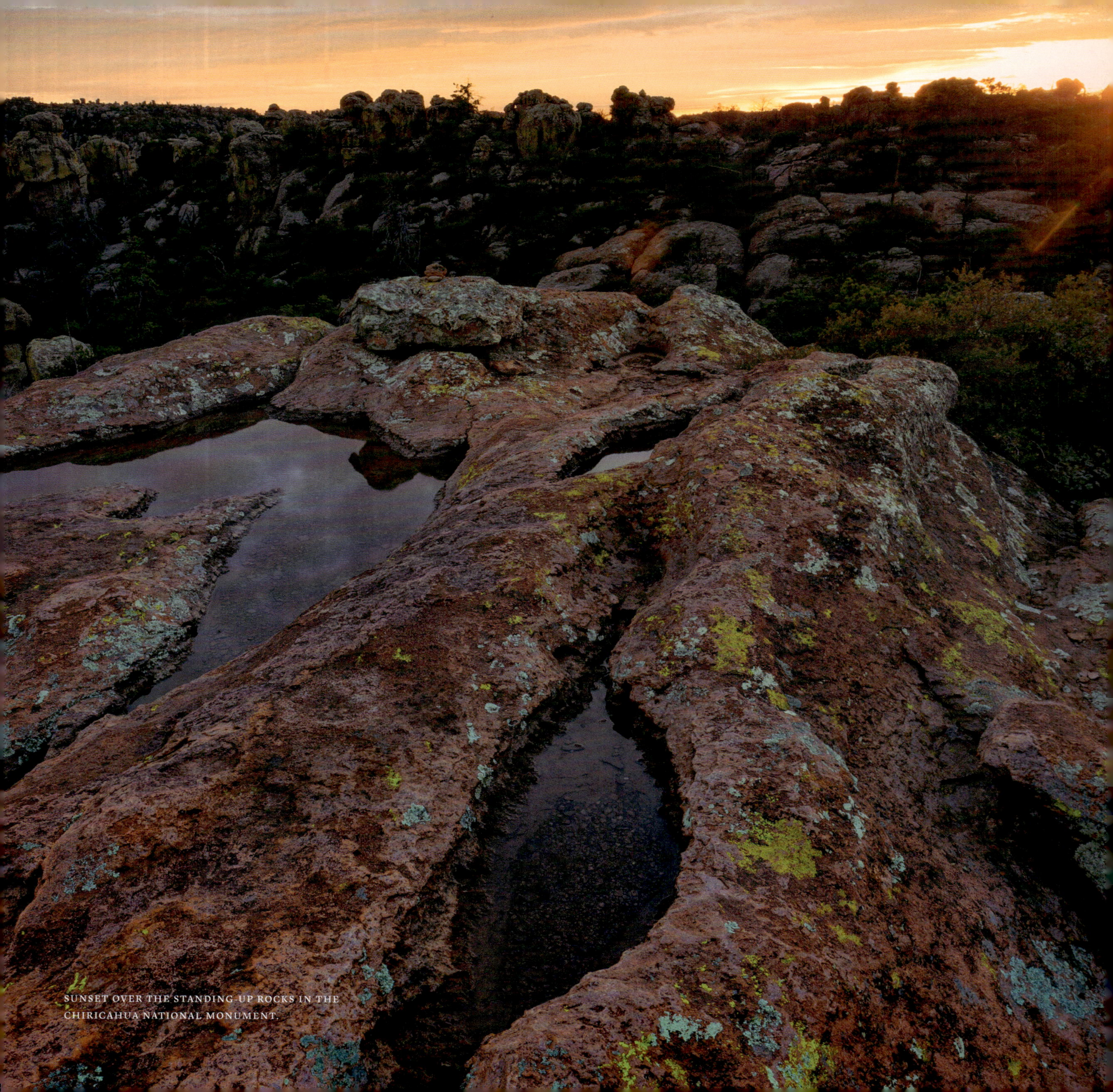

SUNSET OVER THE STANDING-UP ROCKS IN THE
CHIRICAHUA NATIONAL MONUMENT.

# CHIHUAHUAN DESERT

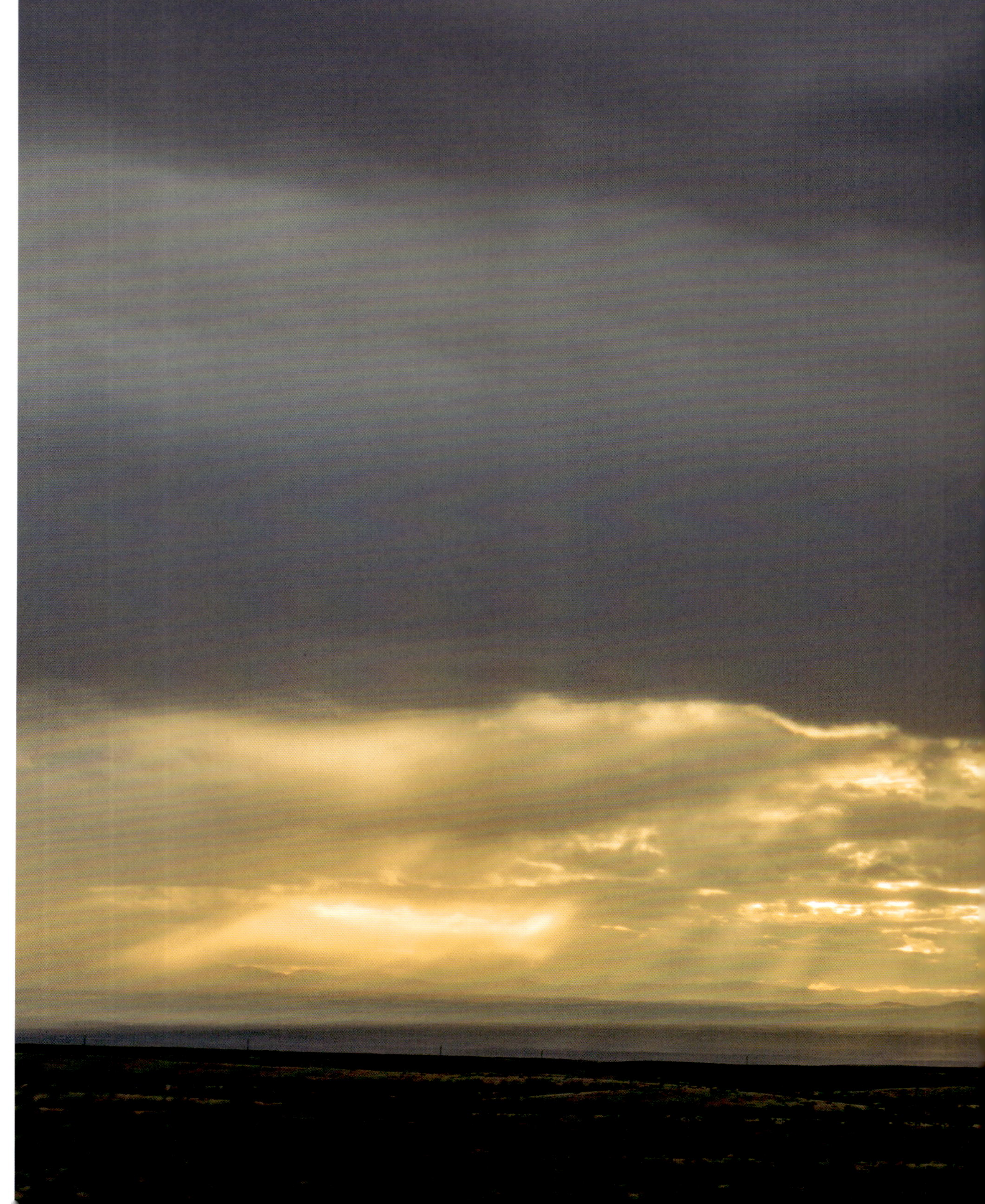

RAIN BREAKS OVER
THE HUACHUCA
MOUNTAINS ABOVE
THE SAN PEDRO
RIVER VALLEY.

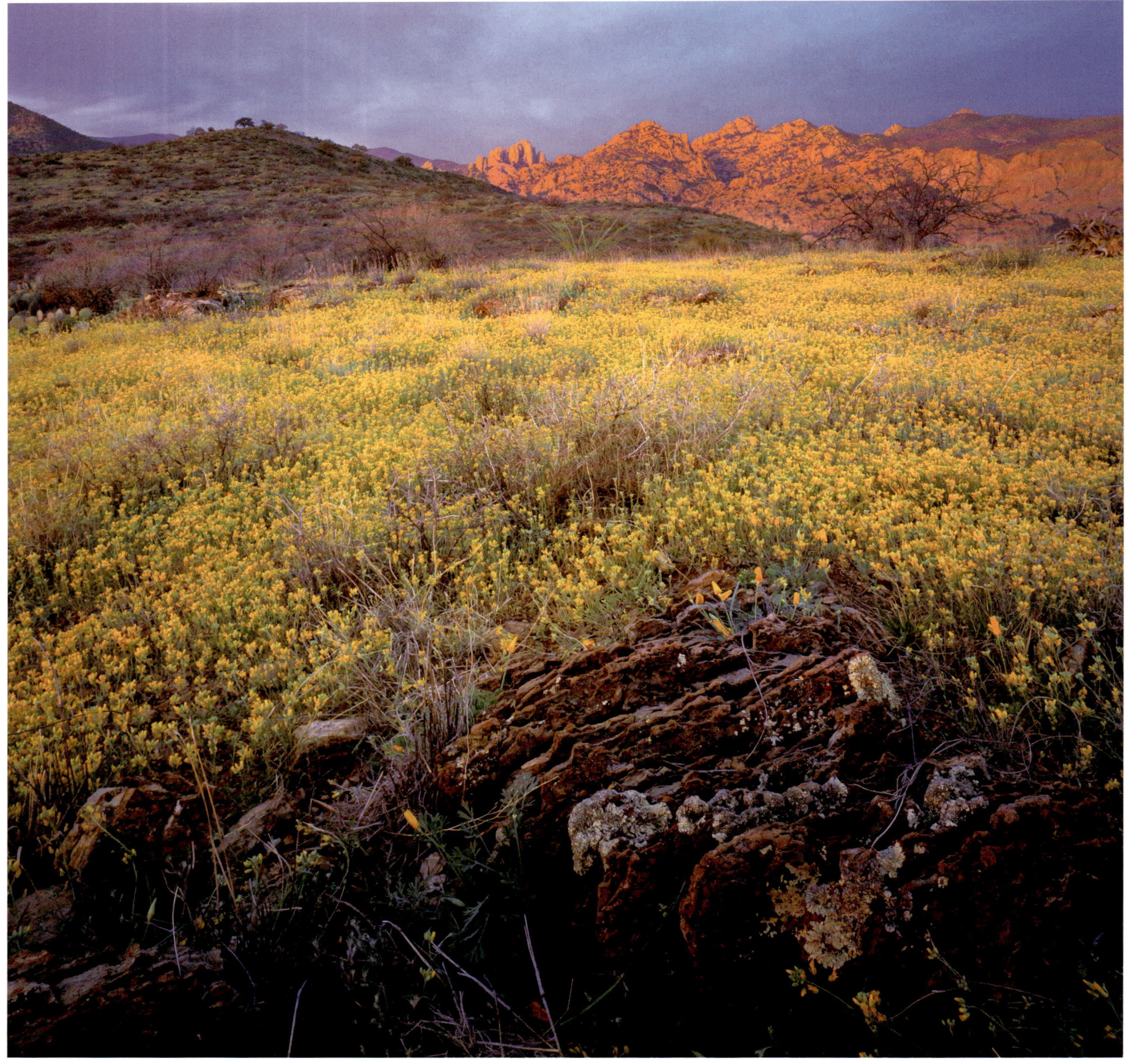



CHINCHWEED AND POPPIES FORM A LUSH YELLOW CARPET IN THE COCHISE STRONGHOLD.

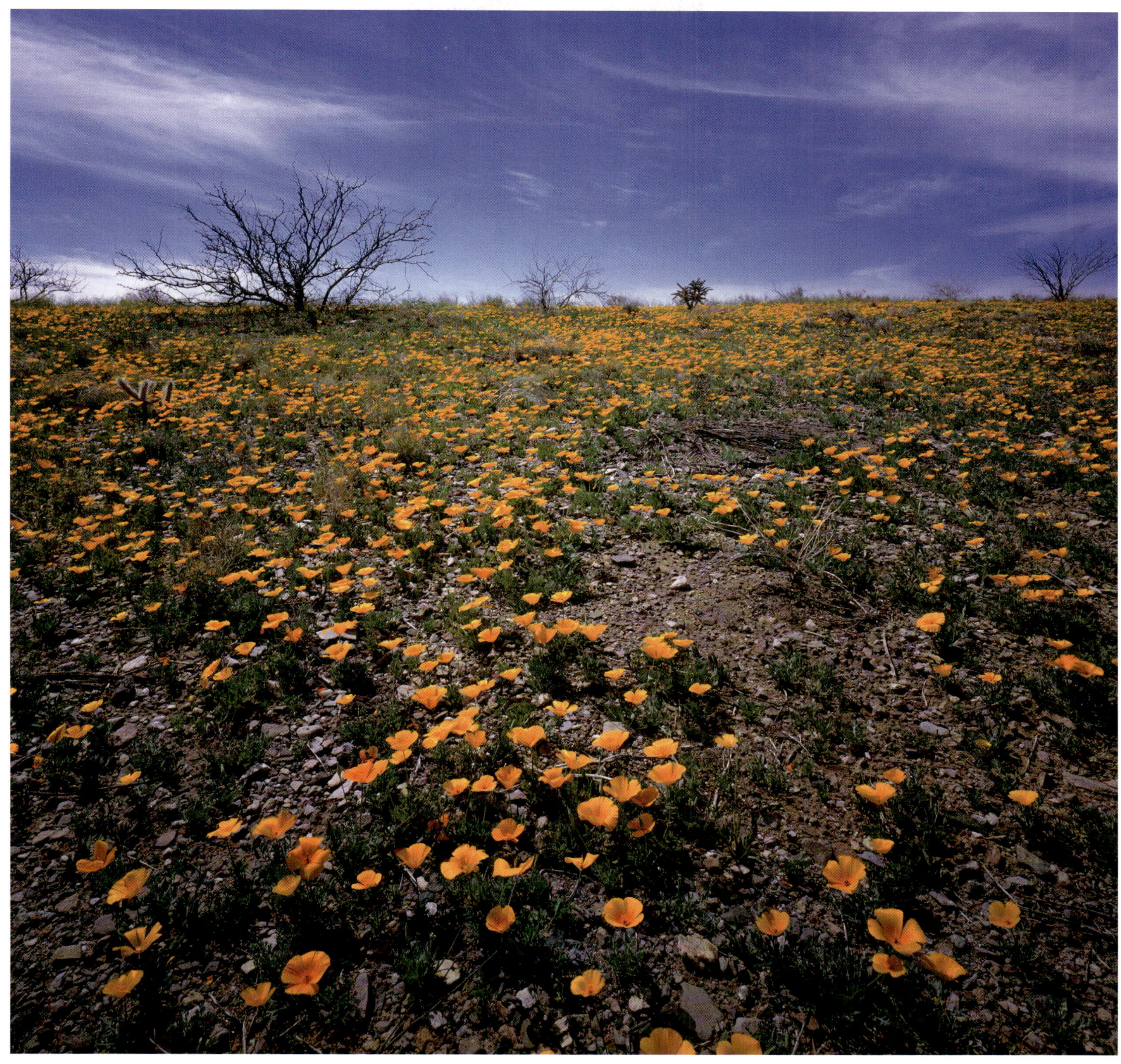

THE CHIHUAHUAN DESERT NEAR FORT BOWIE COMES ALIVE WITH POPPIES.

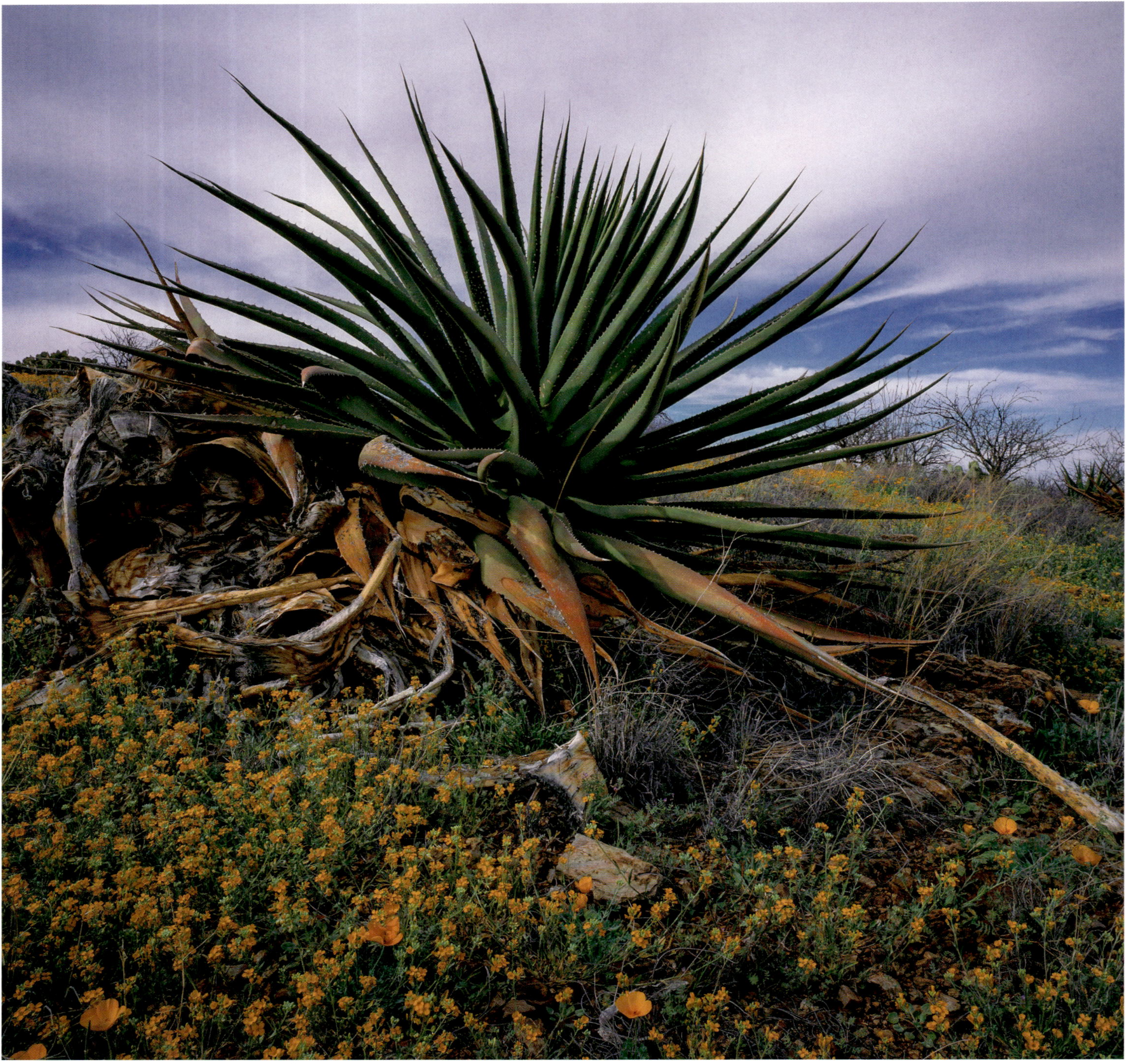



A GNARLED CENTURY PLANT RESTS IN THE ROLLING FOOTHILLS OF THE DRAGOON MOUNTAINS.

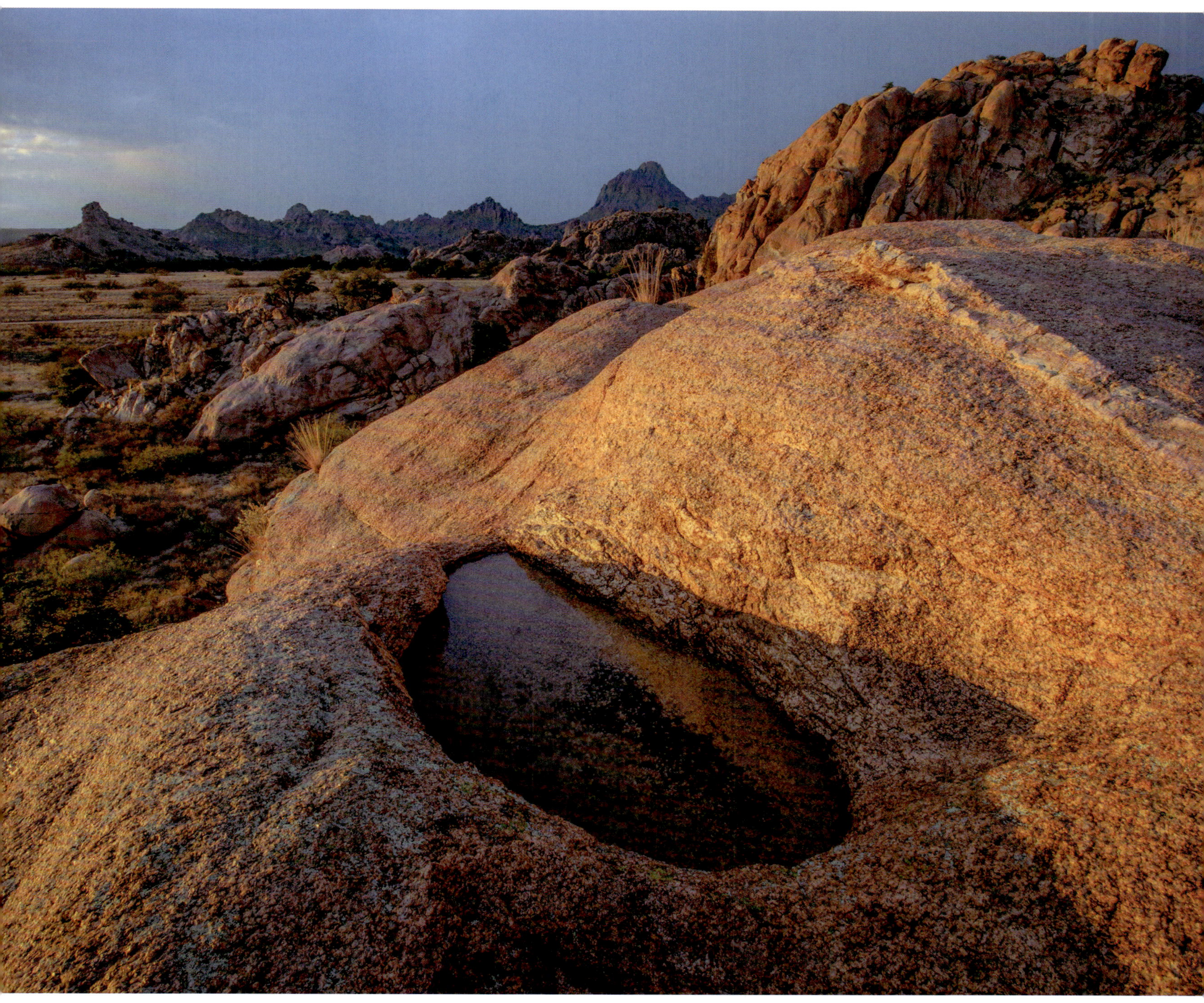

WINTER RAINS COLLECT IN POTHOLES IN THE GRANITE ROCK OF THE DRAGOON MOUNTAINS.

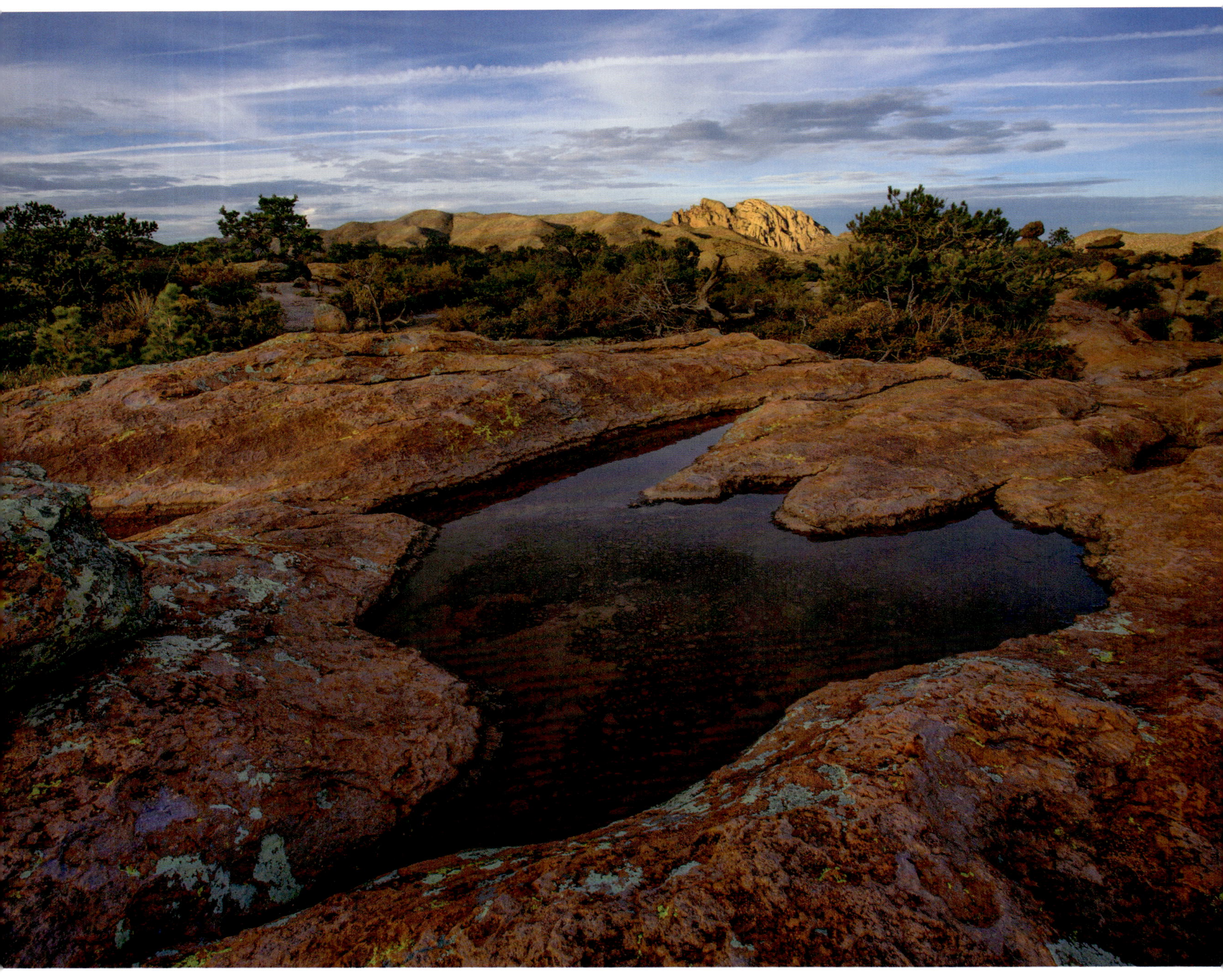



THE LATE EVENING LIGHT ILLUMINATES COCHISE HEAD, A PROMINENT PEAK IN THE CHIRICAHUA MOUNTAIN RANGE.

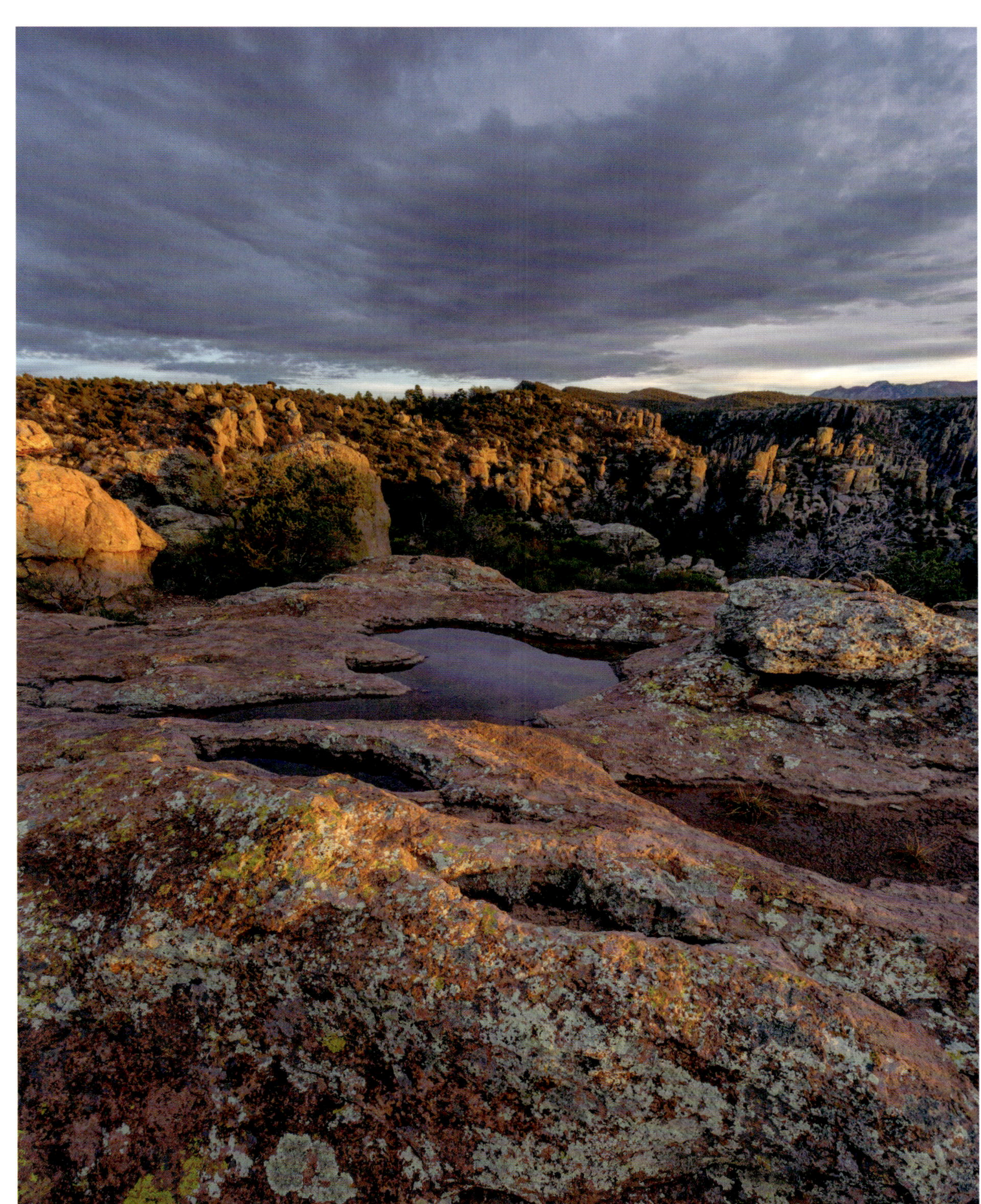

A PANORAMIC VIEW
OF THE STANDING-UP
ROCKS VALLEY IN THE
CHIRICAHUA NATIONAL
MONUMENT.

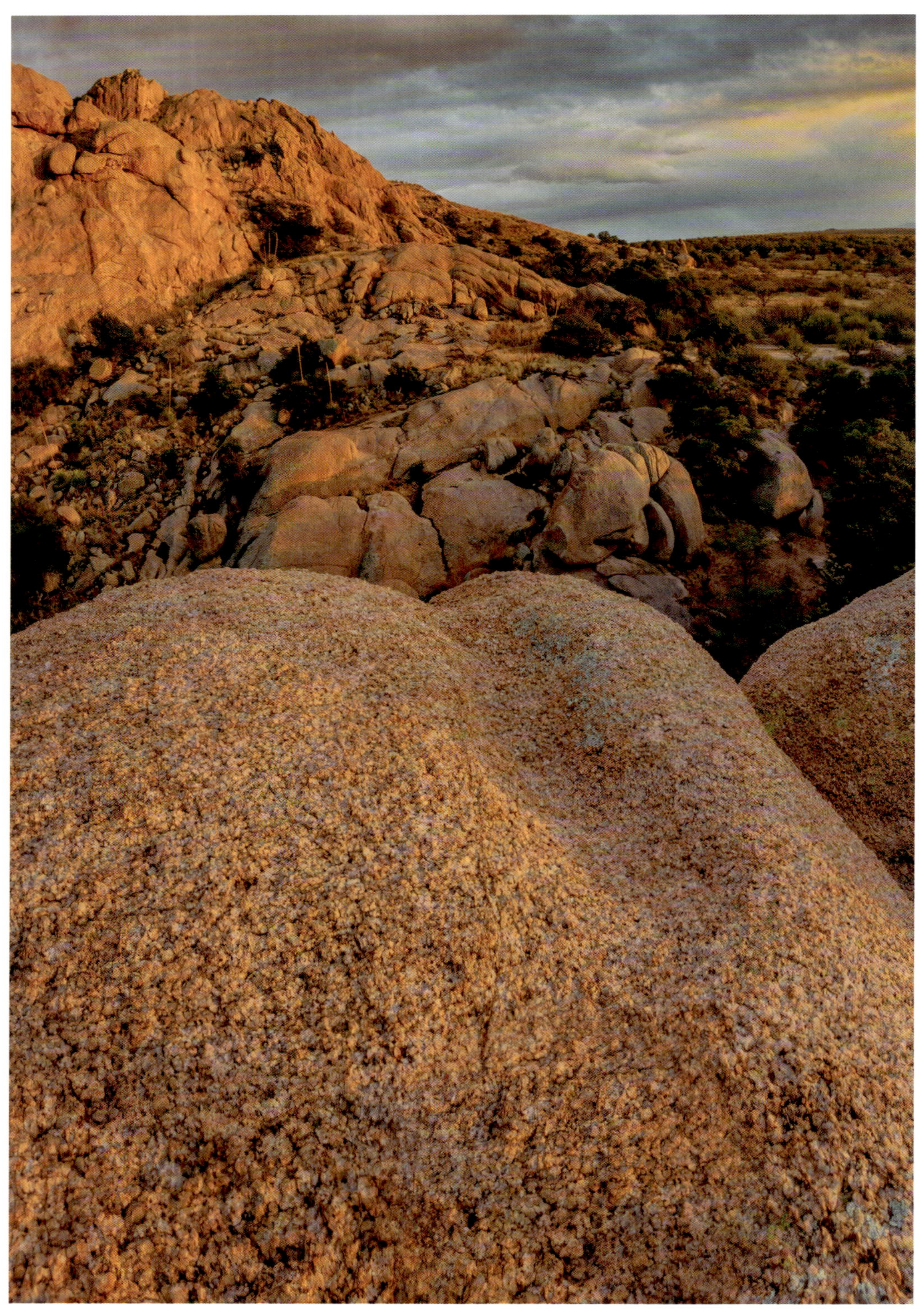

THE DRAGOON MOUNTAINS
NEAR TOMBSTONE ARE A
PICTURESQUE AND POPULAR
CLIMBING SPOT.

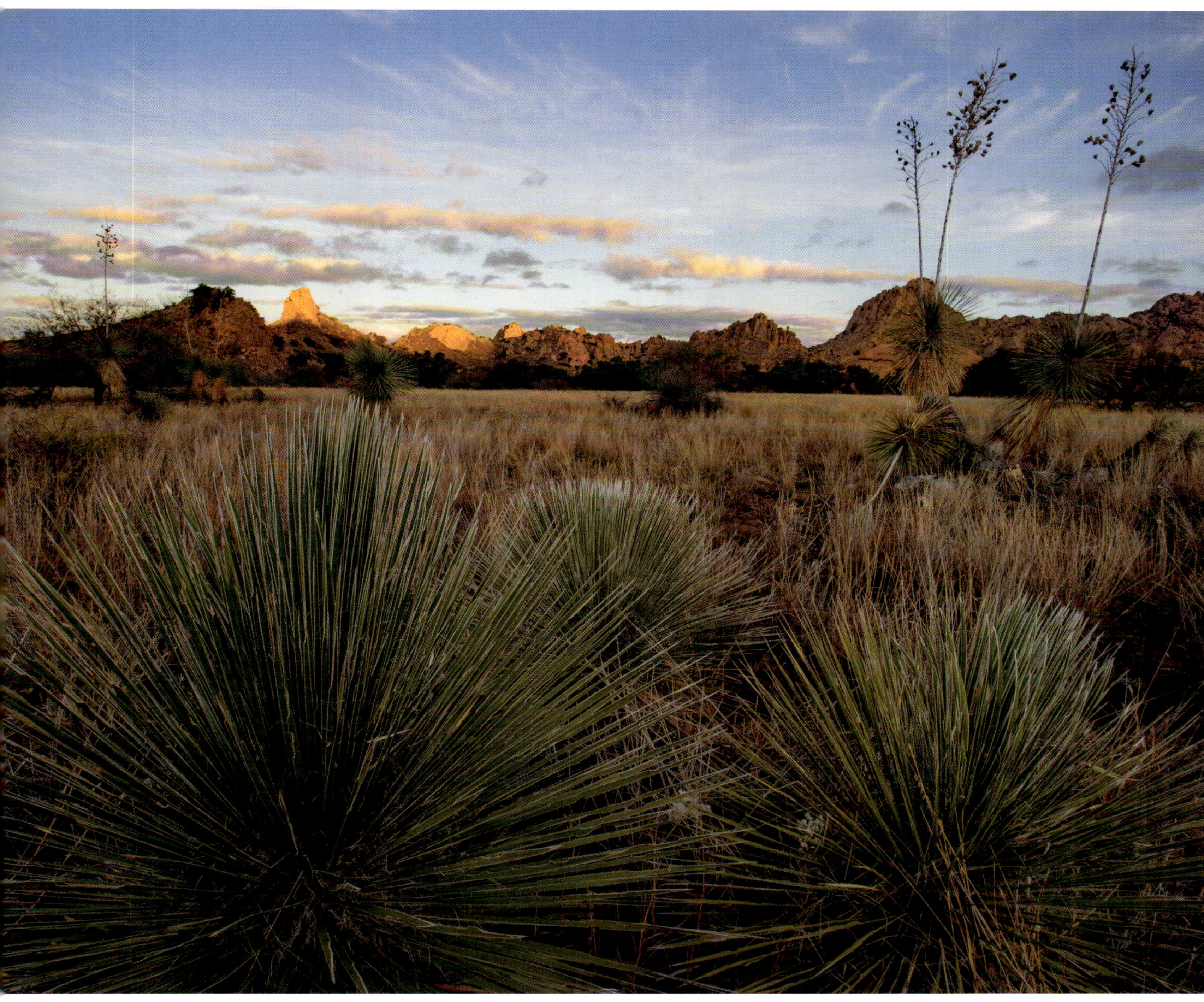

LONG GOLDEN GRASSES LINE THE EDGE OF THE SAN PEDRO RIVER VALLEY.

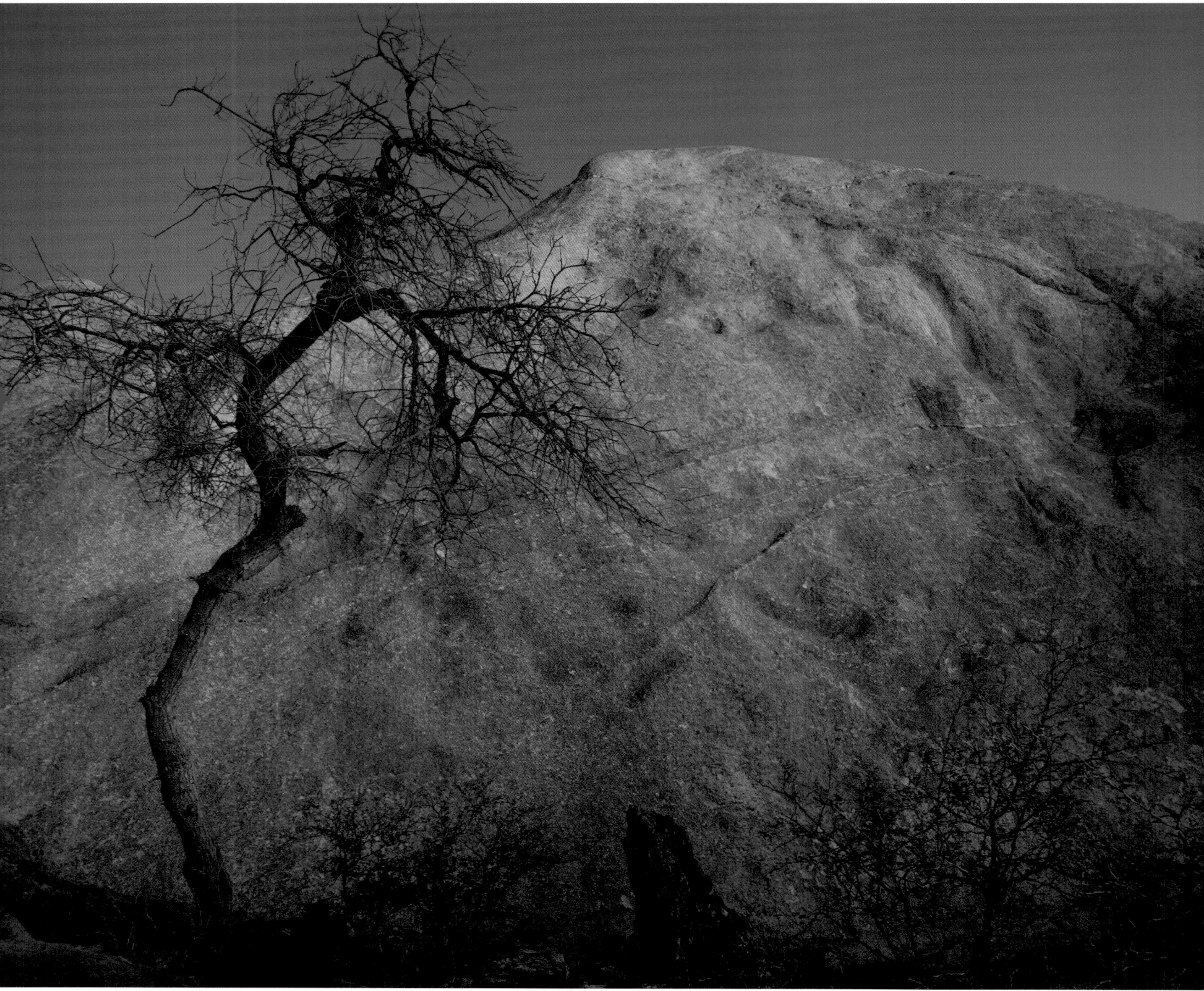

AN AMBER GLOW HIGHLIGHTS GRANITE ROCK IN THE COCHISE STRONGHOLD.

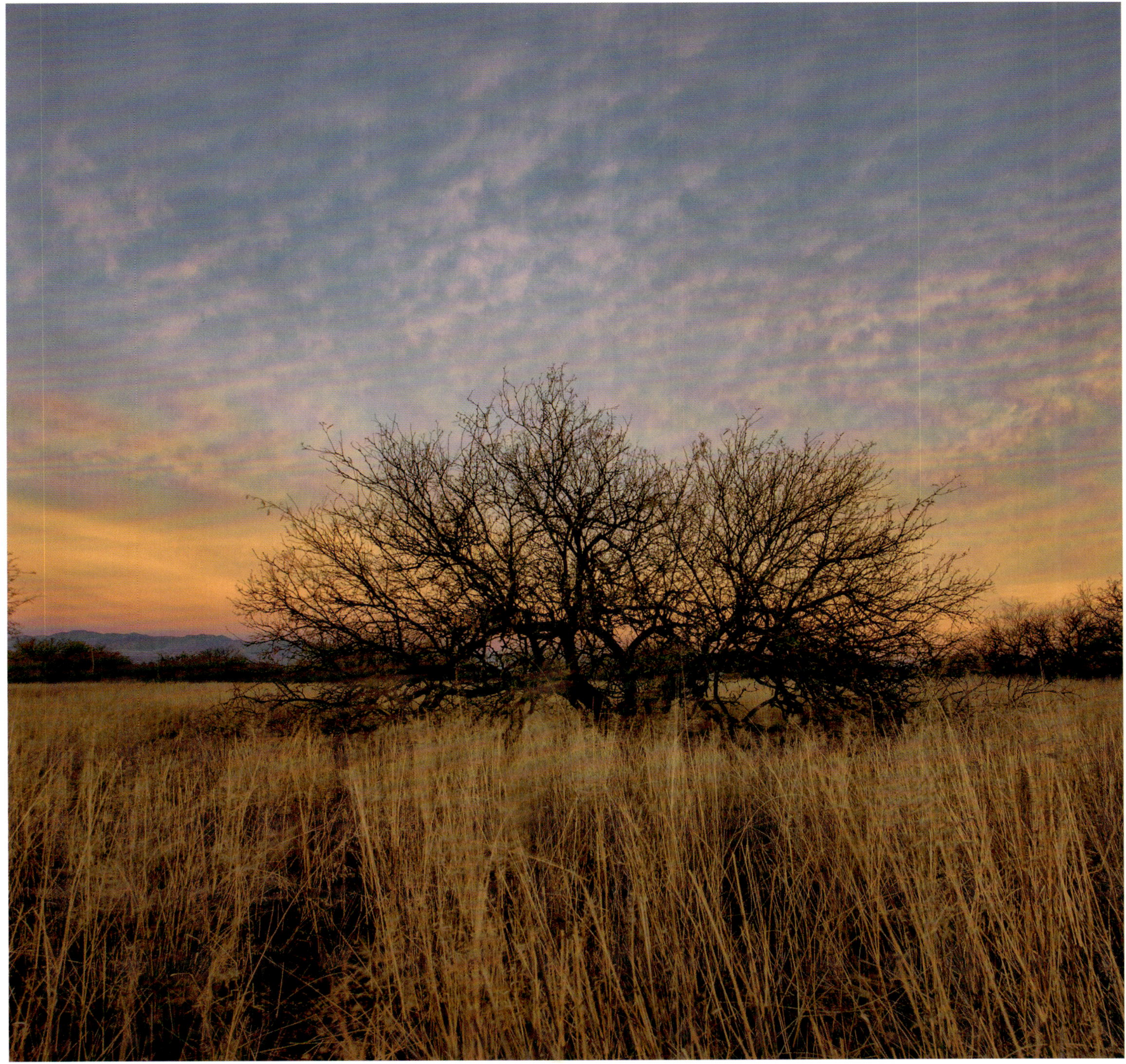

MESQUITE TREES IN THE TALL GRASS PLAINS OF THE SAN PEDRO RIVER VALLEY.

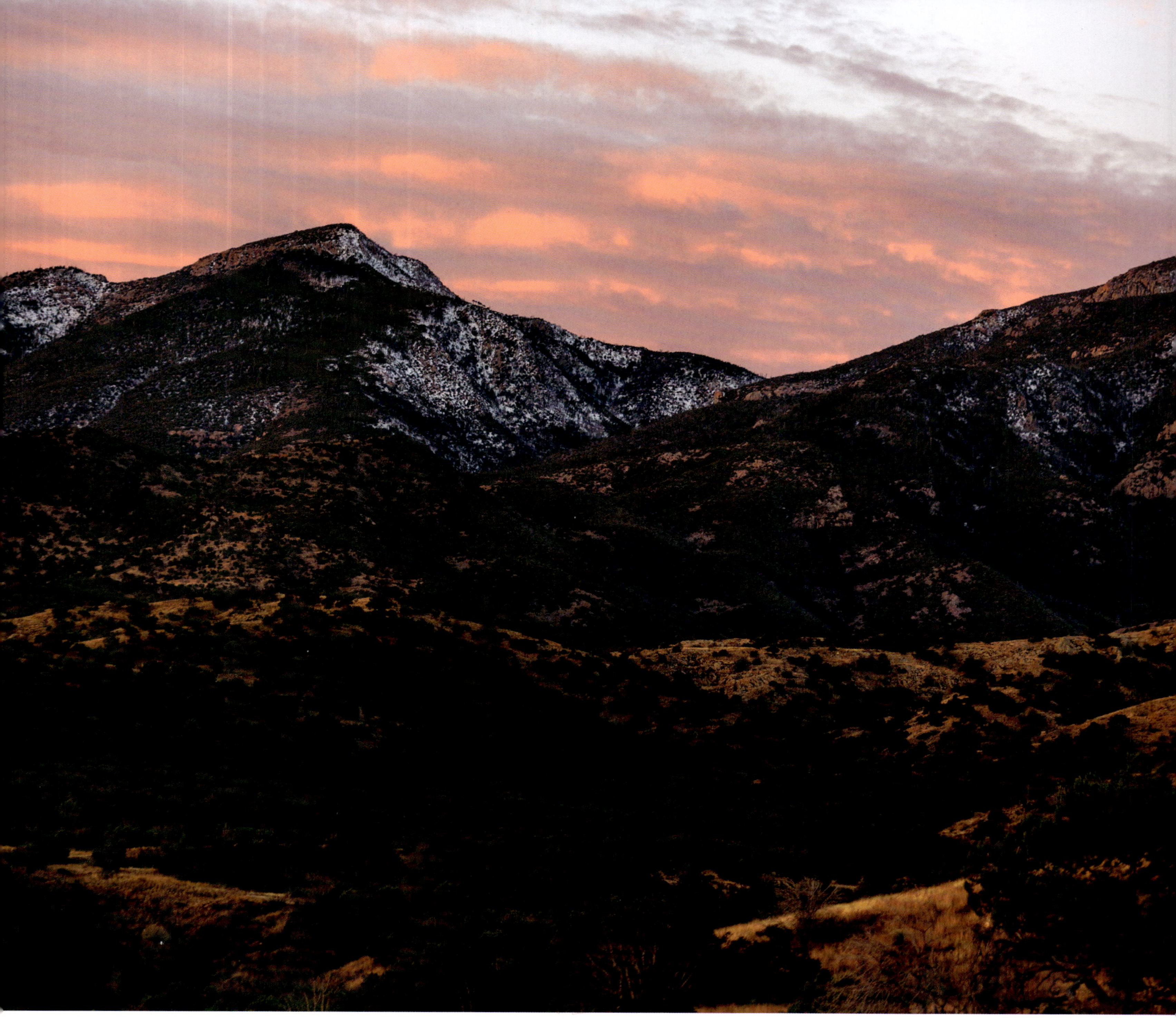

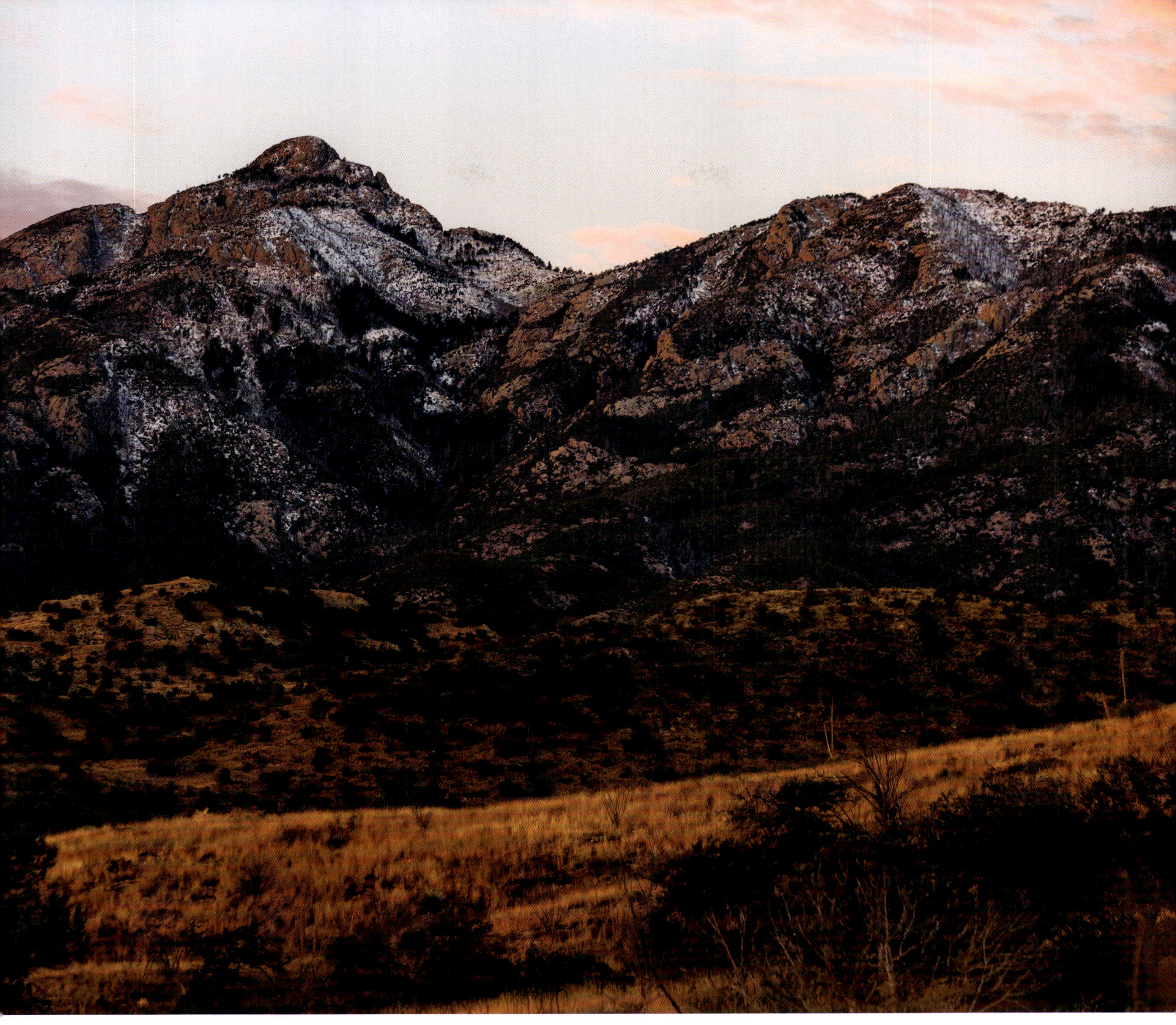

THE SANTA RITA MOUNTAINS RISE TO AN ELEVATION OF 9453 FEET NEAR KENTUCKY CAMP.

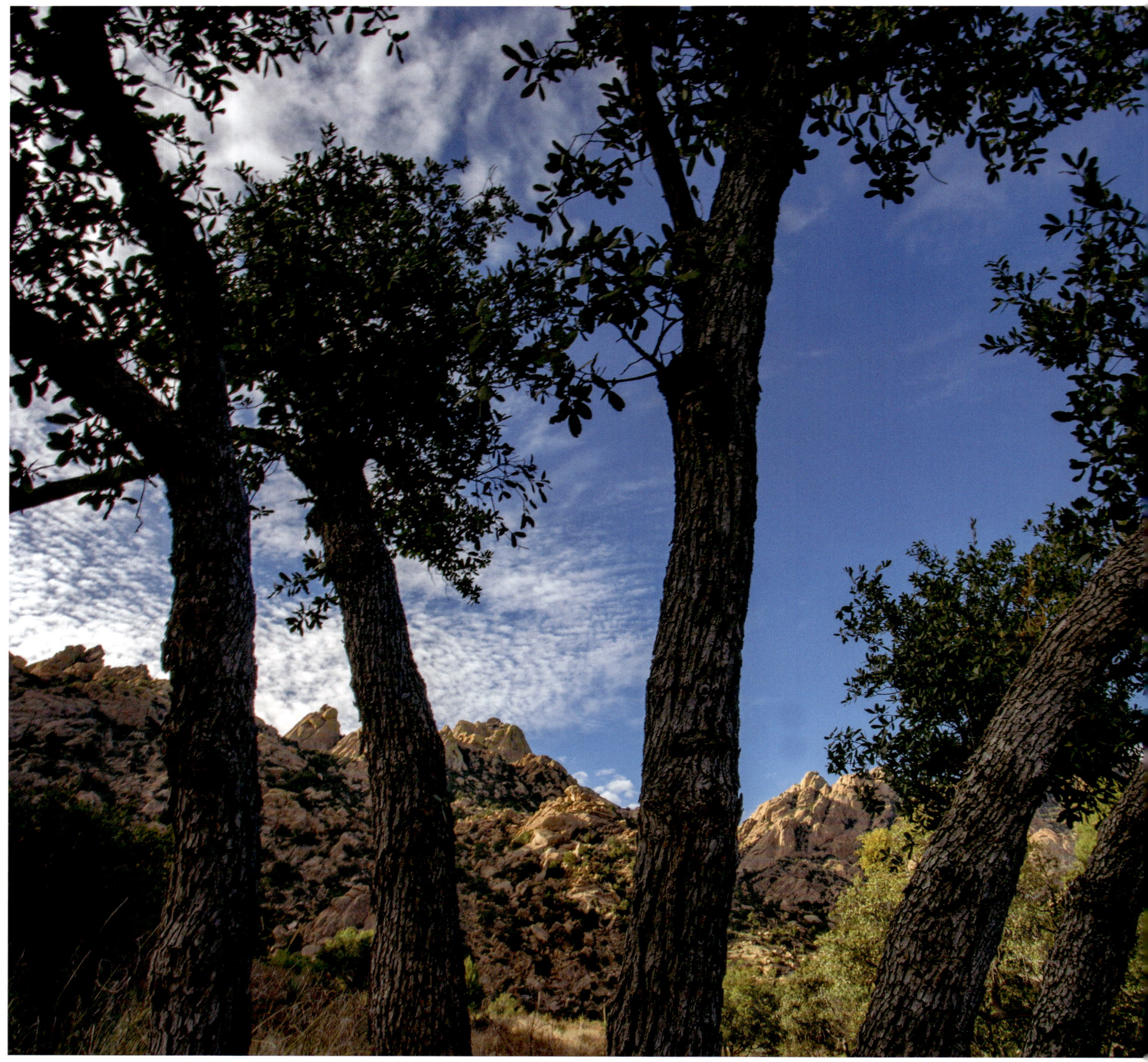

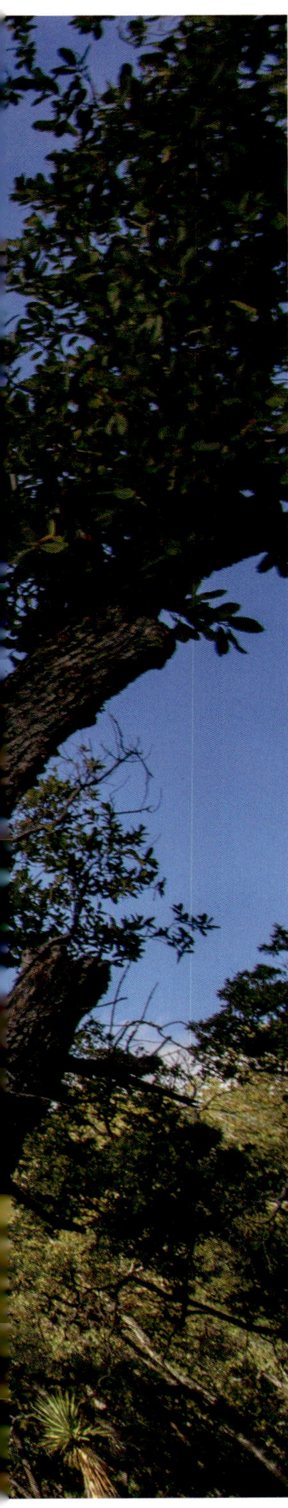

WHITE OAK TREES CREATE A
MUCH-NEEDED SHADE CANOPY
IN THE COCHISE STRONGHOLD
DURING THE WARM MONTHS.

DETAIL OF TWISTED
ARIZONA WHITE OAKS IN THE
COCHISE STRONGHOLD.

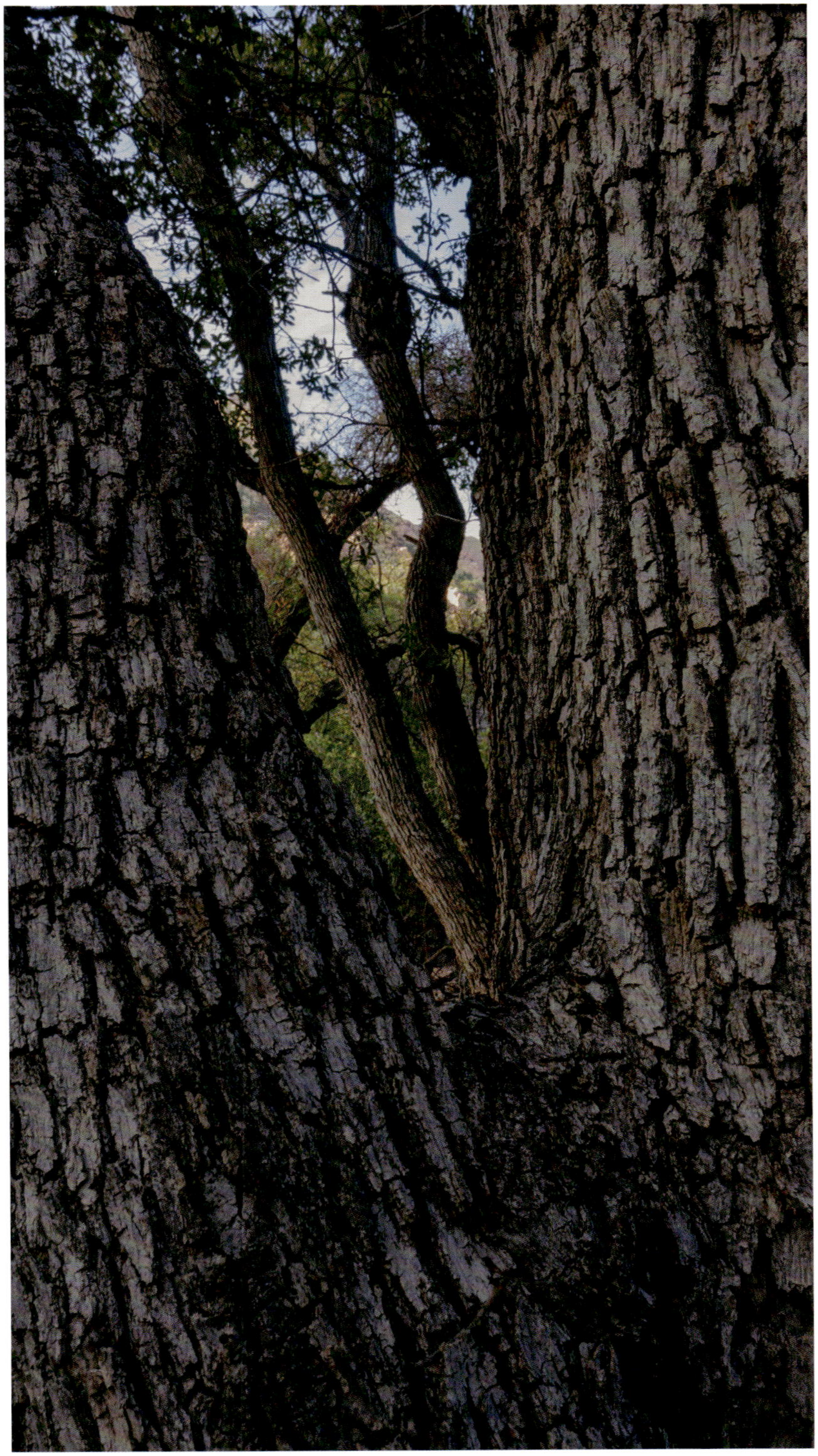

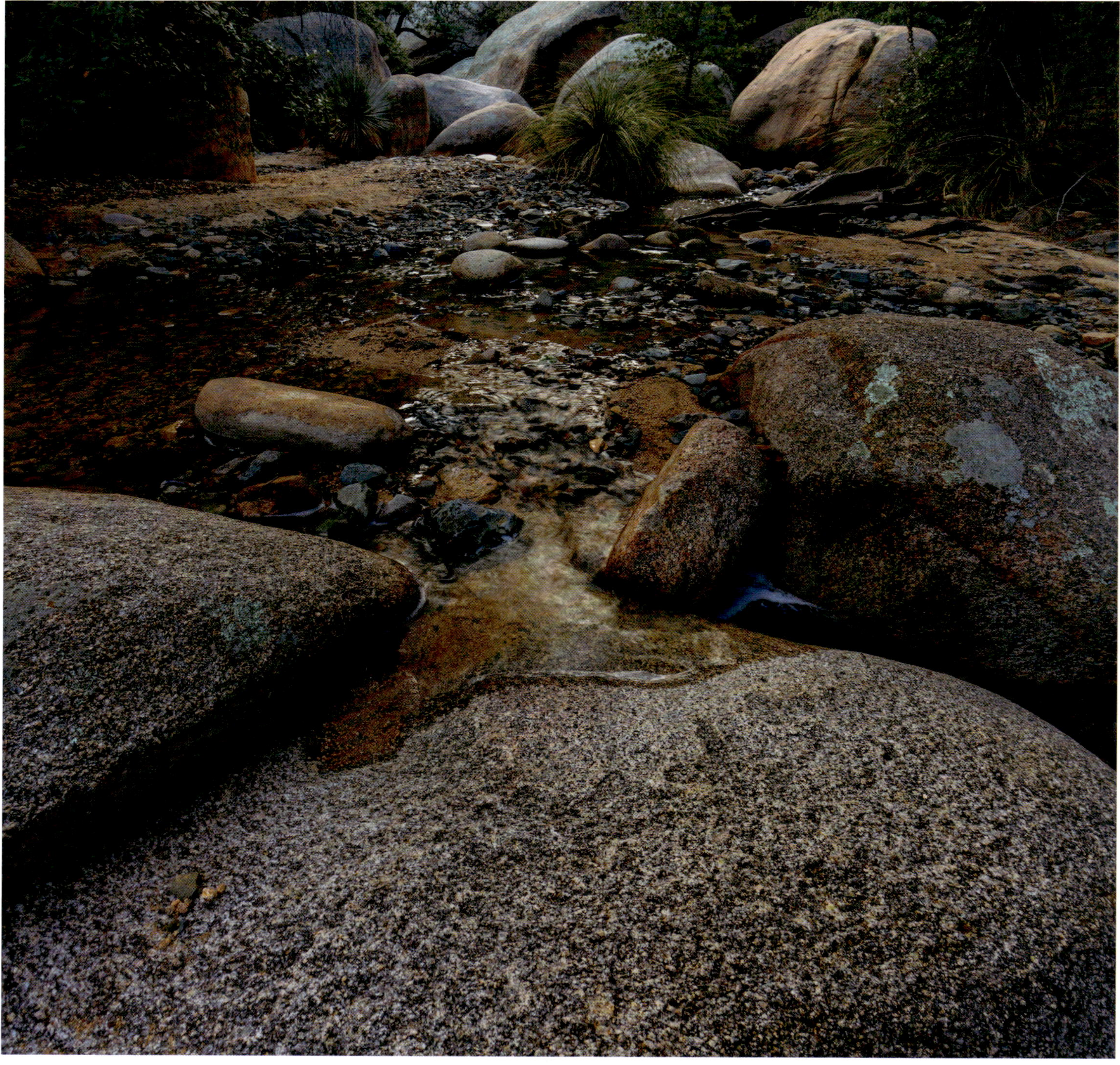



COOL, STILL POOLS GATHER AROUND BOULDERS IN CREEKS THAT RUN DURING THE RAINY SEASON.

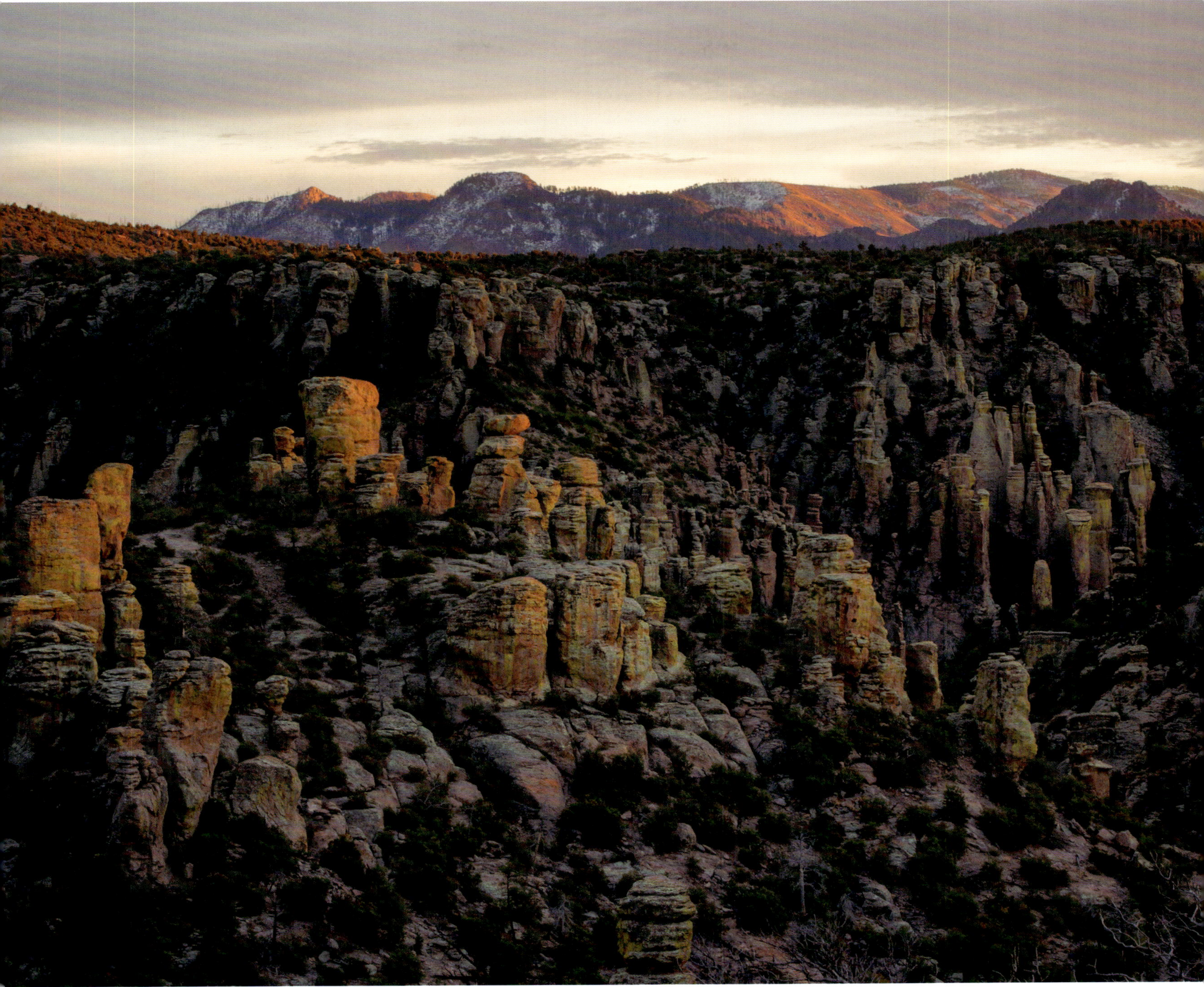

COCHISE PEAK TOWERS OVER THE STANDING-UP ROCKS IN THE CHIRICAHUA NATIONAL MONUMENT.

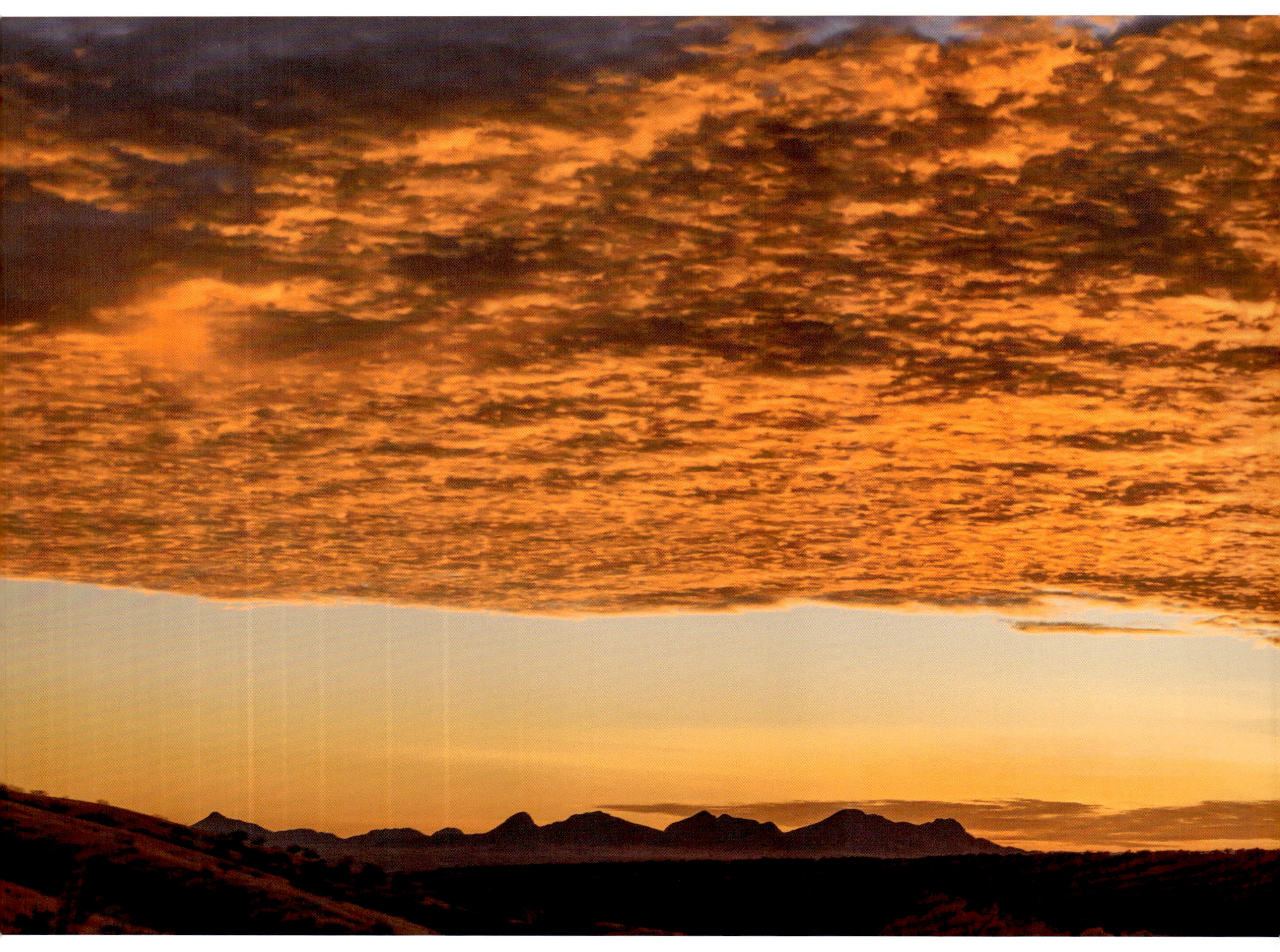

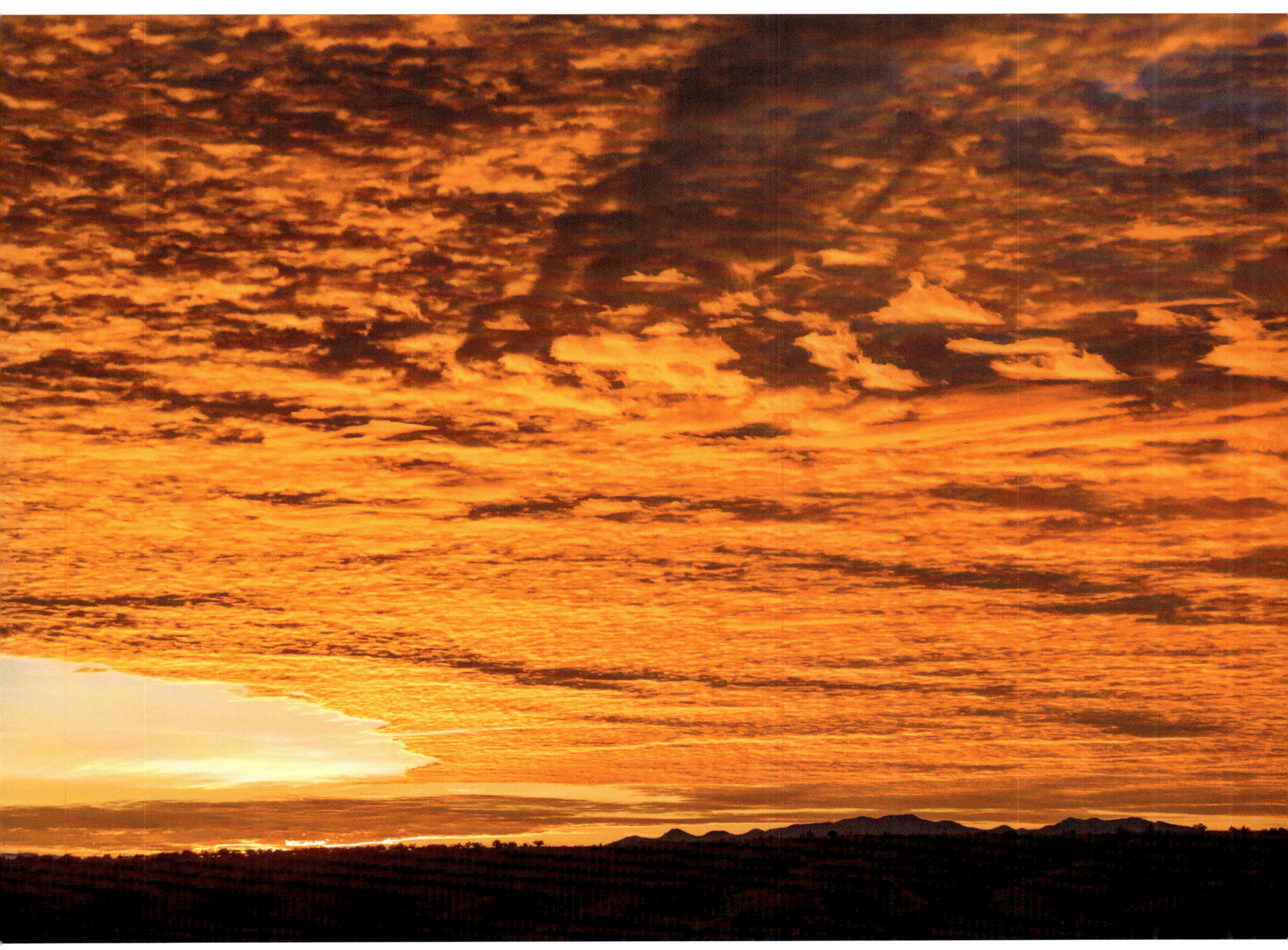

A HUGE STORMFRONT MOVES OVER THE CANELO HILLS IN THE CORONADO NATIONAL FOREST.

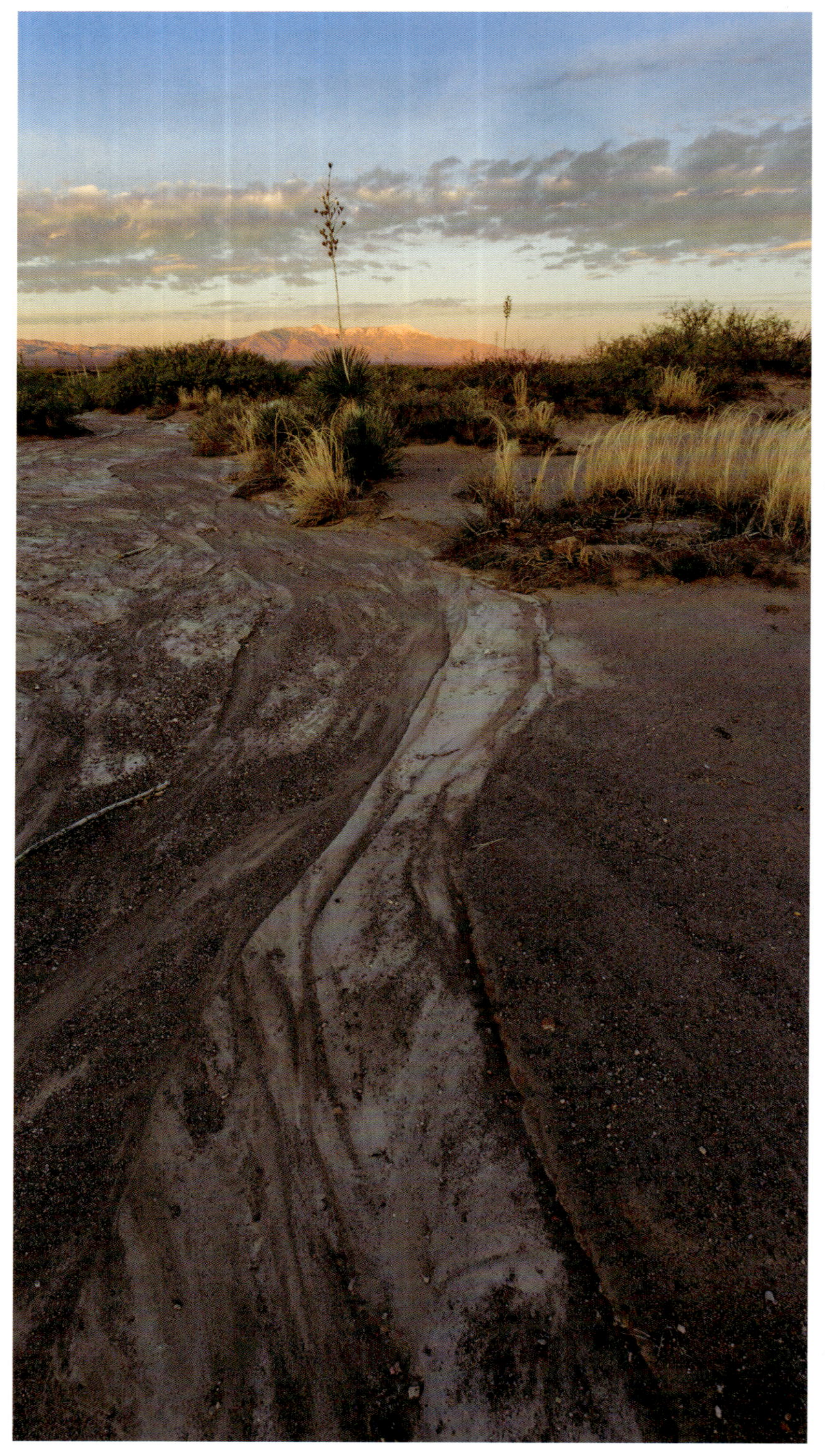



THE PEAKS OF THE PINALEÑO
MOUNTAIN RISE ABOVE THE
SAN SIMON RIVER VALLEY.



THE SUN BREAKS ON
SNOW-DUSTED PEAKS OF THE
SANTA RITA MOUNTAINS.

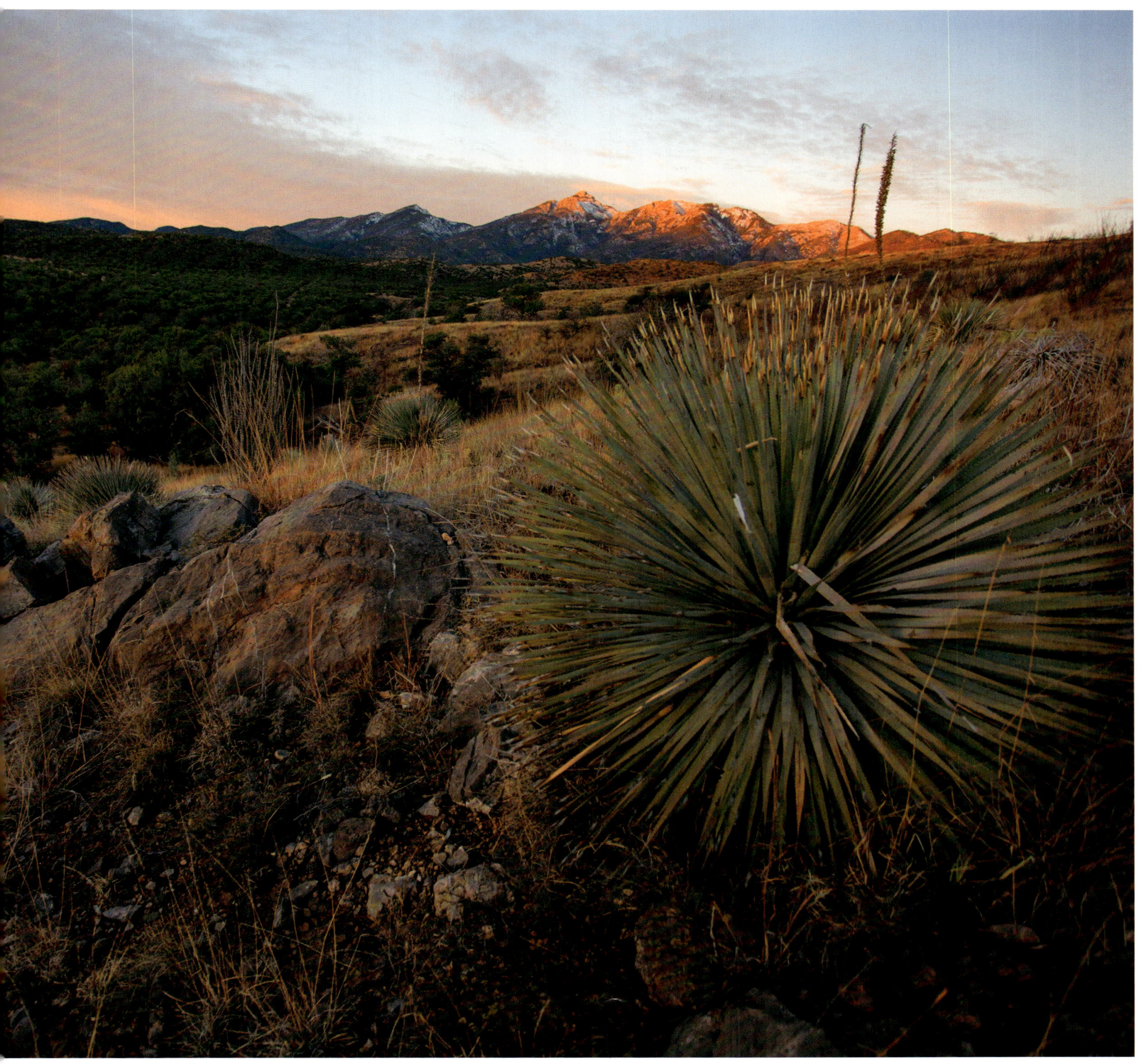

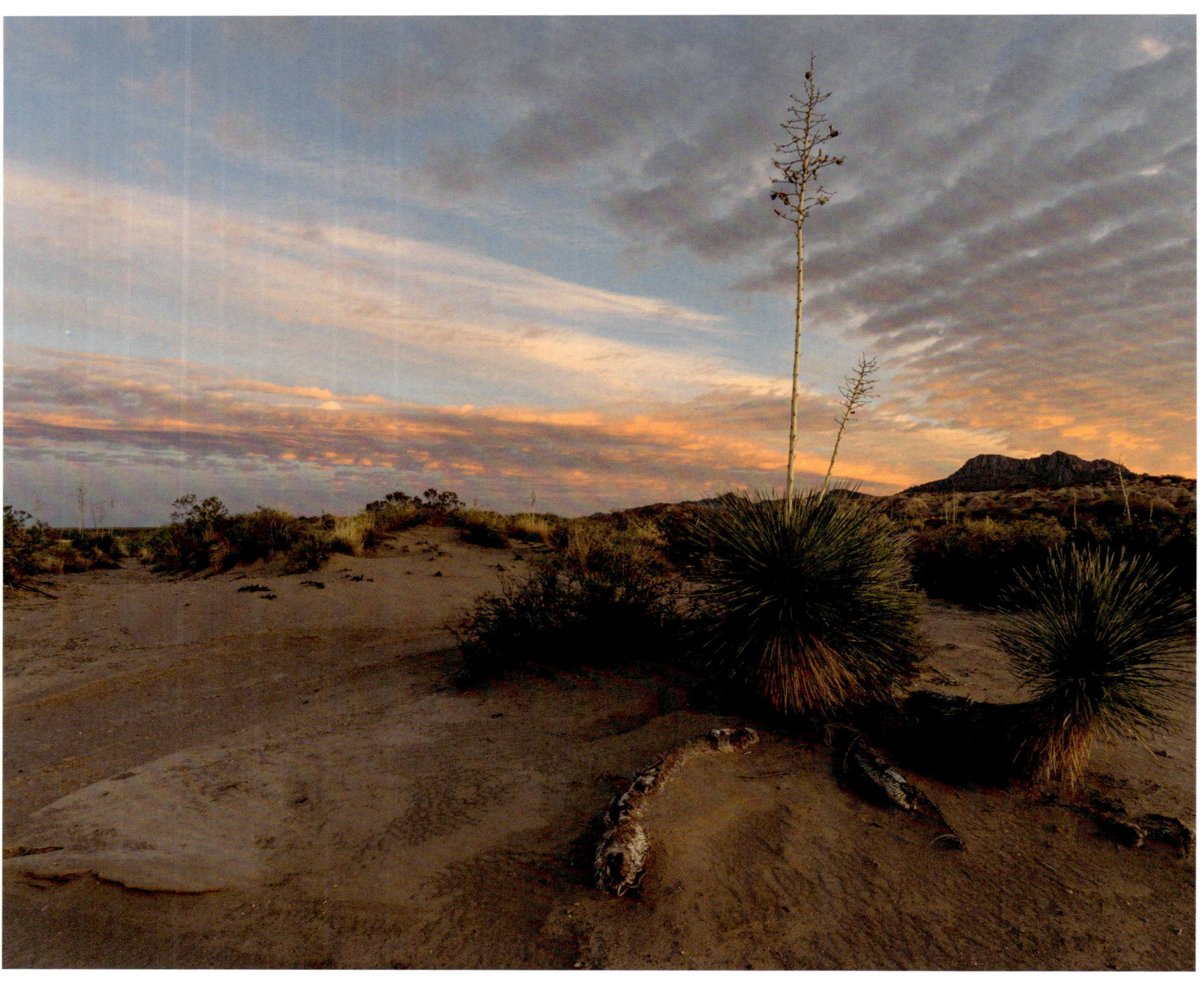



A BRISK WINTER DAY BRINGS CLOUDS TO JAVELINA PEAK IN THE HOT WELL DUNES RECREATION AREA.

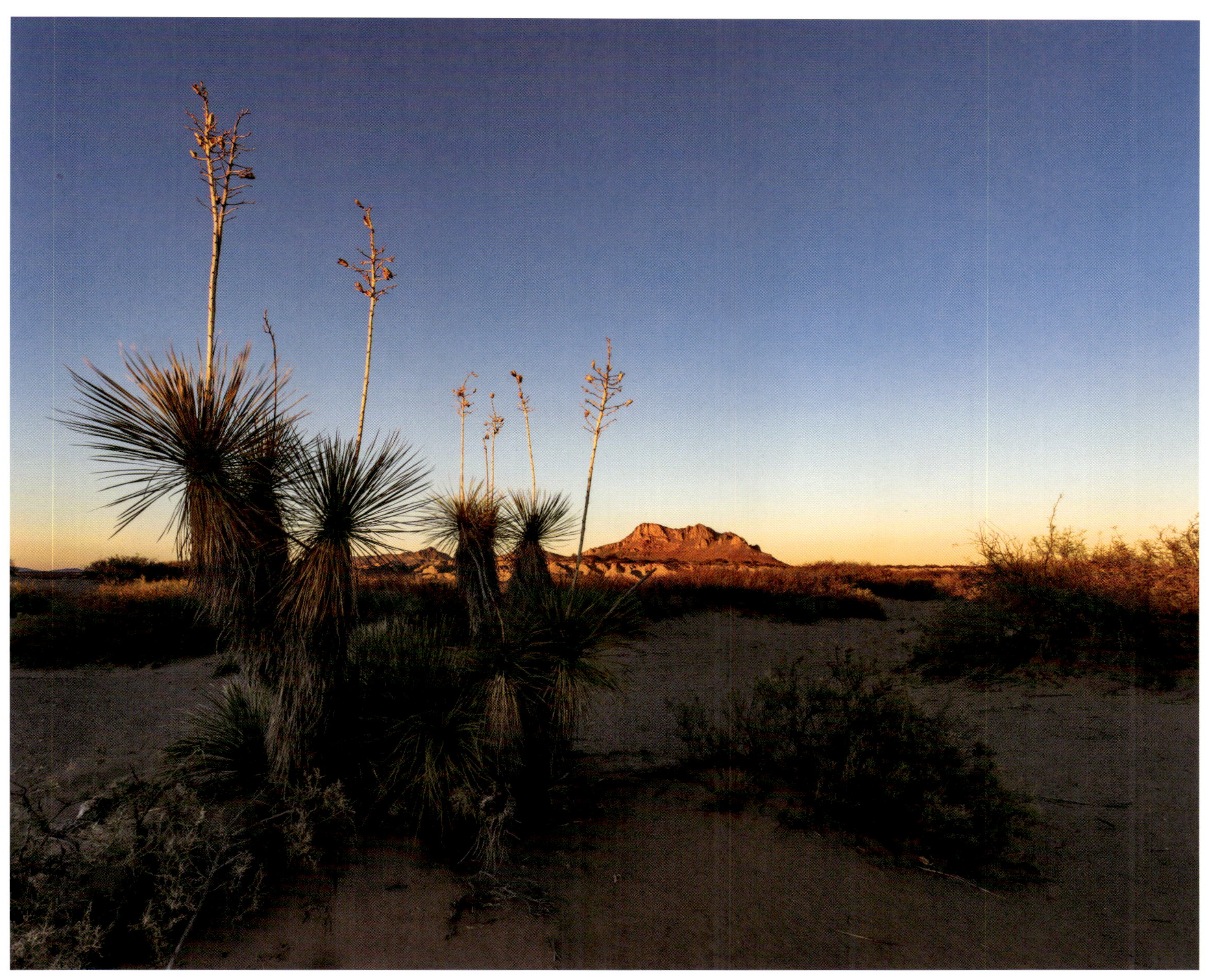

CLEAR BLUE SKIES EMPHASIZE THE DRY BLOOMS OF A SOAPTREE YUCCA IN THE WHITLOCK MOUNTAINS.

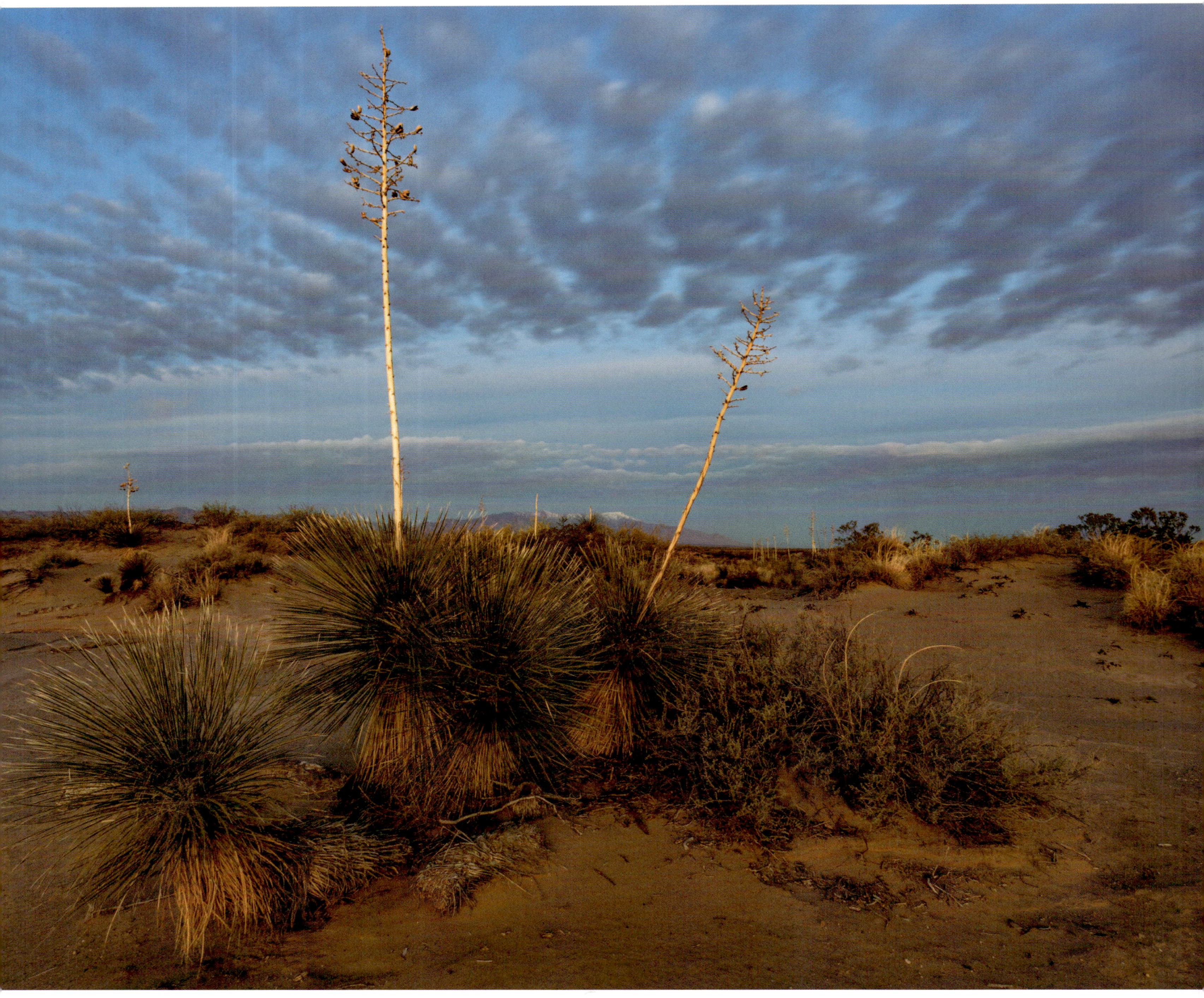



DRIFTING DUNES AND SOAPTREE YUCCAS IN THE HOT WELL DUNES RECREATION AREA.

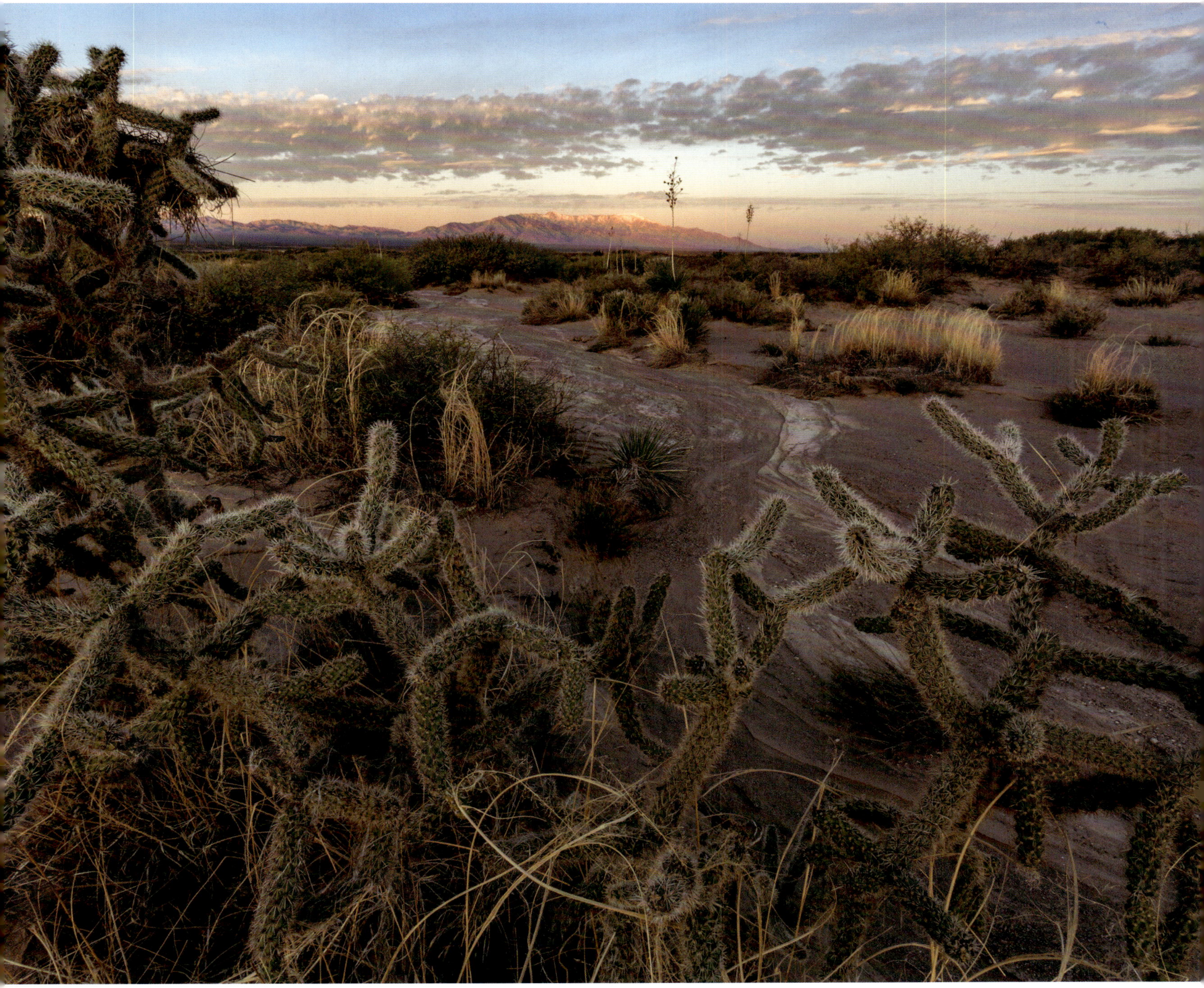

THE PINALEÑO MOUNTAINS SOAR ABOVE THE SAN SIMON RIVER VALLEY.

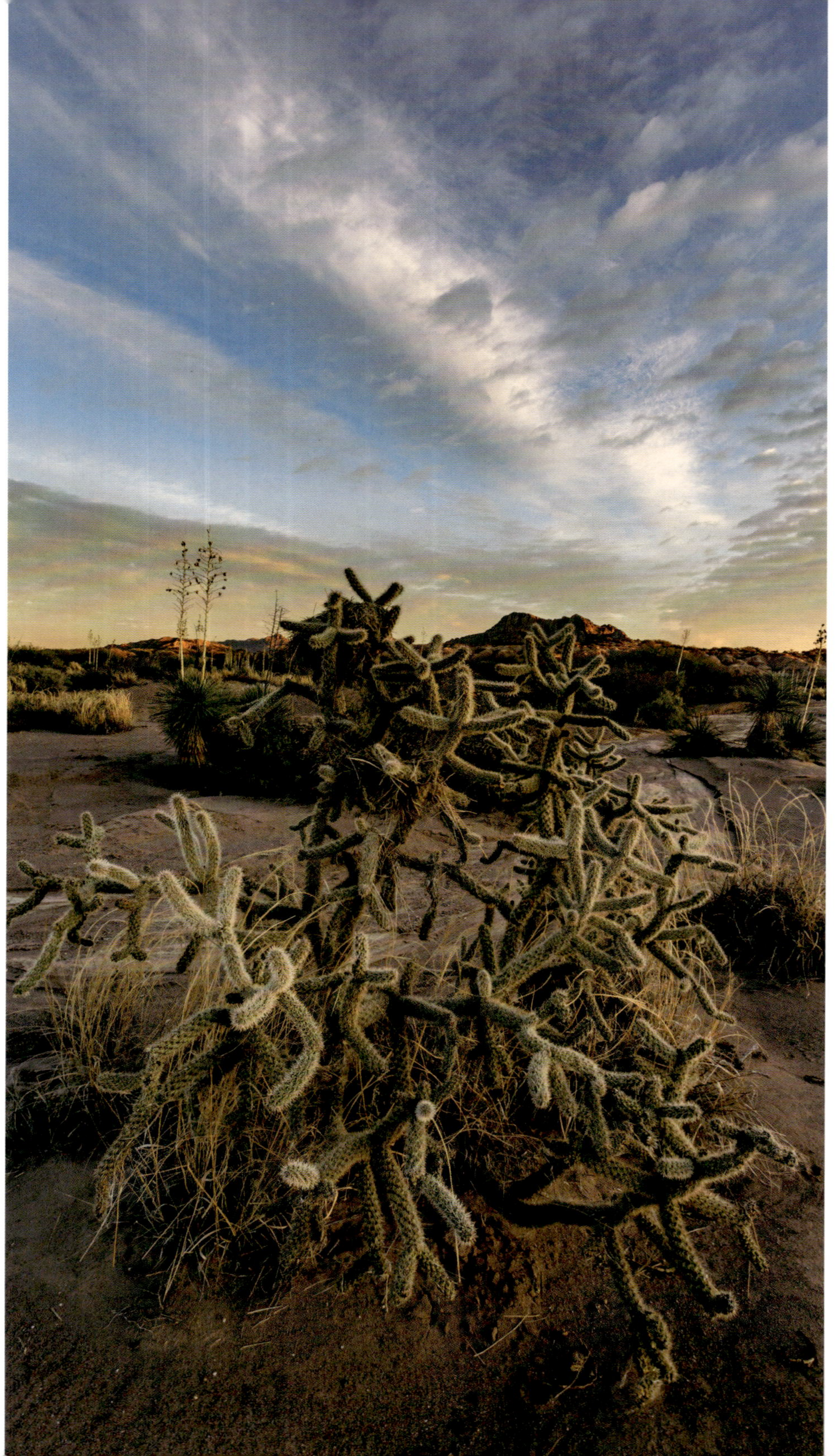

CHOLLA AND SOAPTREE YUCCA ON THE ROLLING
DESERT FLOOR OF THE SAN SIMON VALLEY.

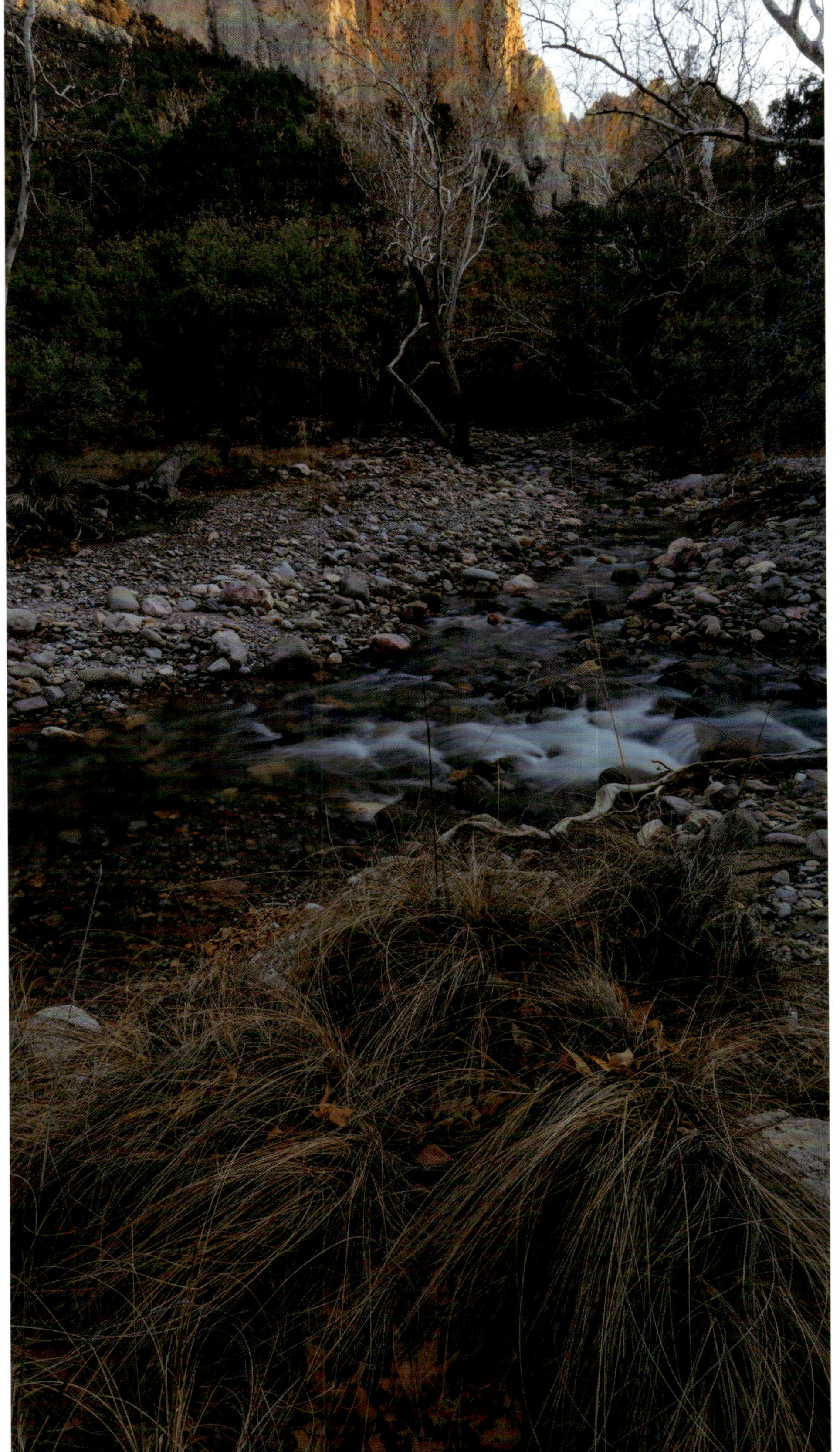

THE SOUTH AND NORTH FORKS OF CAVE CREEK
IN THE CAVE CREEK RECREATION AREA.

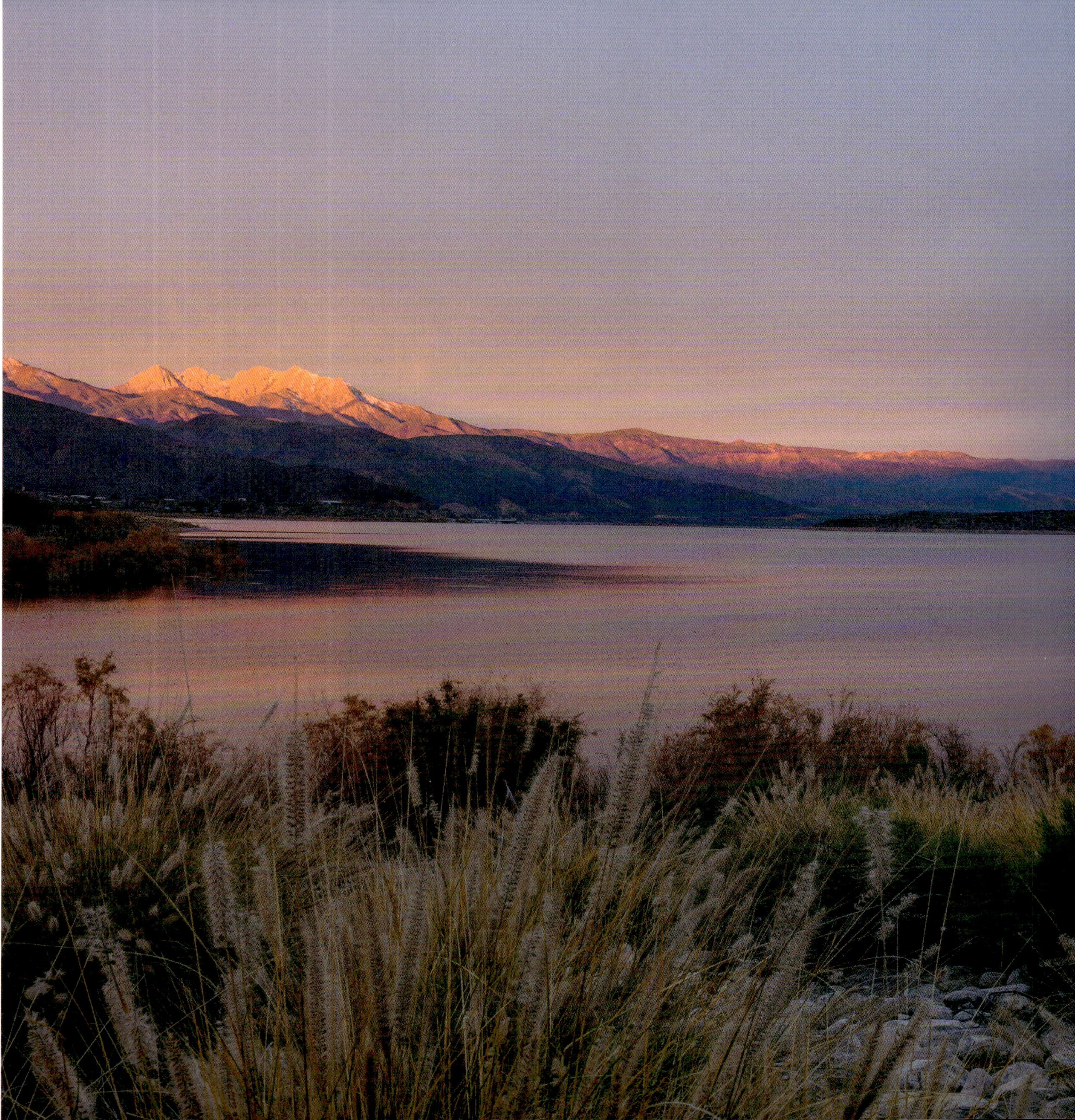

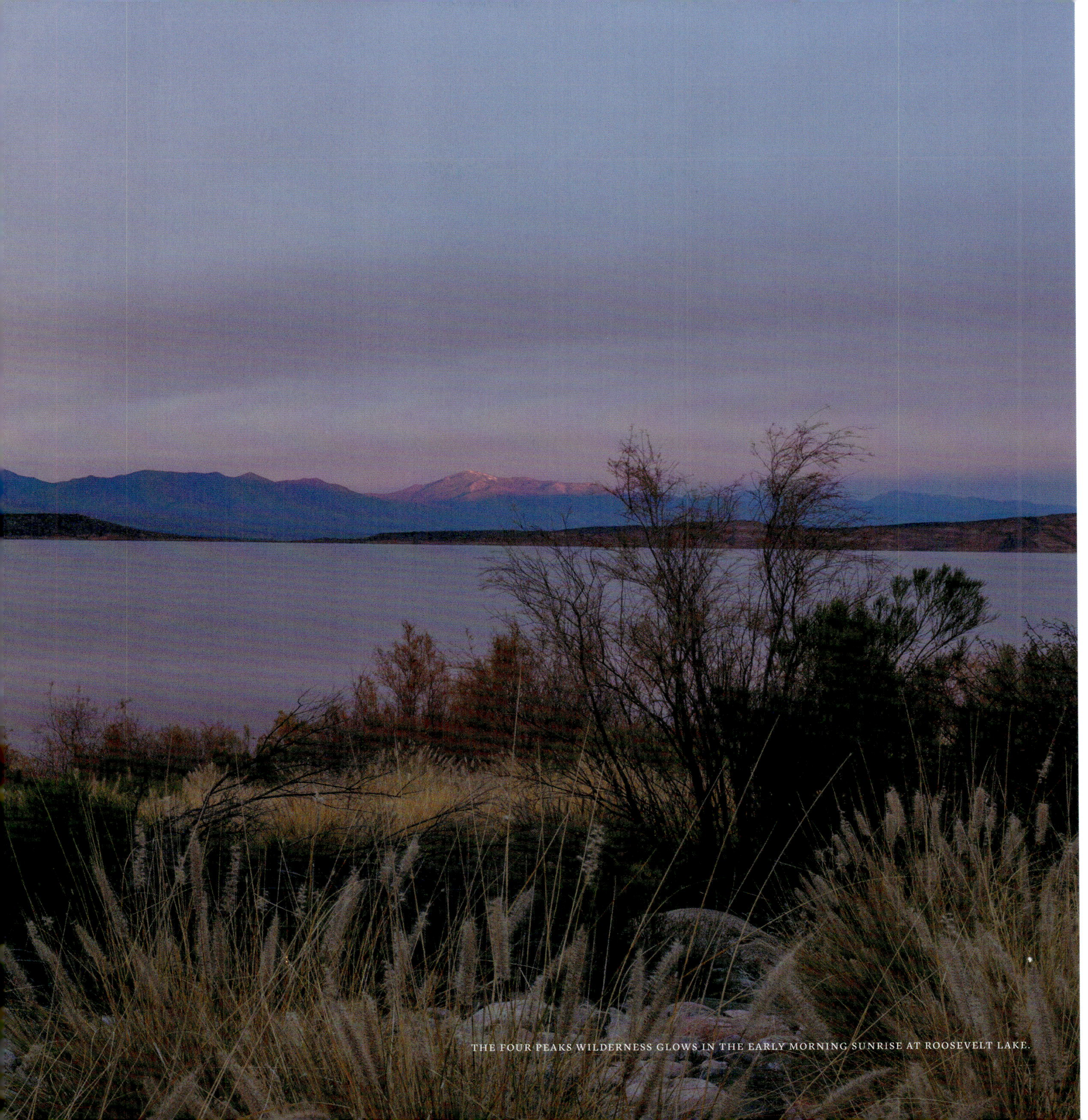

THE FOUR PEAKS WILDERNESS GLOWS IN THE EARLY MORNING SUNRISE AT ROOSEVELT LAKE.

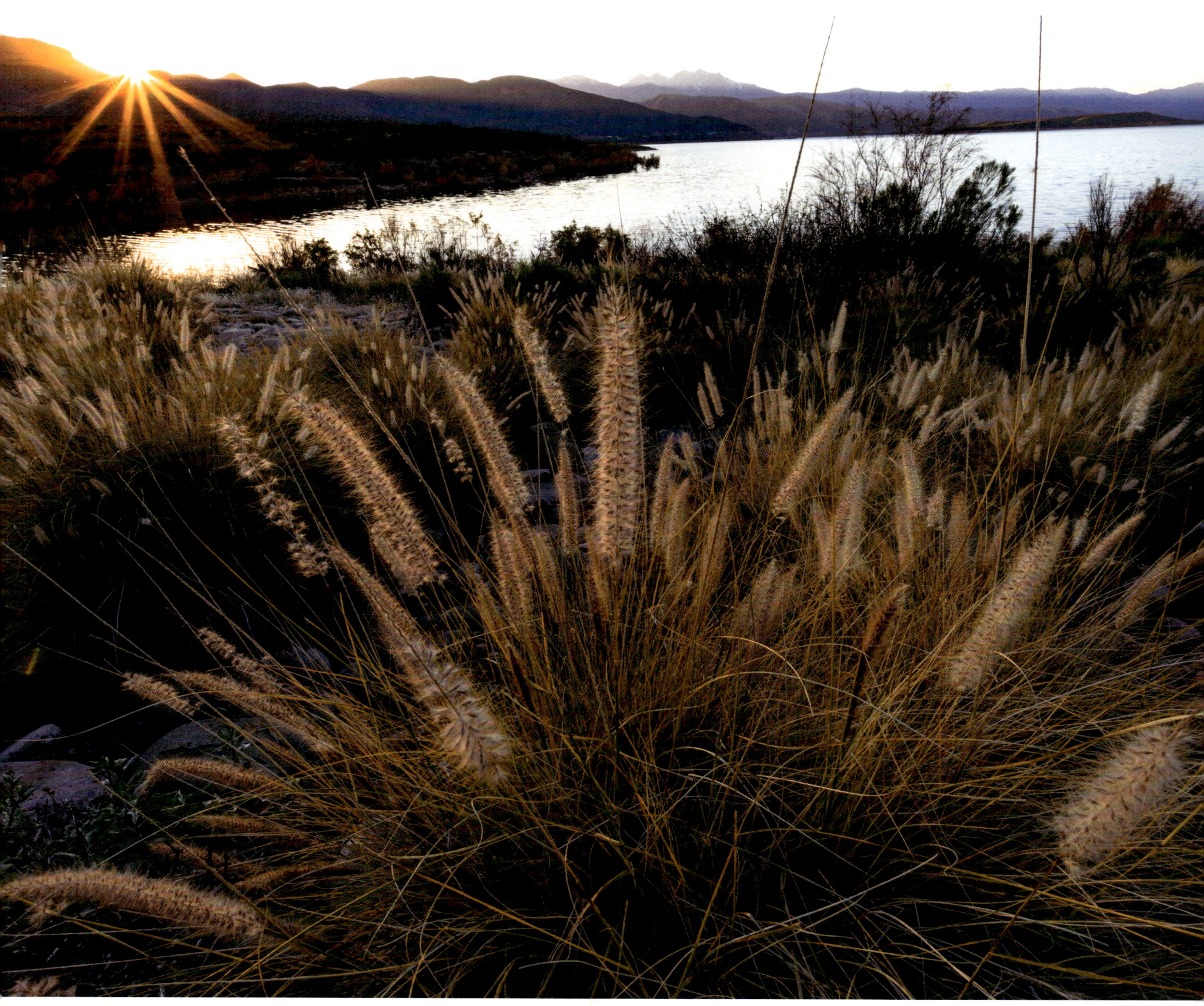



A WARM SUN BREAKS THE HORIZON AT ROOSEVELT LAKE.

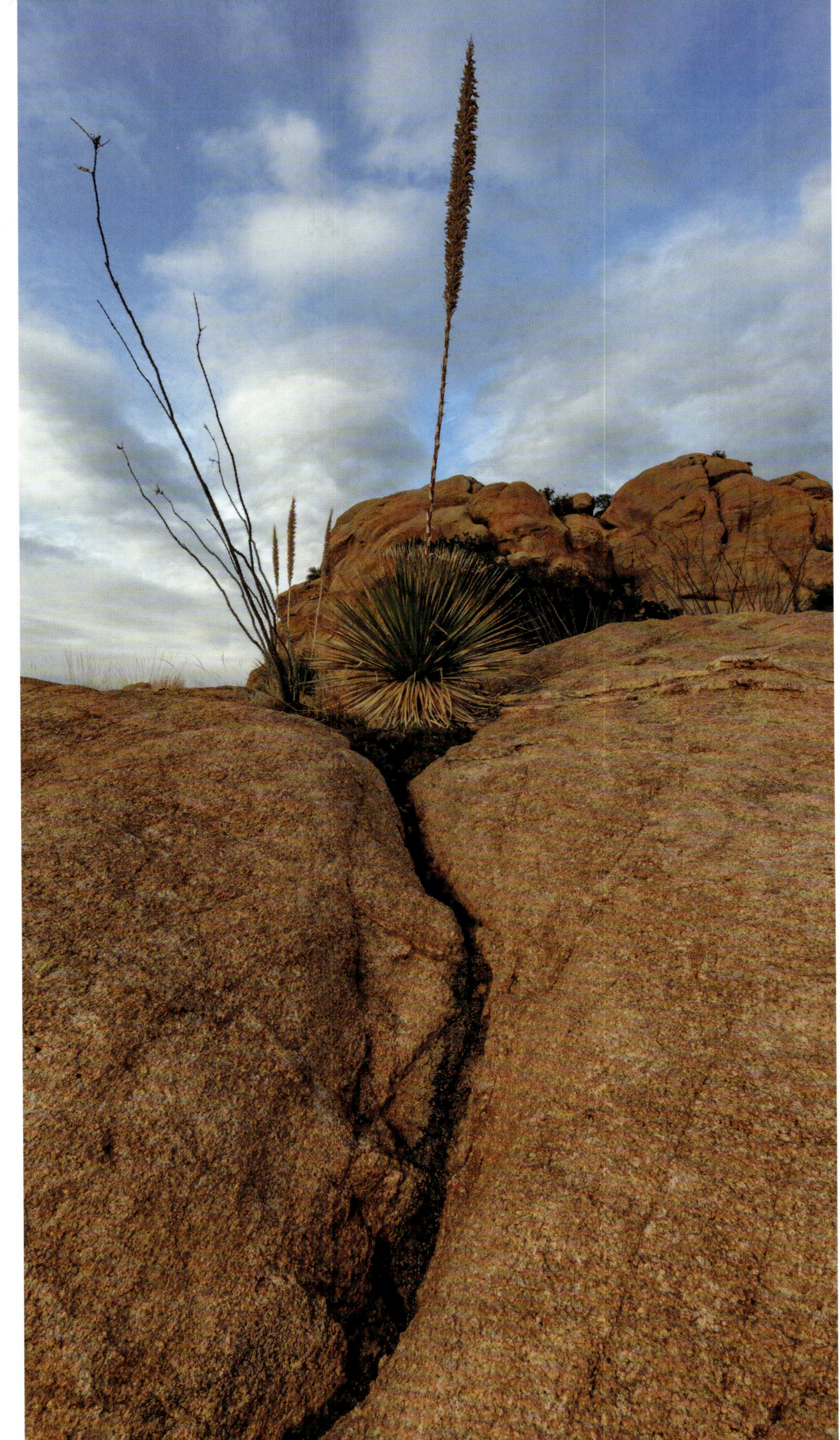

OCOTILLO AND SPANISH BAYONET YUCCA
TAKE ADVANTAGE OF SMALL PLOTS OF
EARTH IN TEXAS CANYON.

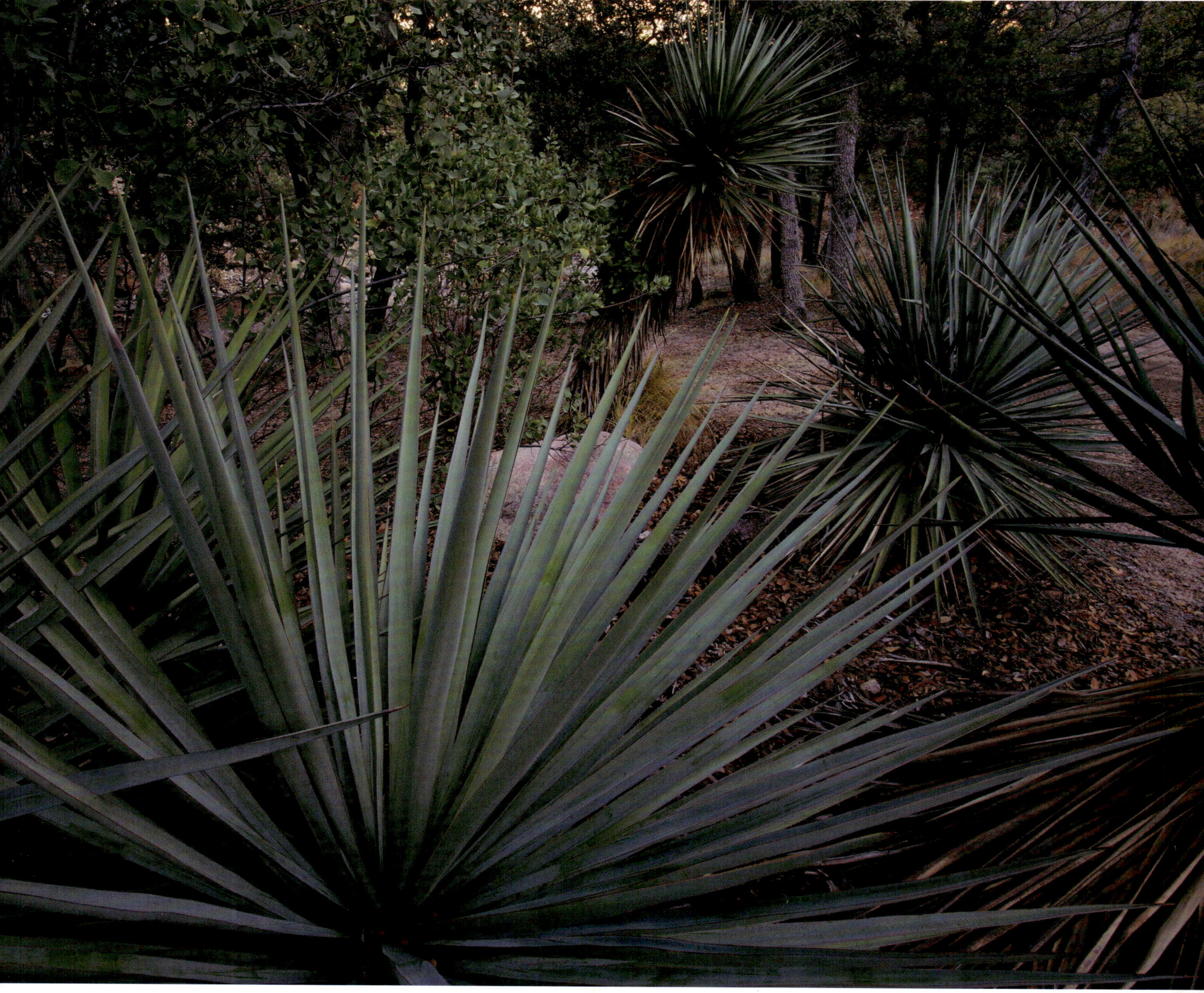



WHITE OAK AND YUCCA CREATE A COOL CANOPY AT THE COCHISE STRONGHOLD CAMPGROUND.

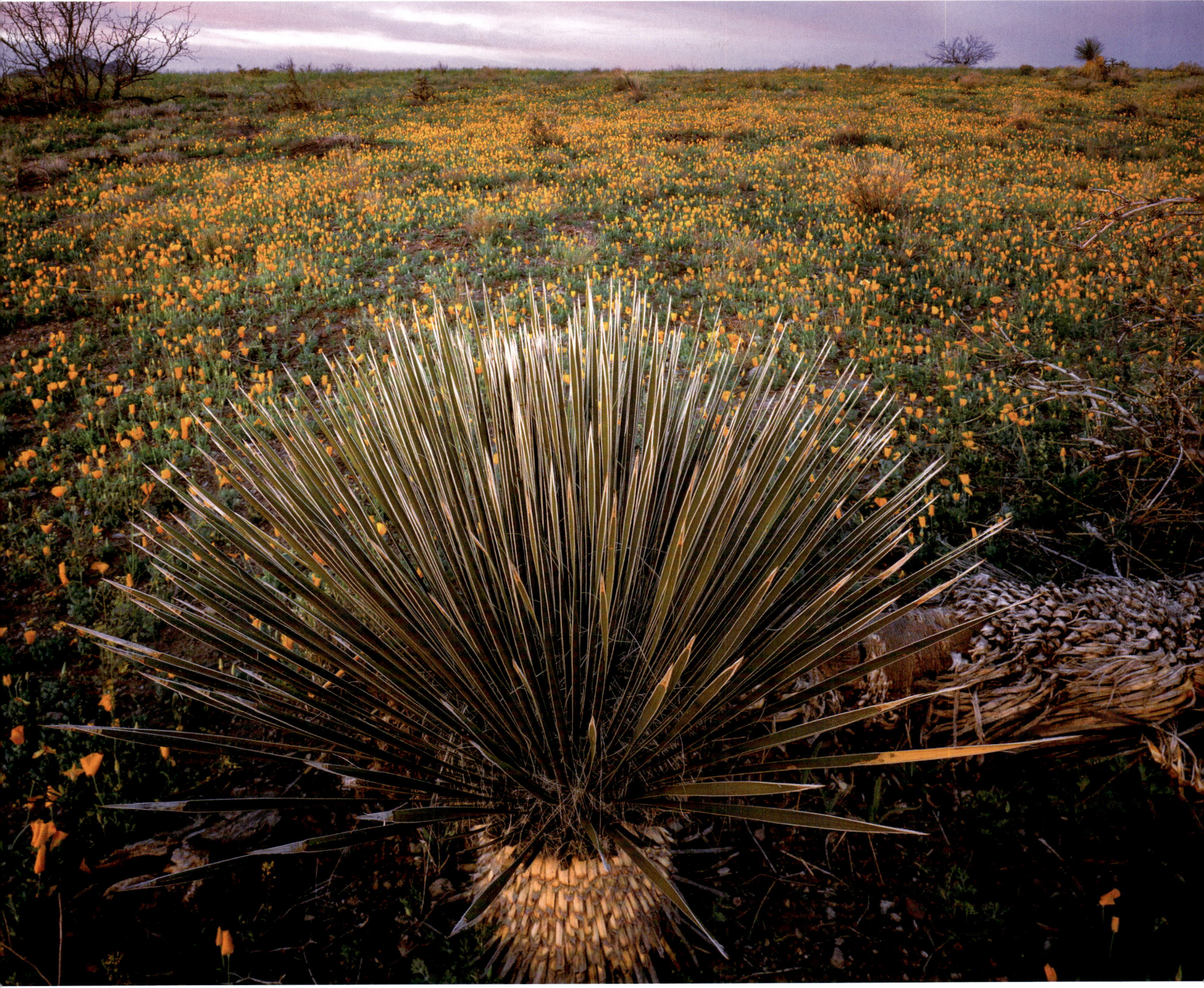

POPPIES COVER THE CHIHUAHUAN DESERT FLOOR NEAR THE DOS CABEZAS MOUNTAINS OUTSIDE OF WILLCOX.

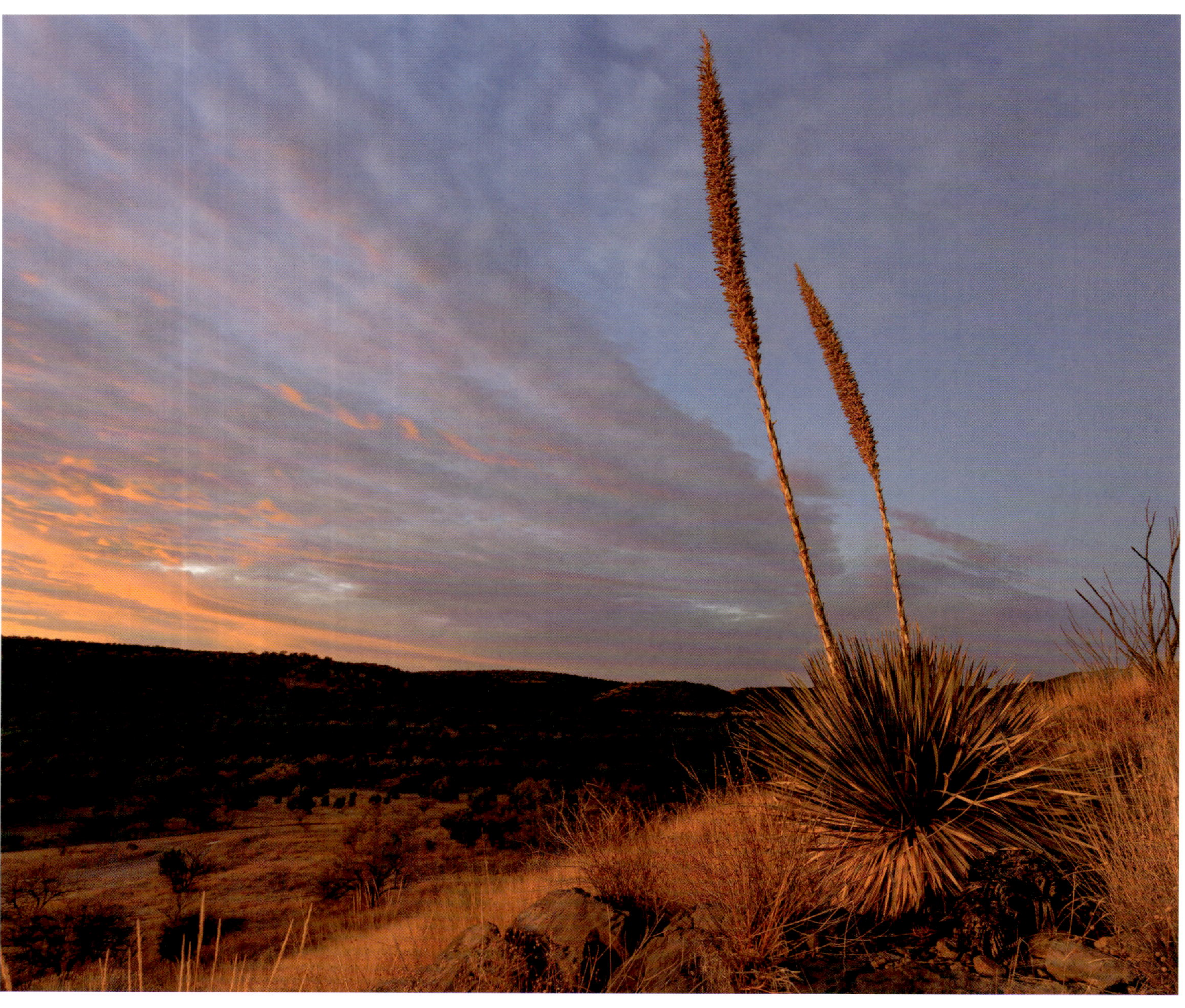



A BRILLIANT SUNRISE ILLUMINATES THE ROLLING HILLS OF GARDNER CANYON IN THE CORONADO NATIONAL FOREST.

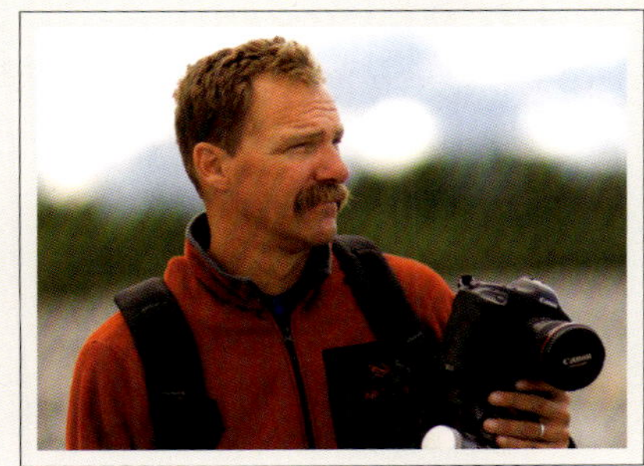

Mark Lisk has long roamed the deserts, mountains, and river canyons of the American West by foot. A graduate of the Brooks Institute of Photography, Mark climbs from the sea to high ridges and plains, gathering within his camera worlds of color and expanse that few ever see or capture in any form. From dry curls of patterned lake bottom to the tiniest brilliant lichen set before a vast line of granite peaks, Mark's foregrounds set him apart. His work fits whole universes of wilderness into single frames under glass. Mark has recently rediscovered his passion for the black-and-white image. His strong sense of composition complements black and white tones, giving the viewer a sense of isolation, alone in a wide, sweeping landscape. Mark's photographs stand alone in nine other books: *Idaho Impressions* (1997), *Salmon River Country* (2004), *Desert Water* (2005), *Idaho: Portrait of a State* (2007), *Owyhee Canyon Lands* (2008), *The Owyhee Canyonlands: An Outdoor Adventure Guide* (2013), *Void* (2013), *Sawtooth-White Cloud* (2016), and *Idaho: The Gem State* (2019).

# ABOUT FAMILIUS

Familius is a global trade publishing company that publishes books and other content to help families be happy. We believe that happy families are key to a better society and the foundation of a happy life. The greatest work anyone will ever do will be within the walls of his or her own home. And we don't mean vacuuming! We recognize that every family looks different and passionately believe in helping all families find greater joy, whatever their situation. To that end, we publish beautiful books that help families live our 10 Habits of Happy Family Life:

- Love together
- Play together
- Learn together
- Work together
- Talk together
- Heal together
- Read together
- Eat together
- Laugh together
- Give Together

WEBSITE: WWW.FAMILIUS.COM
FACEBOOK: WWW.FACEBOOK.COM/FAMILIUSBOOKS
PINTEREST: WWW.PINTEREST.COM/FAMILIUSBOOKS
INSTAGRAM: @FAMILIUSBOOKS
TIKTOK: @FAMILIUSBOOKS

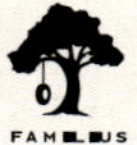

The most important work
you ever do will be within
the walls of your own home.